THE WORL

PLUT
SELECTED
DIAL

PLUTARCH was born about AD 50 at Chaeronea in central Greece, and lived there most of his life, teaching and writing. His most famous work is the *Parallel Lives*, biographies of Greek and Roman statesmen and generals, which have been extraordinarily influential in forming our picture of the Greco-Roman world. But he also wrote a large number of dialogues, treatises, and essays, of which this volume contains a selection. They have much charm, and have been an important model for writers like Montaigne and Emerson; and they give a vivid and individual view of the religious, moral, and political concerns of Plutarch's age.

DONALD RUSSELL was a Fellow of St John's College, Oxford, from 1948 to 1988, as tutor in Classics and latterly as Professor of Classical Literature. He is a Fellow of the British Academy, and has held visiting professorships in the United States, at Chapel Hill and at Stanford. His books include *Plutarch* (London, 1972), *Criticism in Antiquity* (London, 1981), *Greek Declamation* (Cambridge, 1983), as well as commentaries on Longinus (Oxford, 1964), Menander Rhetor (with N. G. Wilson, Oxford, 1981) and Dio Chrysostom, *Orations* 7, 12, 36 (Cambridge, 1992), and a collection of translations of ancient critical texts (with M. Winterbottom, Oxford, 1972; abridged in World's Classics, *Classical Literary Criticism*, 1989).

THE WORLD'S CLASSICS

PLUTARCH
SELECTED ESSAYS AND DIALOGUES

PLUTARCH was born about AD 50 at Chaeronea in central Greece and lived there most of his life, teaching and writing. His most famous work is the *Parallel Lives*, biographies of Greek and Roman statesmen and generals, which have been extraordinarily influential in forming our picture of the Greco-Roman world. But he also wrote a large number of dialogues, treatises, and essays, of which this volume contains a selection. They have much charm, and have been an important model for writers like Montaigne and Emerson; and they give a vivid and individual view of the religious, moral, and political concerns of Plutarch's age.

DONALD RUSSELL was a Fellow of St John's College, Oxford, from 1948 to 1988, as tutor in Classics and latterly as Professor of Classical Literature. He is a Fellow of the British Academy, and has held visiting professorships in the United States, at Chapel Hill and at Stanford. His books include *Plutarch* (London, 1972), *Criticism in Antiquity* (London, 1981), *Greek Declamation* (Cambridge, 1983), as well as commentaries on Longinus (Oxford, 1964), Menander Rhetor (with N. G. Wilson, Oxford, 1981) and Dio Chrysostom *Orationes* 7, 12, 36 (Cambridge, 1992), and a collection of translations of ancient critical texts (with M. Winterbottom, Oxford, 1972; abridged in World's Classics, *Classical Literary Criticism*, 1989).

THE WORLD'S CLASSICS

PLUTARCH

Selected Essays and Dialogues

Oxford New York

OXFORD UNIVERSITY PRESS

1993

Oxford University Press, Walton Street, Oxford OX2 6DP
Oxford New York Toronto
Delhi Bombay Calcutta Madras Karachi
Kuala Lumpur Singapore Hong Kong Tokyo
Nairobi Dar es Salaam Cape Town
Melbourne Auckland Madrid
and associated companies in
Berlin Ibadan

Oxford is a trade mark of Oxford University Press

First published as a World's Classics paperback 1993

British Library Cataloguing in Publication Data
Data available

Library of Congress Cataloging in Publication Data
Plutarch.
[Moralia. English. Selections]
Selected essays and dialogues/Plutarch.
p. cm.—(World's classics)
Includes bibliographical references.
1. Dialogues, Greek—Translations into English. 2. Greek essays—Translations into English. I. Title. II. Series.
PA4374.M7 1993 888'.0107—dc20 92–18159
ISBN 0–19–283094–5

1 3 5 7 9 10 8 6 4 2

Typeset by Pure Tech Corporation, Pondicherry, India.
Printed in Great Britain by
BPCC Hazells Ltd.
Aylesbury, Bucks

CONTENTS

PREFACE

THIS selection of Plutarch's miscellaneous works is designed to illustrate his thought on a variety of subjects. It comprises less than a quarter of the extant corpus of the *Moralia*, and it has been planned so as to complement, with few overlaps, the recent Penguin volume by Robin Waterfield and Professor Ian Kidd. I owe much to many helpers: especially to the staff of the Classics Office in Oxford, and to Dr S. C. R. Swain, who has read and corrected a lot of my work. I hope the result will make these 'essays and dialogues' accessible and enjoyable to new readers and to students who know something of them already, but wish to know a little more.

D.A.R.

Note: Plutarch's 'mosaic' calls for a lot of explanation. I have tried to give the essentials economically by providing: some notes; a glossary of proper names; a list of references to his quotations. I hope that readers of various interests will find that, between them, these three aids supply most of their needs, though there is naturally no place for scholarly discussion of problems.

REFERENCES

REFERRING to parts of the *Moralia* is difficult. Greek, Latin and English titles are not generally agreed, though there is usually no difficulty in seeing what is meant. The tradition has been to use the pages of the Frankfurt edition of 1599, a revision of that of H. Etienne (1572); these page-numbers are given in the right-hand margins of this translation and are used for reference in the Notes, List of Quotations, and Glossary. Individual pieces are identified in the Introduction and Notes either by Arabic numerals (1–78), referring to the list given on pp. xxiii–xxix, or by Roman numerals I–XVII, referring to the Table of Contents. The treatises are also divided by editors into chapters, and the numbers of these are given in bold type in the text.

INTRODUCTION

PLUTARCH (*c.* AD 50–*c.*120) came of a leading family in the Boeotian town of Chaeronea, the scene of Philip of Macedon's defeat of the Greek cities in 338 BC, and Sulla's defeat of Mithridates' general, Archelaus, in 86 BC. Scholar and teacher, deeply read in history and philosophy, he was also a man of affairs in his little world, a magistrate in Chaeronea, an official and priest at the great oracular shrine of Delphi, some twenty miles away. Unlike most of the intellectuals of his time, Plutarch was a home-keeping man; indeed, he prides himself on this (*Demosthenes* 2) as a mark of local patriotism. He did however spend long study-periods in Athens, which was still a great centre of learning and was close enough to make frequent visits easy. He was in Egypt at least once, and in Rome for two or three spells, sometimes lecturing there, and no doubt acquiring influential friends. The dedications of his books reveal that he moved, or wished to move, in high circles: they include addresses to proconsuls and governors: to C. Minicius Fundanus, consul of 107 and a friend of Pliny (29), and to Q. Sosius Senecio, twice consul under Trajan, and the recipient of Plutarch's most important work, the *Parallel Lives*. Plutarch himself was a Roman citizen—L. Mestrius Plutarchus—as, probably, was his father before him. In later life, he is said to have received marked but insubstantial honours from the emperor: *ornamenta consularia*, and an honorific appointment as imperial procurator in the province of Achaea.

Chaeronea, Delphi, Athens, Rome: the places define an intellectual world. Plutarch's local pride and patriotism were grounded in his deep sense of history. His philosophy was centred on making a rational case for traditional belief in prophecy and providence. His public activity and counsel took account both of common principles of humanity (*prāotēs*, 'gentleness', and *philanthrōpia*, 'humanity', are key words with him) and of the power of Rome to set the agenda of Greek political life. These attitudes commended him to posterity. In the fourth century, the Athenian sophist Himerius calls him the educator of mankind; and the Christian fathers—especially Clement of Alexandria and the Cappadocians, Basil and Gregory of Nyssa—found him among the most acceptable of pagan moralists and theologians. His works were carefully collected in Byzantine times; and the Renaissance in the West discovered in them a coherent and convincing image of the classical world.

His potency rested, of course, mainly on the *Parallel Lives.* But these present the pageant of Greek and Roman history in a very special way. One can construct a history from them, but they are not quite history. For one thing, the 'parallelism' between Greece and Rome was vitally important in Plutarch's conception of what he was doing; he wanted to show the underlying likeness between the heroes of the Hellenic past and those of the Roman Republic. Now this likeness—and the consequent possibility of making valid comparisons—rested, in his view, not so much on similar circumstances as on similar moral responses and qualities. Moreover, these responses and qualities were the same as those which deserve praise or blame in ordinary social or political life, such as we all experience. *Rules for Politicians* (VII = 52) is in a way the best commentary on Plutarch as a biographer, for almost every point made is illustrated by reference to some event related in the *Lives*. Indeed, something like this may be said of most of Plutarch's miscellaneous works: they form an indispensable complement to the biographies. In this selection, *Socrates' Daimonion* (IV), *The Fortune of Rome* (VI), *How to Profit from your Enemies* (VIII), and *Virtues in Women* (XVI), are obvious examples.

Byzantine scholars assembled a corpus of nearly eighty of these miscellaneous works, and they accidentally included a few that are not Plutarch's. They knew the titles of other books too; Plutarch's total production was formidable indeed. They called their collection *Ethica*, in Latin *Moralia*, 'works on morals'. The name really applied to a group of treatises (1–21) which they placed at the head of the collection. As a description of the whole, it is misleading, and it may well have discouraged readers. There is certainly a strain of response through the centuries that makes curious reading if you have come to be fond of these books. 'Thou hast read Plutarch's morals now, or some such tedious fellow', says Ben Jonson's Clerimont in *The Silent Woman*, ' 'Fore God, twill spoil thy wit utterly'. But this is a minority response: the admirers are many and powerful. Three witnesses may suffice. The first is Montaigne. Amyot's great translation, *Morals* as well as *Lives*, was his 'breviary', a book without which 'we ignorant folk would have been lost'. Plutarch and Seneca were the sources 'whence I draw water like the Danaïds, filling and pouring without cease', and Plutarch was the better of the two, because he was more manly and more persuasive, with a mind whose motions are 'more assured and better regulated'. Montaigne valued the stability and steadiness; if he found in Seneca something more strident, more suggestive of insecurity, he was surely right. A second witness is Jeremy Taylor, who also knew and studied Montaigne. In the index to Bishop Heber's edition, there are two long columns of Plutarch references, and this is no exhaustive list. It is not that Plutarch is named all that often, but that he is constantly used, especially in 'The Marriage Ring', which is full of *Advice on Marriage* (XIV), and in 'Holy Living'. More important, the manner of writing is Plutarchan, a mosaic of reference and allusion, pagan and Christian, quite in the tradition of Plutarch and the Greek fathers. That some of the quotations are in Latin—which means that Taylor used a bilingual edition—hardly affects the main fact that he is the most Plutarchan of all our moralists. The third of our witnesses has to be Emerson, a great enthusiast, who often alludes to and uses Plutarch and wrote a splendid introduction to W. W. Goodman's revision (1870) of the standard eighteenth-century version of the entire *Moralia*. This version itself, by various hands, not all highly skilled, was published from 1684 onwards, and finally issued in a complete form in 1718. It was evidently a favourite bedside-book of Emerson's, not only for its content, but because he regarded it as a monument of the English language at a period of 'singular vigor and freedom of style'. It had in fact replaced the earlier version of Philemon Holland (1603) in much the same way and for much the same reasons as 'Dryden's' *Lives* had replaced North's: namely, that the prose of the earlier period had come to seem quaint and formless, and people wanted something tighter and more akin to ordinary speech. Emerson's picture of Plutarch must in some way have been affected by the English dress in which he encountered him; but his judgement is penetrating and very interesting. His Plutarch, it seems, has a 'poetical', not a 'profound' mind: 'I embrace the particular and carry a faint memory of the argument', he writes; 'a poet might rhyme all day with hints drawn from Plutarch, page on page.' Imaginative, sympathetic, and fanciful, this Plutarch is certainly to be found in the texts. Emerson's comment is a useful warning that we should not always look for a rigorous connection of thought, but let ourselves be carried along by the variety of the detail, the allusions, the analogies, and the colourful language. Most readers echo this.

This volume contains seventeen pieces, less than a quarter of the whole corpus. I have called them 'essays' and 'dialogues', to indicate the main generic division among them. The word 'essay' is of course a tribute to Montaigne, the inventor of the term; but not all these little books are as personal or as informal as the word suggests. None indeed have the informality of style that Montaigne praised and practised; for it was perhaps a defect, more probably a necessity, in Amyot, that he did not reproduce in French the generally regular periodic style in which Plutarch, somewhat paradoxically, casts his rambling and discursive thoughts. But there are some treatises that are less like 'essays' in that sense than others. A few, for example, are obviously speeches. Plutarch, like most of his contemporaries, practised epideictic oratory—that is, oratory as entertainment or celebration, not as pleading or counsel—and a certain number of these speeches survive: whether they were successful as performances one can well doubt, for they often seem confused and stuffed too full of learning, and Plutarch, as we have seen, chose a private life at home rather than one of running around the world as a visiting sophist. *The Fortune of Rome* (VI = 20) and *Against Borrowing Money* (XII = 54) are in this class: there are others as well (8, 9, 21, 22, 33, 34, 50, 62, perhaps V = 75). Others are collections of anecdotes, which may not be from Plutarch's own hand (15–19), or brief discussions of antiquarian, or philological, or philosophical problems (18, 59, 67). Again, there is a group of technical works on philosophy, interpretations of Plato (68), polemic against Stoics (70–2) or Epicureans

(73–4), and these naturally lack a good deal of the colour and variety that are so conspicuous in the more popular works. So the 'treatise' or 'essay' form is very varied; nor indeed are the 'dialogues' in the mode that Plato usually used, the Socratic elenchus with its remorseless cross-examination of the victim. Plutarch worked rather in another tradition, represented in Greek literature by Aristotle and other Peripatetics, and in Latin especially by Cicero. This prescribes setting out rival positions in formal debating-speeches, and presumably represents the type of disputation which had become common in philosophical schools. It does not exclude a good deal of vividness in the portrayal of the setting and the characters. These could be either historical (IV = 43, 13, XVII = 64) or contemporary (as in II = 26, III = 25, XIII = 47, and a number of others, note especially 46, the nine books of *Table Talk*). Plutarch (unlike Plato) allows himself to appear in his dialogues, but the most important function of the setting is to compliment and give literary immortality to friends and family; Plutarch is specially fond of presenting his brother Lamprias, and himself draws attention (31, 484E) to the way in which Plato brought his own brothers forward 'in his best writings'.

My seventeen pieces have been selected so as not to overlap too much with the Penguin volume translated by Robin Waterfield (Penguin Books, 1992). I am grateful to him and to Professor Ian Kidd for advance knowledge of their plans. It seemed right that, between us, we should make available as much Plutarch as possible within the limits of our two volumes. But neither party was willing to forgo *Socrates' Daimonion* (IV = 43) or the Consolation to Plutarch's wife (45 = XV). The reasons for this are worth stating. *Socrates' Daimonion* is Plutarch's most splendid dialogue. It displays both his narrative skills—the tale of the conspiracy is told with greater freedom than in the *Life of Pelopidas*, where it also appears—and his colourful and imaginative myth-making. Its subject embraces almost all the interests that were dear to his heart. The scene is classical Thebes, his great hero Epaminondas has a part. The main themes are divine guidance, immortality, and divination: these are the concerns with which his life as a priest of Delphi was bound up. Socrates,

Plato's teacher, is the exemplar of the philosophic life. In this one dialogue, all these things come together; it is the quintessence of Plutarch. The 'Consolation' also is essential reading. An infant daughter had died while Plutarch was away from home. He writes to his wife to praise her calm bearing in the emergency, sympathizes with her grief, and gently warns against superstitious indulgence in the process of mourning. The piece is clearly meant for a wider public: the private bereavement is given literary grace and erudite adornment, and the sympathy and warning are set in a context of serious philosophical and moral principles. As in *Advice on Marriage* (XIV = 12), we see philosophy in the home, as comforter and guide. We also coincide in the choice of the last piece in this selection, 'Gryllus', which shows Plutarch in a lighter mood.

I have arranged these seventeen pieces in a way which is meant to exhibit Plutarch's main areas of interest. First, man in his relations with god: cult, divination, the notion of providence (I–V). Second, man in his political dealings: the Greek city, its duties and limitations (VI–VIII). Third, the daily social round: characters one encounters, faults one notices in oneself and wants to correct, ways in which behaviour may be virtuous or the opposite (IX–XII). Fourth, the relationships of love and family (XIII–XVI). I conclude (XVII) with one of Plutarch's few pieces about animals; it happens also to be one of his most amusing dialogues. This order is nothing like the order of the Byzantine collection which is followed in all editions (see pp. xxiii–xxix). Nor is it chronological, for we know very little, despite much speculation, about the relative dates of Plutarch's works. It does, of course, leave out a lot: nothing about education (2, 3) or literary criticism (2, 56, 57); and nothing too technical or specialist. I regret most the omission of 'Table Talk' (46), which contains discussions of almost everything that Plutarch found important, and presents a memorable gallery of his friends and relations.

Whatever the subject, there are two features of Plutarch's work that always seem to obtrude themselves. One is his involvement with the Greek past. It would be unfair to say he lived in the past, but he was certainly very conscious of its immediacy. As a

Roman citizen, aware of the limitations of Hellenic 'liberty' in his own day, he had to base his Hellenic patriotism on past glories; and he found these in the literary record, even more than in the surviving monuments. Indeed, the visible evidences of the civilization—statues, buildings, paintings—must have been overwhelmingly from Hellenistic or more recent times. Even in places like Delphi, where the classical past was most obtrusive, new splendours were appearing, as he observes himself (below, III. 409). It was the poets, historians, and philosophers who were the real heritage. Plutarch saw it as his life's work to display this ancient wisdom as an exemplar and an inspiration for his own age. It spoke not only to Greeks, but to Romans, for all educated Romans read Greek. The most important audience, however, was the Greek ruling élite to which Plutarch himself belonged, many of whom were in this period rising to positions of importance in the Roman administration. To appeal to them, and to his Roman patrons, and to put Greek history in a wider perspective embracing Rome, he integrated into the canon of stories and examples about Pericles, Alcibiades, Alexander, Socrates, and so on, what we may call the historical mythology of Rome: the tales of the heroes of the Republic, and the daemonic geniuses and philosophic martyrs of the Civil Wars. He was, of course, not the first to take this line—Valerius Maximus' Latin compilation of *exempla* shows that it was familiar in the rhetorical schools—but he carried it through on a grander scale and with a profounder understanding than any before or after him.

The programme, then, was to make the past part of the present. It demanded a corresponding literary technique. This was what Erasmus called Plutarch's *opus musaicum*, a mosaic of examples, quotations, similes, and antitheses. There is no pagan author as rich as Plutarch in this kind of allusiveness; but the fathers of the church found him a profitable model, and added biblical quotations and references to the mix. His examples, naturally, come mainly from classical Greek history, or from Roman; but there is also a substantial input from the annals of Hellenistic kings and the lives of the flatterers and philosophers who frequented their courts. The quotations seem innumerable; a glance at the Sources of Quotations (pp. 389–99) will show

how thick and fast they come. They are not always signalled, and not always identifiable. Their purposes vary, from authoritative confirmation to a mere touch of ornament. Most of them come from the classical poets: Homer, Hesiod (on whom Plutarch wrote a commentary), the lyric poets (especially Pindar), the tragedians, Menander. But again there is a Hellenistic element: poets like Callimachus, Aratus, Euphorio, Eratosthenes are named, and there are quite a few unnamed quotations which are almost certainly of the same period. Finally, the similes and antitheses. These are very various, and often rather bookish: mythology, medicine, popular natural history are favourite fields. In all this 'mosaic', the classical past gives the dominant motifs, but there is also a contribution from the post-classical and contemporary worlds. The same situation is reflected in Plutarch's language. His contemporaries, especially the younger ones and even more the generation that followed, generally tried to write Greek that would pass muster for classical Attic of the fourth century BC. This taste, analogous to the fashion of copying or imitating classical sculpture, originated in the rhetorical schools, but came to extend to history, popular philosophy, and *belles lettres* generally. Plutarch did not share it. He does not tell us what he thought of it; but he does make fun of Isocrates, who was supposed to have taken ten years to write a speech, spending immense trouble on keeping vowels from clashing with one another. This was pedantry to Plutarch, or worse; it meant worrying about linguistic trivialities when you ought to be attending to the health of your soul. The odd thing is that Plutarch himself avoids vowel clashes, constructs careful periods, has regular rhythmical habits, and obviously seeks to make his teaching sound impressive. In other words, he is not careless of form, but he is not an 'Atticist'. It was probably the nature of his own literary talent that kept him in the mainstream of earlier writers, and apart from his Atticizing contemporaries. His imagination was too discursive, his memory too full, he had not the patience to curb his exuberance or to select a single word when two or three came into his mind.

These considerations give a clue to understanding Plutarch's thought more generally. If his field of reference and his language show this *mélange* of tradition and contemporaneity, the same should be true of his religion, his politics, his morals, his approach to love and to family duty.

And it does seem to be true of his religion. In Delphi, where he served for so long as a priest, the cult of Apollo and Dionysus and the service of the oracle, constantly brought to mind the classical past, the days when the god advised colonists, took sides (or was prudently ambivalent) in international disputes, and received precious donations from Greek and barbarian rulers. The Pythian dialogues (24; 25 = III; 26 = II; 41) are full of pride in Delphi's past as well as satisfaction with the present. Daily cult too—funerals, marriages, household worship—was set in old ways, and Plutarch approved of this. *Patrios eusebeia*, the piety of our fathers, was his ideal. It was to be set against not only disbelief but the opposite extreme, the excesses of superstition (14 = I), and superstition, in Plutarch's day, came in part from the influx of foreign cults. But it was not because they were foreign that Plutarch rejected certain practices and beliefs; much religious wisdom originated in Egypt and the East, and he was concerned with these things—he wrote a book on *Isis and Osiris* (23), and this is one of his most important theological statements. It was because they were 'barbarian' in a somewhat different sense, 'non-Greek', not conforming to the old Hellenic standards of decency and dignity. In eighteenth-century terms, Plutarch was against 'enthusiasm'. His critique was not confined to the new or the exotic; there were aspects of classical religion which were wrong, and more recent insights which pointed the right way. Cruel sacrifices, mysterious rituals, and tales representing the gods as perverse, jealous, or immoral, had long been the target of philosophers and moralists. Against all such things Plutarch brandishes the Platonic truth that 'God is good and can do no evil', and the criterion of probability (*eikos*), which, in his theology just as much as in his history, determines our judgement in favour of the morally acceptable whenever motives or actions are in dispute. Many philosophers, especially the Stoics—with whom Plutarch conducted a professional polemic (70–2), which nevertheless did not inhibit him from using their ideas a good deal—relied on allegory as a way of reconciling tradition with truth. Plutarch's attitude to this is ambivalent. In general, he distrusts it, as Plato did, but there are traces of a more positive view, at least in *Isis and Osiris* (23), which seems to advocate a more sophisticated interpretation of Egyptian myth, something approaching the sort of metaphysical symbolism which later Neoplatonists practised. But allegory was not a primary concern with Plutarch. His underworld myths (in 41, 43, and 60), like Plato's, are meant to be imaginative 'probable stories' about the fate of the soul after death, rather than parables in which the agents and actions in the fiction stand for the agents and actions of reality. What concerned him most in theological matters was the question of the ways in which god communicates with men. How does prophecy (*mantikē*) work? If this question cannot be answered with reasonable probability, there is no point in serving the oracle at Delphi, and the centre of Plutarch's life and faith is removed. One attempt at an answer is canvassed at length in *Oracles in Decline* (26 = II): the mediators between gods and men are the half-divine, half-mortal beings called *daimones* of whom we learn in certain classical texts of Hesiod and Plato. The notion of *daimōn* is obviously important to Plutarch, and there are various ambiguities about it (see especially 43 = IV); but the doctrine set out by Cleombrotus in *Oracles in Decline* is certainly not Plutarch's own best answer. In *Why are Delphic Oracles No Longer Given in Verse?* (25 = III), there is a much less clear-cut picture, and the debate seems to end with an affirmation of faith and the acceptance of possible alternative rational explanations. It was much the same with the other pillar of his faith, the belief in immortality. One can hardly doubt that the belief was real, and that the mysteries into which he had been initiated were its guarantee. On the other hand, the 'probable' tales in which he portrays the fate of the human soul are remarkably fanciful. His imagination riots in scientific fantasy; mathematics and astronomy, which played a large part in the education and culture of people like Plutarch, provided a setting, mysterious but plausible, for the cosmic adventures of the soul and the *daimones*. And his imagination is extraordinarily vivid; the effects of colour and movement are overwhelming. It has been customary, and it is quite right, to compare these visions not only with Plato but with Dante. Our example, the myth of Timarchus (43 = IV, below, IV. 590), is one of the most striking; but in vividness and horror it is second to the great myth in *God's Slowness to Punish* (41). Later tradition, as represented by a dream-book (Artemidorus 4. 47), seems to have identified (or confused) Plutarch with his fictional visionaries, for it is said that, a few days before he died, he had two dreams: one that he ascended into heaven under the guidance of Hermes; and one in which he learned that the first dream was a sign of great good fortune.

But let us come down to earth. Past and present mingle also in Plutarch's political (VI–VIII) and moral (IX–XVI) writings. In *Rules for Politicians* (52 = VII), most of the examples come from classical Greek history—Pericles, Cleon, Alexander—though there are many also from Rome, and one or two from recent experience of the Greek world under the Roman boot. Plutarch makes the connection clear. However much the world has changed, the basic principles of personal conduct in politics remain. The *demos* still has to be cajoled or controlled, in Roman Sardis as in classical Athens. Eloquence, money, and ingenuity are still the statesman's tools. There are still the same standards of honourable behaviour. Indeed, more may be expected in the way of humanity and generosity in these peaceful times, when there is no external danger, and after centuries of exposure to philosophical teaching. Some modern scholars seem to be shocked by this. They see it as 'camouflage and dissimulation', thinly covering the raw exercise of power by an élite of the wealthy and well-born. This is perhaps just a piece of liberal self-righteousness; it is certainly unfair. Plutarch did indeed have a critical view of the *demos*, both in classical Athens and in the cities of his own time. It was all too often fickle and cruel, for all its good intentions and good feelings. From his classical texts he could have imbibed both a fairly favourable view from the orators and a hostile and satirical one from Plato; perhaps the thought of the urban mobs in the great cities of the Empire inclined him more to the less kindly attitude. In any case, his hints on how to get your way are not dependent on a particular perception of democracy. They surely strike a chord in the mind of anyone who has had to manipulate opinion and get things done, whether on a small scale or a large. What distinguishes him from the cynical manipulator is his emphasis—not at all common in ancient writings on politics—on the qualities of gentleness and humanity (*praotes*, *philanthropia*); the Plutarchan politician is a good man, sympathetic, hard-working, and unselfish. He models himself on the good things in a Pericles or a Phocion, but he knows his limitations, and he has resources of literature and philosophy that they lacked.

There is no clear line to be drawn between the political writings and those which deal with private behaviour. It is noticeable, though, that Plutarch finds it possible to address treatises on anger (29), mental tranquillity (30), and brotherly love (31) to some very important people, high up in the Roman administration, to whom he would hardly dare to give political advice. It is noticeable also that, even when the subject admits a good deal of humour (e.g. curiosity (IX), talkativeness (X)), he is anxious not to make it seem too trivial; the garrulous man is not just a bore, he may be a danger to the community, because he cannot keep a secret. All these books are meant to be very practical; the fault is diagnosed, exercises to cure it are suggested, wise sayings are rehearsed, in the hope that they will stick in the mind and prevent further lapses. This is the fruit of Plutarch's activity as a counsellor, and of the emphasis on practical morals in the Hellenistic philosophical schools, especially the Stoics. But, once again, the literary material is classical, and the expectation is that people going about their ordinary affairs will be helped by seeing the circumstances they encounter in the light of texts they have learned at school. In this sort of subject, these texts come largely from comedy—especially Menander—but also from a philosophical tradition, from Aristotle's *Ethics* and especially, it seems, from the works of Aristotle's successor, Theophrastus. We possess only Theophrastus' *Characters*, a set of little sketches of various sorts of vanity, loquaciousness, and stinginess, which are in fact more amusing, and apparently less serious, than the corresponding characterizations in Plutarch. But he also wrote on ethical problems in a graver vein, and it is a reasonable conjecture that he is among Plutarch's main literary sources. There have always been bores and busybodies, braggarts and toadies; and Plutarch evidently thought it was helpful to see one's own experiences in this way in the light of comedy and philosophy. But the main lesson is not, as one might expect, to be tolerant of others; it is to mend one's ways, and heal one's soul.

One particular area of Plutarch's morals—family life and sexual ethics—has often attracted attention. It has frequently been said that his attitudes are more humane, more consonant with modern feeling, than those of most classical writers. Four books in this selection (XIII–XVI) contain the main material that bears on this question. It seems to be clear from *Eroticus* (47 = XIII) that he is not prepared to follow the 'philosophical' line, supposed to be Plato's, that homosexual love between males is a higher and more divine experience than heterosexual love. Plutarch, speaking in his own person, seems clear about this; and it is significant that the fictional defender of homosexuality in the dialogue, Pisias, is made to end by being a willing wedding-guest. But the Plutarchan ideal of marriage, which emerges from *Advice on Marriage*, is surely very distant from modern perception—though not from Jeremy Taylor's. The husband stands to the wife as soul to body, the natural leader and guide. She is to have no friends other than his, and to let him be the standard by which she rules her life. What does mark Plutarch out (though not Plutarch alone, for some Stoics, like Musonius, argued similarly) is a strong emphasis on the need for the wife to be educated. And this means education in philosophy, and indeed in mathematics. This is intended to help her not so much to develop natural virtues as to have a 'philosophical' attitude to life, accepting its vicissitudes with dignity and equanimity, and refraining from recourse to superstition or magic. If we are moved by *Advice on Marriage*, and find it congenial in many ways, this must be because of the insistent note of *philanthropia*, tolerance and humanity, which Plutarch sees as the guiding principle for both parties in a relationship which, however harmonious, is certainly unequal. The gap between Plutarch and Plato or Aristotle is less than is sometimes alleged.

Plutarch is the voice of the first Greek Renaissance. No wonder that he was so congenial to the Renaissance of early modern Europe. He looked to the past to give shape and principle to the present. This is how he came to give so homogeneous a picture of the classical world, and one so well calculated to appeal to a culture which yearned for just such a model. But the appeal of these 'essays' and 'dialogues' is not confined to people with a Renaissance cast of mind. It rests on the richness of detail and imagery, the personal voice, the sense of a good man, maybe rather conservative in his ways and inclined to talk too much, but someone whom we would be glad to know, and who still has a few useful things to say about how civilized people should conduct their public and private affairs.

PLUTARCH'S *MORALIA*

THIS is a list of the *Moralia* in the traditional order. There is a complete Greek text with English translation in the Loeb Classical Library, and a nearly complete one, with French translation, in the Collection Budé. There are two complete English translations: one by Philemon Holland (1603, 1657), and one by 'various hands' (1684–1718), revised by W. W. Goodwin (5 vols.; Boston, Mass., 1874–8). There is a selection of Philemon Holland in Everyman's Library (ed. E. W. Blakeney), and a selection of the Goodwin version in one volume (1878). There are other selections in English also, notably the versions by T. G. Tucker (1, 3, 4, 12, 13, 35, 36, 50, 51) and A. O. Prickard (24, 25, 26, 41, 43, 14) (Oxford, 1913, 1918), and the 1992 Penguin selection by R. Waterfield and I. G. Kidd (3, 4, 5, 22, 29, 30, 41, 43, 45, 64).

Both the Latin and the English titles are a matter of editors' choices, and vary somewhat in editions and translations.

[1] 1A–14C
'The Education of Children' (*Peri paidōn agōgēs, De liberis educandis*). Spurious: a very influential book in Renaissance educational writing.

[2] 14D–37B
'On Reading the Poets' (*Pōs dei ton neon poiēmatōn akouein, Quomodo adulescens poetas audire debeat* (*De audiendis poetis*))

[3] 37C–48D
'On Listening to Lectures' (*Peri tou akouein, De recta ratione audiendi*)

[4] 48E–74E
'Friends and Flatterers' (*Pōs an tis diakrineie ton kolaka tou philou, Quomodo adulator ab amico internoscatur* (*De adulatore et amico*))

[5] 75A–86A
'Progress in Virtue' (*Pōs an tis aisthoito heautou prokoptontos ep' aretēi, Quomodo quis suos in virtute sentiat profectus* (*De profectibus in virtute*))

[6] 86B–92E
'How to Profit from Your Enemies' (*Pōs an tis ap' echthrōn ōpheloito, De capienda ex inimicis utilitate*)

[7] 93A–97B
'On Having Many Friends' (*Peri poluphilias, De amicorum multitudine*)

[8] 97C–100A
'Fortune' (*Peri tuchēs, De fortuna*). Incomplete; declamatory in manner.

[9] 100B–101D
'Virtue and Vice' (*Peri aretēs kai kakias, De virtute et vitio*). Incomplete; declamatory in manner.

[10] 101E–121D
'Consolation to Apollonius' (*Paramūthētikos pros Apollōnion, Consolatio ad Apollonium*). Spurious; a useful collection of consolatory commonplaces.

[11] 122B–137E
'Advice on Health' (*Hugieina parangelmata, De tuenda sanitate praecepta*)

[12] 138A–146A
'Advice on Marriage' (*Gamika parangelmata, Coniugalia praecepta*)

[13] 146B–164D
'The Banquet of the Seven Sages' (*Tōn hepta sophōn sumposion, Septem sapientium convivium*)

[14] 164E–171E
'Superstition' (*Peri deisidaimonias, De superstitione*)

[15] 172A–208A
'Sayings of Kings and Commanders' (*Basileōn apophthegmata kai stratēgōn, Regum et imperatorum apophthegmata*). Preface is forged, and the whole work spurious, even if it uses Plutarch's material.

[16] 208A–242D
'Spartan Sayings' (*Apophthegmata Lakōnika, Apophthegmata Laconica*)

[17] 242E–263C
'Virtues in Women' (*Gunaikōn aretai, Mulierum virtutes*)

[18] 263D–291C, 291D–304F
'Roman Questions, Greek Questions' (*Aitia Rōmaïka, Aitia Hellēnika, Quaestiones Romanae, Quaestiones Graecae*)

[19] 305A–316B
'Minor Parallels' (*Sunagōgē historiōn parallēlōn Hellēnikōn kai Rōmaiōn, Parallela minora*). Spurious.

[20] 316B–326C
'The Fortune of Rome' (*Peri tēs Romaiōn tuchēs, De fortuna Romanorum*)

[21] 326D–345B
'Fortune and Virtue in Alexander the Great, 1–2' (*Peri tēs Alexandrou tuchēs ē aretēs, i–ii, De Alexandri magni fortuna aut virtute, i–ii*)

[22] 345D–351B
'The Glory of Athens' (*Poteron Athēnaioi kata polemon ē kata sophian endoxoteroi, Bellone an pace clariores fuerint Athenienses* (*De gloria Atheniensium*))

[23] 351C–384C
'Isis and Osiris' (*Peri Isidos kai Osiridos, De Iside et Osiride*)

[24] 384D–394C
'The Delphic "E" ' (*Peri tou E tou en Delphois, De E apud Delphos*)

[25] 394D–409D
'Why Are Delphic Oracles No Longer Given in Verse?' (*Peri tou mē chrān emmetra nūn tēn Puthian, De Pythiae oraculis*)

[26] 409E–438E
'Oracles in Decline' (*Peri tōn ekleloipotōn chrēstēriōn, De defectu oraculorum*)

[27] 439A–440C
'Is Virtue Teachable?' (*Ei didakton hē aretē, An virtus doceri possit*)

[28] 440D–452D
'Moral Virtue' (*Peri ēthikēs aretēs, De virtute morali*)

[29] 452E–464D
'The Control of Anger' (*Peri aorgēsias, De cohibenda ira*)

[30] 464E–477F
'Quiet of Mind' (*Peri euthūmias, De tranquillitate animi*)

[31] 478A–492D
'Brotherly Love' (*Peri philadelphias, De fraterno amore*)

[32] 493A–497E
'Love of Offspring' (*Peri tēs eis ta ekgona philostorgias, De amore prolis*). Incomplete.

[33] 498A–500A
'Is Vice a Sufficient Cause of Misery?' (*Ei autarkēs hē kakia pros kakodaimonian, An vitiositas ad infelicitatem sufficiat*). Incomplete.

[34] 500B–502A
'Ills of the Body and Ills of the Mind' (*Peri tou poteron ta psuchēs ē ta sōmatos pathē cheirona, Animine an corporis affectiones sint peiores*). Fragmentary.

[35] 502B–515A
'Talkativeness' (*Peri adoleschias, De garrulitate*)

[36] 515B–523B
'Curiosity' (*Peri polupragmosunēs, De curiositate*)

[37] 523C–528B
'Love of Money' (*Peri philoploutias, De cupiditate divitiarum*)

[38] 528C–536D
'Bashfulness' (*Peri dusōpias, De vitioso pudore*)

[39] 536D–538E
'Envy and Hatred' (*Peri phthonou kai misous, De invidia et odio*). Fragmentary.

[40] 539A–547F
'Self-Praise without Offence' (*Peri tou heauton epainein anepiphthonōs, De laude ipsius*)

[41] 548A–568A
'God's Slowness to Punish' (*Peri tōn hupo tou theiou bradeōs timōroumenōn, De sera numinis vindicta*)

[42] 568B–574F
'Fate' (*Peri heimarmenēs, De fato*). Spurious: a 'middle Platonist' work of some historical importance.

[43] 575A–598F
'Socrates' *Daimonion*' (*Peri tou Sōkratous daimoniou, De genio Socratis*)

[44] 599A–607F
'Exile' (*Peri phugēs, De exilio*)

[45] 608A–612A
'Consolation to My Wife' (*Paramūthētikos pros tēn gunaika, Consolatio ad uxorem*)

[46] 612C–748D
'Table Talk, I–IX' (*Sumposiakōn biblia ennea, Quaestionum Convivialium libri ix*)

[47] 748E–771E
'Eroticus' (*Erōtikos, Amatorius*)

[48] 771E–775E
'Love Stories' (*Erōtikai diēgēseis, Amatoriae narrationes*). Spurious.

[49] 776A–779C
'Philosophers and Princes' (*Peri tou hoti malista tois hēgemosi dei ton philosophon dialegesthai, Maxime cum principibus philosopho esse disserendum*). Fragmentary.

[50] 779E–782F
'The Uneducated Prince' (*Pros hēgemona apaideuton, Ad principem ineruditum*). Fragmentary.

[51] 783A–797F
'Old Men in Politics' (*Ei presbuterōi politeuteon, An seni sit gerenda res publica*)

[52] 798A–825F
'Rules for Politicians' (*Politika parangelmata, Praecepta gerendae reipublicae*)

[53] 826A–827C
'Monarchy, Democracy, and Oligarchy' (*Peri monarchias kai dēmokratias kai oligarchias, De unius in republica dominatione, populari statu, et paucorum imperio*). Incomplete.

[54] 827D–832A
'Against Borrowing Money' (*Peri tou mē dein daneizesthai, De vitando aere alieno*)

[55] 832B–852C
'Lives of the Ten Orators' (*Bioi tōn deka rhētorōn, Vitae decem oratorum*). Spurious; an important source for ancient knowledge of the Attic orators from Antiphon to Dinarchus.

[56] 853A–854D
'Comparison of Aristophanes and Menander' (abridgement) (*Sunkriseōs Aristophanous kai Menandrou epitomē, Comparationis Aristophanis et Menandri compendium*)

[57] 854E–874C
'Herodotus' Malice' (*Peri tēs Hērodotou kakoētheias, De Herodoti malignitate*)

[58] 874A–911C
'Doctrines of the Philosophers' (*Peri tōn areskontōn philosophois phusikōn dogmatōn, De placitis philosophorum*). Five books; not Plutarch's own work.

[59] 911C–919E
'Natural Questions' (*Aitia phusika, Quaestiones naturales*). Incompletely preserved.

[60] 920A–945E
'The Face in the Moon' (*Peri tou emphainomenou prosōpou tōi kuklōi tēs selēnēs, De facie quae in orbe lunae apparet*)

[61] 945F–955C
'The Primary Cold' (*Peri tou prōtōs psuchrou, De primo frigido*)

[62] 955D–958E
'Which is More Useful, Fire or Water?' (*Poteron hudōr ē pūr chrēsimōteron, Aquane an ignis sit utilior*). Declamatory; authenticity suspected.

[63] 959A–985C
'The Intelligence of Animals' (*Potera tōn zōōn phronimōtera, ta chersaia ē ta enudra, Terrestriane an aquatilia animalia sint callidiora* (*De sollertia animalium*))

[64] 985D–992E
'Gryllus' (*Peri tou ta aloga logōi chrēsthai, Bruta animalia ratione uti* (*Gryllus*))

[65–66] 993A–999B
'On Eating Flesh, 1–2' (*Peri sarkophagias i–ii, De esu carnium i–ii*). Two speeches; incompletely and badly preserved.

[67] 999C–1011F
'Platonic Questions' (*Platōnika zētēmata, Platonicae quaestiones*)

[68] 1012A–1030C
'The Creation of the Soul in Plato's "Timaeus" ' (*Peri tēs en Timaiōi psuchogonias, De animae procreatione in Timaeo*)

[69] 1030D–1032F
Epitome of 68.

[70] 1033A–1057C
'Contradictions of the Stoics' (*Peri Stōikōn enantiōmatōn, De Stoicorum repugnantiis*)

[71] 1057C–1058D
'Stoic Paradoxes are Stranger than Poets' ' (*Hoti paradoxotera hoi Stōikoi tōn poiētōn legousin, Stoicos absurdiora poetis dicere*). Incomplete.

[72] 1058E–1086B
'Common Notions: Against the Stoic View' (*Peri tōn koinōn ennoiōn pros tous Stōikous, De communibus notitiis adversus Stoicos*)

[73] 1086C–1107C
'Not Even a Pleasant Life is Possible on Epicurean Principles' (*Hoti oud' hēdeōs zēn estin kat' Epikouron, Non posse suaviter vivi secundum Epicurum*)

[74] 1107D–1127E
'Against Colotes' (*Pros Kōlōten, Adversus Colotem*)

[75] 1128A–1130C
' "Live Unknown" ' (*Ei kalōs eirētai to 'lathe biōsas', An recte dictum sit latenter esse vivendum* (*De latenter vivendo*)). Declamatory.

[76] 1131A–1147A
'Music' (*Peri mousikēs, De musica*). A history in a dialogue setting: not by Plutarch.

[77–8]
Two brief pieces on: whether desire and grief are psychical or somatic phenomena; whether the affective element in man should be regarded as a part or a faculty of his soul.

Fragments. These are collected by F. H. Sandbach: in the Teubner *Moralia*, vol. vii; in the Loeb, vol. xv.

FURTHER READING

THERE are recent general books on Plutarch by R. H. Barrow (*Plutarch and His Times*, London, 1967), D. A. Russell (*Plutarch*, London, 1973), C. P. Jones (*Plutarch and Rome*, Oxford, 1971); a general introduction to the *Moralia* by R. Flacelière forms the Introduction to vol. i of the Budé *Œuvres Morales*, pp. vii–ccxxvi. The article 'Ploutarchos' by Konrat Ziegler in Pauly and Wissowa, *Realenzyklopädie*, (Stuttgart, 1964) xxi 636–962, remains the basic work of reference. Guidance on some of the pieces in this volume (I, III, IV, V, X, XIII, XV, XVI) may be found in H. D. Betz (ed.), *Plutarch's Theological Writings and Early Christian Literature*, (Studia ad Corpus Hellenisticum Novi Testamenti, Leiden, 1975) and in the companion volume on *Plutarch's Ethical Writings* (1978). *Ploutarchos*, the journal of the International Plutarch Society, reviews current work and announces conferences and colloquia.

On Plutarch's influence, R. Hirzel's *Plutarch*, (Leipzig, 1912) has not been superseded; for the French tradition, see especially R. Aulotte, *Amyot et Plutarque* (Geneva, 1965); and for Emerson, E. G. Berry, *Emerson's Plutarch* (Cambridge, Mass., 1961).

I

SUPERSTITION

Deisidaimonia, which we translate 'superstition', is literally 'fear of *daimones*'; but the reference is not particularly to *daimones* in the special sense of intermediaries between gods and men (see Introd. p. xviii), but to any kind of cult or belief that may lead to excess. Plutarch argues that piety is a mean between unbelief (atheism) and superstition, and that the latter is much the worse of the two extremes, because it is not just a cold conviction but a morbid state of the emotions. His picture is grim; he does not so much laugh at ridiculous eccentricities (as Theophrastus did in his character of the Superstitious Man) as denounce the dark horrors of a life led in the shadow of obsessive fears. The tone is often like that of the Epicurean Lucretius' denunciation of *religio* as the source of barbarous cruelties and fears that cannot find reassurance. This has led some scholars to believe that 'Superstition' is an early work, not representing Plutarch's true religious attitudes, or else that it is a rhetorical exercise, one of a pair, in which its lost partner contained a parallel attack on atheism. Neither hypothesis is needed. There is nothing here that contradicts his usual stand on religious matters, though the presentation is somewhat more rhetorical than elsewhere.

Jeremy Taylor makes considerable use of this essay in his sermons on 'Godly Fear' (*Eniautos: Twenty-five Sermons*, vii) and 'The Entail of Curses Cut Off' (*Eniautos: twenty-seven sermons*, iii).

[1] Ignorance or incomprehension of the gods divides at source, 164
as it were, into two streams. One makes atheism grow on the hard ground of obstinacy, the other develops superstition in the soft soil of a tender heart. Any false judgement, particularly about this subject, is, of course, to be deplored—and all the more so when emotion is involved. Emotion is like an inflamed wound. Just as dislocations of joints are more serious if there is also a wound, so distortions of the mind are more serious when there is an accompanying emotion. That atoms and void* are the basic principles of the universe is a false doctrine; but it produces no ulcers, no throbbing, no distracting pain. The belief that wealth is the greatest good, on the other hand, is a false- 165
hood with venom in it; it ravages the soul, drives you mad,

denies you sleep, fills you with wild impulses, pushes you over precipices, strangles you, and takes away all freedom of speech. Again: there are people who believe that virtue and vice are corporeal: a shameful piece of ignorance, no doubt, but not deserving mourning and lamentation. It is when we come to judgements and attitudes like that expressed in the lines:

> O wretched Virtue, you were but a word;
> yet I pursued you as a real thing[1]

giving up 'the wealth-producer, Wrong' and 'Intemperance, the mother of all pleasure', that we should feel both pity and disgust, because these attitudes breed many ills and diseases, like so many worms and maggots, in the soul.

[2] But let us come to our subject. Atheism, being the false judgement that there is no such thing as a blessed and eternal being, seems to conduce to absence of emotion, because of its disbelief in the divine. But the very name we give to superstition in Greek—*deisidaimonia*, 'fear of the daemonic'—itself declares that this is an emotional attitude, a position which tends to produce a fear which humiliates and crushes the man who believes that there are indeed gods, but that they cause harm and distress. Atheists do not respond to the divine at all; the superstitious make a wrong and perverted response. Ignorance makes the former disbelieve in a helping god, and the latter believe in a harmful one. Thus atheism is a mistaken doctrine, superstition an emotional condition arising out of a mistaken doctrine.

[3] All morbid emotions of the mind are ignoble, but some possess a certain pride, sublimity, and elevation, by virtue of their very volatility, and there is hardly one that is without some active impulse. Indeed, the common charge brought against all emotions is that their impulses to action exercise a driving and compelling force upon reason. It is only fear, which is as deficient in confidence as it is in power of reasoning, whose irrationality is inactive, impotent, and irresolute. That is why it is called in Greek *deima* or *tarbos*, from *deon*, 'binding', because it ties the soul up, and *taratton*, 'troubling', because it also troubles it. Now the most inactive and impotent fear of all is this 'fear of the daemonic', this superstition. No one fears the sea un-

less he travels on it, no one fears war unless he is serving in the army; the stay-at-home has no fear of brigands, the poor man no fear of informers, the private citizen no fear of malice. Men are not afraid of earthquakes in Gaul,* or of lightning strikes in Ethiopia. But he who fears the gods fears everything—land and sea, air and sky, darkness and light, voices and silence.*

The sleeping slave forgets his master, sleep lightens the prisoner's chains; suppurating wounds, savage ulcers, and gripping pains all vanish when we rest:

> O sleep's dear charm, that lightenest my disease,
> how sweet thy coming in my hour of need![2]

This is something superstition will never let you say. It alone makes no truce with sleep; it never lets the soul relax and regain courage in those hours by thrusting aside its bitter and depressing concept of god. On the contrary, it turns the sleep of the superstitious into a hell, rousing up terrifying visions, monstrous phantoms, and avenging spirits. It racks the wretched soul, and hounds it from its slumbers with nightmares; and that soul suffers torments of self-flagellation and self-chastisement in the belief that these are inflicted on it by another, and accepts the most dreadful and bizarre instructions. Nor, when he gets up, can the superstitious man set all this at naught or make fun of it, or feel pleased that none of the things that troubled him was real. He escapes the shadow of a harmless deception only to 166
deceive and trouble his waking self and waste his money on charlatans and wizards who say

> 'Should some nocturnal phantom scare you
> or hellish Hecate's rout come near you[1]

summon the old witch to smear you all over,* dip yourself in the sea, or sit all day on the ground.'

> 'O barbarous evils that the Greeks invent'[2]

in their superstitious fear—smearing with mud and muck, keeping sabbaths, falling on the face, undignified sessions of sitting down in public, performing bizarre acts of devotion. Supporters of traditional music used to advise singers to the lyre to keep 'a true mouth': I am suggesting that we should pray to the gods with a 'true' and right mouth, and not commit the absurdity of examining the tongue of a sacrificial victim to see if it is clean and true, while disgracing our own tongues by distorting and polluting them with extraordinary words and barbarous phrases and offending against the traditional and divine dignity and piety. A comic poet has an amusing remark about people who have gold-plated or silver-plated beds:

> Sleep is the only thing the gods give free:
> why make it so expensive to yourself?[3]

Similarly, one can say to the superstitious man: 'Why make a permanent and painful house of correction for yourself out of something the gods gave us to make us forget and rest from our troubles? Your poor soul can't escape to another sleep!' Heraclitus says that the waking have a single common world, but in sleep everyone retires into his own private one.[4] The superstitious man has no such common world and no private world either. He has no use of his reason when awake, and no relief from anxiety when at rest. His reason is always dreaming, his fear is always awake. He has no escape or change.

[4] Polycrates was a dreaded tyrant on Samos, as Periander was at Corinth; yet nobody continued in fear of them who migrated to a free and democratic city. But if a man fears the rule of the gods as a grim, inexorable tyranny, whither shall he migrate, whither shall he flee? What land, what sea can he find that has no gods? In what corner of the world, poor wretch, can you sink and hide yourself, confident that you have escaped god? The law permits slaves who despair of winning their freedom to apply to be sold and pass to a kinder master; but superstition offers no change of gods, there is no way of finding a god who will not be feared by the man who fears the gods of his ancestors and his family, who shudders at the powers of salvation and beneficence, who goes in fear and trembling at the thought of those from whom we ask wealth, prosperity, peace, concord, and the success of our noblest words and actions. And yet these people regard slavery as a misfortune and say

> For man or woman it is dire disaster
> to be a slave and have a cruel master.[5]

How much worse, though, to have masters whom it is impossible to escape or flee or desert! The slave has his altar of refuge, the robber his sanctuary in many a temple, escapers from battle feel safe if they can touch a statue: but the superstitious man goes in fear and terror of these very aids in which men place their hopes when they fear the worst. Do not drag the superstitious man from the shrine: it is there that he is punished and tormented. In a word: 'Death limits life for all mankind',* but it does not limit superstition, which crosses the frontiers of living, prolongs fear beyond life, links death with an expectation of undying evils, and, at the very moment when our troubles cease, imagines the start of troubles that will never cease—a gate of
Hell, deep down, that opens for us, rivers of fire mingling with 167
branches of Styx, darkness filled with fanciful forms of hideous shape and piteous cry; there are judges and executioners, gulfs and chasms full of innumerable horrors. This god-cursed fear of gods, this superstition, makes the terrors it has escaped in life inescapable in expectation.

[5] None of these consequences attends atheism. Its ignorance is indeed grievous. To be blind in so important a matter is a great misfortune to the mind, which loses thereby the brightest and most vital of its many eyes, its perception of the divine. Yet the opinion is not automatically accompanied, as we have seen, by the additional element of emotion, of ulceration, of confusion, and of abject submission. Plato tells us that music, the creator of harmony and balance, was not given to man by the gods as a luxury to titillate the ear; its function is to unravel and restore to due order that erratic turbulence of the soul's cycles and harmonies which is so often rampant in the body through disorder and lack of control, when Muse and Grace are lacking.

'But the creatures Zeus loves not', says Pindar, 'feel terror when they hear the Muses cry',[1] and grow savage and angry. Tigers, we are told, are maddened and driven distraught by the noise of drums around them, and end by tearing themselves to pieces. And so to be insensitive and unresponsive to music, out of deafness or impairment of faculties, is actually the lesser evil.

It was Tiresias' misfortune not to see his children or his friends, but it was a greater misfortune for Athamas and Agaue to see them as lions or stags. It would have been better for Heracles in his madness* not to have seen his sons or been aware of their presence than to treat his nearest and dearest as the enemy.

Is not this precisely the difference between atheists and the superstitious? The former do not see the gods at all, the latter see them wrong. The former do not believe in their existence, the latter mistake their kindness for terror, their fatherliness for despotism, their care of us for cruelty, and their superiority to anger for savageness and brutality.

Again, they follow the artists in stone and bronze and wax in believing that the gods have bodies in human shape, and they fashion and adorn and adore such images; but they pay no attention to the philosophers and statesmen who demonstrate that the majesty of God implies his goodness, his generosity, his kindliness, and his care.

So the atheist is insensitive to, and incredulous of, divine help, while the superstitious react to that help with fear and confusion. In short, atheism is a failure to respond to the divine or to form a conception of its goodness, while superstition is an excessive response which views good as evil. The superstitious fear the gods, but take refuge with them. They flatter them, but abuse them. They pray to them, but blame them. It is man's common lot not to be consistently happy:

> Illness, old age and pain
> only they escape
> who have passed the roaring straits of Acheron[2]

says Pindar. Human affairs and experiences are bound up with the ever-changing flow of chance.

[6] Consider the atheist in time of trouble. Observe his disposition. If he is a generally well-balanced person, he will cope with circumstances quietly and provide his own help and comfort. If he is impatient or indignant, he will direct all his
168 complaints against chance and fortune, and cry that there is no justice or providence in the world, but that human affairs go their purposeless way in confusion and disorder. Not so the superstitious man. If some little accident happens to him, down he sits and builds a great pile of insoluble problems on top of his

grief. He fills himself with fears and terrors, suspicions and panics, and is racked with groans and lamentations. It is not man, nor fortune, nor the times, nor himself that he blames for everything: it is god. From god, he says, flows the fated stream of disaster that has struck him. He thinks himself chastised and punished by the gods, not as an unfortunate, but as one whom they hate; and he conceives that all his sufferings are deserved and are his own fault. In illness, again, the atheist recalls his excesses of food and wine, the irregularities of his daily life, unusual fatigue, or unaccustomed changes of climate or place. If he gets into political difficulty, or finds himself unpopular with the people or discredited with the ruler, he looks for the cause in himself, and asks himself

> In what was I at fault? what did I do?
> Or what was not done though it was my duty?[1]

The superstitious man, on the other hand, treats everything as a blow from god or an assault of some daemonic power. It does not matter what it is: illness, financial loss, the death of a child, ill-luck or failure in politics. He has not the heart to help himself, to sweep the accident aside, or to take steps to remedy or resist it, for fear of seeming to fight the gods and kick against his punishment. So, if he is ill, the doctor is sent away; if he is in mourning, he will not admit the philosopher who could advise and console him. 'Sir', he says, 'let me pay the price, impious creature that I am, cursed by the gods and loathed by *daimones*.' If an unbeliever is in deep distress, one can wipe his tears, cut his hair, or change his mourning-clothes: but what can you say to the superstitious man? How can you help him? He sits outside in sackcloth or clad in filthy rags, he rolls naked in the mud and proclaims his sins and trespasses—he ate or drank something, or took some path that heaven forbade. On the best assumption—that is, that he has only a mild attack of superstition—he sits at home being fumigated and smeared all over, while the old women, as Bion says, 'come and use him as a peg* to hang anything on that they please'.[2]

[7] The story goes that Tiribazus, when arrested by the Persians, drew his scimitar and showed fight (he was a powerful man); but when they called out that they were arresting him on

the king's orders, he threw his weapon down and let them tie his hands. This is just the sort of behaviour we see in the superstitious. Whereas most men fight misfortune and thrust trouble aside, finding ways of avoiding or diverting disaster, the superstitious man says to himself, without any prompting from others, 'You are suffering because providence wills it and God commands it.' He therefore abandons hope, surrenders, runs away, and fends off anyone who tries to help.

Superstition makes many small troubles fatal. Midas of old, so we gather, being depressed and troubled by a dream, fell into such despair that he did away with himself by drinking bull's blood. Aristodemus, king of Messene, during the war with Sparta,* killed himself because he too became totally despondent and without hope, because the dogs howled like wolves, and dog's-tooth grass* started growing on his family hearth, and the diviners regarded these as ominous signs. And it might have been better for the Athenian general Nicias* to be rid of his
169 superstition in that way, instead of allowing himself, just because he was frightened by a lunar eclipse, to be hemmed in by the enemy wall, and then be captured and die an inglorious death, after losing 40,000 men, killed or taken prisoner. There is nothing alarming about the interposition of the earth, nothing terrible about the conjunction of its shadow with the moon at the due point of the cycle; what is truly terrible is the power of the darkness of superstition to confuse and blind the intellect of the man who falls into it at the very moment when he most needs his intelligence:

> Glaucus, see the troubled water: out at sea the waves run high:
> and that cloud upright on Gyrae signals that the storm is nigh.*[1]

When the helmsman sees this, he prays to get away and calls on the saviour gods; but, while he prays, he pulls on the tiller, lightens the yard, and 'runs in off the darkening sea with shortened sail'.[2] Hesiod tells the farmer to pray to 'Zeus of the Earth and holy Demeter'[3] before ploughing or sowing—but to pray with his hand on the plough. Homer[4] says that, when Ajax was going to fight Hector in single combat, he told the Greeks to pray to the gods for him; but while they prayed, he put on his armour. It is only after Agamemnon has told his fighting men to 'sharpen your spears and put your shields in place'[5] that he prays to Zeus 'Grant me to lay Priam's palace on the ground'.[6]

God is the hope of courage, not the excuse of cowardice. The Jews* sat in their new clothes on the sabbath while the enemy set up their ladders and seized the walls. They simply waited for them, trapped in the net of their superstition.

[8] If these are the results of superstition in difficult and critical moments or circumstances, it has no advantages over atheism on happier occasions either. Festivals, temple celebrations, initiations, mysteries, prayer, and veneration of the gods are among man's greatest pleasures. Observe the atheist on such occasions. He laughs madly or sardonically at the performance, and probably mumbles to his friends something about the stupidity and idiocy of people who think this is done for the gods, but that is the sum total of his error. The superstitious man, however, would like to be happy and enjoy the occasion; but he cannot. His soul is like the plague-stricken city 'with incense filled, with hymns, and yet with sighs'.[7] He grows pale under his festive garland, sacrifices in terror, prays with a tremulous voice, puts the incense on with shaking hand, and generally proves that Pythagoras was talking nonsense when he said: 'We are at our best when we visit the gods.' It is just then that the superstitious are at their worst and their most miserable. You would think they were going to bears' dens or snakes' lairs or sea-monsters' caverns, not temples and shrines of gods.

[9] It therefore seems extraordinary to me to call atheism impiety and not say the same of superstition. Yet Anaxagoras was charged with impiety because he called the sun a lump of stone, but no one calls the Cimmerians impious because they do not believe in a sun at all. If the unbeliever is unholy, is not the man who holds views of the gods like those of the superstitious guilty of a much greater unholiness? I would much rather have men say that I do not exist, and there is no such person as Plutarch, than that Plutarch is unstable, unreliable, quick 170
to anger, indiscriminately vindictive, and prone to take offence at trifles; or that, if you give a dinner and leave him out, or are too busy to call on him or speak to him, he will seize you and

eat you up, or kidnap your baby and beat it to death, or let a wild animal loose on your crops and ruin your harvest.

When Timotheus performed his *Artemis* at Athens and came to the line 'maddened, manic, frantic, frenzied',[1] the lyric poet Cinesias stood up in the audience and cried 'I wish you a daughter like that!' Yet the superstitious have a similar or worse opinion of Artemis:

> Whether hasting from a hanging
> or tormenting one in childbirth,
> whether fresh from viewing corpses
> you have come indoors polluted,
> or have robbed the crossroads offering
> or embraced the blood-stained killer . . .*

Nor do they have any more favourable idea of Apollo or Hera or Aphrodite. They go in fear and trembling of them all. Superstition teaches these fools worse blasphemies than ever Niobe committed. They believe the goddess shot down that poor lady's 'six daughters and six sons in flower of youth',[2] simply because she felt insulted: she was so implacable, they think, and had such an appetite for other people's troubles! But if she really had been angry and a hater of vice, hurt by the evil things said of her, and enraged rather than amused at human ignorance and stupidity, the people she ought to have shot down were those who falsely attributed such cruelty and bitterness to her and spread such tales in speech and in writing. We criticize the savagery and inhumanity in Hecuba's words, when she says, 'let me get his liver in my teeth and eat it!'*[3] Yet our superstitious friends believe that, if you eat sprats or anchovies, the goddess of Syria* will gnaw your shins, burn your body with ulcers, and liquefy your liver!

[10] Can it be, then, that it is wicked to speak evil of the gods, but not wicked to think it? Or is it his thought that makes the blasphemer's words so wrong? We commonly treat evil words as a sign of bad feeling, and think that those who speak ill of us are also ill-disposed to us and therefore our enemies. In this light, consider what the superstitious feel about the gods. They assume them to be excitable, faithless, changeable, vengeful, cruel, and offended by trifles. They must therefore inevitably hate and fear the gods, since they think that their greatest troubles have come about, and will come about, through their agency. And if a man hates the gods and fears them, he must also be their enemy. There is no need to be surprised that they kiss their hands to them, sacrifice to them, and spend time in their temples. People are polite to tyrants, grovel before them, and erect golden statues in their honour, though they hate them silently 'with a shake of the head'.[4] Hermolaus was a courtier of Alexander's, Pausanias served in Philip's bodyguard, Chaereas in Caligula's: but they all said to themselves as they went about their duties 'Had I the power, I would take vengeance on you.'*[5] The atheist does not believe there are any gods; the superstitious man wishes there were none, but unwillingly believes they exist, because he is afraid not to believe it. He would be as glad to escape the fear that oppresses him as Tantalus would be to avoid the rock that hangs over his head, and would find the atheist's state of mind enviable freedom. As things are, however, the atheist has no tinge of superstition in him, while the superstitious person is an atheist in intention, but too cowardly to hold the opinions about the gods that he wishes to hold.

[12] Not that the atheist is in any way responsible for supersti- 171
tion. On the contrary, superstition both gave rise to atheism in the first instance, and has subsequently provided it with a defence—an untrue and ignoble one, indeed, but not without plausibility. Men have never thought the universe godless on the ground of detecting some fault in stars or seasons, in the periods of the moon or the movements of the sun around the earth, those 'craftsmen of day and night',* or some disorder or error in the way animals are nourished or crops grow. It is the ridiculous things that superstition does and endures—the words, the movements, the sorcery and witchcraft, the capering, the drumming, the impure purifications and filthy taboos, the lawless and barbarous chastisements and befoulings in the temples—this is what makes some people say that it would be better if there were no gods at all than gods that accept and enjoy such things, and are so violent, so petty, and so prone to take offence. Would it not have been better for the Gauls and the Scyths to have no concept or image or tradition about the gods, than to believe that gods exist who enjoy the blood of slaughtered humans and think this the

most perfect sacrifice and act of worship? Would it not have been better for the Carthaginians to have had Critias or Diagoras for lawgiver and acquired no belief in gods or *daimones*, rather than sacrifice to Cronus in the way they do? They were not like the animal sacrificers, of whom Empedocles* says:

> The form is changed, but 'tis his son
> the father raises up and kills, and says the prayer,
> fool that he is![1]

No; the Carthaginians knew what they were doing when they sacrificed their children.* Childless fathers would buy children from the poor, just like lambs or chickens. The mother stood by, unweeping, uncomplaining. If she wept or screamed, the money was forfeit, but the child was dead just the same. The area in front of the statue echoed with the music of pipes and drums, to drown the cries and screams. If the Titans or Giants had driven out the gods and established their rule over us, this is the sacrifice they would have enjoyed, this is the service they would have demanded. Amestris, the wife of Xerxes, buried twelve men alive, to save her own life, in sacrifice to Hades—to that very god, that is, who (as Plato tells us[2]) takes his name from his kindness and wisdom and wealth, and controls the souls by reason and persuasion.

The philosopher Xenophanes gave an apt reminder to the Egyptians whom he saw beating their breasts and mourning at the festivals. 'If they are gods',[3] he said, 'do not mourn them: if they are men, do not sacrifice to them.'

[13] There is no sickness so rich in aberrations and sufferings as superstition, nor so deeply involved in contradictory and conflicting attitudes. We must indeed avoid it—but at the same time not fall into the error of people who try to escape from the attack of robbers or wild animals or fire without proper thought or consideration, and find themselves in a wilderness of gulfs and precipices. Yet that is what happens to some people; trying to escape superstition, they fall into the harsh and obdurate ways of the atheist, leaping right over piety, which lies between.

II

ORACLES IN DECLINE

This dialogue is set in Delphi, in AD 83/4. The dramatic date is given by the reference to Callistratus at the beginning, and fits well with an exploration of Britain by Demetrius (see chap. 18) under the governorship of Agricola. The date of composition may be considerably later. The narrator is Plutarch's brother Lamprias. The question under discussion is the reason why oracles are now less vocal and important than in the classical past. We are given suggestions from the Cynic Didymus (that men are now too wicked) and from Plutarch's Platonist teacher Ammonius (that the population has declined, so that there is not so much demand for prophecy). But the two main contributors to the discussion are Cleombrotus of Sparta, a much-travelled enthusiast for religious and philosophical lore, and Lamprias himself. Cleombrotus (see Introd. p. xviii) attributes prophecy to *daimones*, the intermediaries between gods and men of whom Hesiod and Plato spoke. Lamprias takes a much more rationalizing line, suggesting that the natural prophetic power of the human soul is stimulated by 'streams' or 'spirits' emanating from special places on earth. Ammonius and the others are somewhat shocked by the materialism of this, and its tendency to weaken belief in divine providence; and Lamprias, in the concluding chapters, defends himself against this charge. Included in the discussion, though only faintly germane to the main theme, is a lengthy argument about the number of worlds (*kosmoi*) in existence: one, or five, or (as Cleombrotus has it on the exotic authority of an Oriental sage) 183. Lamprias and Ammonius are both professional Plato scholars; and their involved 'mystical mathematics' and ingenious dovetailing of various Platonic texts give a vivid impression of the style of speculation—philosophical, scientific, pseudo-scientific, and antiquarian—which Plutarch and his circle enjoyed.

[1] The story is, my dear Terentius Priscus, that certain eagles or swans, flying from the ends of the earth towards its centre, met here at Pytho at what they call the Navel;* then, in a later age, Epimenides of Phaestus, wanting to test the story by questioning Apollo, received an obscure and ambiguous answer, whereupon he exclaimed: 409

Then after all there is no Navel, centre of earth or sea,
Or, if there is, 'tis God that sees it, human eyes cannot.[1]

Apollo had good reason to fend him off, if he was trying to test an ancient story by touch, like a picture.

410 [2] Now shortly before the Pythian festival held under our contemporary Callistratus, there chanced to come together here in Delphi, from the opposite ends of the earth, two holy men: Demetrius the grammarian, on his way home from Britain to Tarsus: and Cleombrotus the Spartan, who had often travelled in Egypt and in the country of the Troglodytes, and sailed far up the Red Sea. Cleombrotus' object was not trade; he was a studious and curious person, who had means enough and was not greatly interested in having more than enough. He therefore used his leisure in these pursuits, and was collecting information to serve as material for a philosophy having, as he would put it, 'theology' as its goal. He had recently visited the oracle of Ammon and obviously had no great admiration for much of what he saw there. He did, however, give a very interesting account of the lamp that never goes out, based on what the priests had told him. He informed us that it used up less oil every year, and that the priests regarded this as proof of a variation in the length of the years, making each succeeding year shorter than its predecessor; less oil, they pointed out, would naturally be used in a shorter time.

[3] The company marvelled at this, but Demetrius declared it was quite ridiculous to pursue such large issues on such trivial evidence—not drawing 'the lion from his claws',[1] as Alcaeus says, but revolutionizing the whole celestial universe with the aid of a lamp and a wick, and utterly subverting the principles of mathematics. 'Neither of these difficulties will trouble our friends,' replied Cleombrotus: 'they will not yield to the mathematicians in point of accuracy, because they think those people are more likely to be wrong in timing such remote motions and cycles than they are themselves in measuring the oil, especially as they keep a constant watch on the peculiar phenomenon, just because it is so extraordinary. Secondly, Demetrius, the idea that we should not allow that small things may be the sign of great would be an obstacle to many arts. Many demonstrations

and many forecasts would be taken from us. You scholars prove the significant fact that the Homeric heroes shaved with razors from a passage in Homer that mentions a razor;[2] and that they lent money at interest from the line "a debt is owed me, neither new nor small",[3] where, you say, the word for "is owed", *ophelletai*, in fact means "grows". Again, when Homer calls night "sharp",* you pounce eagerly on the word and say that he means precisely that the shadow of the earth is conical, because it is the shadow of a spherical object. And would a person who denies the claim of small signs to indicate great events allow the medical profession to prophesy an unhealthy summer on the evidence of an abundance of spiders' webs or when the spring lettuces look like crows' feet? Would he let the size of the sun be measured by pints and quarts of water,* or the acute angle made by the plinth* here with the ground to be regarded as a measure of the elevation above the horizon of the pole that is always visible? That's the defence I can hear those prophets making. So anyone who wishes to leave the sun in undisturbed possession of his traditional position had better find some other answer to them.'

[4] 'Not only the sun, you should say,' exclaimed the philosopher Ammonius, who was one of the company; 'it applies also to the whole celestial sphere. It follows necessarily that the sun's passage from solstice to solstice will be shortened, so as
not to occupy as large a segment of the horizon as the astrono- 411
mers say; it will contract, and the southern parts be brought steadily closer to the northern, so that our summers will become shorter and cooler, because the sun will be turning within a narrower circle and will reach the solstices at lower parallels. The gnomon at Syene* will no longer cast no shadow at the summer solstice. Many fixed stars will have disappeared under the horizon and some will touch and merge together when the distance between them vanishes. If, on the other hand, they are going to tell us that everything else remains as it is and only the sun's movements become irregular, they will be unable to adduce any cause capable of imparting acceleration to the sun alone among so many other bodies; many phenomena will be disturbed, the moon utterly so. There will be no call for measures of olive oil to demonstrate the difference. Proof enough will come from

eclipses of the sun, which will be in conjunction with the moon more often, and of the moon herself, because she will enter the earth's shadow more often. Other consequences are plain. I need not spend more time exposing the pretentions of the argument.'

'All the same', said Cleombrotus, 'I saw the measure with my own eyes. They exhibited many measures, and last year's was a good deal less than the earliest.'

'Then I suppose', interjected Ammonius, 'that it went unnoticed by other people who tend fires that never go out* and keep them alight for years without number! Anyway, if one did suppose the story true, would it not be better to find the cause in some coldness or dampness of the air, such as is likely to make the fire languish and fail to absorb or need much fuel? I have heard it said that fire burns better in winter, because it is forcibly concentrated and condensed by the cold, whereas in times of drought it weakens and grows thin and faint, and if it burns in sunshine, it is less effective, takes hold less vigorously, and uses its fuel more slowly. Best of all, however, would be to attribute the cause to the oil itself. It is perfectly reasonable to suppose that it was originally watery and deficient in nourishment, deriving from a young plant, but subsequently, when matured and strengthened in the adult tree, has come to possess greater strength and fuel-value, quantity for quantity, than before. At any rate, this is what one can say if one really needs to defend the bizarre and outlandish statements of the men from Ammon.'

[5] I took up where Ammonius left off. 'Tell us rather about the oracle, Cleombrotus,' I said. 'The ancient fame of that holy site is very great; but these days it seems to be fading.'

Cleombrotus looked at the floor and said nothing.

'There's no need to ask questions and puzzle about Ammon in particular,' said Demetrius, 'when we see the dimming of the oracles here, or rather the eclipse of them all, barring one or two. The question to ask is why they have become so enfeebled. Why mention others, when even in Boeotia, which echoed with oracular voices in olden times, the streams, as it were, have totally failed, and there is a great dearth of prophecy in the land? Only at Lebadea now does Boeotia have anything to offer seekers after the waters of prophecy. The other oracles are silent, or indeed quite deserted. And yet at the time of the

Persian Wars,* the oracle of Amphiaraus and that of Ptoion
were both famous, and Mardonius consulted both. Indeed, the 412
prophet at Ptoion, who had previously spoken Aeolic, on this occasion delivered an oracle in a foreign tongue, so that none of the priests present could understand it, though Mardonius' envoy did. The prophet's possession surely demonstrates that the Greek language is never available to serve the commands of barbarians! Again, the Lydian who was sent to the oracle of Amphiaraus dreamt that the god's servant appeared to him and first ordered him out, because the god was absent, and then tried to push him out by main force; when he stood his ground, the servant picked up a big stone and hit him on the head with it. This in a way corresponded to what was going to happen. Mardonius was defeated when the Greeks were under the command not of a king but of a king's deputy and servant, and he died of a blow from a stone, just like the Lydian in his dream. This was also the heyday of the oracle at Tegyrae, where they say the god was born, and where the Orchomenians to this day call one of the streams that flow by the oracle "Palm", and the other "Olive".* Now, at the time of the Persian War, when Echecrates was the prophet there, Apollo foretold victory and success in war for the Greeks. Again, in the Peloponnesian War, the Delians,* expelled from their island, received (it is said) an oracle from Delphi bidding them seek the place where Apollo was born and perform certain sacrifices there. It surprised and puzzled them that Apollo should have been born anywhere but in their native Delos, but the priestess added that a crow would show them the place. On their way home from Delphi, they stopped at Chaeronea, and heard the landlady of the inn talking about the oracle at Tegyrae to some strangers who were going there. As they left, the strangers took leave of the woman by her name—Corone, which means "crow". So the Delians understood the oracle, carried out their sacrifice at Tegyrae, and accomplished their return home before very long. There have been some more recent manifestations at these oracles also, but they have vanished now; so it is worth while debating the reason in the presence of the god of Pytho.'

[6] By this time, we had moved from the temple to the door of the Cnidian Meeting-House.* We went in, and saw the friends whom we were on our way to meet sitting waiting for us. There was nothing else happening. At that time of day people were anointing themselves or watching the athletes. Demetrius smiled. 'Shall I lie', he said (quoting Homer),[1] 'or tell the truth? You seem to me to have no serious question in hand. I see you're sitting very comfortably, and you look very relaxed.'

It was Heracleon of Megara who answered him. 'Well,' he said, 'we are not discussing which of its two L's the verb *ballo** loses in the future tense, nor what is the positive adverb corresponding to "worse" and "better" and "worst" and "best".* Such things no doubt do produce a tense and worried expression. Other researches, on the other hand, can be perfectly well undertaken in peace, without dislocating the eyebrows or shooting horrid glances or getting angry with your companions.'

'Well then,' said Demetrius, 'welcome us, if you will, and with us the discussion which has just been sprung upon us. It is appropriate to the place, and, for Apollo's sake, relevant to us all. And don't knit your brows as you all argue about it.'

[7] We found ourselves places to sit down among them, and
413 Demetrius proposed the question for discussion. Immediately, up jumps the Cynic Didymus, the man with the nickname Planetiades.* He struck the ground with his stick two or three times, and cried out 'Ho, ho! That's a difficult question you've brought with you, and one that needs a lot of research! Is it to be wondered at, when there's such a flood of wickedness in the world, if not only Shame and Nemesis,* as Hesiod says, have abandoned mankind, but divine providence too has packed up its oracles and vanished from everywhere? I put to you the opposite question: why has this oracle also not given up, and Heracles or some other god taken the tripod away, loaded as it is with shameful, impious questions put to the god by people who want to test his skills like a sophist, and others who inquire about hidden treasures or legacies or unlawful marriages? Pythagoras is overwhelmingly refuted when he alleges that men are at their best when they go to visit the gods. What in fact they do is to bring the god, bare and unconcealed, mental diseases and passions that it would be well to deny and hide in the presence of one's human elders!'

He was wanting to go on in this vein, but Heracleon took hold of his cloak, and I, being pretty well his closest friend,* said 'My dear Planetiades, stop provoking the god! He is slow to anger and gentle, and, as Pindar says "adjudged to men the kindest";[1] and whether he is sun, or lord and father of the sun and beyond the visible world, it is unlikely that he would judge today's men unworthy of his voice, since he is the cause of their birth and nurture, their being and their thought. Nor is it likely that providence, the good and kindly mother that provides and preserves everything for us, should be ungenerous in this one matter of prophecy, and take from us what she gave in the beginning, as though there were not even more wicked men around in the larger population of the age when oracles were established in many parts of the world! Come here and sit down again; make a Pythian truce* with vice—you're always castigating it—and join us in investigating the cause of this alleged disappearance of oracles. But keep Apollo your friend, and avoid his anger.'

These remarks of mine succeeded only in making Planetiades make his exit through the door, without saying a word.

[8] There was a brief silence, broken by Ammonius addressing me.

'Lamprias,' he began, 'consider what we are doing, and apply your mind to the argument. We must take care not to remove responsibility from the god. If you believe that the disappearance of the vanished oracles is due to any cause other than god's intention, you raise the suspicion that you believe their creation and existence is not due to god, but came about in some other way. I make this point because there is in fact no greater or superior force capable of destroying and annihilating prophecy, if it is god's work. Planetiades' argument displeases me in many ways—particularly the inconsistency it attributes to the god, who one moment rejects and disapproves vice, and the next somehow accepts it, like a king or tyrant who excludes bad men by one door, only to admit them and do business with them by another. Moderation, adequacy, and an economical completeness of provision are the proper characteristics of the work of god. On this principle, one could argue that Greece has suffered particularly badly from the common depopulation due to the

414 disorders and wars that have affected practically the whole inhabited world. She could now scarcely raise the 3,000 hoplites that the single city of Megara sent to Plataea. The only reason, then, for the god's abandoning many of the oracles would be to demonstrate the depopulation of Greece. I would give such an argument full marks for ingenuity. For to whose benefit would it be that there should be an oracle at Tegyrae as there once was, or at Ptoion, where it is a day's portion to meet one man keeping his flock? Even our oracle here, the oldest and most famous, is said to have lain deserted and unvisited for a long time because of the terrible dragon.* But this explanation is the reverse of the truth: it was the desert that produced the dragon, not the dragon that produced the desert. And when, god having so decided, Greece grew strong in her cities, and the area became populous, they employed two prophetesses who took turns on the tripod, with a third designated to wait in reserve. Now, however, there is only one; and we do not complain, for she suffices for the inquirers. There is nothing in this to make us blame Apollo: the power of prophecy that exists and persists is adequate for all and sends every inquirer away satisfied. Agamemnon employed nine heralds* and could scarce keep the assembly in order because it was so numerous; here, in the theatre, in a few days' time, you will see that a single voice reaches everybody. So with prophecy: in the old days, it employed more voices to reach more people; now, on the other hand, we should have good reason to be surprised at Apollo, if he let his prophecy run away like water to no purpose, or echo like the rocks to the cries of shepherds and flocks in the wilderness.'

Ammonius ended here, and I kept silent. Cleombrotus turned to me. 'Have you conceded the point, then,' he said, 'that it is the god who both creates and destroys these oracles?' 'No, I have not,' I replied: 'I do not believe that any oracle or place of prophecy is destroyed by god's responsibility. As god creates and prepares many things for our benefit, and nature then destroys or negates some of them—or, to be more accurate, matter, which is a privation, often destroys and undoes what a superior cause creates—so, as I conceive it, there are various obscurations and destructions of prophetic powers, because, though god gives man many beautiful things, he gives none that is exempt from death. As Sophocles says, "Gods' works do die, though they themselves do not." The essence and power of these works, say the men of piety, must be sought in nature and matter; their origin, it is only right, must be reserved to god. It is foolish, indeed childish, to believe that god himself, like the ventriloquists* who used to take the name Eurycles and now take the name Python, enters into prophets' bodies and uses their mouths and voices as his instruments. To mix god's nature with human needs is to fail to respect his dignity or safeguard the status and greatness of his excellence.'

[10] 'Quite right,' said Cleombrotus, 'but since it is difficult to define precisely how and to what extent providence should be invoked, both those who deny that god is responsible for everything, and those who make him responsible for practically everything, alike fail to achieve a reasonable and appropriate solution. There is certainly truth in the view that Plato relieved philosophers of many serious problems by his discovery of the element underlying created qualities, which is now called matter and nature; but in my judgement even more problems, and more serious ones, have been solved by the discovery of the
race of *daimones* that comes between gods and men and some- 415
how links and brings together the community to which we both belong, whether this doctrine comes from Zoroaster's magi, or from Thrace with Orpheus, or from Egypt or Phrygia, as we may conjecture from the initiatory rites of both these countries, when we observe the many elements of mortality and grief involved in their orgiastic and dramatic rituals. Among Greeks, Homer seems still to use the two words indiscriminately, sometimes calling his gods *daimones*. It was Hesiod* who first set out clearly and distinctly the four classes of rational beings—gods, *daimones*, heroes, and lastly men—and as a consequence, apparently, wrote of the change of the Golden Race into many beneficent *daimones*, while the *daimones* are changed separately into heroes. Others assume changes in souls corresponding to those in physical objects: as water is produced from earth, air from water and fire from air, as the basic substance rises, so the better souls pass from men to heroes and from heroes to *daimones*; and from *daimones* some few of them, completely

purified over a long time because of their virtue, finally achieve divinity. Some, however, lack self-control: these give way and sink back into mortal bodies, where they continue a dark, dim existence, like wisps of vapour.

[11] Hesiod also thinks that *daimones* die after certain periods of time. Speaking in the person of the Naiad* he hints at the time involved:

> nine generations lives the squawking crow
> of human youth: four crows the stag survives,
> three stags the aged raven, while the phoenix
> equals nine ravens, and we fair-tressed nymphs,
> daughters of Zeus, outlive ten phoenixes.[1]

Those who misinterpret the word "generation" make this an enormous length of time. In fact, it means "year", so that the total length of the life of the *daimones* is 9,720 years, less than many mathematicians think, but more than Pindar meant when he said that nymphs have "a tree's life span", and so call themselves "hamadryads".'[2]

Demetrius interrupted. 'How can you say, Cleombrotus', he cried, 'that a generation of man means a year? The period of human "youth" or "eld"* (as some scholars read in this passage) is not that at all. Those who read "youth" interpret a generation as thirty years, following Heraclitus, that being the period in which a parent produces a child capable of procreation; those who read "eld", on the other hand, allow 108 years to a "generation"; they argue that fifty-four marks the mid-point of a human life, this number being composed of the unit one, the first two plane numbers, the first two squares, and the first two cubes (1 + 2 + 3 + 4 + 9 + 8 + 27 = 54). These are the numbers Plato uses in his account of the generation of the soul.* Hesiod's narrative as a whole seems also to be an allegorical account of the final conflagration,* when (we may suppose) the disappearance of all liquid substances implies the disappearance of the nymphs "whose dwelling is the forest fair, the streams and grassy meadows".[3]

[12] 'I have heard that from many people,' said Cleombrotus, 'and I note that the Stoic conflagration not only ravages the verses of Heraclitus and Orpheus but sets fire to Hesiod too. But

I cannot admit the reference to the destruction of the cosmos, 416 and the impossibilities in the lines you quote about the crow and the stag seem particularly to go against those who take the exaggerated view.* The year comprehends in itself the beginning and end of almost everything "that seasons bring or earth gives life to": is it not also appropriately called the "generation" of men? You scholars agree that Hesiod calls human life "generation", don't you?' 'Yes,' said Demetrius. 'But it is also clear', went on Cleombrotus, 'that the measure and the thing measured are often denoted by the same term—pint or quart or gallon or bushel. So just as we call the unit, which is the smallest measure and principle of all number, a number itself, so Hesiod called the year, which is the primary measure of human life, by the same name as that which is measured by it, namely "generation". Now the numbers arrived at by these people have none of the recognized features of significance and distinction that we expect in numbers; but the number 9,720 derives from the sum of the first four numbers, multiplied by 4, or from 10 multiplied by 4: both of these sums produce the number 40, and this multiplied by 3 to the power of 5 [243] produces 9,720. But there's no need to quarrel with Demetrius about this. Whether the time needed for the soul to change to the life of *daimon* or hero is longer or shorter, the proposition he wants will be demonstrated by unambiguous ancient witnesses: there are indeed beings on the frontier, as it were, between gods and men, susceptible to mortal passions and necessary changes, whom we are right to follow our fathers' tradition in believing to be *daimones* and worshipping under that name.

[13] 'Plato's pupil Xenocrates illustrated this by the paradigm of triangles. He drew an analogy between the equilateral triangle and the divine, the scalene and the mortal, and the isosceles and the *daimones*, the first being equal on all sides, the second unequal on all sides, the third equal in one way and unequal in another. Similarly, the nature of *daimones* is to have the passions of mortality and the power of divinity. Nature displays perceptible images and visible likenesses of the gods in the sun and the stars, and of mortals in lights and comets and shooting stars, as Euripides suggested in the lines

> just now, he flourished in the flesh; now, like
> a falling star, his light is out, his spirit
> released to the air,[1]

while, in the moon, nature shows us a mixed physical structure, which is indeed a model of the *daimones*. And it is the observation that the moon is susceptible of visible waxing and waning and change of phase in harmony with the revolutions of that class of being, that has made men call her the "earthy star" or the "Olympian earth" or "Hecate's estate"—Hecate being both a chthonic* and a heavenly power. Now if one were somehow to extract and remove the air between the earth and the moon, one would leave an empty and disconnected space in the middle, and thereby destroy the unity and community of the whole.* Similarly, to deny the existence of *daimones* is to deny communication and mediation between men and gods, by abolishing what Plato called the "interpreting and ministering"[2] nature; alternatively, it is to force us to introduce total confusion into the universe, by involving god in human passions and affairs and dragging him down to do our business, as Thessalian witches
417 are supposed to pull down the moon. *Their* tricks, indeed, earned credence among women, because a certain lady astronomer, one Aglaonice, daughter of Hegetor, pretended, whenever there was an eclipse of the moon, to be pulling it down by her spells. We should take a different line. On the one hand, we should not listen to claims that there are prophecies outside divine control, or ceremonies or rituals to which gods do not attend. On the other, let us not suppose that god is actually active and present in these events; let us rather attribute such things, as is right and proper, to the servants of the gods, their ministers and secretaries, and believe in *daimones* as overseers of ritual and celebrants of mysteries, and other *daimones* as the roving avengers of great and overweening crimes. Hesiod grandly calls others of them "holy wealth-givers, royal in privilege",[1] because to do good is the mark of a king. For there are various levels of goodness among *daimones*, as there are among men: in some, the emotional and irrational element is reduced to a feeble and vestigial residue, while in others it remains strong and irrepressible; sporadic traces and signs of this are

preserved and maintained in many places in sacrifices, rituals, and myths.

[14] 'The most impressive indications and revelations of the truth about *daimones* are to be found in the mysteries; but on this subject, if I may quote Herodotus, "Let my mouth stay silent."[2] I turn instead to those feasts and sacrifices which are like days of ill omen and gloom, when there is eating of raw meat and tearing of flesh,* fasting or beating of the breast, or (as often happens) obscene words uttered in holy places, or "frenzies and screams, as they leap with necks twisting and turning".*[3] All this, in my submission, is done as an act of appeasement and placation, not to any god, but to avert evil *daimones*. It is unbelievable that the gods should have demanded or tolerated the human sacrifices* that were once performed; nor would kings and generals have put up with handing over their own children for sacrifice or putting the knife into them for no good reason. No: the purpose of these acts was to avert and satisfy the anger and resentment of cruel and malicious spirits, or sometimes their manic and despotic love. These beings neither can nor will unite with bodies or through the medium of bodies. As Heracles besieged Oechalia for a girl,* so these strong and violent *daimones* often demand a human soul dwelling in a body, and bring pestilences to cities and death to the land, and stir up wars and revolutions, until they obtain the object of their love. Some have a different destiny. When I was making a long stay in Crete, I learnt of a strange festival at which they put on show the image of a headless man, and say that he was Molus,* father of Meriones, who raped a nymph and was found headless.

[15] 'All these rapes and travels of gods, concealments, exiles, and servitude, of which we hear in myth and song, are not things that befall gods: they are the sufferings and adventures of *daimones*, remembered because of their valour and power. Aeschylus was wrong to write of "holy Apollo,* god exiled from heaven".[4] Sophocles' Admetus was wrong to say, "my cock's crow sent him forth to work my mill".[5] Furthest of all from the truth are the Delphian theologians who believe that Apollo once fought a serpent here for the oracle, and who allow poets and speakers to tell this in the competitions in the theatre, as though deliberately offering evidence against their holiest rites.'

418 Philip the historian, who was present, expressed surprise at this, and asked Cleombrotus against which rites he thought the competitors were 'offering evidence'.

'The rites relating to the oracle,' replied Cleombrotus, 'in which the city has now initiated all the Greeks beyond Thermopylae and has gone all the way to Tempe. The hut* erected here near the Threshing Floor every nine years does not represent the dragon's lair, but the palace of a king or tyrant. And the silent approach to it by what is called the Dolonia, where they conduct with lighted torches a boy* whose parents are both living,* and then set fire to the hut, overturn the table, and run out of the sanctuary through the gate without ever turning back—all this, and the subsequent wanderings and servitude of the child, and his purification at Tempe, give a hint of some great and audacious act of impiety. Surely it is ridiculous, my friend, to think that Apollo flees to the furthest bounds of Greece seeking purification for having killed an animal, and then pours libations there and performs the rituals men perform when they aim to avert and placate the wrath of the *daimones* they call Alastores and Palamnaioi, because they pursue the memory of unforgotten (*alēsta*) and ancient (*palaia*) pollutions.* The account I have heard of this flight and migration is totally bizarre and paradoxical; but if there is any truth in it, let us not think that what happened at the oracle in those days was any trivial or ordinary event. But I don't want to give the impression of doing what Empedocles describes as

> adding head to head, and never finishing
> a single path of lore.[1]

So let me add the conclusion that properly belongs to what I said first. We are there already. Let us have the courage to say what many have said before us: when the daemonic powers assigned to oracles and places of prophecy fail, the oracles fail with them; when they flee or migrate, the oracles lose their force; when they return in course of time, the oracles speak once more, as musical instruments do when their users are there to control them.'

[16] When Cleombrotus had finished, it was Heracleon who spoke first. 'Of course', he said, 'we have no one with us who belongs to the profane and uninitiated*, or has views of the gods incompatible with ours; all the same, Philip, let us beware of introducing strange but important assumptions into our argument without being conscious of it.'

'Well said,' said Philip, 'but just what is it in Cleombrotus' propositions that embarrasses you?'

'I am sure', said Heracleon, 'that it was perfectly right to suppose that the oversight of oracles belongs not to the gods, who ought to be free of earthly concerns, but to their servants the *daimones*. But I find it a somewhat audacious and barbaric hypothesis, to give these *daimones*, as it were, whole handfuls of the sins and dooms and god-driven wanderings that we find in the poems of Empedocles,* and to end by attributing death to them as to men.'

Cleombrotus asked Philip who this young man was, and where he came from. When he knew his name and city, he turned to him.

'I am well aware myself, Heracleon,' he said, 'that I have reached a very strange position. But one cannot get to probable conclusions about important things without calling into play important principles. You have failed to notice that you are taking away the concession you have made me. You admit that *daimones* exist, but by demanding that they should not be evil or mortal you fail to maintain their essential character as *daimones*. How do they differ from gods if they are in essence imperishable and in character exempt from suffering 419
and sin?'

Heracleon reflected on this, but said nothing.

'But, Heracleon,' said Philip, 'it's not only Empedocles who admits bad *daimones*, but Plato, Xenocrates, Chrysippus, and even Democritus, whose prayer to "encounter fortunate idols"* surely implies that he recognized the existence of unpleasant ones, with nasty impulses and purposes. As regards the death of such beings, I heard a story* from a man who is neither a fool nor given to telling tall tales. This was Epitherses, father of the rhetor Aemilianus, whose lessons some of you have heard. He was a fellow citizen of mine, a teacher of literature. His story was that he was once sailing to Italy on board a ship carrying merchandise and a large number of passengers. In the evening, off the Echinades, the wind dropped, and the ship drifted close to Paxi. Most of them were awake, and some were still having their after-dinner drinks. Suddenly a voice was heard from the island of Paxi, calling out for someone named Thamous. It was amazing. Thamous was the Egyptian helmsman, whom few of the passengers or crew knew by name. Twice he was summoned, and did not reply. At the third call, he answered. The voice then grew louder. "When you reach Palodes",* it cried, "announce that Great Pan is dead." Epitherses told me they were all amazed when they heard this, and discussed among themselves whether it would be best to obey or to let the matter rest and not get involved. Thamous decided that if there was a wind, he would sail quietly by, but if there was no wind and the sea was calm in the area, he would announce what he had been told. When they arrived off Palodes, there was no wind and no swell. So Thamous looked out from the stern towards the land and cried, just as he had been told, "Great Pan is dead!" Scarcely had he spoken, when a great cry of lamentation and surprise arose, not of one voice but of many. There were many witnesses to this, and so the story soon circulated in Rome, and Thamous was sent for by Tiberius Caesar, who believed the story so thoroughly that he proceeded to make inquiries about Pan; and the many scholars at his court came up with the conjecture that it was the son of Hermes and Penelope.'

Several of those present confirmed Philip's account, having heard the story from old Aemilianus.

[18] Demetrius then said that there were many scattered uninhabited islands off Britain,* some of them named after *daimones* or heroes. He had himself sailed to the nearest of these islands on a mission from the emperor, to explore and study it. The inhabitants were few, and were all treated by the Britons as holy and inviolate. Shortly after his arrival, there was a great turbulence in the air, and many significant signs, violent storms of wind and waterspouts. When this gave over, the islanders said that one of the Great Ones had gone. "Just as lighting a lamp has nothing frightening about it", they explained, "but snuffing it is disagreeable, so great souls are beneficent and

harmless in their shining forth, but their extinction and destruction often, as now, produces gales and storms, and often infects 420
the air with pestilence." There was one island, they told him, where Cronus lay asleep,* imprisoned and guarded by Briareos: sleep was the bond contrived to bind him, and there were many *daimones* with him as servants and attendants.'

[19] 'I could tell tales like that too,' interjected Cleombrotus, 'but for our present purpose it is enough that there should be no obstacle or hindrance to thinking these things so. The Stoics, I know, not only hold my view about *daimones* but believe in only one eternal and immortal god among so many, holding that the others were born and are doomed to die. As for the Epicureans, we have no call to be frightened of the scorn and ridicule they direct even at providence, which they describe as a "myth". *We* can just as well use the word "myth" of that infinity of theirs, which doesn't produce a single world, among so many, governed by divine reason, but has them all coming into existence and subsisting spontaneously. If there is any place for laughter in philosophy, we should laugh at their dumb, blind, lifeless "idols", herded like sheep, appearing and circulating everywhere over vast periods of years, some emanating from living creatures, some from creatures long since burnt or rotted away. Such are the bubbles and shadows they introduce into science! And yet, if one asserts, relying not only on nature but on logical demonstration, that there are *daimones* which possess the power to maintain themselves and continue for a long time, they feel aggrieved!'

[20] 'It seems to me', said Ammonius, at the end of this speech, 'that Theophrastus was right when he declared: "What is there to prevent us accepting a respectable and highly philosophical statement? Dismissing it destroys many propositions which are possible but not demonstrable: accepting it does not involve accepting any proposition which is impossible or unreal."* What I understand to be the Epicureans' objection to Empedocles' *daimones* is simply foolish: namely, that it is impossible for bad, sinful beings to be at the same time blessed and long-living, because vice implies great blindness and vulnerability to forces of destruction. On this showing, Epicurus will be a worse man than the sophist Gorgias, and Metrodorus than the comic poet Alexis, since Alexis lived twice as long as Metrodorus, and Gorgias one and a half times as long as Epicurus. When we speak of the "strength" of virtue or the "weakness" of vice, we are not referring to the continued existence or dissolution of the body; even among animals, many that are slow and sluggish of temper, many that are undisciplined and disorderly, live longer lives than the intelligent and clever. It is therefore not a good argument to make the eternity of god depend on his capacity to guard against and repel destructive forces. For freedom from suffering and destruction ought to have been a characteristic of the nature of the "blessed", on the Epicurean view, without any need for effort. But maybe it is impolite to argue against the absent. Cleombrotus has an obligation to take up again the argument he let slip, about the migration and flight of "daemonic" powers.'

[21] 'It would surprise me', began Cleombrotus, 'if this argument did not seem stranger to you than what has already been said. It has, however, a scientific aspect, and Plato gave the keynote—not by making a simple statement, but by cautiously offering an enigmatic hint, based on dimly grasped opinion. Nevertheless, the other philosophers have done a great deal by
421 way of shouting him down! We have before us a mixed bowl of myth and argument. And where could one find more sympathetic listeners before whom to test the foreign currency, as it were, of these notions? I have no hesitation about making you a present of the story of a barbarian. It was only by long travels, and at great expense, that I found the man at last, by the Red Sea, and enjoyed his talk and his friendship. He meets with men only once a year, and spends the rest of the time (so he told me) with nomad nymphs and *daimones*. He was the most beautiful man I ever saw, and never suffered any illness, eating the bitter medicinal fruit of a certain herb once a month. He was practised in many languages, but to me he spoke a most melodious Doric.* And when he spoke, the whole place was filled with fragrance from the sweetness of his breath. Learning and understanding were always with him; but one day a year he was inspired also with prophecy and he came down to the coast and prophesied, and princes and royal scribes came to see him and then departed. He attributed his prophetic power to *daimones*;

he spoke much of Delphi, and knew all the stories told here of Dionysus, and the rituals performed. All that, he said, related to the great sufferings of *daimones*, as did what we have been discussing in the story of Python. The slayer, in his version, was exiled for nine years, not to Tempe, but to another universe, whence he returned purified in nine cycles of Great Years, and became in truth Phoebus, the Brilliant One, and took possession of the oracle which was under Themis' guardianship. He gave a similar account of the stories of Typhon and the Titans. There had been battles of *daimones* with *daimones*, and then exile for the defeated, or punishment by the gods of such as had sinned, as Typhon is said to have sinned against Osiris, or Cronus against Uranus.* Thus their honours have faded among us or disappeared altogether, because they have migrated to another universe. I have myself heard that the Solymi, neighbours of the Lycians, honoured Cronus particularly; but when he killed their founders, Arsalus, Dryus, and Trosobius,* and went into exile—they cannot tell us where—he came to be neglected and Arsalus and the others to be called the Hard Gods, and the Lycians pronounced curses, both public and private, in their names. Mythology contains many similar instances. "And", continued the stranger, "there is no need to feel surprise that we call some *daimones* by the traditional names of the gods. Each one tends to be called after the god to whom he is assigned and whose power and honour he shares. After all, among us also, people are called Dius or Athenaeus or Apollonius or Dionysius or Hermaeus,* and some are lucky enough to have been given these names rightly, though most acquire divine appellations which are inappropriate and wrongly assigned." '

[22] Cleombrotus was silent. Everyone thought his speech remarkable. Heracleon, however, asked what this had to do with 422
Plato and how he gave the 'keynote' for the doctrine.

'Thank you for reminding me,' said Cleombrotus. 'Plato rejected an infinite number of worlds outright, but he was at a loss to propose a finite number; so while conceding probability to the hypothesis of one world for each element, up to the number of five, he himself settled for a single world.* This view seems to be peculiar to Plato. Other philosophers are afraid of any plurality, on the ground that those who don't limit matter to one world, but go beyond, fall at once into the clutches of an indeterminate and unmanageable infinity.'

'Did your stranger', I asked, 'define the number of worlds in Plato's way, or did you not sound him out about this when you were with him?'

'That above all,' said Cleombrotus, 'was a thing about which I was bound to be an eager and persistent pupil, as he made himself so friendly and obliging. He said that the number of worlds was not infinite, nor one, nor five, but 183, arranged in a triangle, sixty on each side, with three fixed at the angles: each lightly made contact with the next as they revolved, as in a dance; and the area within the triangle was the common hearth of the universe, and was called the Plain of Truth.* "Here", he said, "principles, forms, and exemplars of things past and things to come lie undisturbed, surrounded by eternity, out of which time flows like a stream towards the worlds. The sight and spectacle of these things is granted to human souls once in 10,000 years, if they have lived well; the best of our initiations here are dreams of that revelation and initiation. Philosophical discussions are meant to recall that beauty to our recollection; otherwise, they are futile." 'And that,' concluded Cleombrotus, 'is the myth which I heard him tell about these matters. It was just like a mystery or initiation, for he offered no demonstration or confirmation of his statements.'

[23] I turned to Demetrius. 'How do those lines go', I said, 'in which the suitors express their wonder at Odysseus' handling of the bow?'

Demetrius reminded me.

'Well,' I went on, 'it occurs to me to say the same of this stranger: "surely he hath seen or stolen"[1] doctrines and theories of all kinds, has travelled far in books, and is indeed no barbarian at all but a Greek, full to bursting of Greek culture. His number of worlds gives him away: it is neither Egyptian nor Indian, but Dorian out of Sicily, from a citizen of Himera named Petron. I have not read the book myself—I don't know if it is extant—but Hippys of Rhegium, quoted by Phanias of Eresus, reports that this was Petron's doctrine: there were 183 worlds, touching one another "in a row";* what he meant by "in a row" he does not explain, nor does he say anything to make his statement convincing.'

'What convincingness can there be in such things?' interjected Demetrius; 'Even Plato dropped the argument, without having made any sensible or probable statement.'

'All the same,' said Heracleon, 'we hear you scholars attributing the theory to Homer, who is supposed to divide the universe into five worlds—heaven, water, air, earth, and Olympus. Of these, two are common to all—earth at the bottom and Olympus at the top of the universe—while the three in the centre are assigned to the Three Gods.* So too Plato: when he assigns the primary and most beautiful forms and shapes of bodies to the different elements within the universe, he appears to call them 423
five worlds—the worlds of earth, water, air, fire, and finally the element that surrounds them all, to which he assigns the plastic and flexible form of the dodecahedron, as the figure most fitting and appropriate to the cycles and motions of the soul.'

'Why are we raising Homer at this point?' said Demetrius. 'We have had myths enough. Plato is far from calling the five different elements of the world "five worlds". Indeed, where he opposes the proponents of an infinite number of worlds, he asserts his personal belief in a single world, the beloved and unique child of god, whole and complete and self-sufficient, formed out of the whole mass of corporeal being. It would be surprising, therefore, if, having given a true account himself, he then proceeded to hand the others the principle of an unconvincing and irrational distribution. Denial of a single world, in a sense, implied the hypothesis of the infinity of the universe; but to propose a definite number, neither more nor less than five, is surely quite illogical, and devoid of any plausibility—unless you've got something to say?' he added, turning to me.

'Do you think', said I, 'that we ought really to abandon our discussion of oracles, as though it was finished, and move on to another topic of this magnitude?'

'Not *abandon*,' replied Demetrius; 'we are simply facing up to an argument which has got a grip on us. We shall not spend longer on it than is required to investigate its plausibility, before returning to our original subject.'

[24] 'Well then,' I said, 'in the first place the considerations which debar us from positing an infinite number of worlds do not debar us from positing a plurality. It is possible for god,

prophecy, and providence to exist in a plurality of worlds, while chance intervenes very little, and most things, and those the most important, come to be and change in regular order. Infinity allows nothing of this. Secondly: it is more consonant with reason that god should not create a unique, isolated world. Being perfectly good, he lacks no virtue, above all the virtues of justice and affection, for these are the noblest of all and the most appropriate to gods. Again, it is god's nature to have nothing useless or in vain. Therefore there are other gods and other worlds beyond, in relation to which he employs his social virtues. Justice, favour, and goodness have no function in relation to oneself or to a part of oneself, but only in relation to others. So it is improbable that this world should toss about in an infinite void without friend or neighbour or contact. We see that nature also groups individuals in races and species, like so many seeds in pods or envelopes. There is nothing in the sum of existing things that does not possess a generic description, nor does anything acquire an appellation of a certain kind, unless it possesses a certain quality, either common or particular. Now the world is not said to have a common quality. Therefore it has a particular one, derived from the difference between it and other kindred or similar objects. For if neither man nor horse nor star nor god nor *daimon* exists in nature in a unique example, what is there to prevent nature also having several worlds rather than one unique one? The argument that nature contains only one land and sea, misses the obvious point about "similar parts". We divide land into parts which have the same name, and sea likewise, whereas a part of the world is not a world, but made up of different constituents.

424 **[25]** 'Some thinkers want to use up all matter in the formation of our world, because they are afraid that, if there were any left outside, it might disturb the structure of this world by obstruction or collision. This fear, however, is misplaced. If there is a plurality of worlds, each of which is joined with its own substance and matter of finite measure and limit, there will be no disordered or unorganized excess, as it were, left to fall outside. This is because the principle (*logos*) of each world, being in complete command of the matter assigned to it, will not allow any rejected or errant element to impinge upon another world,

or to come from another to its own, because nature admits no indefinite or infinite quantity and no irrational and disorderly motion. If there *is* any emanation from one world to another, it must be homogeneous and congenial, combining easily with all things, like the rays and influences of the stars; and the worlds must take delight in glimpsing one another, and enabling contacts and friendliness to exist between the many excellent gods which each contains. None of these ideas is impossible or fabulous or paradoxical—unless, of course, people are going to suspect that Aristotle's theory* has a basis in natural causes. According to Aristotle, since each element has its own proper place, earth must always move towards the centre, and water, because of its weight, rest upon earth but underneath the lighter elements. So if there are more worlds than one, it will happen that earth will be above fire and air in many of them, but below them in many others; similarly, air and water will sometimes be in their natural places and sometimes not. This being impossible, on his view, there cannot be two or more worlds, but only one, composed of all substance and organized naturally according to the proper differences between the elements.

[26] This, however, is more plausible than true. Look at it like this, my dear Demetrius,' I went on, 'when he says that some elements move down towards the centre and some upwards from the centre, and others circularly round the centre, in relation to what does he define "centre"? Not presumably in relation to the void, because on his view this does not exist. Moreover, for those who do believe in it, the void has no centre, any more than it has a beginning or an end, since there are limits, and void is infinite and illimitable. And if one were to force oneself, against all reason, to admit a "centre" of the void, what would be the difference in the movements of the various bodies in relation to this? Bodies have no force in the void, nor do they possess any purpose or impulse to make them desire the centre or tend towards it from every direction. Similarly, it is impossible to conceive either a self-originating movement of inanimate bodies towards an incorporeal and undifferentiated space, or an attraction exercised upon them by that space. It remains that "centre" must be meant with reference not to a location but to a body. Since our world possesses a unity and order made up of a number of dissimilar bodies, the differences between them inevitably produce differences in movements and directions. This is clear from the fact that when bodies undergo a change of substance they also undergo a change of place: processes of separation lift matter upward and away from the centre and distribute it around, whereas processes of combination or concentration drive it towards the centre and compress it.

[27] 'But there is no need to discuss these matters further here. Whatever cause is assumed to produce these phenomena of change will be sufficient also to ensure the continuance of
425 each world within itself. Each world has its own earth and sea;* for each has its own centre, its physical phenomena of change, its nature, and its force, which preserves and maintains each element in place. Whatever is outside the world, be it nothing or infinite void, has no centre, as we have said; if there is a plurality of worlds, each has its own centre, and therefore its own set of movements, towards, from, and around its centre, if I may use these philosophers' division of movements. The theory that if there are many centres, all weights tend towards the same one, is no more reasonable than the notion that all men's blood flows into one and the same vein, or all men's brains are contained in one and the same meninx. It implies thinking it monstrous that all solid bodies or all fluid bodies should not have one, single location! Both ideas are absurd in their refusal to admit that wholes have parts of their own, possessing their own natural position and order within each whole. It would be absurd, of course, to say that a thing is a world which has a moon in it anywhere;* it would be like saying that a creature is a man who has his brains in his heels or his heart in his temples! On the other hand, there is no absurdity in assuming a plurality of worlds and assigning limits and divisions not only to the wholes but to the parts. Earth, sea, and heaven in each world will have their several natural and appropriate places, and each world will have an "up" and a "down", an "around", and a "centre" in itself with reference to itself.

[28] 'When some thinkers posit a stone outside the world, it's not easy to conceive it as either at rest or in movement. If it possesses weight, how can it be either at rest or in motion in relation to the world, like other weights, since it is neither a part of the world nor assigned a place in its substance? On the other hand, if an earth is contained and fixed in another world, we ought not to be puzzled as to why it does not break off from the whole and migrate to our world, if we observe the natural tension by which each part is held in place. If we take "up" and "down" not in relation to the world, but outside it, we shall find ourselves in the same difficulty as Epicurus, who moves all his atoms to the regions under our feet, as though the void had feet, or infinity allowed one to conceive of an "up" and "down" within it. This is what gives us cause to wonder at Chrysippus—or rather, to feel puzzled about the reasons that made him allege that the world is in the centre and that its perpetual occupation of this central position is what most contributes to its permanence and virtual indestructibility. This is what he advances in *On Possibilities IV*, where he dreams up a "centre" space in the infinite, and even more absurdly attributes the cause of the word's permanence to this non-existent "centre". And this though he often says elsewhere that substance is controlled and held together by movements to and from its centre!

[29] 'And who would take fright, then, at the other question raised by the Stoics—how can there be one destiny and one providence, and not many "Zeuses" or "Zens",* if there are many worlds? First: if it is absurd for there to be many Zeuses or Zens, the Stoics' own conclusions are even more absurd, for they invent an infinite number of suns and moons, Apollos, Artemises, and Poseidons, in their infinite cosmic cycles.* Secondly: what need is there of many Zeuses for many worlds, instead of a single god to rule and guide the whole, possessed of intellect and reason, like the god whom we call lord and father 426
of all? What will there be to prevent all the worlds being subject to the destiny and providence of Zeus, with Zeus supervising and directing them in turn, giving to all the impulses, seed, and principles of all that is put into effect? Here on earth we often find a single body formed of distinct elements—an assembly, an army, or a choir—each of which comes to live, think, and understand, as Chrysippus believes. Why then is it impossible for there to be ten or fifty or a hundred worlds in the universe, using one and the same reason, and subject to one governance? Indeed, such an organization is very appropriate to god. We

surely shouldn't imprison our gods, like ruler-bees* in the hive, with no way out, nor incarcerate them in matter, as the Stoics do when they describe the gods as states of air or combinations of fire and water, making them born when the world is born and burnt up when the world is burnt up. This is not treating them like free, independent charioteers or steersmen—it is to nail them and solder them down like statues to their bases, locked and bolted into the body of the world, to share its fate even to its total destruction, dissolution, and change!

[30] 'Nobler and grander, surely, is the doctrine that makes gods independent and their own masters. The sons of Tyndareus* come to the aid of sailors in a storm,

> softening the onset of the violent sea
> and the swift blasts of the winds,[1]

not by joining the ship themselves and sharing its dangers, but by appearing on high to rescue it; so too we should believe the gods to visit one world after another, enticed by the pleasure of the spectacle, and joining nature in guiding each one. True, Homer's Zeus does not divert his gaze* very far, when he turns his eyes from Troy to Thrace and the nomads of the Danube; but the real Zeus enjoys a changing vision of appropriate beauties in the many worlds; he does not look out upon an infinite void, nor inward upon himself (as some have thought),* but contemplates the many works of gods and men and the many movements and revolutions of the stars in their cycles. For god does not abominate change, but rejoices in it, if we may judge by the celestial alterations and cycles in the phenomena we observe. Infinity, of course, possesses no thought, no reason, no way of welcoming god; chance and accident are its instrument for everything. But, in my judgement, there is just as much glory and effort in care and providence exercised over a finite number of worlds as in a providence that enters into a single body and cleaves to it, reshaping and reforming it an infinite number of times.'

[31] I stopped here. Philip did not wait long before answering. 'I certainly shouldn't like to say for certain', he said, 'whether this is the truth about these things or not. But if we make god go beyond one world, why do we make him the creator of five and not more? What is the relation between this number and

plurality generally? I am more anxious to understand this than the reason for the dedication of the famous E* here! Five is not a triangular number* or a square one, or a perfect number* or a cubic one; it doesn't seem to offer any attractiveness to the people who like and admire that sort of thing. And the argument from the elements, at which Plato himself hinted, is extremely hard to grasp, and reveals nothing of the plausibility which induced him to think it probable that, because there are inherent 427
in matter five equiangular and equilateral solids* bounded by equal planes, there should therefore be exactly the same number of worlds formed out of them.'

[32] 'Well,' I said, 'Theodorus of Soli seems to give a good account of the argument in his exposition of Plato's mathematics. Here is how he does it. The pyramid, octahedron, icosahedron, and dodecahedron, Plato's basic figures, are beautiful because of the symmetries and equalities of their proportions. No better, or indeed comparable, figure remains for nature to fashion. But they do not all have the same structure or a like origin. The pyramid is the most delicate and smallest of all, the dodecahedron the largest and most complex. Of the other two, the icosahedron contains more than twice as many triangles as the octahedron. It follows that they cannot all originate from the same matter at the same time. The small, delicate, and less complex figures must necessarily be the first to obey the mover and fashioner of matter, and be finished and come into existence before the denser figures, with their more numerous parts, whose construction requires more labour, such as the dodecahedron. Consequently, the pyramid is the only first body, and none of the others deserve that name, because they have a naturally slower development. Now the remedy for this disconcerting feature is the division and separation of matter into five worlds, in each of which one of the basic figures—pyramid, octahedron, icosahedron, dodecahedron—will exist *first*. The others will then derive their being from it, combination and division of parts being the universal method of change, as Plato himself explains in his very detailed account. It will suffice for us to be brief. Air comes into existence as fire is extinguished, and then in turn produces fire out of itself as it becomes more tenuous. The phenomena and the change must therefore be seen in terms

of the seed of both elements. The seed of fire is the pyramid, composed of twenty-four primary triangles. The seed of air is the octahedron, composed of forty-eight of the same. Thus one basic unit of air is made by the combination and union of two of fire, and the unit of air, when split, forms two units of fire. Compressed and condensed a second time, it turns into the form of water. In all cases, therefore, the previously existing element easily provides for the production of all the others by a process of change. Thus it is not only *one* that is "first", but that term applies to them all, because in the different world-structures, different elements have the movement which can initiate and anticipate the process of creation.'

[33] 'That's a very courageous and ambitious effort by Theodorus,' said Ammonius, 'but I should be surprised if we don't find that his assumptions destroy each other. On the one hand, he believes that all the five basic forms are not put together at the same time, but that the most delicate and most easily constructed comes into existence first; but then he adds—as a consequence, not as a contradiction of this—that it is not necessary for all matter to introduce the simplest and most delicate form first, but in some circumstances the heavier and more complex emerge from matter in advance of the others! And apart from this, assuming that there are five basic physical structures and therefore just five worlds, he presents plausible arguments for only four of these. He spirits away the cube, as he would the die in a board game, because it can't change into the others or give
428 the others the possibility of changing into it. This is because the triangles are not of the same kind. In all the other forms, the common element is the "half-triangle",* but in the cube alone it is the isosceles, which permits no convergence or unifying continuation with the other. So if there are five primary bodies and five worlds, in each of which one of the bodies holds the primacy of generation, then none of the others can exist where the cube is primary, since it cannot change into any of the others. I pass over the fact that they make the basic element of the dodecahedron different from the scalene triangle of which Plato constructs the pyramid, octahedron, and icosahedron. And so', said Ammonius with a laugh, 'you must either solve these difficulties or say something of your own about our common problem.'

[34] 'Well,' said I, 'I have nothing more plausible to add for the moment; and perhaps it is better to have to answer for one's own opinion than for someone else's. So here is my view. I start again at the beginning. There are two basic natures, the one sensible, subject to change by birth and destruction, and to constant variation; the other intelligible, in the realm of being, always constant and the same. It is absurd, then, my friend, to believe the intelligible to be divided and have differences within itself, while indignantly rejecting any view which does not leave a coherent and internally unified corporeal and passive nature, but seeks instead to divide and separate it. It is surely more appropriate that the divine and enduring should hold together and, so far as possible, escape any severance or division. Yet even here, the power of Otherness produces inequalities of principle and form in the intelligible which are more important than differences of place. This is why, in opposing those who hold the universe to be unique, Plato enumerates the categories of Being, Sameness, Otherness, Motion, and Rest.* These being five in number, no wonder if each of the five corporeal elements is a model or replica in its nature of one of these—not indeed a pure and unmixed replica, but one that takes its character from the predominance in it of one or other of the categories. Thus the cube is obviously a body specially appropriate to Rest, because of the stability and firmness of its surfaces. And anyone can see the fiery, mobile quality in the pyramid, in the tapering of its sides and the acuteness of its angles. The nature of the dodecahedron, which contains all the other figures, is well thought of as an image of Being in the whole corporeal realm. Of the other two, the icosahedron more particularly partakes of the nature of Otherness, and the octahedron of Sameness. Thus the octahedron produced air, which holds all being together in a single form, and the icosahedron water, which can be transformed into the greatest number of different kinds of qualities by mixture. So, since nature demands balance in all things, it is probable that there are neither more nor fewer worlds than there are "models", so that each "model" can have a dominant position and power in one, just as they do in the construction of the primary bodies.

[35] Perhaps this may reassure anyone who feels surprised at our dividing the world of change and becoming into so many categories.

'The next point I would like you all to consider is this. Of the two highest principles—the One and the Indefinite Dyad*—the latter is the basis of all formlessness and disorder, and is called infinity, whereas the One limits and encompasses the void, irrational, and indefinite element in infinity and gives it shape, making it somehow capable of sustaining and accepting the categorization that accompanies our judgements of sensible
429 objects. These principles appear first in connection with number. To be more precise, plurality does not become number unless the One, emerging from the infinity of the indeterminate as form from matter, cuts off portions of various sizes, greater and less. At this stage, each plurality becomes a number, because it is delimited by the One. If the One is removed, the Indefinite Dyad once again introduces confusion and makes everything patternless, infinite, and immeasurable. Now since form is not the destruction of its underlying matter but its shape and order, number must have inherent in it the two principles from which the first and greatest difference and dissimilarity arises. The indefinite principle creates the Even, the better principle the Uneven. The first even number is 2, the first uneven number is 3. From these two added together comes 5, which shares both categories in virtue of its components, but is actually an uneven number. Now, since the perceptible and corporeal world is divided into parts, the number of these parts had to be not the first even, nor the first uneven, number, but a third number derived from these: only then could the world originate from both principles, both that which creates the even and that which creates the uneven. Neither of these could be isolated from the other, for both have the nature and power of a first principle. When they joined forces, the superior principle prevailed over the indeterminacy that sought to divide the corporeal world, and, as matter tended to split into two, it set the One in the centre and so prevented a division of the whole universe into two halves. Nevertheless, the Otherness and Difference of the Indeterminate did produce a plurality of worlds, which the power of Sameness and Limit made an uneven plurality, uneven

in the way that did not allow nature to proceed beyond what was good. For if the One had been pure and uncontaminated, matter would have had no extension; as it is, being mixed with the divisive properties of the Dyad, it admitted severance and division, but stopped at the present state, because the Even was overpowered by the Uneven.

[36] 'This is why the ancients used to call counting "fiving".* I suspect too that the Greek word for "all", *panta*, is derived from *pente*, "five", because the "pentad" is composed of the first two numbers. Numbers other than 5, when multiplied, come to totals ending in various numbers; but 5, multiplied an even number of times, makes a perfect 10, and multiplied an uneven number of times, it always produces itself. I pass over the fact that 5 is the first number composed of the first two squares—1 and 4—and that it is the first number which, when squared, is equal to the sum of the squares of the two numbers preceding it, and so produces the most beautiful right-angled triangle.* I pass over also the fact that it is the first number to produce the proportion 3 : 2. All this is barely relevant to our present theme. What does concern us is this number's natural power of division and the fact that nature makes great use of it in its distribution of things. Nature gives us five senses and five parts of the soul*—vegetable, sensitive, appetitive, spirited, and rational—five fingers on each hand, and sperm which has maximum fertility when divided into five, since we never hear of a woman having more than five children at a birth.* The Egyptians also say that Rhea* gave birth to five gods, and this is an enigmatic way of describing the birth of the five worlds from matter. Again, there are five zones surrounding the earth and five circles dividing the heavens: two arctic, two tropic, and one equatorial. Five also are the orbits of the planets,* since the Sun, Phosphorus [= Venus] and Stilbon [= Mercury] have one common 430
course. The whole structure of the world is harmonious, just like the harmony of our music, which we see in the five notes of the tetrachord—lowest, middle, conjunct, disjunct, and highest—and the five musical intervals—quarter-tone, semitone, tone, triple half-tone, double-tone. So nature seems to take pleasure in making everything in fives, more than she does in making everything spherical, as Aristotle would have it.

[37] 'So Plato refers the number of five worlds to the five basic figures, and says of the fifth structure* that "God used it for the universe when he drew its plan." Why then, one may ask, does he profess uncertainty about the number of worlds, question whether it is right to say there is really one or five, and give the clear impression that conjecture begins at this point? Well, if we are to apply the criterion of probability to his meaning, let us look at it like this. Differences of movements necessarily follow from differences of bodies and figures; this is Plato's own teaching, shown in his demonstration that things undergoing separation or combination suffer a change of location together with their alteration of substance. If fire develops out of air, the octahedron being broken up into pyramids, or air out of fire, which is compressed and crushed into octahedral form, they cannot stay where they are; they escape and move into other locations, forcing their way through and resisting obstacles and pressures in their way. Plato makes it clearer by an image, when he compares "grain shaken and winnowed by the shovel and other implements employed in cleansing it"[1] to the shaking of matter by the elements and the elements by matter, in which like always attaches itself to like, so that they all occupy different places, even before the universe whose order is made up of them comes into being. Matter then being in the state in which the universe must surely be in the absence of god, the five primary qualities moved apart according to their several tendencies, yet never completely or absolutely separated, because in the universal confusion the weaker elements followed the stronger even against their own nature. They therefore created as many divisions and separations as there were different kinds of variously moving bodies—a division not of pure fire, but fire-like, one not of pure ether but ether-like, one not of pure earth, but earth-like. In particular, air and water were subject to mixture, because, as I said, these liquids became filled with foreign substances of all kinds. It was not god who divided and separated being. It was divided by itself, and moved on its own in all that disorder, until he took and organized it by proportion and the mean. And then it was that he set up reason as governor and guardian, and created as many worlds as there are types of primary bodies.

'Let this, for Ammonius' sake, be our homage to Plato. For my own part, I should not insist that there are just so many worlds; but the view that there are more than one—but a finite number—seems to me just as reasonable as the two opposing views. I observe, you see, that the natural tendency to fracture and division in matter, while it prevents total stability, is none the less inhibited by reason from proceeding to infinity. But here, if anywhere, we must remind ourselves of the teaching of 431
the Academy,* strip away any excessive dogmatism, and merely try to keep our balance on the slippery ground of the theory of infinity.'

[38] 'Lamprias' advice is good,' said Demetrius, as soon as I had finished. ' "The gods deceive us oft with many forms"[1]—not of trickery, as Euripides says, but of fact, whenever we have the hardihood to pronounce on such important matters as though we understood them. But—to quote Euripides again—"we must haul back our talk"[2] to the original subject. We suggested that, as *daimones* depart and abandon oracles, these are left idle and silent, like musicians' instruments when the musicians have gone; but this raises an even larger question concerning the causative power by means of which they render prophets and prophetesses inspired visionaries. We cannot blame the silence of oracles on their abandonment by *daimones* unless we are convinced about the way in which their presence and control makes the oracles active and articulate.'

'But have you any other view', interjected Ammonius, 'than that the *daimones* are souls who, as Hesiod has it, travel round "in mist apparelled"?[3] It seems to me that the difference between a soul and a soul fitted with a body suitable for our present life is the same as the difference between a man and a man acting a part in a tragedy or a comedy. So there is nothing unreasonable or paradoxical in the idea that souls can produce visions of the future in other souls, just as we often convey to one another both past events and indications of the future, not always by voice but sometimes in writing or simply by a touch or a look—unless you've something else to say, Lamprias? We had a report the other day that you had had a long conversation on this subject with some visitors at Lebadea,* but our informant didn't remember it very well.'

'No wonder,' I replied, 'for there were a lot of incidents and distractions to interrupt us, because there was a consultation of the oracle and a sacrifice, and these broke up our conversation and fragmented it.'

'Well,' said Ammonius, 'now you have an audience that has the leisure and is anxious to ask questions and learn without any feeling of contentiousness or controversy. As you see, we've given every argument a sympathetic hearing and freedom of expression.'

[39] The others joined him in encouraging me. I was silent for a while before replying. 'As it happens, Ammonius,' I began, 'you have yourself provided a sort of introduction to the arguments we had on that occasion. For if, as you say and the divine Hesiod says, souls that have parted from bodies, or never had bodies at all, are *daimones*, "holy watchers over mortal men on earth",[4] then why do we deprive embodied souls of the power which *daimones* have of foreknowing and foretelling the future? It is improbable that souls should have any power or faculty when they leave the body which they did not have beforehand. The likelihood is rather that they possess such powers in perpetuity, but in an inferior form so long as they are tied up with the body. The faculty will be either entirely invisible and hidden, or else weak and faint and slow and laborious—like seeing through fog or moving through water; it will need much care in the healing and reviving of its native force, not to speak of the removal and cleansing of the environment that envelops it. The sun doesn't *become* bright when it emerges from the clouds; it always *is* bright, but it seems dim and faint to us because of the mist. Similarly, the soul doesn't acquire its power of prophecy
432 when it emerges from the cloud of the body, as it were: it possesses it even now, but is blinded by its contamination and confusion with mortality. There is no need to find this surprising or unbelievable. Consider the mental faculty which corresponds to prophecy: we call it memory. Think of the marvellous work memory does in preserving and safeguarding the past—no, not the past, but the non-existent, since nothing in the past is or subsists, but everything comes to be and passes away in a moment! Deeds, words, events—the stream of time bears all away! Yet this capacity of the soul somehow grasps and invests in appear-

ance and being that which does not exist. The oracle given to the Thessalians about Arne bade them take note of "the hearing of the deaf and dumb, the vision of the blind."* Memory is our hearing of dumb things, and our vision of the sightless. And so, as I said, there is no cause for wonder if the soul which can grasp things no longer present can also anticipate things which have not yet happened. Indeed, these are more closely connected with it, and it has a greater rapport with them. It reaches out and thrusts towards the future, while from the past, from everything that is over and done, it is liberated, except in memory.

[40] 'So souls have this power, innate but dim and vague; but they often bloom and blaze forth in dreams, or some of them at the moment of death, as the body becomes purified and achieves a balance proper to this activity, so as to relax the faculty of thought and reason and dissociate it from present events, while they turn with their irrational and imaginative powers towards the future. Euripides was wrong to say "Best prophet is the man who guesses best".[1] This means the man of reason, who follows the lead of the rational part of his soul, with probability to guide him. The prophetic tablet of the mind, however, has no writing on it, no rational sense, no definition provided by itself. It accepts images and premonitions emotionally, and makes contact with the future without benefit of reasoning processes, at the moments when it has most distanced itself from the present. This distancing, or ecstasy,* happens as a result of the physical balance (*krasis*) and disposition of the body in a moment of change; we call it "enthusiasm"* or possession. It is true, of course, that the body rarely achieves such a disposition on its own. But the earth emits many streams of force which affect mankind, some giving madness, sickness, and death, others good, friendly, and beneficial, all revealed when we chance to encounter them. Of these, the holiest and most divine is the stream and spirit* (*rheuma kai pneuma*) of prophecy, whether borne on its own upon the air or conveyed in a stream of water. When this mingles in our bodies, it gives rise to a balance which is strange and unfamiliar to the soul, the exact nature of which is difficult to state with certainty, though reason gives us many possibilities of making conjectures about it. It is reasonable, for example, to suppose that this stream or spirit opens up, by warmth and dilatation, certain passages which admit visions of the future, just as wine, when it vaporizes in the body, discloses many other movements and words that were hidden and unnoticed,

for bacchic frenzy
and madness have great power of divination,[2]

as Euripides says, whenever the soul becomes heated and inflamed and rejects that spirit of pious caution which mortal prudence often employs to reject or quench enthusiasm.

[41] 'At the same time, one might also reasonably suggest that
433 dryness and heat attenuate the "spirit"* and make it pure and ethereal. "Dry flame, best soul", says Heraclitus.[1] Moisture not only dims sight and hearing; in contact with mirrors, it mixes with vapour, and destroys the brilliance and the light. Nor is the opposite explanation impossible: cooling and condensation of the "spirit" may increase the tension and sharpen the edge of the mind's faculty of foreknowledge, in the way that dipping whets iron. Or again: tin melted down with bronze, which is thin in texture and porous, binds and condenses it, and at the same time makes it brighter and purer. What is there, then, to prevent prophetic exhalations, which possess some quality akin and congenial to the soul, from filling its voids and holding it together by fitting into the spaces? Different substances have different affinities: for example, the addition of beans is supposed to enhance the effect of purple dye, and that of nitre to improve scarlet, and, as Empedocles tells us, "the gleam of the scarlet is mixed in the green flax."[2] And we have heard from you about the Cydnus and Apollo's sacred knife at Tarsus—you told us that Cydnus water cleans no other iron, and no other water cleans that knife. It's like what happens at Olympia, where they use the water of the Alpheus to plaster the ashes down on the altar, and find no other water that will bind them or make them stick.

[42] 'So there is no need to feel surprised if the earth sends many streams up from below but only these produce "enthusiasm" and visions of the future in the soul. And of course there are reports to confirm the theoretical argument. The story goes that the force in this place was first revealed because a herdsman came upon it accidentally and then uttered inspired words; at first people made light of it, but subsequently, when things came to pass as he foretold, they marvelled. Learned men at Delphi actually preserve the memory of the man's name, which they say was Coretas.

'It seems to me, though, that the closest parallel to the way in which the prophetic "spirit" combines and connects with the soul is the way in which the eye relates to the kindred qualities of light. An eye may have the power of sight, but there is no exercise of that power without light; and similarly, the soul's prophetic "eye", as it were, needs something akin to itself to kindle and sharpen it. This is why many early thinkers believed Apollo and the sun to be one and the same god, while those who understood and honoured the beauty and wisdom of proportion conjectured that the sun is to Apollo what body is to soul, sight to intellect, and light to truth: they demonstrate that the sun is in fact Apollo's offspring, the ever-coming-into-being child of the ever-being god. The sun kindles, excites, and encourages the visual power of sense in the same way as Apollo does the prophetic power of the soul.

[43] 'Those, however, who believed that the two were one and the same god, very naturally dedicated the oracle to Apollo and earth together, in the belief that the sun induced in the earth that disposition and balance which give rise to the prophetic exhalations. Now my view is that the earth itself is eternal and indestructible, as Hesiod thought—he shows a better notion of it than certain philosophers when he calls it "safe base of all things".[3] Its forces, however, may be expected to fail in some places and develop in others, or to move and divert their flow from one region to another; indeed, we may expect such cycles to be repeated over and over again in the long course of time. There is evidence in the phenomena to support this. Ponds and rivers, and especially hot springs, fail or dry up altogether in some places, and in others run away, as it were, and dive underground, until the time comes for them to reappear, flowing in or 434
near the same area. We know also of recent instances of the exhaustion of mines—for example, the silver mines of Attica or the copper mines of Euboea, from which cold-beaten swords

were once produced, as mentioned by Aeschylus in the line "seizing his sword, self-whetted, from Euboea".[1] Indeed, it's not long since the rocks of Carystus ceased yielding their soft, flexible ribbons of stone.* I am sure some of you will have seen napkins and nets and hair-nets made of this substance, which are never consumed by fire. If this material is soiled in use, people throw it into fire and recover it clean and translucent. But now it's disappeared, and there are just a few fibres or thin traces of it here and there in the mine.

[44] 'Aristotle and his school, however, declare that the exhalation is the creator of all these phenomena in the earth; all such substances must then be exhausted or change or flourish as the exhalation itself varies. We should think the same about prophetic "spirits": their force is not eternally nor perpetually vigorous, but also subject to change. They may well be extinguished by excessive rains or dissipated by lightning strikes; in particular, they may be shifted or totally aborted by earthquakes producing subsidence or massive collapse deep down. They say the effects of the great earthquake here,* which destroyed the city, still persist. At Orchomenus, so it is said, when there was a plague which carried off a large part of the population, the oracle of Tiresias ceased altogether to function, and remains silent and inactive to this day. And if, as we hear, there are similar phenomena in Cilicia, there's no one could tell us about it better than you, Demetrius.'

[45] 'I don't in fact know what's happening now,' said Demetrius; 'as you know, I've been abroad for a very long time. But when I was at home, the oracles of Mopsus and Amphilochus were still flourishing. And I can tell you, from being at the oracle of Mopsus, a very extraordinary story. The governor of Cilicia was a man who had not formed any clear religious opinions—owing to the lack of strength in his unbelief, I suspect, for in other ways he was a violent and vicious person—but he was surrounded by a group of Epicureans, whose marvellous scientific approach, on their own showing, leads them to heap insults on everything of the sort. Well, this man sent a freedman to the oracle, briefing him like a spy going into the enemy camp, with a sealed tablet on which was written a question that no one else had seen. The man spent the night in the shrine, as is the custom, and slept there; and in the morning he reported his dream. A handsome man had stood over him and uttered the one word "black",* and then disappeared. This seemed strange to us and gave rise to a good deal of discussion. The governor, however, was quite astounded and prostrated himself. Then he opened the tablet and showed the question, which was "Shall I sacrifice a white bull or a black?" Even the Epicureans were put out, and the governor performed the sacrifice and always thereafter honoured Mopsus.'

[46] Demetrius had no more to say; I felt, however, that we should have a proper conclusion to the discussion, and so turned back to Philip and Ammonius, who were sitting together. I thought they wanted to say something, and so I waited again.

'Well, Lamprias,' said Ammonius, 'Philip too has an observation on what we have been saying. Like most people, he believes that Apollo and the sun are one and the same god. My difficulty, however, is more serious and concerns more serious 435
matters. A little while ago, we somehow managed to let the argument shift the responsibility for prophecy from the gods to certain *daimones*; and now we seem to be expelling these also from the oracle and the tripod here, by resolving the principle, or rather the very essence and force of prophecy, into a matter of "spirits", vapours, and exhalations. For the more these balances and warmings and temperings are bound up with physical causes, the more they turn our thoughts away from the gods, and suggest the sort of calculation of causes that Euripides makes his Cyclops use when he says

> The earth bears grass of sheer necessity,
> whether she will or not, and fattens my flocks.[1]

But Cyclops, of course, says he doesn't sacrifice to the gods, but to himself and "greatest of *daimones*, Belly", while we sacrifice and pray at the oracle. But why should we, if souls bring prophetic powers with them and it's some sort of mixture of air or "spirit" that excites it? What is the point of our drenching the victim with water, and not proceeding with the consultation unless the whole animal trembles and quivers down to its feet, as the water pours over it? As you know, it is not considered enough that the head should shake, as in other sacrifices; the quivering and trembling has to extend to every part of the body with an audible shudder. If this doesn't happen, they declare the oracle is not functioning, and they do not bring the Pythia in. Now these are reasonable procedures and beliefs if you put the main cause in the activities of gods or *daimones*; but on your hypothesis, they make no sense, for, whether the victim shudders or not, the exhalation would be bound to produce enthusiasm and affect the soul, and not only of the Pythia, but of any person it comes in contact with. It is idiotic, on this view, to employ one woman for the oracle and give her a hard life by insisting on lifelong chastity and purity. Coretas, whom the Delphians tell us was the first to encounter the force of the place and make it known, was presumably no different from other shepherds and goatherds. But perhaps all that is fable and unfounded invention, as I think myself. Moreover, when I reflect on the great blessings that this oracle here has conferred on Greece, in wars, in founding cities, in times of plague or famine, I think it quite shocking that the discovery should be put down to chance and accident rather than to divine providence. And now I should like to hear Lamprias' reply! Are you going to wait?'

'Of course I am,' said Philip, 'and so are all these people. Your argument has stimulated us all.'

[47] 'It's not only stimulated me, Philip,' I replied, 'it's dismayed me, if all you experienced persons should think that I take a childish pride in the plausibility of an argument at the cost of subverting or undermining our true, pious beliefs concerning the divine. I shall defend myself; and I produce Plato both as witness and as advocate. Plato, you see, found fault with the old philosopher Anaxagoras* because he was too much bound up with natural causes and persisted always in pursuing the necessary effects of bodily events, paying no attention to the superior causes and principles of purpose and agent. It was Plato himself who investigated these two causes first, or at least more seriously than other philosophers. He made god the first
436 principle of what is due to reason, while not depriving matter of the necessary causes of becoming; for he saw that the entire sensible universe, organized as it is, is not pure or unmixed, but came into existence as a result of the combination of matter with reason. Consider this point first as it applies to human

craftsmen. The famous basis and stand of the mixing-bowl* here, which Herodotus called the Underbowl, had material causes—fire, iron, softening in fire, and tempering in water—without which there was no way in which the object could have been made; but the more important first principle, which set these things in motion and acted through them, was given by art and reason. Even these representations and pictures are inscribed, as you see, with the name of the artist and maker: "Polygnotus of Thasos, Aglaophon's son, painted the sack of Ilium's citadel."[1] Now without pounding and blending colours, nothing could achieve this sort of arrangement or appearance; but does it deprive the craftsman of his fame if, in the effort to find the material cause, you investigate or indeed teach the changes and effects produced by mixing vermilion with ochre, or Melian white with black? Or again, does it diminish the responsibility of the craftsman for his work if we research into the hardening and softening of iron, to show how it becomes malleable and yielding to the workman when it is softened by fire, and then, when plunged suddenly into water, is condensed and compressed as a result of the preceding stage of lower density and lower hardness due to the fire, and thus ends by acquiring the tension and firmness which Homer calls "the might of iron"?[2] I just don't believe it. After all, some people study the qualities of medicaments without thereby destroying the art of medicine. And when Plato demonstrated[3] that we see as a result of contact between the ray emanating from our eyes and the light, and hear as a result of a vibration in the air, he did not thereby refute the proposition that we have been made capable of seeing and hearing by a rational providence.

[48] 'There are—this is my doctrine—two general causes of all coming-to-be. The ancient theologians and poets chose to pay attention only to the superior of the two. They applied to everything the general maxim: "Zeus the beginning, Zeus the centre; all things come from Zeus."*[4] They were not interested thereafter in necessary and natural causes. More recent thinkers, however—those whom we call natural scientists—wandered away from the beautiful and divine first principle, and set everything down to the account of physical objects and what happens to them—impacts, changes, mixtures. Both parties' theories fall

short of what is wanted. The latter group ignore or omit the final and efficient causes; the former ignore or omit materials and media. The philosopher who first distinctly grasped both sets of causes, and took into account both the rational principle of activity and motion and also the necessary passive substratum, thereby freed us too from any suspicion or misrepresentation. We do not make prophecy an irrational or godless activity by treating the human soul as its material element, and the possessing "spirit" and exhalation as, as it were, the plectrum that strikes the instrument. For first, the earth, who gives forth the exhalations, and the sun, who imparts to the earth her whole power of mixture and change, are gods according to the traditional religion of our fathers. And, secondly, we shall not be guilty of anything unreasonable or impossible if we accept the existence of *daimones* as supervisors, sentries and guardians of the harmony, as it were, of this mixture, tightening or loosening
437 the strings as occasion demands, taking away excess of ecstasy or disturbance, and imparting its stimulus painlessly and harmlessly to the users.

[49] 'Nor indeed do our preliminary sacrifices, or the garlanding and drenching of the victim, contradict my argument. Do the priests and *hosioi** say that they sacrifice and pour water over the victim, and watch its movements and trembling, for any reason other than to receive some sign that the god is prepared to prophesy? The sacrificial victim must be pure in body and in soul, undefiled and uncorrupted. Now it is easy enough to detect blemishes in the body; the test of the soul is made, with bulls, by putting out grain, and with pigs by putting out chick-peas. If the animal fails to eat, they take it that it is unhealthy. The goat's test is cold water: failure to react to the drenching signifies an abnormal condition of its soul. For my own part, even if it is certain that the shuddering is a sign of the god's availability and the absence of it a sign that he is not ready, I cannot see anything in this to embarrass my view. Every force produces its natural effect more or less successfully according to the conditions of the moment; and it is only to be expected that god may give us a sign if the moment eludes us.

[50] 'Nor do I believe that the exhalation is always, on every occasion, exactly the same. I think it has periods of lesser and

greater intensity. The fact I adduce as evidence of this is supported by the witness of many visitors and all the servants of the shrine. The building in which they make the consulters of the oracle sit is often, but at no regular intervals, filled with a fragrant smell and breath, which gives off something like the scent of the sweetest and most expensive perfume, which seems to have its source in the inner shrine. The phenomenon is presumably caused by warmth or some other force present there. And if this seems implausible to you, you will doubtless agree at least that, in the Pythia herself, the psychic element with which the "spirit" consorts has different experiences at different times, and does not consistently preserve a single unvarying state, a single tuning of the instrument, as it were. Many conscious—and an even greater number of unconscious—discomforts and disturbances grip her body and insinuate themselves into her soul. When she is under such influences, it is bad for her to go into that place and offer herself to the god, when she is not perfectly pure, a well-tuned and resonant instrument as it were, but emotionally disturbed and unstable. Wine does not always have the same effect on habitual drinkers, nor pipe-music on those who are inclined to be emotionally affected by it; in both cases, the same individuals experience different degrees of frenzy or intoxication as their own inner balance varies. The visionary faculty seems to be particularly liable to outside control and change as a result of alterations in the body. We see this clearly in dreams. Sometimes we experience a lot of very varied visions in our sleep; at other times, all is calm and peace. We know that our friend here, Cleon of Daulis, said that he never had a dream in all the many years he lived; and the same is said of Thrasybulus of Heraea in an earlier age. The cause is the bodily temperament (*krasis*); likewise the temperament of the melancholic is rich in dreams and visions, and they are therefore thought to have veracious dreams—their visionary faculty, in fact, is constantly active in every direction, and, like a person who shoots
many arrows, they quite often hit the mark. 438

[51] 'So "possession" or "enthusiasm" occurs in the prophets whenever their faculty of vision and divination is in tune with the mixture or balance of the "spirit", as though this were a medicine they were taking. When this attunement fails to occur, there is no such possession, or else a delirious, disorderly, and confused episode, such as we know happened to the Pythia who died recently. Some foreigners had come to consult the oracle, and the victim remained unaffected and unmoved by the first drenching. The priests, however, were unduly eager to obtain a result, and kept on trying, until the animal, now completely drenched and soaked, at last gave way. What then happened to the Pythia? She went down into the chamber unwillingly and reluctantly, they tell us; and with the very first replies it was evident from the hoarseness of her voice that she was not recovering; she was like a ship in distress, full of a dumb and evil spirit. In the end she became totally disoriented, rushed to the door with a horrible, inarticulate cry, and threw herself down. The visitors, the priest Nicander, and all the *hosioi* who were there fled. After a while, however, they went in and picked her up, restored to her senses. She lived a few days longer.

'It is for these reasons that the Pythia is obliged to keep her body pure of any sexual activity, and her life generally untouched and uncontaminated by alien associations. This is also why they observe the signs before the consultation, in the belief that it must be clear to the god whether the Pythia is in a condition and disposition to endure possession by him without coming to harm. For the force of the "spirit" does not affect everyone in the same way, nor the same person in the same way at all times. As I said, it provides a kindling or stimulus to those who have a special temperament for these experiences and changes. It is indeed divine and daemonic, but not exempt from exhaustion, destruction, or age; nor can it endure throughout that infinite time in which, as we believe, all things fail that are between earth and moon. Some say, indeed, that the supralunary world also is impermanent, and gives up in the face of infinite perpetuity to endure strange changes and rebirths.

[52] 'This', I concluded, 'is a subject I should wish you and me to debate again and again. There are many objections and doubts which suggest the contrary, but time does not allow us to go into them now. So let us leave this over, as well as Philip's question about Apollo and the sun.'

III

WHY ARE DELPHIC ORACLES NO LONGER GIVEN IN VERSE?

The scene of this dialogue—often called simply 'On the Pythian Oracles'—is once again at Delphi. Philinus (who is T. Flavius Philinus of Thespiae, a close friend of Plutarch) reports to one Basilocles (not otherwise known) a conversation which has happened that afternoon. A party of his friends has been showing a young and intelligent visitor, Diogenianus (his father was a friend of Plutarch), round the monuments. As they proceed, so the discussion develops, through eight episodes. Some of the topics raised are antiquarian—the cause of the blue-green patina on the statues of the Admirals, the explanation of some odd details in one of the dedications, the story of the courtesan Rhodopis—but the main question is introduced quite early, and is addressed by Theon in the long monologue with which the dialogue ends. Why does the priestess no longer deliver her responses in hexameters? In fact, says Theon, she still does, occasionally. But the main reason for the change is the change of the times. Prose is now the vehicle of many subjects once handled in verse—philosophy and astronomy, for instance. Nor have the changes which have led to this more prosaic age been all for the worse, for we now live at peace. Theon—a friend who appears in other dialogues too, as do the poet Sarapion and Boethus the Epicurean—is clearly given the main part. It is therefore fair to assume that what he says is acceptable to Plutarch. It is a more balanced position than that of Lamprias in 'Oracles in Decline', and scholars generally believe that it represents a more refined, and so later, account of Plutarch's own views. Theon is made to develop the theme of the soul as the instrument that the god uses in prophecy, and to show that the innocent virgin-prophetess is an appropriate medium.

The text is unfortunately defective in several places. A visit to Delphi, or reference to a good plan of the site, will make the dialogue much more vivid.

[1] BASILOCLES 394

You've made it a late evening, Philinus, guiding our guest around the monuments. I quite gave up waiting for you.

PHILINUS

We were walking slowly, Basilocles, sowing and harvesting in battle armed and warlike words that kept sprouting and growing under our feet on the way, like the warriors that sprang from the dragon's teeth.*

BASILOCLES

Shall I have to ask some other member of your party, then, to tell me what the words were and who spoke them, or are you willing to do me the favour?

PHILINUS

It's for me to do that, I think, Basilocles. You won't easily find any of the others in town. I saw most of them again going up to the Corycian cave and to Lycorea* with our guest.

BASILOCLES

He seems to be a most enthusiastic listener and sightseer!

PHILINUS

He's more a man of letters and learning. But even this isn't the
395 most remarkable thing about him; that is his gentle charm, and his combative and questioning intelligence, which never shows any bad temper or stubbornness in debate. A short acquaintance would be enough to make you call him 'good son of a good father'. You know the admirable Diogenianus.

BASILOCLES

I never saw him myself, Philinus, but I've met many people who have a very high opinion of his learning and his character, and say the same of the young man. But what was the starting-point and occasion of your discussion, my friend?

[2] PHILINUS

The guides were going through their regular programme, and paid no attention to us when we asked them to cut short their speeches and most of the inscriptions. Our guest was only moderately impressed by the appearance and the technique of the statues—he has no doubt seen many fine works of art—but he much admired the patina on the bronze, which was not like verdigris or rust so much as like a dye of brilliant dark blue, so that he remarked about the Admirals* (that was where the visit started) that the colour really did make them look like men of the deep sea.

'Was it', he went on, 'some trick of mixture or chemical treatment of the bronze by the ancient craftsmen, like the alleged method of tempering swords, the loss of which led to bronze having a rest from deeds of war? Corinthian bronze* is absurdly supposed to have acquired its beautiful colour by accident, not by art. Fire (it is said) destroyed a house containing some gold and silver and a great store of bronze, all of which were thus fused and melted together, though the preponderance of bronze gave the alloy its name.'

'I have heard a less reputable story,' said Theon, 'of how a Corinthian bronzeworker discovered a cache of gold, and, fearing detection, cut it all up into small pieces and quietly mixed it with his bronze, thereby producing a marvellous alloy, which he was able to sell at a high price because it was much prized for the beautiful colour. But both these stories are fables. There must have been, I imagine, some special preparation and mixture, just as nowadays they mix gold and silver to make the special pale colour which seems to me such a sickly and unbeautiful degeneration.'

[3] 'What then', said Diogenianus, 'do you think is the cause of the colour of the bronze here?'

'Well,' said Theon, 'when, of the four primary, natural elements—fire, earth, air, and water—only air is in contact and association with the bronze, the bronze is obviously affected by it and acquires its special characteristics from this constant companion and neighbour. Or "was this an old song ere Theognis lived,"[1] as the comic poet says, and is your question really about the nature and virtue of the air which enables it to colour bronze by contact?'

Diogenianus agreed that that was his question, and Theon went on: 'It is my question too, young man; so let us investigate it together. Let us first ask, if you will, why it is that, of all liquids, olive oil produces most rust. It cannot be that it actually leaves a trace of rust on the bronze, because it is itself quite pure and clean.'

'Of course not,' said the young man, 'but I have my own view about the cause. It is when rust impinges on a thin, pure, transparent liquid that it is most visible, whereas in other liquids it vanishes.'

'Well done, boy,' said Theon, 'that's a good, scientific answer; but perhaps you would like also to consider Aristotle's account of the cause.'

'Indeed I would,' he said.

'Well, he says that other liquids are of loose and uneven texture, and when they are present this lightness serves to dissipate and scatter the rust unobserved, whereas the density of oil protects it and holds it together. Now if we too can put forward a hypothesis of this kind, we shall not be altogether without some comforting formula in our perplexity.'

396 [4] We agreed that he should go ahead. He began by observing that the air at Delphi, while dense, compact, and of high internal tension because of the resistance of the mountains off which it is reflected, was also subtle and mordant, as is shown by the good digestion of food in these parts. Its subtlety therefore enabled it to penetrate and bite into the bronze and extract large amounts of earthy rust from it, then holding and concentrating this (its density not allowing it to dissipate); the rust then settled down and was enough to produce an efflorescence and develop a sheen and brilliance on the surface. We accepted this account, but the visitor observed that one hypothesis was sufficient to support it. 'The assumption of subtlety', he remarked, 'will appear to be in contradiction to the alleged density, and is unnecessary. As bronze ages, it releases and discharges the rust on its own, and the density of the air then concentrates and condenses this till there is enough of it to be visible.'

'But, sir,' interjected Theon, 'what is there to prevent the same thing from being both subtle and dense, like silk or linen cloth? When Homer says "the liquid oil drips off the linen weave",[1] he means to show the delicacy and fine weave of the cloth from the fact that the oil does not remain on it, but runs away and slips off because the density of the material will not let it through. Moreover, there is another possible function, apart from the extraction of the rust, for the alleged subtlety of the air:

it produces a pleasanter, greener colour, adding light and brilliance to the blue.'

[5] There was silence at this, and the guides once again began on their set speeches. At the mention of a verse oracle, concerning (I think) Aegon, king of Argos,* Diogenianus remarked that he often felt surprised at the poor, commonplace style of the verses in which the oracles were delivered. 'And yet', he said, 'Apollo is the leader of the Muses, and his honour rests on verbal eloquence, and on outdoing Homer and Hesiod in splendour of words, no less than on beauty of song and music. Yet we see that most of his oracles abound in errors and weaknesses both in metre and in language.'

Now there was a poet present, Sarapion by name, who had come from Athens. 'If we believe', he cried, 'that these verses are by the god, how do we dare to say that they are inferior to Homer and Hesiod? Ought we not to use them as models of excellence, and correct our own critical judgement where it has been prejudiced by bad habit?'

He was answered by the mathematician Boethus—who, as you know, was by now going over to the ranks of the Epicureans. 'Have you heard the story of the painter Pauson?' he said.

'No, I haven't,' said Sarapion.

'Well, it's worth hearing. Pauson was commissioned once to paint a horse rolling on the ground, and he drew one running. His client was annoyed, but Pauson simply laughed and turned the picture upside down, whereupon the horse appeared to be rolling on the ground instead of running. Bion says that the same thing happens to some arguments, when they are turned the other way round. So some will say not that the verses are good because they are the god's, but that they are not the god's because they are bad. Now the god's authorship is something we cannot clearly show; but that the verses of the oracles are negligently composed is no doubt perfectly clear to your judgement, my dear Sarapion, because you write poetry that is severe and philosophical in content, but in force, charm, and verbal ornament comes nearer to Homer and Hesiod than to what the Pythian priestess puts out.'

[6] 'Yes, Boethus,' said Sarapion, 'we have a sickness of ear and eye because we have grown accustomed through luxury and

397 comfortable living to regard pleasure and beauty as identical. We shall soon be blaming the Pythia for not making sweeter sounds than the lyre-singer Glauce, and for not using perfume or putting on a purple dress before going down to the oracle, or burning incense of cassia or laudanum or frankincense instead of bay and barley meal. Think of the elegance of Sappho's songs, that so charm and fascinate the listener! And contrast the Sibyl, who, as Heraclitus tells us, 'speaks words without laughter, without adornment, without perfume, from her mad-woman's lips, and reaches through a thousand years with her voice, because of the god'.[1] Pindar says too that Cadmus heard the god performing 'right music'[2]—not sweet, or voluptuous, or effeminate in its tunes, but 'right'. The pure and passionless gives no place to Pleasure; she was cast out here on earth, together with Ruin,* and most of her, it seems, has gathered in the ears of men.'

[7] Theon smiled at these words of Sarapion. 'Well,' he said, 'Sarapion has indulged his habits as usual, and made good use of the tale of Pleasure and Ruin when it came into his mind. But for our part, Boethus, whether these lines are inferior to Homer or not, let us not believe that the god composed them, but only that he initiates the movement, and each of the prophetesses is moved according to her nature. If they had to write the oracles instead of speaking them, I don't imagine that we should complain that the handwriting was not as good as that of royal documents! Voice and sound, diction and metre, belong not to the god but to the woman. He merely puts the concepts into her mind, and gives her soul light to view the future; that is what 'possession' (*enthousiasmos*) means. Taking all in all, there is no way of escape from you prophets of Epicurus—it is plain that you are going that way yourself—because you find fault equally with the ancient prophetesses for making bad verse, and with the modern, who deliver their oracles in prose and commonplace language, so as not to have to account to you people for a line that is a syllable short at the beginning or in the middle or at the end.'

'Don't make a joke of it,' said Diogenianus, 'for goodness' sake. Just solve our present problem. Everyone here wants to find a rational explanation of why the oracle has stopped using hexameter verse.'

'But at present, young man,' interjected Theon, 'we are being rude to the guides, by depriving them of their proper function. Let them do their bit first, and then you can ask any question at your leisure.'

[8] We had by now got as far as the statue of the tyrant Hiero. Our guest knew most of what was told him, but his good nature made him a good listener. It was only when he heard that a bronze pillar given by Hiero had fallen down of its own accord on the very day that Hiero died in Syracuse that he expressed surprise. At the same time, I recalled some similar events: how the eyes fell out of the statue of the Spartan Hiero* before the battle of Leuctra, in which he died; how the stars disappeared which Lysander had dedicated after the naval battle of Aegospotami; and how the marble statue of Lysander himself developed a growth of rough vegetation so abundant as to conceal his face; how the gold dates fell off the palm-tree* at the time of the Athenian disaster in Sicily; how the crown of the Cnidians, which the Phocian tyrant Philomelus had given to the dancer Pharsalia, was the cause of her death, when she was dancing at the temple of Apollo at Metapontum (this was after she emigrated from Greece to Italy), and the boys made a rush for the 398
crown and tore the lady to pieces in their struggles for the gold. 'Aristotle said[1] that only Homer could devise words active enough to possess movement, but I would add that the dedications here are especially capable of moving and giving signs in accord with divine providence; no part of them is empty or senseless, all are replete with divinity.'

'I see,' said Boethus, 'it's evidently not enough to lock the god up in a mortal body once a month; we are to make him an ingredient of every stone and every bronze, as if fortune and chance were not adequate to create coincidences like this.'

'Then do you really think', I replied, 'that all these coincidences look like fortune and chance? Is it plausible that the atoms should slip, dissipate, and swerve at no other time than at the very moment when each of the donors of the offerings was on the point of some failure or success? Epicurus obviously helps you by what he said or wrote 300 years ago; do you believe then that the god has to be incapable of providing impulses to motion or causes of change in any existing thing unless he goes and locks himself up in things and becomes totally mixed up in them?'

[9] That was my answer to Boethus. <We then had a discussion> on the same lines about the oracles of the Sibyl.* This was when we arrived at the rock—opposite the Council Chamber—on which the first Sibyl, who was brought up by the Muses, is said to have sat when she first arrived from Helicon. (Some say, however, that she was the daughter of Poseidon's daughter Lamia, and had come from Malis.) Anyway, Sarapion reminded us of the lines in which she sang her own praises, and foretold that she would not cease from prophecy even after her death, but would go round and round with the moon, as what appears to us as the face in the moon; her spirit, she said, would mingle with air and travel on for ever in rumours and voices, while from her changed body grasses and woods would grow on earth on which sacred animals* would feed, displaying in their organs all kinds of colours, shapes, and qualities from which men would prognosticate the future.

Boethus' ridicule became even more obvious at this. Our guest, however, observed that even if these were fables, there was abundant evidence of the validity of the Sibyl's prophecies, in the many migrations and movements of Greek cities, the many visitations of barbarian armies, and the many destructions of empires. 'And', he went on, 'are not these recent disasters around Cumae and Dicaearchia,* foretold long ago in the Sibylline songs and hymns, a debt that time has now paid in full? The Sibyl spoke of fires erupting from the mountain, boiling seas, rocks and fire cast up by the blast, and many great cities destroyed so utterly that those who visit them on the morrow do not know for certain where they once stood amid the devastation of the land. It is hard enough to believe these things if they happen; it is harder still to foretell them without divine inspiration.'

[10] 'My dear man,' said Boethus, 'is there any disaster that time does not owe nature? Is there any event, however extraordinary and outside our expectation, involving land or sea, city or individual, that one could predict without finding that it actually happens? One cannot even call this prediction; it is simply assertion, or rather it is like throwing a scatter of base-

less words into the infinite, where chance often meets up with them quite fortuitously as they wander around. In my opinion there is a difference between the fulfilment of something said and the statement of something which is going to happen. A statement of the non-existent contains its error in itself. It is not entitled to await fortuitous confirmation or to regard a sub- 399
sequent event as a certain indication that its forecast was made with knowledge. Infinity brings everything to pass. More accurately, the "good guesser", as the proverb describes the "best prophet", is like a stalker tracking the footsteps of the future by probable signs. These Bacises and Sibyls scatter names and expressions applying to every kind of event and occurrence indiscriminately into the uncharted sea of time. Some of the things actually happen by chance, but what is said now is none the less false, even if it later in fact becomes true.'

[11] 'Boethus' statement is perfectly proper', said Sarapion at the close of this exposition, 'so far as indefinite and unspecific statements are concerned—for example, if there is a prophecy of victory for a general and he wins one, or if the destruction of a city is foretold and it is destroyed; but when not only the future event but the manner, time, sequence, and circumstances are given, this is no longer a conjecture about what may happen but a forecast of what will. Take for example the prophecy about Agesilaus' lameness:

> Take care, o Sparta, high though stands thy pride,
> lest, though thy legs be strong, thy realm be lame;
> for long shall toil unlooked-for wear thee down
> and deathly waves of a long-rolling war.

Or take the oracle about the island* that the sea thrust up between Thera and Therasia about the time of the war between Philip and the Romans:

> But when the seed of Troy victorious
> in battle has o'erthrown the Punic power,
> strange things shall follow; sea shall blaze with fire,
> and lightning shafts shoot upwards through the sea,
> mingled with rocks; an isle unknown to man
> shall rise upon the place; and the worse men
> shall lay their betters low by force of hand.

And within a short time, the Romans defeated Hannibal and overcame the Carthaginians; Philip met the Aetolians and Romans in battle and was defeated; and finally an island rose out of the sea with much fire and with boiling waves. Surely no one could say that all these things occurred coincidentally, by chance and fortune. The order proves the foreknowledge. Similarly with the forecast, made nearly 500 years before the event, of the time when the Romans would "war against all nations at once".* This meant the war against their rebel slaves. In all these cases, the prophecy does not give a vague or indeterminate message [*some words unintelligible*]; it offers many guarantees of experience, and shows the road by which destiny advances. For I cannot conceive that anyone will argue that every one of these things happened as foretold simply by chance. Otherwise, what is there to prevent one saying that Epicurus didn't write the *Essential Thoughts*,* but the letters came together by chance and accident until the book was finished?'

[12] As we talked, we continued on our tour. In the Corinthian Treasury we saw the bronze palm-tree, the only offering to survive. The frogs and water-snakes in relief around the root were a surprise to Diogenianus, and indeed to us. For the palm is not, as some other trees are, a water-loving plant of the marshes, nor have the Corinthians any connection with frogs, so that it could be a symbol or sign of the city, in the way that the people of Selinus, for example, are said once to have dedicated a gold celery-plant (*selīnon*) and the people of Tenedos an axe, from
400 the crabs found around the place called Asterion on Tenedos, which are the only crabs to have a mark in the shape of an axe on their shell. We believe too that Apollo himself loves ravens, swans, wolves, and hawks—any animal rather than frogs and water-snakes! Sarapion's suggestion was that the artist wished to symbolize the fact that the sun draws its nourishment, its origin, and the exhalation on which it feeds, from moisture. He had, he thought, perhaps heard Homer's words: 'then rose the sun, leaving the lovely lake',[1] and had observed that the Egyptians represent the first rising of the sun by a picture of a child sitting on a lotus flower.*

I laughed. 'My good friend,' I said, 'why do you keep thrusting your Stoicism upon us, and surreptitiously introducing all these kindlings and exhalations? You're as good as bringing down the moon and sun, as the Thessalian witches* do, by telling us that they grow and are nourished from earth and water! Plato called man a 'plant of heaven',[2] held upright, as it were, by the root in his head; but your school on the one hand makes fun of Empedocles for saying that the sun, being formed by the reflection of heavenly light around the earth, then "with face undaunted casts back rays to heaven",[3] yet, on the other hand, you declare the sun to be a creature of earth or a plant of the marshes, enrolling him as a citizen of the land of frogs and snakes! But let us leave all that to the Stoic melodrama, and make a side-issue ourselves of the artists' sideshow. For artists, clever as they are, do not always succeed in avoiding frigid artificiality. The sculptor who set a cock on Apollo's hand obviously meant to suggest dawn and sunrise; and on the same principle one can see the frogs here as a symbol of spring, the season when the sun begins to dominate the air and dispel winter—if, as your people hold, we are supposed to regard Apollo and the sun as one single god.'

'Don't you believe that?' said Sarapion; 'Do you think the sun and Apollo are distinct?'

'Yes,' I replied, 'just as I think the sun and the moon are distinct. But the moon obscures the sun only rarely and never for everyone, whereas the sun makes everybody ignore Apollo, because he diverts our minds with sense, turning them from reality to appearance.'

[13] Sarapion next asked the guides why they called the building the Treasury of the Corinthians and not the Treasury of Cypselus, who dedicated it. They remained silent—presumably because they had no explanation to give—and I burst out laughing. 'How can we expect them', I said, 'to go on knowing and remembering when they have been so taken aback by our grand talk? We heard them say earlier that, after the collapse of the tyranny, the Corinthians expressed a desire to have the Treasury here and the gold statue at Pisa inscribed as gifts of the city. The Delphians agreed that this was a proper request and granted it, but the Eleans grudged it them, and Corinth therefore banned

Elis from the Isthmian games. The murder of the children of Molione* by Heracles at Cleonae has nothing to do with the banning of the Eleans, though some think it has; on the contrary, that would have given the Eleans reason to ban Corinth from the Olympic festival, if they had quarrelled on that account.'

[14] That was my contribution. But when we had passed the treasury dedicated by the Acanthians and Brasidas,* the guide showed us the place where there once stood the iron spits given by the courtesan Rhodopis.* Diogenianus waxed indignant.

'So the same city', he cried, 'gave Rhodopis room to deposit
401 the tithe of her earnings, and put her fellow slave Aesop* to
death!'

'And what is there to be indignant about in that, my friend?' said Sarapion. 'Look up there and observe, among the generals and kings,* Mnesarete, in gold, set up, as Crates said, to commemorate Greek incontinence!'

The young man looked at the offering. 'So it wasn't Phryne that Crates said that about?' he said.

'Yes, it was,' said Sarapion. 'Her name was Mnesarete, but she was called Phryne—"Toad"—because of her pale complexion. It seems that nicknames often displace real names. Alexander's mother, they say, was originally called Polyxena, but then Myrtale, Olympias, and Stratonice. Eumetis of Rhodes is commonly called Cleobulina, after her father; Herophila of Erythrae, who became a prophetess, was then called Sibyl. And you will find scholars who say that Leda was called Mnesinoe and Orestes Achaios. But how do you'—and he looked at Theon—'propose to answer the charge about Phryne?'

[15] Theon smiled gently. 'By bringing a charge against you', he said, 'for complaining about the most trivial of the offences the Greeks have committed. Socrates, when he is entertained at Callias' house,* makes war only on the perfume, but tolerates the slaves' dances and acrobatics and the kissing and the jesters. You're the same. You try to exclude from the holy place a woman who made an ignoble use of her beauty, but you feel no indignation at seeing the god surrounded by the tithes and first-fruits of murder, war, and robbery, and a temple full of spoil and booty taken from Greeks; nor do you feel pity for the Greeks as you read the inscriptions of shame on these beautiful dedications: "Brasidas and the Acanthians, from Athenian spoils"; "The Athenians from Corinthian spoils"; "The Phocians from Thessalian spoils"; "The Orneates from Sicyonian spoils"; "The Amphictyons from Phocian spoils". It was only Praxiteles, it seems, who caused Crates distress for securing a place here for the woman he loved. Crates ought rather to have praised him for setting a prostitute wrought in gold side by side with these golden kings, and showing thereby that there is nothing admirable or venerable in wealth. Kings and rulers would have done well to dedicate to the god offerings of justice and temperance and magnanimity, not those of that gilded and luxurious prosperity which is open also to those who live the most vicious of lives.'

[16]'Aren't you going to add', interjected one of the two guides, 'that Croesus* dedicated a gold statue of his baking-woman here?'

'He did indeed,' replied Theon, 'but not so as to insult the temple. He had a fair and honourable reason. The story is that Alyattes, Croesus' father, married a second wife, by whom he had a second family. This lady then plotted against Croesus and gave the baking-woman a poison, telling her to make a loaf with it and give it to Croesus. The baking-woman, however, privately warned Croesus, and served the loaf to his step-mother's children. So when he came to the throne he requited the woman's service before Apollo as witness, as it were, and he was right to do so. We should also', he continued, 'honour and approve any such offerings made by cities, like that given by the people of Opus. When the Phocian tyrants melted down many of the gold and silver offerings and coined money out of them, which they circulated among the cities, the people of Opus collected all the Phocian silver they had and made a water-jar which they sent here and consecrated to the god. I also approve the action of the people of Myrina and Apollonia in sending golden ears of corn, and still more Eretria and Magnesia for giv- 402
ing the god the first-fruits of their people,* revering him thus as the giver of harvest, the god of fathers and of birth, and the lover of mankind. On the other hand, I disapprove of the Megarians, who are unique in having set up a statue of the god carrying a spear, in consequence of the victory which expelled the Athenians from their city after the Persian wars. Later, however,

they did dedicate a gold plectrum. No doubt they had taken note of the words of Scythinus* about

> the lyre
> that Zeus' fair son Apollo tunes, and grasps
> end and beginning, with the sun's bright ray
> for plectrum.[1]

[17]Sarapion was on the point of putting in a word at this point, but the visitor spoke first. 'It is pleasant', he said, 'to listen to this kind of discussion, but I feel bound to ask fulfilment of our original undertaking, to explain what has caused the Pythia to give up prophesying in hexameters or other metres. I suggest, if you agree, that we postpone the rest of our sightseeing and sit down here and hear this debate. There is in this an argument which is particularly damaging to the oracle's credibility, as there seem to be two possibilities: either the Pythia does not go near the place where the divine power resides, or the spirit (*pneuma*) is entirely exhausted and the power has faded away.'

So we went round and sat on the southern steps of the temple, looking towards the shrine of Earth and the Water <of Cassotis>. Boethus immediately observed that the place itself helped to solve our visitor's problem. 'There used to be a shrine of the Muses here,' he said, 'near the outlet of the stream, so that they used the water for libations and ritual washing. Simonides speaks of the place

> where is drawn up from below
> for the rite of the washing of hands
> the fair-tressed Muses' holy water.

And again, in a somewhat more elaborate passage, he addresses Clio as

> overseer of the washing of hands,
> golden-robed, to whom the drawers pray,
> who givest the lovely water,
> fragrant from immortal depths.[2]

Eudoxus was surely wrong to believe those who declare this to be what is meant by the water of Styx. They established the Muses here, as assessors and guardians of the prophecy, right by the spring and the shrine of Earth (to whom the oracle is said to have belonged) because of the metrical and musical form of the oracular pronouncements. Some indeed say that the first heroic hexameter was heard here:

> Birds, bring your feathers up hither: bees, bring your wax to me hither!

[*The conclusion of this speech is corrupt and defective; it is not clear what account Boethus gave of the cessation of verses; perhaps the cessation of a cult of the Muses on this site.*]

[18]'That is certainly a more respectable and educated account, Boethus,' said Sarapion; 'for it is essential not to battle against god and demolish providence and the divine along with prophecy. What we ought to do is to seek solutions for apparent objections without abandoning the pious faith of our fathers.'

'Very true, my dear Sarapion,' I said, 'we do not despair of philosophy, as a thing altogether lost and ruined, because philosophers used at one time to present their doctrines and arguments in verse—as Orpheus, Hesiod, Parmenides, Xenophanes, and Empedocles did—but later ceased to do so, and have not used metre since, apart, of course, from yourself; it is through your doing that poetry is once again restored to philosophy and proclaims a stirring, noble message to the young. Nor was astronomy disgraced because Aristarchus, Timocharis, Aris-
tyllus, and Hipparchus wrote in prose, though Eudoxus, Hesiod, 403
and Thales had formerly written in verse—if indeed Thales did write the *Astronomy* attributed to him. Pindar also confesses[1] to being at a loss for a musical technique neglected in his own time, and says that he is surprised [*some words missing*]. There is nothing strange or absurd in investigating the causes of such changes; what is wrong is to deny the existence of arts and faculties just because there has been some change or disturbance in their conditions of activity.'

[19]Theon took me up. 'Nevertheless,' he said, 'while these arts have indeed suffered great changes and innovations, <we know that> many of the <oracles> here, even in the old days, were delivered in prose, though they were about matters of some importance. Thucydides, for example, tells us that when the Spartans consulted the oracle about their war with Athens,

Apollo promised them victory and domination, and said he would help them, bidden or unbidden.[2] He told them also that, if they did not recall Pleistoanax, they would be "ploughing with a silver plough". Again, when the Athenians asked for advice about their expedition to Sicily, he told them to summon the priestess of Athena from Erythrae; that lady's name was Hesychia, which means "Quiet". Then there was Deinomenes the Sicilian's inquiry about his sons. The god replied that three of them would be tyrants.* "And may they suffer for it, Lord Apollo," replied Deinomenes; and the god replied that this too he granted and added to his prophecy. So Gelo, you must know, was ill with dropsy when he came to power, and Hiero with the stone, while the third, Thrasybulus, was caught up in wars and revolutions and fell from power before very long. Procles, tyrant of Epidaurus, put many to death cruelly and illegally; and among them was a certain Timarchus, who had come from Athens with a sum of money, and whom Procles welcomed and entertained hospitably before killing him and putting the body in a basket and sinking it at sea. His accomplice was Cleandros of Aegina; no one else knew. Later, when his affairs became troubled, Procles secretly sent his brother Cleotimus here to Delphi to ask about the chances of exile or emigration. The god replied that he granted Procles exile and emigration, either to the place where he had told his friend from Aegina to sink the basket, or else to the place where stags lose their horns. The tyrant realized that he was being told either to drown himself or to bury himself. Stags, you see, bury and hide their horns* in the ground when they drop. He waited for a time, but then, when things got very bad indeed, went into exile. Timarchus' friends captured and killed him, and threw his body into the sea. But the most important example of all is the code of laws, the *rhētrai*, by which Lycurgus organized the Spartan state. These were delivered to him in prose. And Herodotus, Philochorus, and Istros, the writers most interested in collecting verse oracles, have nevertheless recorded innumerable instances of prose ones. Theopompus, who is second to none in his enthusiasm for the oracle, is severe in his criticism of those who believed that the Pythia did not deliver verse prophecies in those days; but when he wants to prove his point, he can find very few oracles to support it, because most of them were already being delivered in prose.

[20] 'However, even nowadays some come out in metre. One of these has become very celebrated because of the circumstances. There is a temple in Phocis of Heracles,* and the rule is that the priest must not have relations with women during his year of office. They usually therefore appoint very elderly priests. However, a little while ago, an honest but ambitious man, who was in love with a girl, accepted the priesthood. At first, he kept a tight hold on himself and avoided her; but when she came to 404
him one day when he was resting after drinking and dancing, he had his way with her. In great fear and distress he then went to the oracle, and asked the god if there was any remedy or expiation for his sin. He was given the following verse:

The god permits all necessary acts.

But even if one were to grant that no prophecies are delivered in metre in our own day, this would only increase the difficulty about the ancients: why did they sometimes provide answers in verse, and sometimes not? Yet neither practice is unreasonable, my young friend, provided that we hold pure and unerring opinions about the god, and do not believe that it is he himself who used to compose the verses and who now puts the oracle into the Pythia's mouth, like an actor speaking through a mask.

[21] 'But this merits fuller discussion and inquiry on another occasion. For the moment, let us briefly recall what we have learnt. The body uses many instruments; the soul uses the body itself and its parts. The soul is the instrument of god, and the excellence of an instrument lies in its copying its user with whatever power it has and producing the action corresponding to the thought that appears in him, and displaying it, not pure and free of passion or error, as it was in its creator, but mixed with <other elements>; for the thought is in itself not accessible to our view, and when it appears in another object or through another medium it is inevitably imbued with the nature of that medium. I say nothing of wax and gold, silver and bronze, and whatever other kinds of malleable material receive a single shape from the likeness imprinted on them but still contribute their own various distinctive features to the resulting model. I say nothing either of the innumerable distorted images and appearances of a single object that can be produced by plane, concave, or convex mirrors. <Everyone knows about these.> But there is nothing so like <a mirror> as the moon, nothing so obedient to serve as an instrument: yet when the moon borrows fire and brilliance from the sun, she does not transmit it to us in the same form; the fire mingles with the moon, changes colour, and acquires a different force. The heat indeed vanishes altogether, and the light fades through weakness.

'I am sure you know the saying of Heraclitus: "The Lord whose oracle is at Delphi neither speaks nor conceals but gives signs."[1] Combine this with what has been said, and think of the god here as using the Pythia in the world of hearing as the sun uses the moon in the world of sight. He reveals and discloses his thoughts, but only as they are mixed in a mortal body and a human soul that cannot be still or offer itself to the force that moves it in a stable condition, free from its own internal movement, but only, as it were, tossing on its own troubled waters and bound up with the even more disturbing motions and emotions within it.

'Let me make an analogy. An eddy does not totally control falling objects which are also rotating; the combination of the forced rotatory movement with the natural downward fall results in an irregular and disorderly spiral motion. Possession by the god seems similarly to be a combination of two movements, the mind being affected simultaneously by the experience and by its own nature. Inanimate, stationary bodies cannot be used forcibly against their nature: a cylinder cannot be moved like a sphere, or <a cone> like a cube; a lyre cannot be played like a flute, or a trumpet like a harp. There is, it appears, no difference between the skilled use of these objects and their natural use. *A fortiori*, animate, self-moving objects, which possess impulse and reason, can be handled only in accordance with their inherent, pre-existing condition, capacity, or nature. Can one affect
405 an unmusical mind by music, an illiterate mind by the written word, a mind that has no theoretical knowledge or practice in eloquence by eloquence? In no way!

[22]'Homer confirms what I say. His general assumption is that nothing is effected without god's being responsible, but he

does not represent god as using all persons for all purposes, but each according to his skill and capacity. You surely see, my dear Diogenianus,' he went on, 'how Athena encourages Odysseus, when she wants to persuade the Greeks; how she seeks out Pandarus when she wants to break the truce; and how she makes straight for Diomedes when she wants to rout the Trojans. Diomedes is a mighty warrior, Pandarus a foolish archer, and Odysseus a wise and eloquent speaker. Homer, you see, didn't have the same opinion as Pandarus,* if indeed it was Pandarus who wrote "If god so wills, you'll sail upon a mat." He recognized that different capacities and natures are intended for different purposes, each having a different type of motion, even if there is a single motive-force affecting them all. The force cannot make a walking animal fly, or a lisper speak distinctly, or a feeble voice resonant. When Battus came to the oracle to ask advice about his voice, the god sent him to Libya to found a colony, because, though lisping and feeble of voice, he was a natural ruler and statesman of great wisdom. Likewise, an uneducated person who has never heard verses cannot speak poetically. The present servant of the god is a case in point. She has lived from birth as lawful, honourable, and orderly a life as anyone in Delphi, but she was brought up in the house of poor peasants, and when she goes down into the cave of the oracle she takes with her no resources of art or experience or capacity. Like the bride whom Xenophon thinks ought to go to her husband's house "having seen very little and heard very little",[1] she is, for all practical purposes, totally ignorant and inexperienced; she goes to the god truly with the soul of a virgin. Now we believe that the god gives signs by the voice of herons and wrens and ravens, and we do not expect these creatures, because they are heralds and messengers of gods, to indicate everything in a clear and logical manner; yet at the same time we expect the god to make the Pythia's language a sort of tragic performance, not plain and simple, but grand, metrical, elaborate, metaphorical, and with a flute accompaniment!

[23]'Then what of the prophetesses of old? There are several things to be said. First, as we saw, they too spoke for the most part in prose. Secondly, that age produced natures and temperaments with a certain fertility and fluency in poetry. To this were

soon added a willingness, a determination, and an education which produced a readiness of mind needing but small external initiative or stimulus of the imagination. Consequently, not only were astronomers and philosophers, as Philinus reminds us, quickly drawn to the activity natural to them, but, whenever men were drunk or emotional, when pity crept upon them or joy struck them, they would all slip into the voice of song; their drinking-parties were filled with tunes and songs of love, and their books with poetical writings. When Euripides wrote "Love makes a poet of the unmusical",[2] he realized that love does not produce a capacity for poetry or music, but rather stirs and warms one that was unseen or dormant before. Are we to say that nobody falls in love nowadays, my friend, but love has disappeared, because no one now (in Pindar's words) "fires off the arrows of youth's honeyed song"[3] in metre or poetry? That
406 would be absurd. The Loves still move among men, and in strength, but because the minds with which they associate are not gifted or prepared for music, they play no pipe or lyre, though they talk as much and are just as fiery as the Loves of old. It would be very wrong and dishonourable to suggest that the Academy and the circle of Socrates and Plato was without love. They have left no poems, but we have their erotic speeches to read. What is the difference between alleging that Sappho is the only woman who loved, and saying that the Sibyl or Aristonice or the others who delivered oracles in verse were the only women gifted with prophecy? "Wine mingles with the drinker's temperament," says Chaeremon;[1] and prophetic possession, like possession by love, makes use of whatever capacity is available and moves each individual recipient according to his or her nature.

[24]'Indeed, if we consider the workings of god and of providence, we shall see that the change has been for the better. The use of words is like the currency of coin; the usual and familiar is the most acceptable, and its validity varies from time to time. Once upon a time, metre, lyric, and song were the verbal currency. History, philosophy, every experience or subject that needed a certain dignity of utterance was put into poetical and musical form. It is only part of the truth that few people now understand these things, whereas in those days everyone listened to and enjoyed songs—"shepherds and ploughmen and trappers of birds", as Pindar says.[2] It is also true that the aptitude for poetry led most people to use song and lyric for advice, abuse, and exhortation. Fables and proverbs adopted the same form. Hymns, prayers, and paeans were composed in song and metre—by some because they had a talent for it, by others because it was the done thing. And so the god did not deny his prophecy the charm and the splendour of verse, or drive the Muse with honour away from his tripod here. On the contrary, he encouraged poetical natures, stimulating and welcoming them, and himself provided images and helped to develop a luxuriant eloquence, as being both appropriate and admirable. But circumstances and natures changed, and life changed with them. Utility drove out elaboration. Golden hair-ornaments* vanished, long, soft dresses were laid aside, luxuriant hair was cut short, high boots were taken off. Men began, very rightly, to accustom themselves to letting the elegance of moderation rival that of extravagance, and to treat the plain and simple as no less ornamental than the luxurious and elaborate. Speech too shared in the change, and set itself free. History descended from the chariot of metre, and prose became the mark that distinguished fact from fable. Philosophy came to prefer clear instruction to emotional impact and made her inquiries in plain prose. And finally the god stopped the Pythia calling her fellow citizens "fire-burners", the Spartans "snake-eaters", mankind in general "mountaineers", and rivers "mountain-drinkers". He stripped the oracles of their versification, their foreign words and periphrases and obscurity, and made them speak to their clients in the way laws speak to cities, kings address their peoples, and pupils listen to teachers. His aim was intelligibility and persuasiveness.

[25]'We must keep in mind that the god, as Sophocles says, was

> ever a riddling prophet to the wise;
> to fools, a simple teacher of few words.[3]

The coming of clarity made a difference to everything, including confidence. In the old days, the mass of mankind was struck 407
with awe and veneration for the uncommon and unusual, the

truly "oblique"* and the periphrastic, which they regarded as an indication of divine influence. Later, however, they began to take pleasure in clear and easy understanding of detail, without pretentiousness or affectation; not only did they find fault with the poetical form of the oracles, as obstructing their comprehension of the truth, by casting a shadow of obscurity over the meaning, but they also began to be suspicious of metaphors, riddles, and ambiguities which seemed to have been devised to allow the errors of prophecy to find hiding-places and refuges in which to skulk and retire. Many could be heard saying that poetically talented persons sat around the oracle, receiving and taking up the words that were uttered, and constructing a sort of vehicle for the prophecies, in verse, metre, rhythm, using whatever came to hand. I say nothing of the responsibility of people like Onomacritus, Prodicus, and Cinaethon for the oracles, dressing them up as they did quite unnecessarily in pretentious bombast. <There is no need to talk about> these alterations. The greatest discredit to poetry came from the tribe of street-corner mendicants, the altar-scroungers and vagabonds who haunt the temples of the Great Mother and of Serapis. Some of these invented their own oracles, others took them by lot from written lists, and gave them to slaves and women who were captivated by metre and poetical vocabulary. This was the main way by which poetry came to be thought to have prostituted herself to quacks and charlatans and false prophets, and this is why she was banished from truth and from the tripod.

[26]'So I find nothing surprising if the ancients sometimes felt the need of double meanings, circumlocution, and obscurity. It was not a matter of ordinary folk coming down to ask about buying a slave or starting a business. Powerful cities, kings and tyrants, without a modest thought in their heads, came to seek the god's advice about affairs <of great moment>. It was certainly not in the interests of the keepers of the oracle to annoy or alienate such persons by letting them hear a lot of things they would not wish to hear. The god does not in fact follow Euripides' law, if we may call it that: "Phoebus alone must prophesy to men."[1] He employs mortal servants and spokesmen, and it is his duty to care for them and protect them against being destroyed by wicked men while they are in the god's service. And so, though he had no desire to conceal the truth, he did seek to eliminate its unattractive and repellent aspect, by distorting its revelation with poetry, as a ray of light can be reflected and fragmented again and again. There were, of course, things that a tyrant ought not to know, or of which warring parties ought not to have prior information. He covered these up with allegories and ambiguities, which obscured the meaning for others, but did not escape or deceive the inquirers themselves, so long as they paid sufficient attention. Times have changed now, and it is a fool who complains or finds fault because the god now thinks he ought to help us in a different way from before.

[27]'Another point. The greatest advantage that accrues to speech from poetry is that the thought is fixed by being entwined in the metre, and so is more easily remembered and retained. Now the men of old had great need of memory. Much information was given them as they set out on those long voyages, far from Greece: indications of places, moments for action, shrines of foreign gods, secret burial places of heroes that were hard to find. You know about all those leaders of expeditions who had to find their appointed places of settlement by the clues they
were given: Teucer, Cretines, Gnesiochus,* Phalanthus. Some, 408
like Battus, missed the place. He had gone into exile not understanding where he had been sent, and he came back here again, full of complaint. The god answered:

> If you know sheep-rearing Libya better than I do—
> I who have been there, and you who have not—I admire you!

And he sent him out again. Lysander failed to understand about the Orchalid Hill (also called Foxes' Hill) and the river Hoplites,* "and the treacherous serpent, the offspring of earth, that creeps up behind you". And because of that he was defeated and killed there by Neochorus of Haliartus, the sign on whose shield was a serpent. There are many examples of ancient oracles which were difficult to understand and remember; but you all know them, and I need not repeat them here.

[28]'For my own part, I feel very content with the present subjects of the questions men put to the god. All is peace and quiet, war has ceased, there are no migrations or revolutions or

tyrannies in Greece, or any other disorders and evils demanding complicated medication, as it were. There are no complexities, no secrets, no dangers. There are only questions about small, everyday matters, like our school exercises:* "Should I marry?"; "Should I go to sea?"; "Should I lend money?" The gravest prophecies needed by cities relate to harvests or the increase of cattle or the health of the population. In such circumstances, to add metre or circumlocution or foreign words to questions that need only a short and simple answer is work only for an ambitious sophist who wants to make a reputation by prettifying the oracle. The Pythia is herself a woman of splendid character; and when she goes down there and is with the god, she is more concerned <with serving him according to her duty> than with reputation or the praise and blame of men.

[29]'And that perhaps is what our attitude should be also. But instead, we seem to be in an agony of fear, lest this place should lose the reputation it has had these 3,000 years, and certain people come to hold it in contempt, and desert the oracle, like an audience deserting an unsuccessful lecturer! So we construct defences and invent explanations and arguments about things we do not know and have no business to know. We try to appease and convince the complainer, instead of letting him be: for "he himself shall suffer first", if he continues to hold an opinion about the god which involves, on the one hand, admiring the inscriptions of the Wise Men—"Know Thyself" and "Nothing in Excess"—for the conciseness with which they express a pregnant, solid thought in a small compass; and, on the other hand, finding fault with the oracles because they generally convey their message simply, concisely, and in straightforward language. Now these sayings of the Wise Men are like streams confined in narrow channels; they do not allow a clear, transparent view of the thought, but if you consider what has been said and written about them by those who seek to interpret them, it would be hard to find a longer discussion of anything anywhere. The Pythia's speech, on the other hand, has the characteristic that mathematicians attribute to a straight line: it is the shortest line between two points. Her words have no twists or curves, no double sense or ambiguity. They go straight to the truth, they risk the test of belief, they take responsibility for themselves,

and they have never yet been proved wrong. They have enriched the shrine with offerings and gifts from Greeks and barbarians, and adorned it with beautiful buildings and the rich possessions 409
of the Amphictyons. You all see yourselves many new buildings where there were none before, and many ruined and desolate buildings now restored. And as young trees grow up beside those that are already flourishing, so does Pylaea* share in Delphi's vigour and prosperity. Our wealth has given her form and beauty and a splendour of temples and meeting-houses and water-courses such as she has never had for a thousand years. The inhabitants of Galaxion* in Boeotia became aware of the epiphany of the god because of the abundant flow of milk:

> From all the sheep it bubbled,
> milk from their udders like water from the springs;
> they ran to fill their jars;
> no wine-skin, no storage-vat stood empty;
> their wooden pails and pots were brimming full.[1]

But here he gives us a brighter, stronger, clearer sign. He has given us prosperity and splendour and honour, in place of the drought of our former desolation. I love myself for my zeal and service in this cause, with Polycrates and Petraeus. I love also the initiator of this policy,* who takes thought and cares for most of these achievements. But so great a change cannot have happened in so short a time by mere human effort, without the presence of the god among us and his divine guidance of the oracle.

[30]'Yet, just as in the old days there were some who found fault with the obliquity and obscurity of the prophecies, so now there are some who impugn their simplicity. This is a silly, childish attitude. Children get more pleasure and enjoyment from seeing rainbows and haloes and comets than from seeing the sun and the moon; and similarly these critics long for the riddles and allegories and metaphors which are but the reflections of the prophecy in our mortal imaginations. Then, if they fail to satisfy themselves about the reason for the change, they depart condemning the god, instead of condemning us or themselves for being incapable of attaining to the god's thought by the power of reason.'

IV

SOCRATES' *DAIMONION*

This is Plutarch's most elaborate dialogue, and it concentrates within itself many of his main interests (Introd. p. xiii). The setting is a heroic moment in the history of Thebes, the liberation from Spartan occupation in 379 BC. The conspirators planning the *coup* meet at the house of Simmias, an old friend of Socrates who, according to Plato's *Phaedo*, was present at the latter's death. They discuss the problem of Socrates' 'divine sign' (*daimonion sēmeion*), the mysterious warning voice which (according to tradition) deterred him from wrong or rash actions. By coincidence, a Pythagorean has arrived in Thebes, to perform certain ceremonies at the grave of the exiled Pythagorian Lysis. He too—his name is Theanor, 'Man of God'—comes to take part in the discussion. Naturally enough, the explanations offered have much in common with the theories regarding divination which we have seen in II and III. But the notion of *daimon* is here more complex and ambivalent. In Theanor's speech, *daimones* are primarily the 'intermediaries' of Plato and Hesiod; but *daimon* is also identical with *nous*, intellect, the highest and most rational part of man, his only true guide, and this is the key idea in the 'Myth of Timarchus', the revelation which forms the most striking part of the discussion. This myth—one of several in Plutarch, to be compared with those in 'God's Slowness to Punish' (41) and 'The Face in the Moon' (60)—is an extraordinary vision of the fate of the human soul, when it escapes from the body into the starry immensity of the *kosmos*.

The narrative of the conspiracy, taken up at intervals as the discussion proceeds, and dominant in the closing chapters, is exciting and skilfully executed, with plenty of suspense. Plutarch's other account of the events, in the *Life of Pelopidas*, is less vivid and enthralling. Our dialogue thus displays both the life of philosophy and the life of action; it is worth observing that Epaminondas, later to be the great hero of the Theban hegemony, appears here only as a philosophic pupil of the Pythagoreans, and a bystander so far as the main action is concerned. If there is a thematic link between narrative and discussion, it should be sought in the common theme of liberation: as the city was freed, by virtue and good counsel, from the foreign yoke, so does the soul, though not without trials and setbacks, escape by virtue from the trammels of the body.

The 'frame dialogue' is set in Athens, where young Caphisias (not much more than a boy in the main story) is on an embassy (precise date unclear) which gives him the opportunity of informing Athenian friends of the details of the liberation.

[1] ARCHEDEMUS 575

I remember, Caphisias, once hearing a painter use an apt simile to describe people who look at pictures. He said that a layman who had no knowledge of the art was like a man giving a general salutation to a crowd of people, whereas the sophisticated connoisseur was more like the man who greets everyone he meets individually. He was right. The layman has only a general, inexact view of the work of art, while the connoisseur's separate examination of every detail allows nothing, whether good or bad, to pass unobserved or uncommented. It is much the same, I suspect, with real events. For the lazy-minded, it suffices to learn the basic facts and the outcome; but the lover of honour and beauty who views the masterpieces of that greatest of arts, virtue, takes greater pleasure in the detail. Since the issue depends on fortune, while the motivation and execution do not, it is in these that the student can perceive the struggle of virtue with circumstance, or the play of intelligent daring in the face of danger, when reason joins forces with the emotions of the moment. You will, I hope, regard us as students of this kind, and so tell us the story of the whole action from the beginning, including the conversations which took place while you were there. I shouldn't have hesitated to go to Thebes just for this, if I hadn't already been believed by the Athenians to be too much inclined to the Boeotian cause.*

CAPHISIAS

My dear Archedemus, the very fact that your goodwill towards us makes you so anxious to hear what happened would itself have obliged me to come to Athens just to tell it all to you, and to put this, as Pindar says, 'above all business'.[1] But as I am here anyway as an ambassador and have nothing to do till we get our answer from the people, any ill-mannered resistance on my part to the request of so well-disposed a friend would be sure to revive the old reproach about Boeotian lack of culture, though that idea has been on the wane, thanks to <the devotion of people like Simmias and Cebes> to your philosopher

Socrates, and my family's devotion to the holy man, Lysis. But what about our friends here? Do they have time to listen to an account of so many incidents and conversations? It's not a short narrative, since you ask me to put the conversation in also.

ARCHEDEMUS

You don't know them, Caphisias. You should: their fathers were brave men and your friends. This is Lysitheides, nephew of Thrasybulus. This is Timotheus, son of Conon. These are the sons of Archinus. All the rest belong to our group; so your audience is a friendly one, and the story is one that interests them deeply.

CAPHISIAS

Excellent! Now what would be the right point to begin, taking into account what you know?

ARCHEDEMUS

We are pretty well acquainted with the state of Thebes prior to the return of the exiles. We know from our friends Melon and Pelopidas, of whom we saw a great deal during their exile here,
576 how Archias and Leontiadas induced Phoebidas to seize the Cadmea* in a time of truce, and how they expelled some citizens and repressed the rest by the terror of their lawless and violent rule. We have also heard how the Lacedaemonians fined Phoebidas for seizing the Cadmea and dismissed him from his command of the expedition to Olynthus, and then sent Lysanoridas to Thebes in his place with two colleagues, and reinforced the garrison of the citadel. We know also about Ismenias' trial and his horrible death: Gorgidas reported all this by letter to the exiles here. So what remains for you to tell us is the actual return of our friends and the overthrow of the tyrants.

[2] CAPHISIAS

Well, Archedemus, in those days all of us who were involved in the plot were in the habit of meeting in Simmias' house, where he was recovering from an injury to his leg. We would make our necessary contacts with one another there, at the same time openly devoting the time to philosophical discussion. We often brought Archias and Leontiadas along, to allay suspicions. They were no strangers to this kind of talk. Simmias had been abroad a long time, and wandered among many kinds of people, and had not long returned to Thebes, full of all sorts of tales and barbarian lore. So Archias was very pleased to listen, whenever he had time to spare, joining the young men, and happy that we were spending our time in discussion rather than spying on what he and his friends were doing.

Now, on the day when the exiles were due to arrive secretly at the wall when darkness fell, a messenger sent by Pherenicus arrived from Athens. None of us knew him except Charon. He reported that the twelve youngest of the exiles were hunting with hounds on Cithaeron, and hoped to arrive in the evening: he himself, he said, had been sent to give advance warning and to find out who was to provide a safe house for them when they arrived, so that they could go straight there. While we were still puzzling over this, and debating what to do, Charon offered his own house. The messenger thereupon decided to go straight back to the exiles.

[3] At this, Theocritus the prophet seized me by the hand, and gazed at Charon as he was leaving. 'Caphisias,' he said, 'just look at that man. He is no philosopher, and he has no special education like your brother Epaminondas, but he is naturally guided by the law to actions of honour, and volunteers to run great risks for his country. Yet Epaminondas, who thinks himself superior to any Boeotian because he has been educated for virtue, shows no keenness or enthusiasm . . . But what better time is he going to find to make use of his talents and accomplishments?'

'My dear enthusiast,' I replied, 'you and I are doing what we decided to do, and Epaminondas, being unable to persuade us to give it up, as he thinks we should, is very naturally resisting efforts to involve him in something for which he is not suited and which he does not approve. It wouldn't be sensible (would it?) to compel a doctor to operate or cauterize, if he promises to cure the illness without knife or fire.'

<Theocritus agreed>.

'Then we had best leave him alone,' I continued, 'since he undertakes not to put any citizen to death without due trial

except under the most dire necessity, but to join enthusiastically in the efforts of any who wish to liberate the city without civil bloodshed and murder. But as he cannot convince the majority, and as we have embarked on the business this way, he is asking
577 us to let him wait on events, innocent of bloodshed and with no responsibility for it, and then come in on the side of justice and of expediency. The action, he thinks, cannot be limited. Pherenicus and Pelopidas will doubtless confine themselves to the guilty and the wicked, but once fiery and passionate people like Eumolpidas and Samidas get their chance in the night, they will not sheath the sword until they have swamped the whole city with blood and killed many of their private enemies.'

[4] My conversation with Theocritus was interrupted by Galaxidorus, who pointed out Archias and the Spartan Lysanoridas coming down from the Cadmea, apparently hastening to join us. We waited for them; and Archias called out to Theocritus, led him away to join Lysanoridas, and talked privately with him for some time, going off the road a little way below the Amphion.* This made us all anxious. Had they perhaps had some hint or information, and were questioning Theocritus about it?

At this juncture, Phyllidas—you know who I mean, Archedemus; he was clerk at the time to Archias and his fellow polemarchs, but he knew about the arrival of the exiles, and was privy to the plot—seized me by the hand and, in his usual style, made a show of joking about my interest in athletics and wrestling, and then drew me aside and started to ask whether the exiles were holding to the appointed day. I told him they were.

'Well then', he said, 'I was right to arrange the dinner for today at which I shall entertain Archias and make him drunk enough to be an easy prey to our friends.'

'Indeed you were, Phyllidas,' I said; 'do try to get all or most of the enemy together.'

'Not easy,' he said, 'indeed, impossible. Archias is expecting a lady of rank to visit him at the time, and he doesn't want Leontiadas there. So we shall divide them between the two houses. If Archias and Leontiadas are once dealt with, the rest will either take themselves out of the way, or wait quietly and be happy to be liberated.'

'That's what we'll do, then,' I replied, 'but what are they talking to Theocritus about?'

'I don't know for certain,' he said, 'but I heard there had been some signs and prophecies ominous for Sparta.'

<Theocritus now returned to join us> and we were also joined by Phidolaus of Haliartus, who told us that Simmias asked us to wait for a while, because he was having some private talk with Leontiadas about Amphitheus, in an attempt to secure the latter's exile instead of a death sentence.

[5] 'You've come at the right moment,' said Theocritus, 'and as though it were meant. I wanted to ask you what was discovered at Haliartus when the tomb of Alcmena was opened, and what it looked like—if, that is, you were present yourself when Agesilaus sent to remove the relics to Sparta.'

'No, I wasn't present', said Phidolaus, 'and I was very annoyed and angry with my fellow citizens for leaving me out. What was found in the tomb was <not the remains of> a body, but a small bronze necklace and two earthenware jars containing earth long hardened into stone. <Over> the tomb there was a bronze tablet with a quantity of very ancient writing. This showed clearly enough after the bronze had been cleaned, but nothing could be learnt from it; the script was a peculiar one, not Greek, but very like Egyptian writing. Agesilaus therefore, so they said, sent a copy to the king of Egypt, requesting him to show it to the priests, in case they could understand it. Simmias may have something to report about this, since he was in contact 578
with the priests in Egypt at the time, studying philosophy. The people of Haliartus, at any rate, believe that the great famine and the great overflowing of the lake* did not happen fortuitously, but were a visitation of divine anger, come upon them for permitting the excavation of the tomb.

Theocritus paused a moment before replying. 'Well,' he said, 'the divine powers seem to have been angry with the Lacedaemonians also, to judge from the signs that Lysanoridas was just telling me about. He is going to Haliartus now, to rebuild the tomb and pour a libation to Alcmena and Aleos, as instructed, it seems, by an oracle. But he has no idea who Aleos was. When he comes back, he is just the man to try to investigate the tomb of Dirce, which no Theban knows, save those who have held the office of hipparch.* The retiring hipparch, you know, always conducts his successor alone at night and shows him the tomb. They perform certain ceremonies there, not requiring fire, destroy the traces of what they have done, and go their ways separately, still under cover of darkness. However <if he looks for people who know the secret> I <don't think> he will easily find them. Most of those who have held the office legally are in exile—all of them, in fact, except Gorgidas and Plato, and I suspect Lysanoridas and his friends would be too frightened to ask *them*. The present office-holders on the Cadmea simply receive the spear and seal of office, and know nothing <about the tomb>.'

[6] While Theocritus was talking, Leontiadas and his friends emerged. We then went in, and greeted Simmias. He was sitting on his bed. I don't think he had succeeded in his appeal, for he was very sad and thoughtful.

'Heracles!' he cried, as he looked at us all, 'what cruel, savage ways! Old Thales was right. When he came home after a long time abroad, and his friends asked him what was the most extraordinary thing he had found, he replied "A tyrant grown old." Even if one has suffered no personal injustice, disgust for the mere burdensomeness and unpleasantness of living with such people makes one an enemy of unconstitutional and irresponsible power. But maybe God will take care of that. Caphisias,' he went on, 'do you and your family know who this stranger is who is visiting you?'

'I don't know who you mean,' I said.

'Well, according to Leontiadas, a man has been seen at Lysis' tomb, getting up before daybreak, an impressive figure, with a large number of attendants; he seems to have spent the night there in the open, on a makeshift bed, for a bed of *agnus castus** and tamarisk was found, with traces of burnt offerings and libations of milk. In the morning, this man asked the passers-by whether he might find the sons of Polymnis at home.'

'Who could it be?' said I: 'from what you say, he is some exceptional personage, not an ordinary individual'.

[7] 'Indeed not,' said Phidolaus, 'but the time to welcome him will be when he comes. Meanwhile, Simmias, tell us what more you know about the inscription that has been puzzling us.

The priests in Egypt are said to have understood the writing on that tablet which Agesilaus took from us when he dismantled Alcmena's tomb.'

Simmias remembered at once.

'I don't know about that tablet,' he said, 'but the Spartan Agetoridas brought many writings from Agesilaus to Memphis, to the prophet Chonuphis, with whom Plato and I and Ellopion of Peparethus were studying.* The king had sent him with a request to Chonuphis to send a translation of the inscription at once if he could understand it. Chonuphis shut himself up alone for three days, reviewing all kinds of scripts in ancient books, and finally replied to the king, and also told us, that the inscription 579
was a command to celebrate games in honour of the Muses. The alphabet was that in use under King Proteus, which Heracles, son of Amphitryon, had learnt; and the message comprised an exhortation and instruction of the god to the Greeks to dwell together in leisure and peace, competing with one another in philosophy and deciding their rights with the aid of the Muses and of reason, without recourse to arms. We thought well of Chonuphis' interpretation at the time, but even more so when, on our return voyage from Egypt, we were met in Caria by a group of Delians, who asked Plato, because he was a mathematician, to explain an odd oracle that the god had given them. The oracle said that Delos and the rest of Greece would have rest from their present troubles "if they doubled the altar at Delos".* They were quite unable to understand the meaning; indeed they made an exhibition of their stupidity by what they did to the altar, for they doubled each of its four sides, unaware that they were thereby creating a solid eight times the size of the original. This was due to their ignorance of the proportionals by which the linear duplication is obtained. They therefore called Plato to their aid. He remembered the Egyptian, and declared that the god was alluding to the Greeks' neglect of education, ridiculing our ignorance and bidding us give priority to the study of geometry. No weak or dull mind, but only one well trained in the use of geometrical diagrams, could comprehend the method of finding two mean proportionals, which is the only way in which a cube can be doubled in volume by means of an equal extension of each dimension. Eudoxus of Cnidus or Helicon

of Cyzicus would do it for them, he said; but they were not to think that this was what the god really wanted. His command to all the Greeks was rather that they should give up war and evil, consort with the Muses, calm their passions by reason and study, and live a harmless and useful life together.'

[8] While Simmias was speaking, my father, Polymnis, had come in and taken a seat beside him. 'Epaminondas invites you', he said, 'and all these people, to wait here, unless you have something more important on hand. He wishes you to meet our visitor, who is an important personage come on an important and honourable errand from the Pythagoreans in Italy. He has come to pour a libation at the tomb of old Lysis, at the bidding, as he says, of certain dreams and clear visions; he has also brought a large sum in gold, and thinks he ought to repay Epaminondas for his care of the old man. He is most insistent on this, though we neither ask nor want help for our poverty.' Simmias was delighted. 'What a wonderful man!' he said, 'worthy to be called a philosopher; but why does he not come to us at once?'

'He spent the night', replied Polymnis, 'by the tomb of Lysis, and I think Epaminondas took him to the Ismenus to wash. Then they will join us. Before he met us, he had slept by the tomb, intending to take the remains back to Italy, unless he received any daemonic warning during the night.'

[9] When my father had finished, Galaxidorus burst out. 'Heracles!' he exclaimed, 'how hard it is to find anyone free of pretence and superstition! Some are merely the involuntary victims of these failings, through ignorance or weakness; but there are others who ascribe their actions to divine power in order to appear special favourites of the gods, hiding their rational ideas under a cover of dreams or visions or some such pretentious
580 foolishness. That may be a useful trick for politicians, who are forced to deal with obstinate and disorderly people. Superstition will serve as a bridle to rein back the impulses of the masses and divert them into useful outlets. But this kind of decoration is not only indecorous for philosophy, it is quite contrary to her professed aims, if, while claiming to teach the good and the expedient by reason, she acts as though she despised reason, and takes refuge in the gods as principles of action, and scorns her own powers of demonstration only to have recourse to prophecies

and visions, in which the poorest intellect is often no less successful than the finest! This is why your friend Socrates, my dear Simmias, seems to me to have adopted a more philosophical style of education and reasoning, by choosing simple sincerity as the mark of the liberal lover of truth, and blowing away pretentiousness—which is nothing but a smokescreen of philosophy—on to the sophists.'

'What makes you say that, Galaxidorus?' interrupted Theocritus; 'has Meletus convinced you that Socrates despised the divine?* That was the very charge he brought against him at Athens.'

'No, not the divine,' he replied, 'but having found philosophy full of visions and fables and superstitions in the hands of Pythagoras . . . and Empedocles, he rescued her from intoxication, and taught her to be sane in the face of facts and pursue truth by sober reasoning.'

[10] 'Well, then,' said Theocritus, 'what do we say about Socrates' *daimonion*, my friend? Imposture, or what? Nothing of what is told of Pythagoras' power of prophecy strikes me as so impressive or so divine. God seems to have given Socrates right from the start a vision to guide his steps in life, as Homer gives Athena to Odysseus, "in all his labours standing at his side";[1,2] it "went before him and gave light"[3]by itself in dark and doubtful moments, inscrutable to human thinking, in which the sign often agreed with him and lent its divine sanction to his decisions. You must ask Simmias and the other companions of Socrates for all the important examples; but let me tell you something that happened in my own presence. We had gone to see the prophet Euthyphro. Socrates—you must remember this, Simmias—was walking up to the Crossroads* and Andocides' house, asking questions all the time, and confusing Euthyphro in his playful way. Then, quite suddenly, he stopped and was silent for some time, concentrating on his own thoughts. He then did an about-turn, and went down Boxmakers Street, calling back those of his companions who had gone ahead by saying that the *daimonion* had occurred. Most of us, including myself (I was keeping close to Euthyphro) turned round with him, but some young fellows carried straight on, with a view to discrediting the *daimonion*. They dragged with them the piper

Charillus, who had come with me to Athens to stay with Cebes. As they were going down Statuaries Street, near the law-courts, they were confronted by a herd of pigs, very muddy, jostling one another in a dense mass. There was no escape, and our friends were either knocked over or smothered in mud. Charillus came home with his legs and his cloak all muddied, and we always laugh when we think of the *daimonion*, and marvel how divine care never abandoned or neglected Socrates.'

[11] 'Do you really believe, Theocritus,' said Galaxidorus, 'that Socrates' *daimonion* had some peculiar, special force, rather than that he had reliable experience in some department of common divination, and used this to determine his decision on obscure or inscrutable matters? An ounce weight will not tip
581 the scale on its own, but if it is added to a weight already on the balance it may pull the whole thing down. Likewise, a sneeze, a casual word, or any such trivial sign, cannot on its own determine a weighty mind to action, but if it is added to one of two opposing calculations, it solves the problem by tipping the balance, and the impulses and movements follow.'

'As a matter of fact,' interjected my father, 'I heard from a Megarian, who had heard it from Terpsion, that Socrates' *daimonion was* a sneeze,* either his own or someone else's. If someone else sneezed on the right, either in front or behind, it persuaded him to do whatever he was about; if on the left, it dissuaded him from doing it. As to his own sneezes, one that happened while he was hesitating made him go forward; one that happened in the course of the act gave him pause and stopped his impulse. What seems amazing to me is that, if it was a sneeze, he did not admit it to his companions, but always said that the *daimonion* was stopping him or leading him on. Surely to be panicked by a casual word or a sneeze into desisting from a course of action or abandoning an intention like this would be an indication of some sort of vain pretention or pride, not of the simplicity and sincerity which we believe made Socrates such an outstandingly great man. Indeed, Socrates' impulses seem generally to have possessed a consistency and vigour suggesting that their origin lay in a strong, correct judgement. To have persevered voluntarily in poverty all his life, when it would have pleased and gratified others to relieve him; to have been loyal to philosophy in the face of so many obstacles; and ultimately, though his friends' zeal and means were at his disposal to ensure him safety in exile, never to have yielded to their entreaties or evaded the approach of death, but faced the terrible moment with unflinching reason—these are not the acts of a man whose resolution changes at the bidding of an accidental word or a sneeze, but of one guided towards the good by some superior authority and control. I am told too that he foretold the destruction of the Athenian forces in Sicily to some of his friends. Even before that, Pyrilampes, Antiphon's son, who was taken prisoner by our troops in the pursuit at Delium,* and was wounded by a spear, was told by the Athenian emissaries who then came to negotiate a truce, that Socrates, with Alcibiades and Laches, had gone down by the Crossroads* and got home safely. Pyrilampes afterwards often invoked Socrates' name and the names of all the friends and comrades who had been with him in the rout near Parnes, and had met their deaths because they had paid no attention to Socrates' *daimonion*, but had left the battlefield by another route than the one by which he was leading them. Simmias must have heard this also.'

'Yes, indeed,' said Simmias, 'and from many witnesses on many occasions. Socrates' *daimonion* was much talked of in Athens as a result.'

[12] 'What then, Simmias?' said Phidolaus, 'are we to allow Galaxidorus his fun, reducing this great achievement of prophecy to sneezes and accidental words, things which ordinary folk only attend to in a humorous way, and in matters of no moment? When graver designs or greater actions pend, Euripides' words come true: "None plays the fool like that when swords are out." '[1]

'Well, Phidolaus,' retorted Galaxidorus, 'I am ready to listen to Simmias, and be convinced by him as you are, if he heard anything from Socrates' own lips. But it's not difficult to demolish what you and Polymnis have said. In medicine, a throbbing or a blister is no great thing in itself, but it may be a symptom of something far from trivial. A pilot uses the cry of a seabird or a wisp of thin cloud as a sign of wind and rough sea. So it is with 582
prophecy. A sneeze or a word is no great thing in itself, but it is a sign of great events. No art despises the possibility of indicating

great things by small, or many things by few. Imagine an illiterate person, seeing a few poor scratches, and not believing that a scholar could deduce from these great wars of the men of old, foundations of cities, and the deeds and destines of kings. Suppose he were then to say that some 'daemonic' or supernatural source of information must be telling the historian about all these events. You would have a good laugh at the expense of such an ignoramus. So perhaps it is because we are ignorant of the power of particular techniques of prophecy and their relationship to future events that we feel this foolish indignation if a sensible man uses them to reveal something of the unseen, especially if he says himself that it is something 'daemonic' that guides his actions, and not a sneeze or a casual word. And now I turn to you, Polymnis, and the surprise you felt at the idea that Socrates, the man who most of all humanized philosophy by his simplicity and unpretentiousness, should not describe his sign as a sneeze or a casual word, but use the grandiose term *daimonion*. On the contrary, I should have been very much surprised if a skilled dialectician and master of words like Socrates had said that it was a sneeze or a word and not the *daimonion* that signalled to him. It is as though you were to say that the dart which had wounded you was the agent, and not that the thrower was the agent and the dart the instrument; or that the scales were the agent that weighed something, and not the weigher the agent and the scales the instrument. The action does not belong to the instrument, but to the possessor of the instrument; and the sign which the "signaller" uses is, in a sense, his instrument. However, as I said, we must listen to anything Simmias has to say, since he is better informed.'

[13] 'Yes,' said Theocritus, 'but not until we have seen who these people are who are now coming in. I think this must be Epaminondas bringing the stranger.'

We looked towards the door and saw Epaminondas leading the way, and our friends Ismenodorus, Bacchylides, and Melissus the piper with him. Immediately behind followed the stranger, a man of impressive presence, splendidly attired, but with an air of gentleness and kindliness. He sat down beside Simmias, and my brother sat beside me. The rest just took their chance. When silence was restored, Simmias addressed my brother. 'Now Epaminondas,' he said, 'who are we to say the stranger is? How should we address him? Where does he come from? These are the usual preliminaries to meeting someone and getting to know him.'

'His name is Theanor,' replied Epaminondas, 'he comes from Croton, and he is one of the philosophers there who do not disgrace Pythagoras' great fame. And he has made this long journey from Italy to crown a good decision with a good deed.'

'And yet, Epaminondas,' interjected the stranger, 'it is you who are preventing me from doing the best deed of all. If it is honourable to benefit a friend, there can be no dishonour in receiving benefits from a friend. Benefactions require a recipient as well as a donor, both of whom contribute to their honourable completion. To refuse is as bad as dropping a catch when the ball has been thrown well. What target can be pleasanter to hit or more distressing to miss than a deserving person whom one is anxious to benefit? But in sport, it is your own fault if you miss a stationary target; whereas in this business of giving and taking, to decline and step aside is to be unfair to the benefit that cannot reach the target it is aimed at. I have already explained to you, Epaminondas, what reasons led me to make the voyage here. I should like now to explain them to the com- 583
pany, and invite them to judge between you and me.

'After the Pythagorean societies* in the cities were driven out in the various revolutions, the supporters of Cylon set fire to the house in Metapontum where the surviving members were in conference. All died in the fire except the young, strong, and agile Philolaus and Lysis, who managed to escape. Philolaus fled to Lucania, and contrived to make his way safely from there to join our other friends, who were beginning to regroup and get the better of Cylon's party. Where Lysis went was long unknown to us, until Gorgias of Leontini, on his return from Greece to Sicily, brought word to Arcesus that he had met Lysis, who was living in Thebes. Arcesus himself planned to make the voyage, out of his desire to see Lysis; but he was now very old and weak, and instead gave us instructions either to bring back Lysis to Italy alive or, if he was dead, to bring his remains. The ensuing wars and revolutions and tyrannies prevented his friends from accomplishing this task during Arcesus' lifetime.

But when we had a daemonic revelation by certain sure signs* that Lysis was dead, and received reliable information from persons who knew he had lived and been cared for by your family, Polymnis, and how he had died happy, a rich man tended in his old age by a poor household and enrolled as father to your sons, then I was sent, one young man as the representative of my many seniors, who offer the money they have to you who have none, and desire in return to have your favour and friendship. Lysis lies well at rest, and this is your doing. But better in his sight even than his fair tomb is the repayment of his friend's kindness by his other friends and brethren.'

[14] During the stranger's speech, my father wept much at the thought of Lysis. My brother smiled in his usual way, and said: 'What do we do, Caphisias? Do we give up our poverty for wealth and say nothing?' 'No, indeed,' I answered, 'poverty is our "good and loving nurse of youth".[1] Defend her. It's for you to speak.'

'Well, father,' said Epaminondas, 'I was afraid that the family might be susceptible to the lure of money for one reason only—Caphisias' person, and his need of fine clothes to look nice for all his lovers, and of generous rations to make him fit for the gymnasium and his wrestling-exercises. But since he doesn't choose to abandon the family poverty, or let its colours fade, as it were, but prides himself, boy as he is, on a simple life, and is happy with what we have, what useful way of disposing of wealth could we find? Should we gild our armour, and adorn our shields with purple and gold like the Athenian Nicias? Should we buy you a Milesian cloak, father, or a dress for mother with a purple border? I assume we shouldn't use the gift on our stomachs and give them an expensive treat, as though wealth was a burdensome guest to be entertained.'

'Don't talk nonsense, son,' said his father, 'I would rather not live to see such a change in our lives!'

'Neither will we sit at home guarding our money,' went on Epaminondas, 'for the favour would have no favour and our possession of it no honour.'

'What then?' said his father.

'The other day,' said Epaminondas, 'when Jason, Prince of Thessaly,* sent a large sum in gold to us, and begged us to

accept it, I was thought rude and ungracious for replying that he was the aggressor, because, being a lover of absolute power, he was using his money to tempt a private citizen in a free and independent state. Your interest, sir, I accept and greatly 584
appreciate. It is noble, and worthy of a philosopher. But you bring medicine to friends who are not ill. If you had heard we were at war, and had sailed to our aid with weapons and armour, but then found peace and friendship, you would not have thought it right to offer the weapons or leave them with us, because we should not now need them. It is so now. You have come as an ally to fight poverty, as though we were hard pressed by her. But poverty is easy for us to bear. She is a dear member of the family. We need no money to fight one who causes us no trouble. Tell your friends at home that they use their wealth to noble ends, and that they have friends here who use poverty also to noble ends. Lysis himself paid for our care of him in life and in his burial in many ways, and not least by teaching us not to complain of poverty.'

[15] 'Is it ignoble, then,' put in Theanor, 'to complain of poverty, but not absurd to fear and avoid wealth?'

'No, that *is* absurd,' said Epaminondas, 'unless your rejection of wealth is based on reasonable grounds, and is not insincere or derived from some sort of vanity or bad taste.'

'But what reasonable grounds can forbid honourable and just acquisitions, Epaminondas?' said the stranger, 'or rather—and do please make yourself a little gentler in your answers than you were to the Thessalian—tell me now: do you think it is sometimes right to offer money, but never right to accept it? Or is an offer always as bad as an acceptance?'

'Not at all,' said Epaminondas, 'my view is that wealth is no different in this from other things: both generosity and acquisition are sometimes wrong and sometimes good.'

'Then doesn't a debtor who offers his money willingly and readily make an offer that is honourable?'

'Yes.'

'And is not acceptance of an honourable offer itself honourable? Can there be any more justified acceptance of money than from a justified offer?'

'No.'

'Well then, Epaminondas: if one of two friends is under an obligation to give, the other is under an obligation to accept. In a battle, one has to avoid an enemy whose aim is good; but in doing good turns it is wrong to avoid or repulse a friend whose giving is well-directed. If poverty is no hardship, neither is wealth so deserving of dishonour and rejection.'

'No,' said Epaminondas, 'but there are people for whom a gift well offered brings more prestige and honour if they do not accept it. Look at it this way. Desires are many and have many objects. Some are, as they say, "innate", and develop in the body with reference to necessary pleasures. Others are adventitious, stimulated by unsubstantiated fancies. If these latter acquire force and strength as a result of long habit under bad education, they frequently prove a more powerful depressive influence on the soul than do the necessary desires. Now habit and exercise often enable reason to draw off some of the strength of the innate passions; but it is on the intruders, the unnecessary desires, that the main force of exercise must be deployed, to cut them down by restraints and inhibitions and let reason chastise them. If rational resistance to food and drink can even force out hunger and thirst, it is obviously far easier to curtail, and indeed ultimately to eliminate, greed and ambition, by denial and restraint. Would you not agree?'

The stranger agreed.

'Then do you acknowledge a difference between exercise and the activity to which exercise is devoted? In athletics, the activity is the competition with the rival for the crown, while the exercise is the physical preparation in the gymnasium. Would you agree that, in the case of virtue too, there is a distinction between the activity and the exercise?'

He agreed.

'Then tell me first: is it an exercise of self-control, or an activity and demonstration of it, if one refrains from base and unlawful pleasures?'

585 'An activity and demonstration.'

'And what about the practice and exercise of self-control? Is it not this by which you Pythagoreans have always been attracted, when you excite your appetite as an exercise, as though it were some sort of animal, and sit down and wait at a splendid table laden with every kind of food, only to hand it all over to your servants for a feast while you yourselves offer your now chastened appetite a simple meal? The denial of available pleasure, I take it, arms the soul against the forbidden.'

'Yes,' he said.

'Then, my friend, justice also has a way of taking exercise to prevent greed and avarice, not by simply refraining from burgling ones' neighbour's house or mugging and robbing people, nor by refusing to betray friends or country for money. That isn't exercise against avarice, and in these respects fear of the law itself may very well prevent the greedy from doing wrong. No; the man who voluntarily and repeatedly distances himself from perfectly just and permissible sources of profit is also the man who is really exercising and habituating himself to keep away from unjust or unlawful gain. When one is tempted by intense pleasures that are unnatural or damaging, one cannot keep one's thoughts quiet unless one has frequently spurned permitted enjoyments. Likewise, it is not easy to rise above dishonest gain or great material advantage if this comes within reach, unless one has long since chained up one's love of gain and put it under strict guard. If it has been educated to take profit without restraint where it is legitimate to do so, it will wax big at the prospect of crime, and can scarcely be restrained from taking its chance of gain. But when a man has never surrendered to the favours of friends or the gifts of kings, but always rejected every lucky chance and reined in his covetousness wherever it rears up at the prospect of treasure, then his love of gain will not rise in revolt or throw his thoughts into confusion; proud of himself and clear in conscience, such a man will pursue the right without effort. Caphisias and I love these battles, Simmias; and we beg our guest to let us train ourselves on poverty to attain this virtue.'

[16] When my brother had finished, Simmias nodded two or three times.

'He's a great man, a great man, is Epaminondas,' he said, 'and Polymnis here is responsible for that, because he has always given his children the best education through philosophy. You must make your peace with them about this on your own, sir; but if we may be permitted to know, are you moving Lysis from his tomb to Italy, or will you let him stay here with his kind friends, so that he can have our company when we too pass over?'

Theanor smiled, 'Lysis seems to be at home here,' he said, 'and, thanks to Epaminondas, he lacks for nothing that is good. There is a special rite in Pythagorean burials without which we do not think we have the proper blessedness at the end. When we learnt of Lysis' death from a dream—and we can tell from a certain sign whether a dream is a vision of a dead or a live person—many of us judged that Lysis had been buried with other rites in a strange land, and must therefore be moved if he was to have his due place yonder. This was my purpose in coming. I was guided to the tomb by the local people in the evening, and I made my libation and called upon Lysis' soul to return and reveal to me how I must perform my duty. Later in the night, though I saw nothing, I seemed to hear a voice telling me 'not to move the unmovable'. Lysis' body, the voice said, had been buried by his friends with due ritual, and his soul had already departed from it and gone to a new birth, with a new *daimon*.
586 And in the morning, I met Epaminondas and heard how he had buried Lysis. Then I knew that he had been educated well by Lysis even in the secret rites, and had the same *daimon* to guide his own life, if I have any capacity for identifying a pilot by the course he steers. Countless are the paths of life, but few are those in which *daimones* are men's guides.' At this, Theanor glanced at Epaminondas. He seemed to be studying his look and his air afresh.

Meanwhile, the doctor had come in and undone Simmias' bandage to attend to him. Phyllidas had also entered with Hipposthenidas, and asked Charon, Theocritus, and myself to step outside. He led us to a corner of the peristyle. His face showed that he was very much perturbed.

'Has anything new happened, Phyllidas?' I asked.

'Not new to me, Caphisias', he replied, 'I warned you about Hipposthenidas' weaknesses, and begged you not to tell him about our plans or involve him.'

We were aghast at this. 'For goodness' sake, Phyllidas,' said Hipposthenidas, 'don't say such things. Don't ruin both ourselves and the city by mistaking rashness for courage. Let the men return safely, if they are destined to do so.'

'Tell me, Hipposthenidas,' said Phyllidas angrily, 'how many do you suppose are privy to our plot?'

'Not less than thirty, I should say,' he answered.

'Well then,' he said, 'if so many people have agreed on a thing, why have you, and you alone, stopped it and wrecked it, by sending a horseman to the men when they are already on their way, to tell them to turn back and not hurry forward today, when chance has provided almost all the conditions best for their return?'

This speech threw us all into a panic.

Charon stared hard and fiercely at Hipposthenidas.

'Villain!' he cried, 'what have you done to us?'

'Nothing to be alarmed about,' he answered, 'if only you will speak a little less roughly and share the thinking of a man of your own age, with just as many grey hairs as you have. If we are resolved to show to our fellow-citizens a courage that seeks danger and a spirit careless of life, then, Phyllidas, there's plenty of the day left. Let us not wait till evening. Let us seize our swords and go and attack the tyrants. Let us kill or die and not spare ourselves. But, while there is no difficulty in all that, it's very far from easy to rescue Thebes from armed occupation when it is surrounded by such large enemy forces, or to expel the Spartan garrison at the cost of two or three casualties. I don't imagine Phyllidas has got in enough wine for his hospitable party to make Archias' fifteen hundred guards drunk! Even if we kill him, we shall still have Herippidas and Arcesus to deal with during the night, and they will be sober. So why are we so anxious to bring our friends and kindred home to certain death? Even the enemy knows about their return. Why else should orders have been given to the Thespians two days ago to be in arms and hold themselves ready for the Spartan command to summon them? I gather also that they intend to interrogate Amphitheus today and put him to death as soon as Archias is back. Are not these signs that the plot is discovered? Would it not be best to wait only long enough to propitiate the gods? The diviners sacrificing the ox to Demeter* say that the burnt remains portend great turmoil and danger for the city. And there is another thing, Charon, that needs your special attention. Hypatodorus, the son of Erianthes, a good man and a close

587 friend of mine, but knowing nothing of what is afoot, travelled in from the country with me yesterday. On the way, he said "Charon is a friend of yours, Hipposthenidas, but I don't know him well. Would you please warn him to beware of some danger? I had a very strange and unpleasant dream last night. I dreamt that Charon's house was labouring with child and about to give birth; and he and his friends were standing round, praying anxiously. Then the house gave a groan and made inarticulate noises, and finally a fearful fire flared up inside, and most of the city was burnt down, though the Cadmea was only enveloped in smoke, the fire not reaching that far up." That was the vision as he described it to me, Charon; I was alarmed at the time, but now that I have heard today that the exiles are going to lodge in your house, I feel all the more fearful. We may, I fear, be becoming involved in great troubles without achieving anything more significant than causing the enemy some confusion. I am assuming that the city is our side and the Cadmea is theirs.

[18] Charon was about to say something in reply to Hipposthenidas, but Theocritus broke in.

'For my part,' he said 'that is the best encouragement for our venture that I have heard. I have always had favourable indications from sacrifices about the exiles, and this vision points the same way. You tell us that a big bright light shone out of a friendly house in the city, while the enemy stronghold was darkened by smoke, which can only bring tears and confusion. You say that the sounds from our side were inarticulate; so, even if an attempt is made to betray us, our venture will produce no more than a vague reverberation and a dim suspicion, and will be victorious as soon as it is public knowledge. Unfavourable omens from the sacrifice are only to be expected, since the office and the victim belong to the rulers, not to the people of Thebes.' As Theocritus finished, I turned to Hipposthenidas. 'Who did you send to them?' I asked: 'if he hasn't much start, we can catch him up.' 'I had better tell you the truth, Caphisias,' he replied, 'I doubt if you *could* catch him. He has the best horse in Thebes. He is someone you know—the head man of Melon's charioteers. He has been privy to the business from the start, because of Melon.'

'Do you mean Chlidon,' said I—for I had just caught sight of the very man—'the one who won the horse-race last year at the Heraclea?'

'Just so,' he said.

'Then', said I, 'who is this who has been standing at the outer door for some time, looking at us?'

Hipposthenidas turned round.

'By Heracles!' he cried, 'it's Chlidon! I hope nothing dreadful has happened.' As soon as he saw we had noticed him. Chlidon quietly stepped forward. Hipposthenidas motioned to him, and told him to speak before us all. 'I know these men perfectly well,' began Chlidon, 'and when I couldn't find you either at home or in the market-place, I guessed you were with them, and hurried on here, so that you should know everything that has happened. When you ordered me to make all speed to meet the men on the mountain, I went home to get the horse. I asked my wife for the bridle, but she couldn't find it for me. She spent a long time in the store, pretending to look for it and make everything ready. In the end, when she had tricked me long enough, she confessed that she had lent it to a neighbour last night at his wife's request. I was angry, and I said some hard things; and she proceeded to utter some dreadful words, calling down curses on my journey and my return. May the gods visit as much on her! 588
Finally, I was provoked to strike her in anger, and a crowd of neighbours and women soon gathered. I took a disgraceful pounding, and gave as good, and I've only just managed to get away and come to you. Send someone else to them, please. I am quite out of my mind, and I am in a very bad way.'

[19] Our feelings were strangely altered by this. Just before, we had been frustrated by the obstacles; now the urgency of the crisis brought on an agony of fear. No postponement was possible. I turned to Hipposthenidas, and grasped him by the hand to give him encouragement. The gods, I said, were calling us to our work. Phyllidas went off to attend to the reception of his guests, and to lure Archias to the drinking-bout. Charon went <to make preparations to receive the exiles>. And Theocritus and I went back to Simmias, to have an opportunity to talk to Epaminondas.

[20] They were well into the lofty inquiry on which Galaxidorus and Phidolaus had touched, asking what the nature and force of Socrates' *daimonion* might be. What Simmias said in reply to Galaxidorus we did not hear; but we did hear him say that he had himself asked Socrates about this without ever obtaining an answer. He had also (he said) often witnessed Socrates dismissing as impostors people who claimed to have contact with divine beings by visions, while listening carefully, and eagerly questioning anyone who claimed to have heard a voice. 'We therefore began to suspect privately', he continued, 'that Socrates' *daimonion* was not a vision but a perception of a voice,* or an apprehension of words making some mysterious contact with him, just as in dreams there is no voice but we receive some impression or consciousness of words and imagine that we hear them spoken. Generally, however, this kind of understanding actually is a dream; the calm and quiet of the body in sleep just enables the mind to submit to the superior powers, whereas in waking moments, choked by tumultuous emotions and demanding distractions, men are unable to listen or attend to what is thus presented to them. Socrates, however, had a pure, untrammelled intelligence, which involved itself in the body only so far as bare necessity required, and was sensitive and delicate enough to respond quickly to a touch. And the touch, we may conjecture, was not a sound but a word or thought of a *daimon* making voiceless contact with the mind by its bare meaning. Sound is a sort of blow to the mind, which thus receives words forcibly through the ear whenever we talk to one another; but the mind of a higher being guides the gifted soul by a mere thought, for it needs no blow. Such a soul yields to the guide that slackens or intensifies its impulses, for these are not made violent by emotional resistance, but prove soft and pliant, like reins with some give in them. This need cause us no surprise. We see huge merchantmen brought round by the touch of a tiny tiller, we see potters' wheels run smoothly at the touch of a fingertip. These things, though lifeless, are yet built to move easily, and their smoothness makes them yield to the moving force as soon as the inclination is given. The human soul, with all its countless puppet-strings of impulse, is by far the most sensitive machine of all. Handled according to reason, it quickly

responds to any inclination and moves in whatever direction the 589 mind conceives. In man, the strings of emotion and impulse terminate in the thinking mind. If this is disturbed, the strings are pulled, and in turn draw and pull upon the man. We see here the force of thought. Insensate bones and sinews and moist flesh, and the whole mass that these make up, lie heavy and inert. Yet the moment the soul conceives an idea in the mind and excites its impulses in the direction of that idea, the whole mass rises up, taut and tense in every part, and flies into action as though it had wings. And if it is difficult, or impossible, to comprehend the mechanisms of motion, tension, and excitation that thus enable the soul by merely thinking to draw the mass after it by its impulses, although the mere entertaining of an idea moves the body so effortlessly, then we need not be unbelievers either in regard to the notion that a mind may be guided by a superior mind, and a soul by a more divine soul that contacts it from without by whatever kind of contact thought may have with thought, like light with reflected light. We recognize one another's thoughts by means of voice, groping for them as it were in the dark. But the thoughts of *daimones* radiate light, and shine within those who can perceive them with no need of verbs and nouns, which are but tokens which men use among themselves to discern images and reflections of their thoughts, since thoughts themselves they cannot know, unless there should be, as I said, some special 'daemonic' light upon them. Our experience of sound, however, may in a sense reassure the incredulous. It is the moulding of air by articulate utterance and its total conversion into audible words that brings the thought to the hearer's mind. So we should not be surprised if the air, which is very plastic, can be converted by *daimones* into the form of the actual thought, and so imprint the thought of the thinker on men specially favoured by god. The noises made by sappers in a mine, undetectable by any other means, can be detected by a bronze shield, through the echo produced as the sound strikes the shield on its upward path. Similarly, the thoughts of *daimones*, though they pass everywhere, make an echo only in men of untroubled character and calm soul—holy or 'daemonic' men, as we call them. Most people, however, believe that the 'daemonic' power gives inspiration only in sleep; they find it extraordinary, indeed unbelievable, that it should also affect the waking or the wholly sane. But that is like thinking that a musician plays his lyre only when it is unstrung, and does not touch or use it when it is adjusted and tuned. They think this because they do not see the reason, which is their own confusion and tunelessness, from which Socrates was entirely free, as the oracle given to his father when Socrates was a child clearly foretold. The oracle told the father to let the boy do whatever came into his head, and not compel or force him, but let his own impulses rule, simply praying for him to Zeus Agoraios and the Muses, but otherwise taking no thought about him, because he had within himself a better guide for life than ten thousand teachers or tutors.

[21] 'Such are the ideas we have had about the *daimonion*, Phidolaus, both during Socrates' life and after his death. We have nothing but contempt for people who speak of sneezes and accidental words and the like. But I had perhaps better leave unsaid what I heard from Timarchus of Chaeronea about these things, for it is myth or fiction rather than argument.'

'No, don't leave it unsaid,' said Theocritus, 'tell us about it.
Myth does in some sense touch on truth, even if not very exactly.
590 But tell us first who this Timarchus was. I don't know him.'

'Of course you don't, Theocritus,' said Simmias, 'he died young, and asked Socrates to allow him to be buried beside Socrates' own son, Lamprocles,* his friend and contemporary, who died a few days before him. Timarchus was a spirited young man, who had just got his teeth into philosophy; so he was naturally anxious to understand the power of Socrates' *daimonion*. He took Cebes and me, but nobody else, into his confidence, and made the descent into the Cave of Trophonius,* after performing the usual rites at the oracle. He stayed in the cave two nights and a day; most people despaired of him, and his relatives mourned him as dead. But on the second morning, he reappeared, very cheerful. Having performed his act of reverence to the god, and escaped the waiting crowd, he proceeded to tell us of all the wonderful things he had seen and heard.

[22] 'He said that when he descended into the place of the oracle, he first found total darkness. He prayed, and lay there for a long time, not very clear in his mind whether he was awake or dreaming. It seemed to him, however, that there was a noise, and his head was struck, and the sutures of his skull parted to release his soul. It rose joyfully into clear, bright air, and seemed then to relax for the first time after long confinement and pressure, and it felt as though it grew in size like a sail being unfurled. Then he heard, faintly, a whirring going round and round above his head, making a pleasant noise. Looking up, he could not see the earth anywhere; there were only shining islands, beaming soft fire on one another, and colouring the light now with one hue and now with another as they moved around. These islands seemed vast and innumerable, all circular, but not all equal in size. The ether hummed sweetly as they circled round, for the gentleness of the blended music of their harmony seemed to match the smoothness of their motion. In the centre, there stretched a sea or lake, bright with the colours that mingled in its greyness. Some few of the islands sailed through the strait to cross beyond the stream, but most were borne along by it, while <the sea itself> moved <gently and smoothly round>. The depth of the sea varied: in its southern parts it was deep, but elsewhere shallow and marshy; it overflowed in many places, but receded in others, and had no major outlet. Its colour varied too: part was pure like the open sea, part turbid and marsh-like. And whenever the islands emerged from its waves, they would turn back again, not precisely to their starting-points, but making each circuit miss the one before, so that their revolution produced a continuous spiral. Now this sea, or so it seemed to Timarchus, made an angle with the central and widest part of the surrounding space of a little less than eight parts of the whole. It had two openings, receiving rivers of fire which entered it from opposite directions, so that it was lashed and broken into foam, and its greyness turned to white. Timarchus beheld all this with delighted eyes. But when he looked down, he saw a huge, round chasm, like a sphere cut open, very frightening and deep, and full of dark turbulence that kept welling up. Out of this arose howls and groans of living creatures beyond number, the wailing of countless children, the mingled lamentations of men and women, all kinds of noises and dim tumult coming up out of the depths. It terrified him. After a time, a voice spoke, though the speaker could not be seen.

591 "Timarchus," said the voice, "what do you wish to know?" "Everything," he replied, "for what is there that is not marvellous?" "We for our part", replied the voice, "have little to do with what is above. That belongs to other gods. But Persephone's Share, which is our responsibility, which is one of the Four Shares bounded by Styx, is open to your inspection, should you so wish." "And what is Styx?" said Timarchus. "It is the road to Hades," said the voice, "you see it in front of us, and its tip divides the light. As you observe, it rises from Hades. It marks the bounds of the last division of the universe as its revolving point encounters the light. There are four Principles of Things: the first of Life, the second of Motion, the third of Becoming, and the fourth of Decay. The first is bonded to the second by the Monad in the Invisible, the second to the third by Intellect in the Sun, and the third to the fourth by Nature in the Moon. And there is a Fate, a daughter of Necessity, to hold the keys of each of these bonds: Atropos controls the first, Clotho the second, and Lachesis the bond of the Moon, where lies the turning-point of Becoming. The other islands are all held by gods, but the Moon belongs to the *daimones* of the Earth. She barely escapes Styx, and is caught once in every 177 secondary measures.* And when Styx comes near, the souls howl in terror. Many of them slip, and Hades catches them. But the Moon rescues others as they swim up from below. These are they for whom the end of Becoming has come. The foul and unpurified, however, she will not receive. She flashes and roars at them most horribly, and will not let them near her. They lament their fate and are borne away down there once again, to another birth, as you can see." "All I can see", said Timarchus, "is a lot of stars dancing around the chasm, some diving in, others darting up again from below." "Those are the *daimones*," said the voice, "though you do not recognize them. This is how it is. Every soul has some part in Intellect. There is no soul without Reason or Intellect, though the part of the soul that combines with the flesh and its passions is changed by pleasure and pain into an irrational thing. This combining, however, is not always of the same kind. Some souls sink entirely into the body, the confusion extends throughout their whole being, and they are at the mercy of emotions throughout their existence. Others merge in the body to

some extent, but leave their purest element outside, and this is not dragged down with the rest, but floats on the surface as it were, attached to the head of the sinking man and keeping his soul upright, raising up as much of it as is obedient to its pull and is not under the domination of the passions. The part submerged in the body is what is called 'soul'; the part that survives destruction is called 'intellect' by most people, who believe it to be inside themselves, just as they believe reflections to be inside mirrors. Those who have the right view, however, call it *daimon*, and know it is outside them. Now, Timarchus, the stars whose light seems to you to be going out are the souls that are sinking wholly into the body. The lights that come on again and appear out of the depths, shaking off the mire of mist and dark, as it were, are those that are making the upward voyage after death. Try to make out the bond in each, just where it joins the soul." At this, Timarchus (as he told us) looked more closely and saw some of the stars tossing about more violently than others, like the buoys we see marking nets 592
in the sea. Some were describing an irregular and confused spiral, like a spindle as the thread is spun, and seemed unable to stabilize their motion in any straight path. The voice explained that those who exhibited a straight, orderly movement had souls made responsive to the rein by good breeding and education, and an irrational element which was not unduly obstinate or savage. Those which swerved up and down, up and down, in a confused and irregular fashion, as though tearing themselves away from their bonds, were in fact struggling against characters made disobedient and uncontrollable by lack of education, sometimes successfully guiding their course to the right, sometimes twisted by emotion and dragged down by wrongdoing, and then making further efforts to resist and force their way up. The bond is like a curb put on the irrational element in the soul, and when this pulls against it, it produces what is called repentance for wrongs, and shame for lawless and uncontrolled pleasures. For shame is the painful wound felt when the soul is curbed from within by its own controlling and ruling part. This process goes on until repeated chastisements tame the soul and make it obedient to the rein, like a well-broken horse, and able to respond quickly to the signals and signs of the *daimon*, without

blows and pain. "These souls which you see", the voice went on, "are brought to heel and stabilized in the end, however long it takes. It is among those who are responsive and obedient to the *daimon* from the start that we find the race of prophets and inspired men. You will have heard, for example, about the soul of Hermodorus of Clazomenae.* It used to leave his body and wander far and wide by night and by day, returning after many experiences of things said and done in distant places, until his wife betrayed him and his enemies burnt his body in the house while the soul was away. This story cannot be true. Hermodorus' soul did not really leave its body, it merely yielded and loosened its bond with its *daimon*, and let the *daimon* travel and wander and bring back word of all that it saw and heard in the world beyond. Those who destroyed the body while Hermodorus was asleep are still paying the price in Tartarus. You will know more about these things, young man, in two months' time. You may go for the present." The voice stopped. Timarchus wanted to turn round and see who the speaker was. But he again felt a violent pain in his head, as though it was being forcibly squashed together. He lost consciousness; but after a little while he came to again, and found himself lying in the Cave of Trophonius, near the entrance, just where he had lain down in the first place.

[23] 'Well, that was Timarchus' story. He returned to Athens, and died two months later, just as the voice had foretold. We told Socrates the strange tale, and he reproved us for not telling him while Timarchus was alive, because he would have liked to hear it from his own lips and question him in more detail. And so, Theocritus, you have your myth, and your argument too. But perhaps we should ask our guest to join our discussion. This a theme very appropriate to a holy man.'

'Why doesn't Epaminondas offer his opinion?' said the stranger; 'he has had the same training as I have.'

My father smiled. 'That's his way, sir,' he said, 'silent and cautious in speech, but insatiable in learning and listening.
593 Spintharus of Tarentum, who spent a long time with him here, says that he never met anyone who knew more and said less than Epaminondas. Pray tell us what you think yourself about what has been said.'

'My opinion', said Theanor, 'is that Timarchus' discourse should be set aside and dedicated to the god. As to what Simmias has said, it surprises me that anyone should disbelieve it, or speak of sacred swans and snakes and horses without believing in divine and god-favoured men. After all, people regard god as "friend of man", not "friend of birds". And just as horse-fanciers do not take equal care for every specimen of the species, but are always choosing and selecting the best, and training, rearing, and cherishing them above all others, so those who are above us put their brand, as it were, on the best of the herd, and think they deserve special guidance. They use no reins or halters, of course, but guide them by reason, using secret signs of which the common herd have no experience. An ordinary dog does not understand the huntsman's call, nor an ordinary horse the trainer's: but those who have learnt perceive the command from a casual whistle or clacking of the tongue, and readily settle to their duty. Homer clearly understood the distinction I am making. He calls some prophets augurs and priests, but he believes that others foretell the future by understanding the speech of the gods and sharing their thoughts:

> Then Priam's dear son Helenus understood
> the plan the gods in counsel had agreed.[1]

Or again:

> For so I heard the voice of the immortals.[2]

'Kings and generals make their plans felt and understood at a distance by means of beacons and proclamations and trumpet calls; but they tell their faithful friends individually. Similarly, god rarely converses directly with men, and only with a few. To the majority, he gives signs; and this is the origin of what we call divination. The gods themselves order the lives of very few of us, indeed only those whom they choose to make truly blessed and divine; but souls freed from becoming, and henceforth at leisure from the body, free and at ease, are the *daimones* who, as Hesiod tells us,[3] are the carers of mankind. Now athletes who have given up exercise because of their age do not entirely lose their competitiveness and interest in physical excellence. They enjoy watching others exercise, and encourage

them or run along beside them. So also those who have retired
from life's contests and become *daimones* through their souls'
virtue do not entirely disdain human affairs and thoughts and
interest, but feel a friendly concern for those still practising for
the same goal. They enthusiastically encourage them, and urge
them on in their struggle for virtue, when they see that the race
is bringing them within touching-distance of their hopes. For
these *daimones* do not aid all and sundry. They are like people
standing on the beach, who watch silently as they see swimmers
far out at sea, but run down and wade into the water as soon as
they come close, hauling them to safety, and helping them with
hands and voices. Such, my friends, is the way of *daimones*.
While we are swamped by the world, changing from body to
body—from one boat to another, as it were—struggling and
enduring in the effort to save ourselves by our own virtue and
reach harbour safely, they let us alone. But once a soul has run
the long race well and heartily through many births and is at the
594 end of its cycle, enduring the risks, sweat, and effort of landing
in the upper regions, then god is not indignant if that soul's own
daimon goes to its aid; indeed, he gives it permission to do so if
it so wishes. Different *daimones* wish to encourage and rescue
different souls. The souls, who are now close at hand, listen and
are saved. If they do not heed, and the *daimon* abandons them,
they come to no good end.'

[25] At the end of all this, Epaminondas looked at me. 'Time for you to go to the gymnasium, Caphisias,' he said, 'and not give up your friends. We will end this discussion when we think fit, and we will look after Theanor.'

'Let us do that,' I replied, 'but I think Theocritus here, with Galaxidorus and myself, would like to have a few words with you.'

'Fine,' he said, 'he can have them.'

So he got up and led us out to the corner of the colonnade. Standing round him, we all tried to urge him to take part in our venture. He said he knew the date of the exiles' return, and had made plans with his friends, with Gorgidas' help, to meet the situation; but he would not kill any citizen without fair trial, unless under absolute necessity. Also, it was better for the ordinary people of Thebes that there should be some persons without part or responsibility for the *coup*. They would be less open to popular suspicion, and their advice would appear to be given on the highest grounds. We agreed, and Epaminondas returned to Simmias, while I went down to the gymnasium and met my friends. As we changed partners in wrestling, we also exchanged information and prepared for action. We saw Archias and Philip, who, after duly anointing themselves, were on their way to the dinner. Phyllidas, who was afraid that they might execute Amphitheus before we could save him, had intercepted Archias as soon as he returned from escorting Lysanoridas, and raised his hopes that the lady he was in love with would be at the party. He thus persuaded him to unbend, and join his usual companions in indulgence.

[26] It was late now, and getting colder, and the wind was rising. People had therefore gone home early. We soon fell in with Damoclidas, Pelopidas, and Theopompus, and took them along with us. Others welcomed others of the party. The exiles had split up after crossing Cithaeron, and the bad weather made it easier for them to enter the city with safety, well wrapped-up against the cold. Some of them had seen lightning on their right, with no thunder, as they passed through the gate. This was judged a good sign of safety and glory: the venture would surely be crowned with success and free of danger.

[27] When we are all assembled in the house, forty-eight of us, and Theocritus was sacrificing privately in a separate room, there came a loud beating at the door. After a while, someone came to tell us that two of Archias' men were knocking at the outer door, sent on an urgent message to Charon; they had ordered the door to be opened, and were angry at the delay. Charon was greatly put out. He gave orders for the door to be opened, and went himself to meet his visitors, and find out what they wanted. He was still wearing his garland, as though having a drink after the sacrifice. 'We have been sent by Archias and Philip', said one of the two men, 'to ask you to come and see them as soon as possible.' Charon asked what was so urgent as to make it necessary to send for anyone at such an hour, and whether there was any particular news. 'We know no more,' said the man, 'but what shall we tell them?' 'Tell them', said Charon, 'that I've taken off my garland, put on my cloak, and

am following you. If I go with you at this hour, I shall cause a disturbance, because people will think I am being arrested.' 'Do
595 that,' replied the messenger, 'we have to take some instructions from the magistrates to the guard in the lower town.'

When they had gone, Charon came back inside and told us all this. We were all dismayed, thinking the plot must have been revealed. Most of us suspected Hipposthenidas, because he had tried to prevent the exiles' return by sending Chlidon to them, and, having failed and danger being at hand, might well have disclosed the plan out of fear. He had not come into the house with the rest, and he had a general reputation of being vacillating and unreliable. However, we all agreed that Charon must obey the summons and go. First, however, he asked his son to step forward—the most beautiful boy in Thebes, Archedemus, very good in the gymnasium, fifteen years of age, but much taller and stronger than his contemporaries. 'This,' said Charon, 'as you know, is my beloved, only child. I put him in your care, with this solemn injunction—all the powers of heaven be my witness!—that if I prove traitor to you, you are to kill him, and not spare my family. And now, my brave friends, face what has happened, do not hand yourselves over to the enemy like craven cowards. Fight back, keep your hearts unconquered for your country's sake.'

We could not help admiring the pride and nobility of these words of Charon; but we were grieved that he felt unsure of us, and bade him take his son away.

'However,' said Pelopidas, 'we think you were wrong not to move your son to another house. Why should he run into danger by staying with us? He should be sent away at once, to avenge us nobly on the tyrants one day, should we perish now.'

'No,' said Charon, 'he shall stay here and run the same risks as you. It would not be right for him to live in our enemies' power. My boy, have courage beyond your age. You will taste a fight that has to be fought. Run the risk for freedom and honour. You will have many good citizens at your side. There is still hope, and I am sure god looks down on us with favour, for we fight in a just cause.'

Many of us burst into tears at Charon's speech; but he remained dry-eyed and unmoved. He handed his son over to

Pelopidas, and walked away through the door, taking each of us by the hand and giving us encouragement. You would have been even more amazed at the boy's bright, fearless demeanour in the face of the danger. Like Neoptolemus,* he 'neither paled nor showed fear'. He drew Pelopidas' sword and tried the blade!

And now another of our friends, Cephisodorus, son of Diogiton, arrived. He was armed with a sword, and wore an iron corselet under his clothes. Hearing that Archias had sent for Charon, he chided us for our delay, and urged us to march on the enemy houses at once: we should get there first, and even if we did not it would be better to fight in the open against a disorganized and scattered adversary than to shut ourselves up in a building to be smoked out by the enemy like a swarm of bees. Theocritus was also in favour of this course: his sacrifices had promised salvation and honour, and guaranteed our safety.

[29] We were still arming and getting ready when Charon returned. He was cheerful and smiling, and as soon as he saw us told us to take heart: there was nothing to fear, the affair was going according to plan. 'Archias and Philip were already 596
drunk', he said, 'when they heard that I had arrived. Their minds were as useless as their limbs. They could barely struggle to their feet to come out to the door. "We hear", said Archias, "that exiles have entered the city, and are in hiding." "Who are they supposed to be, and where?" I asked, a good deal disturbed at what he had said. "We don't know," said Archias, "and that is why we invited you to come, in case you had heard anything more definite." It took me a moment or two to recover from the shock, but I reckoned that the report was not definite information, and that none of the conspirators had revealed our plot. If there had been any accurate intelligence, they could not have been in ignorance of the house. I guessed that some vague suspicion or report current in town had reached their ears. So I said, "When Androclides was alive, I often knew of rumours and false tales like this, which had no foundation but caused you some trouble. But this time, Archias, I have heard nothing. I will look into it, if you wish, and you shall be told anything I discover that seems worth your attention." "Yes, indeed," said Phyllidas, "let nothing pass without looking into it properly. We must neglect nothing, we must keep a sharp eye on everything.

Forewarned is forearmed." And so he let Archias back into the room where they were drinking. Now, friends, no more delay: let us pray to the gods and go forth to fight.' So we said our prayers, and did our best to give one another courage.

[30] It was now most people's dinner-time. The wind had strengthened, and there was a little snow in it, mixed with light rain. The streets were very empty as we passed through them. The party detailed to deal with Leontiadas and Hypatas, who lived near each other, wore cloaks and had no weapons but their daggers. They included Pelopidas, Damoclidas, and Cephisodorus. Charon, Melon, and the others who were to attack Archias' party with them, put on half-breastplates, and wore thick garlands of fir or pine. Some were dressed as women, for they were meant to be disguised as a group of revellers with their ladies. But our evil fortune, it seems, was bent on evening the odds between the enemy's cowardice and ignorance and our courage and preparedness. Right from the start, it had made our venture into a drama full of perilous episodes, and it was to confront us yet again in the moment of action, producing a sudden, dangerous crisis and an unexpected turn of events.

After Charon had persuaded Archias and Philip to go back home, and while he was still making us ready for action, a letter arrived from Athens from Archias the hierophant to our Archias, who was a friend of his, reporting the return and intentions of the exiles, the house to which they had repaired, and the names of their accomplices. Archias was now far gone in drink, and excited by the prospect of feminine company. So he took the letter, but when the messenger told him it was about serious business, he replied 'Serious business tomorrow,' and put it under his cushion. Then he called for a cup, ordered it to be filled up, and kept sending Phyllidas out to the door to see if the ladies were coming.

[31] These pleasant expectations kept them at their drinking till we arrived on the scene. We pushed past the servants and penetrated to the dining-room. There we stood for a moment by the door, taking in with our eyes everyone present. The garlands and the disguise tricked them. There was silence. Melon was the first to rush in, hand on sword-hilt. Cabirichus, the archon-by-lot, seized his arm as he passed, and shouted: 'Phyllidas, isn't this Melon?' But Melon evaded him and drew his sword, and, as Archias struggled to his feet, he ran at him and struck until the man was dead. Charon wounded Philip in the neck, and then, when he tried to defend himself with the drinking-cups that were at hand, Lysitheus threw him off his couch on to the ground and finished him off. We tried to calm Cabirichus, begging him not to help the tyrants but to help in the liberation of his country, since he was personally bound and consecrated to its service. But, in his drunken condition, he was anything but amenable to reason in a good cause. He got to his feet in a high state of excitement and confusion, and brandished the spear which our archons always carry. I seized it by the shaft, raised it above my head, and shouted to him to let go and save himself, or else be struck down. Theopompus thereupon appeared on his right, and struck him with his sword. 'Lie there', he cried, 'with those whose toady you were! Never wear your garland in a free Thebes! Never sacrifice again to the gods in whose name you called down so many curses on your country in her enemy's cause!' After Cabirichus had fallen, Theocritus, who was close at hand, snatched the sacred spear out of the blood and gore. A few of the servants put up a bit of resistance, and these we killed. Those who caused no trouble we locked up in the dining-room, not wanting them to slip out and carry the news of what had happened until we knew whether our colleagues had been successful.

[32] What had happened to them was this. Pelopidas' party had gone quietly to Leontiadas' outer door, and knocked. They told the servant who answered the door that they had come from Athens with a letter for Leontiadas from Callistratus. The man gave their message and was told to open the door. He removed the bar, and opened the door a little. Then they all rushed it, threw the man to the floor, and dashed through the hall to the bedroom. Leontiadas guessed the truth at once. He drew his dagger and made ready to defend himself. Unjust and despotic as he was, he was a brave man, and strong of arm. But instead of thinking to overturn the lamp and fight his opponents in the dark, he stayed where they could see him. As the door opened, he struck Cephisodorus in the side and engaged the second man, who was Pelopidas, and shouted for the servants to come to his

aid. They, however, had been detained by Samidas, and they had no desire to risk coming to blows with the most distinguished men in Thebes, who were also famous fighters. Pelopidas duelled with Leontiadas in the narrow doorway of the bedroom. Cephisodorus lay dying between them, so that the others could not join in. In the end, our man, having dealt many wounds and himself been wounded in the head, though not seriously, succeeded in throwing Leontiadas and killing him over Cephisodorus' still-living body. Cephisodorus saw the enemy fall, gave his hand to Pelopidas, said farewell to the others, and breathed his last, a happy man. Having done with this business, they turned their attention to Hypatas. There, the door was opened to them by a similar trick, and they chased Hypatas over the roofs to a neighbour's house before cutting him down.

[33] They hurried on then to meet us, and did so outside the Colonnade. We greeted each other and talked; and then made our way to the prison. Here Phyllidas summoned the governor and said 'Archias and Philip order you to take Amphitheus before them at once.' The governor, seeing that it was a strange time for such an order and noticing that Phyllidas was flustered by his fight and was not very calm, suspected a trick. 'And when', he said, 'have the polemarchs ever sent for a prisoner at this hour of day? And when did they ever employ you as a messenger? What password have you got?' 'Here's the password,' said Phyllidas, and drove his cavalry lance through the man's side, and stretched him on the ground. When morning came, many women trampled and spat upon the wretched man's corpse. We went on to hew open the door of the prison, and call on the prisoners by name—first Amphitheus, then any others whom any of us knew. When they recognized a voice, they jumped joyfully out of their beds, dragging their chains with them, while those whose feet were held in the stocks stretched out their arms, pleading not to be left behind. While they were being freed, many of the neighbours joined us, rejoiced to see what was happening. When the women heard about their relations, they lost all their Boeotian restraint, and ran to one another and questioned every passer-by. Those who found fathers or husbands joined them, and no one stopped them. Everyone was moved by pity and the tears and pleadings of these honest women.

[34] I now learned that Epaminondas, Gorgidas, and their friends were assembling at the temple of Athena. So I went to join them. Many worthy citizens had already arrived, and more kept flocking in. When I told them in detail what had been done, and asked them to go to the market-place to help, they immediately summoned the citizens to liberation. Great crowds gathered, and were supplied with arms from the colonnades (which were full of war-booty of all kinds) and from nearby armourers' shops. Hipposthenidas also arrived with his friends and servants, and brought with him the trumpeters who were in town for the festival of Heracles. Some of these sounded a call in the market-place, others in other parts of the town. Everywhere the enemy was in a panic, believing the uprising to be general. The supporters of the Spartan occupation took refuge on the Cadmea, taking with them the Selectmen, as they were called, who were in the habit of camping at the foot of the citadel every night. The garrison on the hill, confronted by this disorderly and confused influx, and noticing us around the market-place, saw noise and confusion everywhere, with no area unaffected. So they had no thought of coming down, though there were about 1,500 of them. Terrified, they excused themselves as having to wait for Lysanoridas, who <was expected back> that day. We understand that the Spartan elders fined him heavily for this absence afterwards, and put Herippidas and Arcesus to death when they were captured at Corinth. The Spartan commanders surrendered the Cadmea to us under truce, and departed with their men.

V

'LIVE UNKNOWN'

This short piece is preserved as one of Plutarch's polemics against the Epicureans (73–5), whom he regarded as little better than atheists, because of their denial of divine providence. It is, however, more a rhetorical exercise than a serious argument; it is a 'destruction' (*anaskeuē*) of Epicurus' famous saying *lathe biōsas*, 'live unknown to anyone', which advocates quietism and absence from public life. It is included here, both as a specimen of rhetorical technique and for the sake of its closing passage, a characteristically warm expression of belief in the afterlife. Unfortunately the ending is badly preserved (see Notes).

1128 **[1]** The man who said this had no wish to live unknown. He said it to be known. He wanted to be thought very clever, he was seeking undeserved fame from the advice to avoid fame.

> I hate the sage whose wisdom's not for himself.[1]

They tell us that Philoxenus, the son of Eryxis, and Gnatho the Sicilian, enthusiastic gourmets, used to wipe their noses on the dishes, so as to discourage other diners and have a monopoly of the food to stuff themselves. Likewise, those whose love of glory knows no bounds or limits try to discredit glory in the eyes of others, their rivals in love as it were, so as to win the prize without a competition. They are really doing the same as oarsmen: the oarsman faces the stern but contributes to the forward movement, because the reverse thrust from the impact of the oar pushes the boat forward. That's just what those who give us this kind of advice are doing; they are chasing glory with their backs turned to it. Why else should he say such things? Why write and publish them for posterity? Or did he want to be unknown to his own generation, but not to posterity?

[2] But let that pass. Surely the concept itself is immoral. 'Live unknown'—is it like robbing tombs unknown? Is life disgraceful, so as to make us all want to be unknown? I prefer to say, 'Don't let a bad life be unknown; be known, be corrected, reform. If you're virtuous, don't make yourself useless; if

you're vicious, don't postpone treatment.' Even more important: define exactly who it is that you are advising. If he is ignorant or wicked or foolish, you are like the man who says 'Conceal your fever' or 'Conceal your madness, lest the doctor should know about you; go and throw yourself down in a dark corner, where you and your troubles will be alike unknown'; or again, 'You too, go and suffer from your incurable, terminal disease of vice, hide your envy and your superstition, as you would your palpitations, because you're afraid to show them to people who could set you right and cure you.' The ancients used to parade the sick in public, and everyone gave whatever help he could, from his own experience of illness or of nursing others. This, they say, is how a great art arose, out of the contributions of experience. They ought also to have paraded unhealthy lives and diseases of character in public, so that we could all have touched and inspected and pronounced on the various conditions. 'Angry?' 'Beware of this.' 'Jealous?' 'Do this.' 'In love?' 'So was I once, but I repented of it.' But as the world is, people deepen their wickedness by denying, concealing, and wrapping it up.

[3] If, on the other hand, it is the good whom you are urging to 'live unknown' and unobserved, you are saying to Epaminondas 'Don't be a general', to Lycurgus, 'Don't make laws', to Thrasybulus, 'Don't kill tyrants', to Pythagoras 'Don't teach', to Socrates 'Don't debate', and to yourself, Epicurus, 'Don't write to your friends in Asia,* don't recruit followers in Egypt,
don't dance attendance on the young men of Lampsacus; don't 1129
circulate books, advertising your wisdom to all men and all women; and don't give instructions for your funeral.' What is the good of your common table, your meetings of beautiful friends, the tens of thousands of lines written to Metrodorus, to Aristobulus, to Chaeredemus, all carefully composed to keep their lives from being 'unknown' even after their death, if your laws prescribe that virtue shall go unremembered, art be ineffective, philosophy silent, and success forgotten?

[4] If you put out the lamp of knowledge at the dinner of life, so that people can do anything they choose for pleasure without being noticed, you can indeed say 'Live unknown.' Of course I will, if I propose to live with my mistress Hedea, or end my

days with Leontion,* and 'spit on honour' and say 'the good' consists in 'the flesh and its titillation'. These rites do indeed need darkness and night, this is what oblivion and ignorance are meant for. But if a philosopher sings the praises of god and justice and providence in his theory of nature, and of law and community and political society in his ethics, and treats honour and not utility as the basis of politics, why should *he* 'live unknown'? So as not to educate pupils, or not to be admired for his virtue or become a paradigm of goodness? If Themistocles had lived unknown to Athens, Greece would never have repulsed Xerxes. If Camillus had been unknown to the Romans, Rome would not have survived as a city. If Plato had been unknown to Dion, Sicily would not have been liberated. Light makes us not only visible to one another, but useful; and similarly knowledge gives virtue not only fame but the power of action. Epaminondas remained unknown to the Thebans till he was forty, and did them no service; but later, when he was trusted and had held office, he rescued the city from ruin and freed Greece from slavery. It was thanks to the light of his reputation that he made his virtue available for action in the time of need. For it is not only a 'house', as Sophocles says, that

> gleams bright in use, like noble bronze,
> but, long inactive, falls[1]

This is equally true of human character, which gathers a sort of rust of age in obscurity and inactivity. Quiet and silence, a sedentary life of secluded leisure, weakens both body and mind. Just as hidden pools become foul, by being overhung with shade, and stagnating because they have no outflow, so, if there is anything of use in an undisturbed life, its natural powers decay and grow old.

[5] Do you not see that, as night comes on, a lethargic heaviness oppresses our bodies, and feeble hesitations overpower our minds? Our reason contracts like a dying fire, and flickers with a few scattered fancies, idle and depressed, barely indicating that the person is alive. But when the rising sun 'scatters the tricksy dreams'[2] and, as it were, brings the actions and thoughts of all men together, and turns them to itself and makes them share the impulse of its light, then, as Democritus says, men 'have new thoughts with day',[3] and rise to go about their various

avocations, drawn, as it were, by the tightened string of their attraction for one another.

[6] Life, and in general birth and participation in the world of becoming, was, I believe, given to man by god for him to be known. Man remains unknown and unseen as long as he moves, a scattering of tiny particles, through the vast universe; but, once born, he comes together, acquires dimension, and is revealed; the unseen is seen, the hidden is made plain. 'Becoming' is not, as some allege, the path to Being; it is the path that Being takes in order to be known. It does not generate what comes to be, it only reveals it. Similarly, destruction is not the 1130
removing of the existent into the non-existent, but the transfer of the dissolved into the unseen. This is why, in our traditional rites, Apollo is called 'Delian' and 'Pythian',* because he is believed to be identical with the sun; while the lord of the other half of the universe, be he god or *daimōn*, is called 'king of blind night and work-forbidding sleep',[1] because we believe that, when we come to our dissolution, we go to a place unseen and invisible, I suspect too that the ancients used the word *phōs* not only meaning 'light', but meaning 'man', because there is innate in each of us, because of our kinship with it, a strong desire to know and be known. Some philosophers indeed hold that the soul is in its essence light. Among their arguments is the fact that the soul is distressed by ignorance, hates the unilluminated, and feels disturbed by darkness, which is full of fear and uncertainty for it. Light, on the other hand, it finds pleasant and desirable, and cannot take delight in any of its natural pleasures in darkness and deprived of light. It is light that makes all pleasures, pursuits, and enjoyments bright and happy, for it is light that, as it were, gives them all a good flavour. The man who casts himself down into unknowing, clothes himself in darkness, and buries his life in an empty tomb, surely finds his birth a burden, and is weary of his existence.

<That the soul does indeed love light and hate oblivion is shown by what is told of>* the Land of the Blessed,

> on whom the mighty sun
> shines through our earthly night
> on meadows of red roses[2]

where a plain is spread out, bright with flowers and rich with shady trees, and peaceful rivers flow gently by; and there they pass their time conversing together, with memories and talk of things past and present . . . But the Third Road is that of those who have lived lawless and unholy lives, and it drives their souls into a blackness and an abyss

> whence the pale rivers of night's gloom
> belch darkness infinite,[3]

receiving and hiding the condemned in oblivion and unknowing. There are no vultures tearing the livers of the wicked as they lie on the ground, for their livers are burnt or rotted away; no monstrous burdens weigh them down or weary the bodies of the chastised, for 'their sinews have no flesh or bones any more',[4] and there is no remnant of body left to the dead which would be capable of sustaining the blows of the crushing punishment. No: those who have lived an evil life have only one real place of punishment: disgrace, oblivion, total annihilation, which bears them off to Lethe's unsmiling river and plunges them into the bottomless chasms of an ocean of uselessness, inaction, unknowing, and infamy, that sucks them all down.

VI

THE FORTUNE OF ROME

This piece also is a rhetorical performance, incompletely preserved, but presumably intended for some public occasion. It is an *agōn*, or competition, in which the allegorical figures of Fortune and Virtue are represented as contending for the honour of being held primarily responsible for the greatness of Rome. Neither 'fortune' nor 'virtue' is very clearly defined: the former covers luck as well as providence, the latter moral excellence generally as well as courage. But there is some splendid *bravura* writing, and Plutarch's knowledge of the details of Roman history is very apparent. It has often been held that this piece, just because it is so 'rhetorical', is a fairly early work. There is no proof of this. In any case, it states a view of the providential destiny of Rome that Plutarch held consistently all his life.

[1] Of all the great contests that Virtue and Fortune have 316
engaged in against each other, this is the greatest. They are disputing about the Roman Empire. Which of them is responsible for it? Which of them created so mighty a power? The victor will win a great witness for her cause, or rather a strong defence against her accusers. Virtue is charged with being noble but useless; Fortune with being good but unreliable. Virtue, they say labours to no profit; Fortune gives gifts we cannot trust. Who will deny, then, that if Rome is adjudged to Virtue, Virtue will be proved profitable, because she has done so much good to good men; if to Fortune, Fortune will be proved reliable, because she has kept up her gifts so long?

The poet Ion, in a prose work,*[1] says that though Fortune is very unlike Wisdom, she is nevertheless the architect of very similar results. Both give cities increase, and man honour; both raise their favourites to glory, power, and empire. Need I lengthen my discourse by enumerating all the instances? Nature herself, who begets and bears all things, is thought by some to be Fortune, by others Wisdom. This debate therefore confers great honour and prestige on Rome, since we are asking the same question about her that we ask about earth and sea, heaven and stars: is it Fortune or Providence that created her?

[2] For my own part, I think it must be right to conjecture that, however much Fortune and Virtue perpetually contend and struggle with each other, the probability is that, in order to form such a mighty power and empire, they made a truce, and collaborated in the execution and completion of this noblest of human works. Plato says[2] that the universe (*kosmos*) was made with fire and earth as its primary and necessary elements, in order that it should become both visible and tangible. Earth contributed mass and stability, fire contributed colour, shape, and movement; the intermediate substances, water and air, softened and suppressed the dissimilarity of the extremes, and combined them to form the mixture of matter. So too with Rome. Time, who, with God's help, laid her foundations, yoked Fortune and
317 Virtue together, so as to use the special powers of both in creating for all mankind a hearth truly 'holy and wealth-giving', a secure 'mooring-cable', an abiding element, an 'anchor in the surge and drift' of this shifting world, as Democritus has it.[1]

The scientists say, however, that there was no 'cosmic order', and that the primary bodies did not wish to come together and give nature a common form by their union; instead, those that were yet small and scattered slid about and avoided inclusion or interlacing with others, whereas the larger bodies, which were already formed, became involved in terrible conflicts and wrestlings with one another, resulting in wave-motions and agitations, and a world full of destruction, uncertainty, and wreck, until such time as earth acquired a certain magnitude from the moving and concentrating atoms, and thus both stabilized herself and provided a stable base for other things in and around herself. This too has an analogy with human affairs. The greatest powers and empires were at one time driven and borne along by chance, because no one man could dominate, though all wished to do so; universal ruin, disorder, and change prevailed, until such time as Rome developed and grew strong, and attached to herself not only nations and peoples but foreign kingdoms beyond the sea; and then at last the world found stability and security, when the controlling power entered into a single, unwavering cycle and world order of peace. All Virtue was present in those who contrived this revolution, and Fortune too made her great contribution, as we shall see as we proceed.

[3] And now, as I approach my theme, I imagine myself looking down, as from a place of vantage, on Fortune and Virtue going forth to the contest that is to pit them against each other. Virtue walks modestly, and with a sober look, but the flush of competitiveness spreads over her face as the contest draws near. She walks well behind Fortune, who is in a hurry, but she has an escort, and a numerous one, of 'warriors in gory armour',[2] scarred with wounds 'on the front', dripping blood and sweat, their feet planted on the broken spoils of war. Would you know who they are? They tell us their names: Fabricius, Camillus, Lucius Cincinnatus, Fabius Maximus, Claudius Marcellus, Scipio. I see Gaius Marius, furious with Fortune, Mucius Scaevola holding out his flaming hand and crying 'Are you making Fortune a present of this?' Horatius Cocles, the hero of the river, weighed down by Etruscan spears, displays his crippled thigh, and cries out from the depths of the current, 'Was it Fortune that made me a cripple?' Thus Virtue's company goes forth, 'heavily armed for the fray, fierce to the foe'.[3]

[4] Fortune's movements, on the other hand, are quick, her thoughts bold, her expectations proud. She is ahead of Virtue, and is near us now—but not 'borne on light wings', or 'standing tiptoe on her globe',* unsure and unreliable, only to vanish again. No: Aphrodite, as the Spartans tell, lays aside her mirror and her finery and her magic belt as she crosses the Eurotas, and takes up spear and shield to make herself fine for Lycurgus; and so Fortune left the Persians and Assyrians behind, flew lightly across Macedonia, and quickly shook off Alexander; she went the rounds of Egypt and Syria, bearing kingdoms as her gift; she visited Carthage, more than once, only to let her sink; but when
she came to the Palatine and crossed the Tiber, she laid her 318
wings aside, stepped out of her sandals, and abandoned her treacherous, rolling globe. She entered Rome, meaning to stay; and it is in this guise that she appears for her trial. She is not 'deaf to entreaty', as Pindar says,[1] nor does she 'wield twin tillers'; she is rather 'sister of Order and Persuasion, daughter of Forethought',[2] according to Alcman's version of her family tree. In her hand she bears the famous Horn of Plenty,* full not of fruit forever ripe, but of all that land and sea, river and mine and harbour bear; and all this she pours out in plenteous effusion.

With her too can be seen famous men, and in no small number. Numa Pompilius the Sabine, Priscus from Tarquinii, both strangers and incomers whom she placed upon the throne of Romulus. Aemilius Paullus magnifies Fortune, bringing home his army from Perseus and the Macedonians without a man lost, and celebrating in his triumph a victory without tears. Caecilius Metellus* magnifies her too, carried to his grave by four sons who were consuls (Quintus Balearicus, Lucius Diadematus, Marcus Metellus, and Gaius Caprarius), two sons-in-law who held the same office, and nephews distinguished for military prowess and political achievement. Aemilius Scaurus, a *novus homo*,* raised by Fortune from a humble life and a humbler family, is inscribed by her as first man on the roll of the Senate.* She it was who took Cornelius Sulla, lifted him out of the embrace of his mistress Nicopolis, and raised him above all Marius' Cimbrian triumphs and seven consulships to the power of a dictator and a monarch. And Sulla in fact made himself, by his actions, an adopted child of Fortune, crying, in the words of Sophocles' Oedipus, 'I count myself as Fortune's child.'[3] In Latin he was called Felix, in Greek he wrote his name 'Lucius Cornelius Sulla Epaphroditus'. The trophy commemorating his victory over Mithridates' forces at my home town of Chaeronea* is thus inscribed, and rightly so: for it is not 'night', as Menander claims,[4] but Fortune that 'shares most in Aphrodite's works'.

[5] May I now, having thus begun at home, call the Romans themselves as Fortune's best witnesses, on the ground that they pay more honour to her than to Virtue? No temple of Virtue was established in Rome till a late date, by Scipio, the victor of Numantia; it was followed by a temple of Virtus and Honor, founded by Marius. It was Aemilius Scaurus, who lived at the time of the Cimbric War, who founded the temple of Mens, that is, 'intelligence'. It was when the city began to be flooded out with rhetoric, sophistry, and chatter that they began to honour such abstractions. Even today there is no temple of Wisdom or Temperance, Magnanimity, Perseverance, or Endurance. But the temples of Fortune are splendid and ancient, almost contemporary with the first foundations of the city. The first to establish a temple of Fortune was Numa's grandson, Ancus Marcius,* the

fourth king of Rome. It was perhaps he also who gave her the name 'Manly', because manliness is Fortune's chief partner in ensuring victory. The temple of Ladies' Fortune was built before the time of Camillus, when the women were the means of repulsing Marcius Coriolanus' march against the city with the Volsci: his wife and mother undertook a mission to him, and succeeded in persuading him to spare the city and remove his
barbarian army. The story goes that, at the consecration of 319
the temple, the statue of Fortune spoke, and said 'Women of the city, piously have you set me up by the city's law.' Furius Camillus, when he had put out the Gallic fires and rescued Rome from the pan of the balance as she was being weighed against her worth in gold, established a temple not of Good Counsel or Courage, but of Rumour and Report,* hard by the New Road, where, they say, M. Caedicius was walking by night before the war and heard a voice bidding Rome expect a Gallic war soon. Fortune on the riverside bears the name 'Fortis'*—which means strong, heroic, or manly—because she holds the power of victory over all comers. They built her temple in the garden bequeathed to the people by Caesar, in the belief that he too—as he himself bore witness—owed his greatness to good fortune.

[6] I should indeed have been reluctant to ascribe Caesar's rise to Fortune, had he not borne witness to it himself. He had sailed out of Brindisi* in his pursuit of Pompey on 4 January, in the middle of winter. He had a safe passage over the open sea, for Fortune put off the stormy weather. He found Pompey in strength, and all his forces deployed by land and sea. Caesar had only a handful of men with him, for Antony's and Sabinus' army was delayed. Nevertheless, he embarked boldly in a small boat, disguised as a servant, unknown to the captain and the helmsman. They struggled against the river current. The waves rose. The helmsman prepared to change course; but Caesar tore off the cloak he had wrapped round his head, and disclosed himself. 'Have courage, my brave friend,' he said, 'do not fear; spread your sails to Fortune, and accept her wind. Be confident: you have Caesar and Caesar's Fortune on board.' So convinced was he that Fortune was at his side in his voyages, his travels, his campaigns, and his commands. It was her business to order the

sea to be calm, winter to turn to summer, the slow to be swift, and the coward to be brave. More incredible still, she made Pompey flee and Ptolemy murder his guest, so that Pompey should die and Caesar not be defiled by the guilt of his death.

[7] And what of Caesar's son, the first to be called 'Augustus', who ruled fifty-four years?* Did he not, when he sent his grandson* to the war, pray the gods to grant the young man Scipio's courage, Pompey's popularity, and his own Fortune? He thus inscribed Fortune's name on himself, like the artist's name on a masterpiece. She had built him up on Cicero, Lepidus, Pansa, Hirtius, Mark Antony; she raised him by their bravery, their strong arms, their victories, wars, and armies, only then to cast down those by whom he had risen, and leave him standing alone. It was for him that Cicero was a statesman and Lepidus a general, that Pansa won victories, Hirtius fell in battle—and Antony wantoned: for Cleopatra too I would count as Caesar's Fortune, since she was the rock on which a great general's ship foundered, leaving Caesar alone. The story goes that, the two being close friends and familiar companions, and often playing ball or dice together, or competing with their fighting cocks or quails, Antony always came off worse. One of his companions, who took some pride in being a prophet, often warned him frankly about this. 'My dear fellow,' he would
320 say, 'why do you deal with this boy? Avoid him. You are more famous, you are senior to him, you have more men under your command, you are well-tried in war, you have greater experience. But your *daimon* fears his *daimon*; your fortune is great, but she bows down before his. If you don't put a good distance between you, she will desert to his side.'

These proofs of Fortune's case come from witnesses. We must next adduce the proofs that come from the facts of history, beginning with the very beginnings of the city. Who could deny that, in the birth, rescue, upbringing, and rise of Romulus, it was Fortune who laid the foundations, and Virtue who built upon them? The circumstances of the birth and begetting of the very founders and establishers of the city are proof of marvellous good fortune. Their mother is said to have been bedded with a god; and, as Heracles is said to have been begotten in a long night,* when the day was supernaturally delayed and the sun slowed his path, so, in the planting of the seed of Romulus, the sun, it is related, was in eclipse, making an exact conjunction with the moon, while the god Mars was with the mortal woman Silvia. And the same thing happened to Romulus, it is said, at his departure from this life: he disappeared during an eclipse of the sun, on the day called Nonae Capratinae,* now celebrated as a great festival. And later, when the twins were born and the tyrant sought to kill them, Fortune ensured that the servant who took them up was no savage barbarian but a man of mercy and humanity, who would not kill them. There was a branch of the river washing a green meadow, shaded with low-growing trees. Here he laid the babies, near the fig-tree later called Ruminalis*. And there was a she-wolf, who had lately borne cubs, and had her teats full of milk. She had lost her cubs, and wanted relief; so she embraced the babies, and gave them suck, relieving her breast as if she had given birth a second time. And the sacred bird of Mars, the woodpecker, came and perched beside them, opening each of the babies' mouths in turn, and dropping a morsel of food into them, sharing his own nourishment with them. The fig-tree is called Ruminalis from the teat (*ruma*) which the she-wolf offered to the babies as she crouched beside it. The people of the locality long preserved the practice of never exposing infants; they would always accept them into the family, out of regard for the similar fate of Romulus. And that they were reared and educated secretly at Gabii, and that it remained unknown that they were Silvia's sons and King Numitor's grandchildren, was clearly another clever trick of Fortune, to make sure that they were not killed because of their family before their moment of action, but were revealed only in the hour of success, displaying their valour as a token of their noble birth. I am reminded here of a fable invented by that great and wise general Themistocles to some of the Athenian generals who were later successful and claimed to be given precedence over him. 'Day After,' he said, 'tried to compete with Feast Day, and said that Feast Day was a day of fatigue and occupation, whereas on *her* day, people enjoyed in peace what they had got ready. "True enough," said Feast Day, "but if I had not existed, where would you be?" And so', continued Themistocles, 'if I hadn't been around in the Persian War, what benefit would there

have been in you?' Romulus' Fortune, I suspect, could say the same to his Virtue: 'Your deeds are brilliant and magnificent,
321 you have indeed proved yourself to be of the blood and race divine; but do you see how far behind me you come? If I had not been beside you, with my kindness and friendship, if I had abandoned the children, how could you have existed, how could your light have shone? Suppose the she-wolf had never appeared, fevered with the abundance of her milk and needing something to feed rather than something to feed on? Suppose she had been fierce and starving? Would not all these fine palaces and temples, theatres, walks, squares, and public offices have been mere shepherds' huts, the abode of herdsmen, owing obedience to some Alban or Etruscan or Latin master? The beginning is the greatest part of every enterprise, and especially of the foundation and building of a city; and Fortune provided this beginning when she rescued and protected the founder. Virtue made Romulus great; Fortune preserved him until he became great.

[9] Numa's long reign too was admittedly guided by marvellous good fortune. It is perhaps a fable that a nymph, Egeria, one of the dryads, a wise *daimon*, consorted with him for love, and gave him tuition and guidance in his policies. Other humans who are said to have unions with divinities or been loved by them—Peleus, Anchises, Orion, Emathion—have not necessarily enjoyed an enviable or painless life; but Numa seems to have had good fortune to share his house, his seat of judgement, and his throne. And this good fortune, finding Rome tossed on the turbulent and troubled sea of neighbours' hostility and savagery, and inflamed by innumerable ills and divisions, calmed the winds of hostile anger and envy; like the sea that saves the fabled halcyons' brood* in storm and helps to rear the chicks, she enveloped Numa's Rome in a calm, free of war and plague, danger and fear, and so gave the newly settled and much-shaken people the chance to root their city in stability, so that it could grow in peace, secure and unhindered. It takes many blows and much force to build a trireme or a merchantman; the hull shakes with hammers and nails, with bolts and saws and axes; and once it is fitted together, it has to rest and settle for a certain time, until the joints hold and the bolts get used to their place; if the ship is launched while the joints are still mobile, the whole

structure will be shaken and loosened and will let in the sea. And so it is with Rome. Her first ruler and builder, who made her out of rough herdsman-stock, from tough oak, as it were, endured much toil and stood firm against great wars and perils, because he was forced to resist those who opposed the creation and settlement of the city. Her second master, thanks to good fortune, gave her time to confirm and secure her growth; it was given him to enjoy times of peace and plenty. If at that time some Porsena had fallen on Rome, bringing his Etruscan host and army to assault its feeble, infant fortifications; if some war-mad tyrant had broken out among the Marsi, or some aggressive, bellicose Lucanian, breathing strife and malice, like Mutilus in later times, or the audacious Silo, or Sulla's last adversary, Telesinus, whose signal made all Italy rise in arms*—if any such enemy had sounded the trumpet over the philosophic Numa when he was at sacrifice or prayer, the incipient city could never have withstood the storm and tempest, nor
developed into a strong and populous nation. The peace of 322
Numa's reign seems now to have been the means whereby Rome prepared for her future wars. After the conflicts of Romulus' time, the people trained, like an athlete, for forty-three years,* in order to produce a force capable of confronting its later adversaries. In all that time, so they say, no famine or plague, no dearth, no unseasonable summer or winter, came to trouble Rome. It was as though divine Fortune, not human counsel, was the guardian spirit of the age. Then too the Double Gate of Janus*—they call it the Gate of War—was closed; it is open when there is war, closed in peace. It was opened after Numa's death, because the Alban war broke out. Countless wars ensued, one following another; and it was 480 years before the gate was closed again, at the end of the war against Carthage, in the consulship of C. Atilius and T. Mallius. After that year, it was opened again, and wars continued until Caesar's victory at Actium. Then Roman arms were idle for a time, but not for long; the Cantabrian disturbances and the outbreaks in Gaul and Germany broke up the peace. These are all further proofs of Numa's good fortune.

[10] His successors also honoured Fortune, as founder, nurse, and, as Pindar has it,[1] 'upholder' of the city of Rome. Servius

Tullius,* the king who did most to increase the power of the people, organize the constitution, and prescribe due forms for elections and military service, and who was the first censor and overseer and controller of men's lives, a man both brave and wise, none the less associated himself with Fortune, and made his rule depend on her. Indeed, Fortune was believed to visit him, entering through a window into the building which they now call the Fenestella Gate. Whether or not this is true, he built a temple of Fortuna Primigenia—that is to say, 'First Born'—on the Capitol, and one of Fortuna Obsequens*—that is, 'Obedient' or, as some translate it, 'Propitious'. But let me leave these Roman names and try rather to explain the functions of the various temples in my own language. On the Palatine, there is a temple of Private Fortune, and one of Fortune the Birdcatcher; this may sound absurd, but there is a meaning in the metaphor, namely that Fortune attracts things from afar and holds them fast when they come to settle upon her. By the spring
323 called Muscosa ('Mossy') there stand to this day a temple of Fortune the Virgin, and on the Esquiline one of Fortune Returning. In the Long Street there is an altar of Fortune of Good Hope, and next to the altar of Aphrodite with the Basket there stands a shrine of Masculine Fortune. There are countless other cults and titles of Fortune also, mostly established by Servius, who knew very well the truth of the saying that 'in all human affairs, Fortune is decisive, or rather she is everything'. He understood this particularly because of his own good fortune, in being raised to the throne despite his hostile and captive origins. It was at the capture of the town of Corniculum by the Romans that a captive virgin named Ocresia, whose bearing and character Fortune could not dim, was given as a slave to King Tarquin's wife, Tanaquil. A 'client' of his—to use the Roman term for a dependant—took her as his wife, and to this couple Servius was born. There is another version of the story, however, according to which the maiden Ocresia always used to take the first-fruits and libations from the king's table back to the hearth; and one day, when she was putting the first-fruits on the fire, the flame went out and a man's genital organ rose up out of the hearth. The girl was terrified, and told no one except Tanaquil. That wise and intelligent lady dressed the girl as a bride and

shut her in the same room as the apparition, which she believed to be divine. Some say the lover was a Hero of the Household,* others that it was Vulcan. Whichever it was, Servius was born, and a flame like lightning played around his infant hands. Antias has yet another story. He relates that, when Servius' wife, Gegania, was dying, he lay down sadly and wearily while his mother watched, and as he slept, the women saw his face enveloped in fiery light, evidence that he was indeed born of fire, and a good omen of his unexpected accession to the kingdom, to which he succeeded through Tanaquil's efforts on the death of King Tarquin. Of all the kings, Servius seems to have been the best-fitted by nature for the kingship, and the least desirous of it. He actually tried to abdicate, but he was prevented, and Tanaquil exacted an oath from him that he would stay in power and not abandon Rome's ancient constitution. Thus Servius' reign was wholly the work of Fortune; he succeeded to the throne against his expectation, he remained on it against his will.

[11] But I have no wish to give the impression of avoiding clear and obvious instances by taking refuge in the dark places of antiquity. Let us leave the kings, and move on to the most famous deeds and most glorious wars of Roman history. Who would not admit that these are proof of daring and courage, and (as Timotheus puts it) 'the shame that works with spearmen's valour'?[1] But the whole tide of events, the surging impulse that led to all this power and greatness, shows, if you think of it fairly, that the empire was not advanced by human hand or counsel, but sped on its way by divine guidance and Fortune's favouring wind. Trophy is raised on trophy, triumph meets triumph; before the first blood cools on Roman weapons, fresh blood washes it away. They count their victories not by the number of dead or the quantity of spoil, but by kingdoms made captive, nations enslaved, islands and continents added to their dominions. One battle cost Philip Macedonia, at one blow Antiochus yielded up
Asia, a single Carthaginian defeat lost Africa. One man in one 324
campaign* won Pontus, Syria, Arabia, Albania, Iberia, right up to Hyrcania and the Caucasus. The Ocean that surrounds our world thrice saw his victories. He drove the Numidians of Libya back to their southern shores; when Spain caught Sertorius'

sickness, he overran it all the way to the Atlantic coast; when the Albanian kings fled before him, he brought them to a stand on the Caspian Sea. All these successes he achieved through the fortune of the Roman people. It was his own individual destiny that overthrew him. The great *daimon* of the Romans does not dispense favour for a day, or flourish for a space, like that of Macedon; it is not confined to dry land, like that of Sparta, nor to the sea like that of Athens. It was not slow to awake, like that of Persia, nor quick to cease, like that of Colophon. It was with the city from its birth: young with it, growing to strength with it, joining it in all its political life, it stood by loyally on land and on sea, in war and in peace, against barbarians and against Greeks. This great power wasted and exhausted the torrent of Hannibal's armies in Italy, when envy and political hostility stopped any reinforcement reaching it from home. This same great power scattered and separated the Cimbri and Teutones over vast distances and intervals of time, so that Marius could fight each in turn, and Italy escape the cataclysm of 300,000 invincible warriors descending upon her at once. By the agency of the same power, Antiochus was distracted while Philip was attacked, and Philip cowered in defeat when Antiochus was in danger. Mithridates was preoccupied with wars with the Sarmatians and Bastarnae while the flames of the Marsian war encircled Rome. Tigranes was divided from Mithridates at the height of his success by suspicion and envy, and in defeat he joined him only to share his ruin.

[12] And was it not Fortune that set the city on its feet in its greatest disasters? When the Gauls camped round the Capitol, and besieged the citadel, Fortune 'sent plague among the host, and the people died',[1] and it was Fortune and Chance that detected the night attack, which no human being noticed. Perhaps I may take a little time telling this story in more detail. After the great defeat of the Romans at the Allia, the arrival of the routed troops in Rome filled the people with terror and scattered them in panic. Some few, however, made ready the Capitol, and held their ground there. Those who retreated to Veii after the rout elected Camillus dictator; this was a man whom the people had rejected and put down in their pride and prosperity—he was accused of embezzling public funds—but,

frightened and humiliated after the defeat, they now recalled
him, and gave him absolute authority. Now, in order that it
should be clearly seen that Camillus accepted this power legally
and not in the heat of the emergency, and was not getting him-
self elected by the arms of a scattered, homeless army, it was
vital for the senators on the Capitol to ascertain the soldiers'
will and take their votes. A brave man named C. Pontius under-
took to be the messenger to take their decision to the Capitol. It
was a dangerous mission; the road lay through the enemy, who
had surrounded the fortress with guards and fences. He descended
to the river at night, tied broad sheets of cork to his chest,
and, trusting their lightness, let the current bear him down- 325
stream. The river was slow and still, and he reached the further
bank in safety. Once landed, he made for a place where no light
showed, thinking that the darkness and silence indicated that
there was nobody there. He clung to the cliff, and trusting to
whatever slope or turn or roughness of the rock gave him a hold,
scrambled to the top, where he was taken in charge by the sen-
tries and reported the decision to the authorities on the Capitol.
He was given the decree, and departed again to return to Camil-
lus. When day came, one of the Gauls, who was patrolling the
area, noticed toe-marks and indications of slipping; he observed
also that, where there was soil, the grass was bruised and
broken, and there were signs of a body having been dragged
across the space and pressed upon the ground. He told the others
what he had seen. They concluded that the enemy had shown
them the way up; and they set about accepting the challenge.
They waited till the quietest hour of the night, and then began
their ascent. They went undetected by the guards, and even by
the watchdogs of the garrison, which had gone to sleep. Yet
Rome's fortune found a voice to reveal and disclose the danger.
There were sacred geese in the temple of Juno, bred in the ser-
vice of the goddess. Now the goose is an easily disturbed crea-
ture, frightened at everything; and at this time the geese were
neglected, because of the shortage of food in the fortress, and
their sleep was light and hungry. They became aware of the
enemy the moment they appeared over the edge of the cliff, and
they cackled and attacked with vigour. The sight of the weapons
disturbed them all the more, and they soon filled the place with

their shrill, harsh screeching. This roused the Romans, who soon understood what was happening, and pushed the intruders down the cliff. In memory of these events, there is still a ceremonial procession* which includes a crucified dog and a goose that sits proudly on an expensive coverlet on a litter. The sight well illustrates the strength of Fortune, the resource she draws from the strangest sources in any eventuality; when she is the manager and commander of an operation, she inspires the foolish and irrational with wisdom, and the coward with strength and courage.

Anyone who reflects upon the dejection of those times and the present prosperity of the city must surely be truly amazed and filled with admiration. Behold the splendid temples, the wealth of offerings, the competitions of artists, the generous gifts of cities, the crowns given by kings! Think of all the products of land and sea, of islands and continents, rivers, trees, animals, plains, mountains, and mines! See how all these combine to make Rome beautiful, in a vision of splendour and grace! And yet all this nearly did not come to pass at all. When all was bowed low in defeat, in fire and darkness, fear and gloom, with the swords and murderous hearts of the savages threatening death, these everyday, irrational, cowardly birds gave the signal of salvation! Those great champions and leaders, the Mallii and Servilii, Postumii and Papirii, founders of houses famous in after times, came near death, and were only roused to defend the gods of their fathers and their country by the geese!

Even if what Polybius tells us in Book II of his *History* is true,[1] namely that the Gauls who captured Rome made peace with Camillus and retreated because they learnt that their home country was being devastated by an incursion of neighbouring barbarians, this does nothing to diminish Fortune's claim to
326 have been the saviour by distracting the enemy or drawing them unexpectedly away from Rome.

[13] But why spend more words on these stories? There is nothing certain or definite in them, for the written records of the Romans were destroyed, and their annals lost, as Livy tells us.[1] Later events, plainer and more evident, equally display the good will of Fortune. To her too I would attribute the death of Alexander, the man who, by the successes and brilliant achievements of his invincible courage and spirit, darted like a shooting star across the universe, from the rising to the setting sun, and was already beginning to direct the flashing light of his arms towards Italy. The massacre of Alexander the Molossian* at the hands of the Bruttians and Lucanians at Pandosia was only an excuse for the expedition; it was his love of glory and empire, driving him on against all mankind, that conceived the ambition to lead armies beyond the limits which Dionysus and Heracles* had reached. Alexander had heard of the strength and valour of Rome, the point of steel drawn up for battle in defence of Italy. The name and reputation of the Romans had reached his ears, as a people of athletes trained in countless wars. 'Not without bloodshed had the fight been won',[2] if the pride that would not brook slavery had met the army that had never known defeat. The Romans were 130,000 strong, all men of warlike spirit and manly heart,

> on horseback skilled to fight,
> or stand on foot where needed.[3]

VII

RULES FOR POLITICIANS

This is the work in which Plutarch engages most closely with the political problems of his own time, though viewing them always in the light of classical examples and parallels. The addressee, Menemachus, is a rich and influential citizen of Sardis, embarking on a political career. Plutarch's advice (Introd. p. xix) clearly recognizes the limited powers of Greek cities under Roman rule, and warns against going beyond the permitted bounds. Many of the examples seem to come straight out of the *Parallel Lives*, and it would seem that this work is a product of the research that went into the writing of these, and is therefore a fairly late composition. This is borne out by the style, and the resemblances with *Old Men in Politics* (51), which is confessedly late. However, in collecting examples to illustrate the demands of particular kinds of occasion or crisis, Plutarch is following an old tradition; and it is likely that some Peripatetic work on politics, such as that by Theophrastus, was an important source. He also draws to some extent on recent events, as in the warning story of Pardalas (815, 825), of which unfortunately we know no details.

798 [1] Not one of all the Achaeans will find fault
or contradict your words; but you've not gained
the full conclusion of your argument.[1]

This passage* is often useful, Menemachus; and never more so than when it is applied to philosophers who exhort but offer us no instruction or suggestion. They are no better than people who trim their lamps but don't put the oil in. Now I can see that you have been stimulated by theoretical arguments to a political career, and you want to be 'a speaker of words and a doer of deeds'[2] in your own country, in a style befitting your great family. But you do not have the time to observe an actual philosopher's life in the open, with all its political actions and public contests, or to see with your own eyes exemplary events going on in the real world. So you ask me for some political rules. It would be wrong of me to refuse; I only hope the outcome will prove worthy of your enthusiasm and my readiness to help. As you requested, I have used a great variety of examples.

[2] Political activity must first have a firm and secure foundation, as it were, in motives which are based on judgement and reason, not on the emotional excitement of vanity or combativeness, or mere lack of other occupation. Just as people who are not happy at home spend most of their time in the agora, even if they have no call to be there, so too there are persons who throw themselves into public life because they have no private interests worth troubling about. Their politics is their pastime. With many, again, it is chance that has led them to put their hands to public affairs; then, when they have had enough of it, they find it hard to escape. They are like persons who go for a sail for the sake of the movement, and then find themselves carried out to sea. They peer over the side, sick and distressed, but they have no choice but to stay and make the best of their circumstances:

> over the gleaming calm
> the fair-faced loves of a ship's
> benches that furrow the sea
> misled them into terrible outrage.[3]

These people particularly discredit their activities by their regrets and distress, whenever they either hope for glory and find disgrace, or expect to awe others by their power and then find themselves drawn into danger and confusion. Nothing of this disturbs or unhinges the man who embarks on a public career out of rational conviction, in the belief that it is noble work and particularly right for him. It is wrong to enter upon public life as a money-making business, like Stratocles and Damoclides, who invited each other to the 'golden harvest', which was their name for the speaker's platform. It is also wrong to take it up out of a sudden access of emotion, like C. Gracchus, who, having withdrawn from politics in the immediate aftermath of his brother's fall, subsequently took fire at the insults and abuse of certain people, and plunged into public life in a passion; he was soon weary both of the work and of the fame, but, however much he tried and wanted to revert to a quieter life, he could find no way to lay down his power,
because it was now so great, and he lost his life before he could 799
do so. Again, people who construct an image of themselves, like

actors on the stage, with an eye to competitiveness or reputation, are sure to repent of it; they either become the servants of those they hope to control, or offend those they wish to please. Politics is like a well. If you fall in accidentally and unexpectedly, you are upset and regret the step; but if you descend quietly and after due preparation and reflection, you will make reasonable use of your circumstances, and not have cause to complain, because the sole object of your actions will be honour.

[3] So, having established our motives in our own minds, and secured them against change or vacillation, we have next to consider the character of our fellow citizens—I mean the perceived dominant character resulting from the combined characters of them all. It is neither easy nor safe to try to shape or change the character of the people oneself; it takes a long time, and great influence. However, just as wine is at first controlled by the character of the drinker, but gradually, as it penetrates and warms him, shapes and modifies that character, so should the politician act: until he has firmly established his power of leadership on reputation and confidence, he must adapt himself to the current mores, and keep them in his sights. He needs to know what the people like, and by what means they are naturally led. The Athenians, for example,* are swift to anger, but swift also to change to pity, quicker to form instantaneous suspicion than to accept quiet demonstration. Anxious to support men of no standing or repute, they are likewise fond of humour and jokes in speeches, and have a preference for such things. They like those who praise them, but they do not get angry with those who make fun of them. Their formidableness extends to their rulers, their humanity to their enemies. The Carthaginian character is different. Bitter, grim, subservient to rulers and arrogant to subordinates, they are at their worst in moments of fear, at their most savage in moments of anger. Once they have made a decision, they persevere in it. No amusement, no charm softens their severity. If Cleon had asked them to postpone the Assembly because he had sacrificed and was about to entertain guests, they would not have laughed, applauded, and broken up their meeting. If Alcibiades had let a quail fly out of his lap as he was speaking,* they would never have joined eagerly in the chase and given it back to him. They would have put both of them to

death for frivolously insulting them. Why, they actually accused Hanno of aiming at tyranny and exiled him, because he had a lion to carry his baggage on campaign. Nor do I think the Thebans, if they had come into possession of enemy correspondence, would have behaved like the Athenians, who captured Philip's couriers* carrying a letter addressed to Olympias, and declined to open it or disclose the private expression of affection of an absent husband to his wife. On the other hand, I cannot imagine that the Athenians would have tolerated Epaminondas' contemptuous pride when he refused to answer the charges against him, and walked out through the Assembly to the gymnasium. And most certainly the Spartans would never have endured the rude humour of Stratocles, the man who once persuaded the Athenians to hold a victory celebration, and then when the real news of defeat came, and they displayed their anger, simply asked them what harm they had suffered from 800
enjoying themselves for three days because of what he had done. Court flatterers, just like bird-catchers, mimic their masters' voices and copy them so as to insinuate themselves into favour and win the kings over by deceit. The politician, by contrast, is not allowed to ape the popular character, but he has to understand and use the features which make each particular society amenable. Ignorance of the character of the people produces mistakes and failures in political dealings just as much as in royal friendships.

[4] So it is not until you are powerful and trusted that you should attempt to mould the character of your fellow citizens. Lead them gradually into better ways, take them in hand gently. It is a laborious business to change the many. You will yourself henceforth be living on an open stage. Discipline and order your ways. If it is hard to rid yourself completely of your vices, do at any rate remove or restrain the most conspicuous and obvious faults. You have heard how Themistocles,* when he was thinking of a political career, kept himself aloof from drink and riotous parties. Sleepless, sober, and serious, he would tell his friends that Miltiades' trophy* kept him awake. Pericles actually made a change in his appearance* and style of life; he came to walk slowly, talk softly, maintain a composed expression all the time, keep his hands inside his cloak, and take one road

only—the road to the Assembly and the Council House. The populace is not something that can be easily won over, and not everyone can win it, even to save its life; one should feel very pleased if it accepts control without shying at sights and sounds like a restive and suspicious horse. If it's right to pay special attention even to little things like these, how can it not be right to ensure that your life and character should be free from reproach or scandal of any kind? Men in public life are not responsible merely for their public words and actions. Their dinners, their bed, their marriage, their amusements and interests are all objects of curiosity. I hardly need mention Alcibiades!* For all his supreme efforts in the public cause and his unbeaten record as a general, the indiscipline and audacity shown in his daily life both ruined him and robbed the city of the benefit of his other good qualities, all because of his extravagance and lack of self-control. The Athenians even found fault with Cimon for drinking, as the Romans did with Scipio for his sleeping-habits, because they had nothing else to complain about. Pompey's enemies, too, abused him because they saw him scratch his head with one finger!* A birthmark or a wart on the face causes more distress than brandings or deformities or scars elsewhere on the body; and similarly small faults appear great when they are seen in the lives of leaders and statesmen. This is because of the view of the ordinary people that authority and government are very great things, which are expected to be entirely free of eccentricity or aberration. It was therefore only natural that the demagogue Livius Drusus should be so well thought of. He had a house, many parts of which were overlooked by his neighbours. An architect undertook to remove this disadvantage at a cost of only five talents. 'Make it ten,' said Drusus, 'and make my whole house open, so that my fellow citizens can see how I live.' He was in fact a temperate and orderly man. Maybe, though, he didn't need this kind of public exposure: ordinary
801 people can see into the character and plans and actions and lifestyle of public figures even when they seem to be well wrapped up. Popular love and admiration, like popular contempt and dislike, are based as much on private as on public habits. 'What? Don't cities make use of persons who live a dissolute and lavish life?' Yes. Pregnant women long for stones, seasickness victims

long for cabbage and food like that, but they soon reject it. Similarly, a democracy will employ whatever leader is at hand, however much they detest and despise him, either out of sheer insolence and perversity, or because there is none better to be had. They even enjoy it when such things are said against them. The comic poet Plato, for instance, puts the following into the mouth of Demos:

> Hold my hand, hold my hand; I'm just about
> to elect Agyrrhius general

and he calls for a bowl and a feather to make himself sick, and says

> it's coming up—to my platform—it's Mantias,

and

> he's feeding stinking Cephalus, vile disease.[1]

And when Carbo solemnly promised the Romans something, and added an oath and a curse, the people took an oath themselves—that they did not trust him. At Sparta, when a man of bad character put forward a proper proposal, the people threw it out; the ephors, however, then chose by lot one of the elders to make the same speech, thus decanting the idea, as it were, from a dirty vessel into a clean one, in order to make it acceptable to the many. Confidence in character, and the opposite, are decisive factors in politics.

[5] But this doesn't mean that we should rely entirely on virtue and neglect the charm and power of speech. Rhetoric should be seen not as the 'maker' of persuasion but as its assistant. Menander's line 'the speaker's character, not his word, is what persuades'[2] needs some correction. It is a combination of character and word that persuades—unless, of course, you're going to tell me that, just as the helmsman, not the rudder, steers the ship, and the rider, not the bit, guides the horse, so it is character and not the word that political virtue uses as its rudder or bit to guide a city, putting a controlling hand on it, as it were, from behind, that being the quarter from which, as Plato tells us,[3] the animal is most easily directed. Those great kings, the 'born of Zeus', as Homer calls them, used to puff themselves out with

purple robes and sceptres and bodyguards and oracles, enslaving the common people by their grandeur as superior beings. Nevertheless, they sought also to be 'speakers of words' and did not neglect the charm of speech 'or the assemblies where men's greatness shows'.[4] They felt the need not only of Zeus of Good Counsel and Ares the Warrior and Athena of the Host; they also called on Calliope, 'who is the attendant of respected kings',[5] and controls the stubbornness and violence of nations by her persuasions and her magic. How then can a private person, with the dress and the looks of a man of the people, have strength to control the masses in the city he hopes to guide, unless he has speech to persuade and to attract? Ships' captains employ others to shout the commands, but the politician needs to have in himself both the mind that steers and the word that gives orders. He ought not to need another's voice. He ought not to be like Iphicrates,* who said, when Aristophon had out-talked him, 'My opponents have the better actor, but I have the better play.' He ought not to have many occasions to quote Euripides' lines:

802 O that the seed of wretched man were speechless![1]

and

> alas, that facts themselves do not have voices,
> that clever speakers might not count at all![2]

We may perhaps allow this escape-route to craftsmen and workers with their hands—an Alcamenes, a Nesiotes, an Ictinus—who renounce any claim to power of speech. There were once two architects in Athens, competing for a public contract. One was glib and fluent, and swayed the people by the carefully practised speech in which he expounded his plan; the other, a better craftsman but an incompetent speaker, came forward and simply said, 'Gentlemen, what he has described, I will perform.' Athena of Craftsmen is the only divinity served by those who fashion inanimate matter that obeys their blows 'on anvil with heavy hammer', as Sophocles has it.[3] The spokesman for Athena Polias and Themis of the Council, 'who summons and dismisses men's assemblies',[4] sets his city in order with one tool only at his disposition—the word: with this he shapes and joins, and softens or smooths down the obstacles to his work—the knots in the wood, as it were, or the flaws in the iron. It was the power of the word that produced Pericles' government—'in word democracy,' as Thucydides says, 'but in fact rule by the first man'.[5] Cimon had been a good man; so had Ephialtes; so had the Thucydides who once answered King Archidamus of Sparta, who asked him whether he or Pericles was the better wrestler, by saying 'No one knows; when I throw him, he says he has not been thrown; so he wins and convinces the spectators.' Now this power of speech brought not only fame to Pericles, but salvation to Athens. While Athens listened to him, she preserved her existing prosperity and refrained from external adventures. Nicias had the same intentions, but he lacked that sort of persuasiveness; the speech with which he tried to deter the people* proved an ineffectual curb. He neither restrained them nor controlled them. He was whisked away to Sicily and came to grief with the rest. They say you can't hold a wolf by the ears; but it is by the ears that you need to take hold of your city, not—like some of the uneducated, who look for holds that need no culture or skill—by the belly with feasts, or by the purse with hand-outs, or by organizing ballet-performances or gladiators all the time, so as to be leaders, or rather wheedlers, of the people. Leadership belongs to those who persuade by the word; these other ways of domesticating the masses are no different from trapping and taming animals.

[6] A politician's style of speech must not be extravagant or theatrical, as though he was orating at a festival and weaving a garland of soft and flowery words. Nor on the other hand, must it 'smell of the lamp'* (as Pytheas said of Demosthenes' style) or of sophistic elaboration, all sharp epigrams and periods measured out by rule and dividers. Music critics expect the touch on the strings to show sensibility, not mere mechanical skill. The same principle applies to the speech of the politician who gives advice or holds office: there should be no ingenious tricks about it, one shouldn't be able to applaud it by saying 'What facility!' 'What skill!' 'What organization!' No: the speech should be overflowing with sincerity, genuine pride, a father's frankness, forethought, and caring intelligence. Its 803
nobility of content should be given the charm and attractiveness of dignified language and individual and convincing thoughts.

Political oratory admits more generalizations, more history, myth, and metaphor than does forensic speaking, and moderate and timely use of these elements is very effective—as in 'Do not put out one of the eyes of Greece!'* or Demades' 'I govern the shipwreck of the city',* or Archilochus'

> let not the rock of Tantalus*
> hang over this our isle[1]

or Pericles' counsel to 'remove the eyesore* from the Piraeus', or Phocion's observation on Leosthenes' victory—'Fine for the sprint, but I'm apprehensive about the long distance.' As a general rule, however, an impressive dignity is more appropriate to the man of affairs. The *Philippics* provide a model, and also (among the speeches in Thucydides) the address of the ephor Sthenelaidas, King Archidamus' speech at Plataea, and Pericles' after the plague.[2] As for the rhetoric and the periods of Ephorus and Theopompus,* which they rehearse when they have got their armies under arms and drawn up for battle, the best comment is the line of Euripides: 'none plays the fool like that, when swords are out!'[3]

However, jest and laughter do sometimes form part of a political speech, if they are meant as salutary reproach or criticism, and not as insults or vulgar jokes. The most successful examples of this are in answers and repartees: to premeditate or initiate a joke is what the professional comic does, and it can earn a reputation for malice, as happened to Cicero's jokes and the elder Cato's, and to those of Aristotle's friend Euxitheus.* All these were in the habit of joking, and often started it off. The circumstance of having to defend yourself, on the other hand, both excuses and lends charm to the jest. So it was with Demosthenes' retort to the the suspected thief who made fun of his habit of writing all night: 'I realize that it is a trouble to you that I keep my lamp burning.' Or again: Demades cries out 'Demosthenes wants to put me right! It's a case of Athena and the pig!'* and Demosthenes retorts 'This Athena was caught in adultery last year.' Another neat retort was what Xenaenetus* said to the citizens who reproached him with running away when he was general: 'Well, it was with you, dear souls.' One must avoid going too far in the ridiculous, or giving pain to the audience unseasonably, or making oneself, as speaker, appear low and contemptible. This last mistake was made by Democrates, when he said, as he was going up to the Assembly, that, like the city, he had 'not much strength but a big puff'; and again, when he addressed the people in the crisis of Chaeronea, he began 'I wish the city was not in such dire straits as to make you ready to listen even to me.' This second remark marks the small man; the first is that of a lunatic. Neither is right for the politician. In Phocion, they admired also his conciseness. Polyeuctus used to say that Demosthenes was the greatest orator, Phocion the most forceful speaker, because his dicourse held the greatest amount of sense in the smallest number of words. Demosthenes indeed, though he despised the rest, used to say, when Phocion rose to speak, 'Here comes the chopper to chop up my speech.'

[8] Try, if possible, to address the people with a well-considered speech, meaningful and without slips. Pericles, you know, used to pray, before making a speech in the Assembly, that not so much as a word inappropriate to the situation should enter his mind. At the same time one needs a flexible and well-exercised technique of meeting objections. Situations move fast;
there are a lot of sudden emergencies in politics. Demosthenes, 804
so they say, was less good at this than many others, because he tended to hesitate and hold back at crucial moments. Alcibiades, according to Theophrastus, thought carefully about what to say and how to say it, and often fished for words and tried to put his phrases together as he was actually speaking, so that he hesitated and was lost. But it is the man who rises to speak under the pressure of the moment who most affects his audience, wins them over and changes their hearts. Leon of Byzantium* arrived once to speak to the Athenians when they were in political turmoil. They laughed to see such a small man named 'lion'. 'I wonder what you'd say', he retorted, 'if you saw my wife; she barely comes up to my knee.' More laughter. 'None the less,' he went on, 'small as we are, Byzantium isn't big enough for us when we quarrel.' The orator Pytheas was once speaking against honours offered to Alexander, when someone interrupted him by saying, 'How can a young man like you dare to speak about such important matters?' 'Well,' he replied, 'Alexander, whom you propose to make a god, is younger than I am.'

The struggles of politics are not easy, they take all one's fighting strength: so the power of speech you bring into the fray must be thoroughly trained for healthiness of voice and strength of lungs, so that it doesn't faint or fail or let itself be beaten by some

> 'screaming robber, roaring like a waterfall'.[1]

Cato, if he thought it impossible to persuade Senate or people, because they were already prejudiced by favour or interest, used to rise and speak all through the day, and so get the question postponed.

These indications should suffice for a competent person to draw further conclusions for himself regarding the preparation and use of speech.

[10] There are two approaches, two roads, to public life. One is quick, splendid from the point of view of reputation, but not without its dangers. The other is slower, more pedestrian, but safer. Some plunge into politics straight off the cliff-top, as it were, of some great and famous but daring deed. They believe in the truth of Pindar's words:

> at a work's beginning, set
> a front that shines afar.[2]

The mass of the people are actually readier to accept a beginner, because they have had their fill and are weary of the familiar figures. It is the same with audiences and actors. Power and authority that have had a quick and brilliant rise put envy quite out of countenance. As Ariston said, fire produces no smoke and fame no envy if it flares up suddenly and quickly; it is those who grow slowly or step by step who find themselves attacked from various quarters. This is why many fade away before they come into bloom on the platform. But if, as men say of the sprinter Ladas,* 'the crack of the starting-rope still rings in his ears'[3] while he is being presented with the crown for some distinguished embassy or triumph or military command, then envy and contempt have no power over him. That is how Aratus won his reputation, by making the deposition of the tyrant Nicocles the first achievement of his career, and Alcibiades by arraying the Mantinean alliance against the Lacedaemonians. Pompey

expected a triumph before he was ever in the Senate; Sulla refused it him, but gave way when Pompey retorted that 'more people worship the rising sun than the setting.' It was no ordinary circumstance that made the Romans elect Cornelius Scipio consul, against the provisions of the law,* when he was only a candidate for the aedileship; they had admired his single combat 805
and victory in Spain as a lad, and later his actions as a military tribune at Carthage, which made the elder Cato exclaim 'he alone has a mind, the rest but flit like shadows.'[1]

These days, however, when the state of our cities requires no leadership in war, no deposition of tyrants, no formation of alliances, what starting-point can one find for a distinguished and brilliant public career? Well, there are still public lawsuits and embassies to the emperor. These need a man of zeal, with a combination of boldness and good sense. It is open to us also to win support by reviving some of the good practices in our cities which have been neglected, or changing some things which have crept in through bad habits, to the shame or detriment of the city. There have been instances of men making a notable start in public life by the successful conduct of an important legal case, by loyal advocacy of the weak against a powerful adversary, or by plain speaking to a bad ruler in a just cause. Indeed, not a few owe their rise to enmities, having attacked persons whose position made them objects of envy and fear; in such cases, the influence of the vanquished passes to the victor, and a better reputation with it. On the other hand, there is no honour, and no expediency, in making a malicious attack on a good man who owes his leading position to his own good qualities, as Simmias attacked Pericles, Alcmaeon* Themistocles, Clodius Pompey, or the orator Meneclides Epaminondas. This is because, when the people have treated a good man wrongly, and then (as soon happens with anger) repented of it, they very rightly think that the easiest defence is to crush the man who persuaded them in the first place. By contrast, it makes a brilliant opening-scene for the drama of your political life if you can rise up and destroy and humiliate a wicked man who has got the city in his clutches through his reckless audacity and cunning, like Cleon and Cleophon at Athens. I know, of course, that some, like Ephialtes at Athens or Phormio at Elis, have attained influence and fame by curtailing the power of an oppressive oligarchic Council; but this is a very dangerous thing for one beginning his career. Solon made a better start. Finding the community divided into three factions—Mountain, Plain, and Coast, as they were called—he joined none of them, but, by remaining impartial and working for concord in all his actions and speeches, got himself chosen as lawgiver to effect a reconciliation, and so established his rule.

Such are the different ways in which a distinguished entry on to the public stage may be achieved.

[11] Many famous men, however, have chosen the safe and slow way: Aristides, Phocion, Pammenes of Thebes, Lucullus and Cato at Rome, Agesilaus at Sparta. Each one of these, as a young unknown, attached himself to an older man of repute, like ivy that entwines itself round a strong tree and grows with it. They were gradually raised by the older men's influence, shared its development, and so rooted themselves firmly in the political world. Aristides was brought on by Clisthenes, Phocion by Chabrias, Lucullus by Sulla, Cato by Fabius Maximus, Pammenes by Epaminondas, Agesilaus by Lysander. Agesilaus, however, later violently rejected his political mentor because of Lysander's reputation for untimely ambition and jealousy. The others continued to the end in an honourable and statesmanlike
806 spirit to respect their teachers, and indeed to add to their glory, enhancing and illuminating by their efforts the source of their own brilliance, as objects that face the sun reflect its light. Scipio's detractors actually called him the actor, and his friend Laelius the author of the play; but none of this made Laelius conceited, and he remained consistently anxious to promote Scipio's achievements and reputation. Pompey's friend Afranius, though of humble origin, expected to be made consul; but when Pompey supported others, he gave up his ambitions, saying that the distinction he would have by gaining the consulship was less than the pain and trouble it would give him if he had it without Pompey's help and approval. He waited a year, no more, and then achieved the office without losing the friendship. Those who have others to hold their hand on their way to fame can both win the favour of the masses and be less actively disliked if anything troublesome occurs. This is why Philip

advised Alexander to win friends while he could, while another king was on the throne, by treating people generously and being their friend.

[12] The beginner in politics should choose as a guide not simply the man who has power and reputation, but one who has achieved these things by his goodness. Not every tree will welcome or bear the vine that twines around it; some choke and destroy the growth. So also in politics: those who love honours and power, but have no real love of the good, do not sacrifice opportunities of action in favour of young men; they prefer, out of envy, to crush them and make them wither away, because they regard them as stealing from them their own food of glory. Marius owed many successes to Sulla, in Libya and again in Gaul, but he then ceased to employ him. The real reason for this was that he was angry at Sulla's rise, but the pretext was his signet-ring: for Sulla, when quaestor under Marius in Libya,* had been sent by him to Bocchus and brought back Jugurtha as a prisoner, and, being an ambitious young man enjoying his first taste of fame, did not bear his good fortune very modestly, but had a representation of Jugurtha's surrender engraved on the signet-ring he wore. This was the thing Marius complained of when he threw him aside. Sulla therefore went over to Marius' opponents, the excellent Catulus and Metellus, and soon succeeded in expelling and deposing Marius, in the civil war, when the latter had come near to ruining Rome altogether. Sulla himself, on the other hand, helped young Pompey to rise in the world, standing up and uncovering his head when he approached, and gave other young men opportunities for command, sometimes even encouraging the reluctant; by which means he inspired his armies with ambition and enthusiasm. He mastered them all by wanting to rule alone but to be the first and greatest among many great men. These are the men to fasten on to and hold tight, not in order to steal their fame—like the wren in Aesop* who was carried on the eagle's shoulder and suddenly flew off and raced the eagle—but to accept it from them in a friendly and benevolent spirit. As Plato tells us, no one can rule who has not first served well.[1]

[13] Connected with this is the decision that has to be made about one's friends. This should not accord either with

Themistocles' principle or with Cleon's. Cleon, when he first decided to enter politics, called his friends together and broke off his friendship with them, on the ground that friendship often distorts or emasculates right and just policies. He would have done better to put aside the greed and aggressiveness in his own
807 personality, and purge himself of envy and malice. Cities don't need men who have no friends or companions; they need men of good, sound character. But, as it was, Cleon drove out his friends, 'and a hundred wheedling heads (confound them!) licked and fawned upon him,'[1] as the comic poets say. Harsh and oppressive to the better people, he submitted to the many to gain their favour, 'taking the old man's arm and offering wages',[2] and making the worst and most corrupt elements of the people his allies against the aristocracy. Themistocles took the opposite line. When someone said to him that he would do well in government if he treated all men equally, he replied: 'May I never sit on any bench where my friends have no advantage over those who are not my friends!' But he was no more right than the other; it was wrong to mortgage policy to friendship, and to subordinate the common good to private favours and interests. Yet when Simonides made an improper request of him, he answered: 'A poet is no good if he sings out of tune, and a ruler is not fair if he grants favours contrary to the law.'

The helmsman chooses his sailors, the captain chooses the helmsman,

> well-skilled to hold the tiller at the stern,
> and make the yard-arm fast as the wind rises.[3]

The architect chooses the assistants and craftsmen who collaborate best in the work, not ruin it. So it would be a terrible paradox if the statesman, whom Pindar calls 'craftsman supreme',[4] a maker of good government and justice, is not to choose like-minded friends to serve and share his zeal for the good, but always different persons who bend him, forcibly and unjustly, to serve their different ends. He will seem just like a builder or a carpenter who ignorantly or mistakenly uses squares and rules and plummets which are going to distort his work. Friends are the living, thinking tools of the statesman. One must not take a tumble with them when they transgress, but

take steps to ensure they don't go wrong without one's knowing about it. This is what disgraced and discredited Solon with his fellow citizens. Having formed the plan of alleviating debt and introducing his 'unburdening' (a euphemism for cancellation of debts), he communicated his intention to his friends, who then behaved very wrongly. They stepped in to borrow large sums, and then, when the law was made public shortly afterwards, they were found to be in possession of splendid houses and land purchased with the money they had borrowed. Solon was accused of being their accomplice, though in fact he was their victim. Agesilaus, too, was at his weakest and feeblest in dealing with his friends' interests. Like Pegasus in Euripides, he 'crouched and cowered the more, the more he wanted'.[5] His excessive eagerness to help in their misfortunes made him seem as bad as they were. For example, he rescued Phoebidas, who was on trial for having seized the Cadmea without orders, by saying that such things had to be done on the spur of the moment. He also organized the escape of Sphodrias, who was charged with a particularly heinous breach of the law (he had invaded Attica, Athens being at the time a friendly ally), because his resolve was broken by the pleas of his own son, who was Sphodrias' lover. Again, there is recorded a letter from
Agesilaus to a tyrant, which runs thus: 'If Nicias is not guilty, 808
let him go; if he is, let him go for my sake. In any case, let him go.' Phocion, on the other hand, did not even go into court to support his son-in-law Chariclus, who faced a charge arising out of the Harpalus scandal. He merely said 'I made you my kinsman for all honest ends,' and went his way. Timoleon of Corinth, finding himself unable, despite all his arguments and pleas, to dissuade his brother from making himself tyrant, collaborated with his assassins. One's obligation, in fact, is not, as Pericles put it, to be 'a friend as far as the altar'—that is, not committing perjury—but to be a friend as far as law, justice, and expediency allow; neglect of this rule leads to great damage even to the public cause, as in the failure to punish Sphodrias and Phoebidas, for these were the people mainly responsible for plunging Sparta into the war of Leuctra. Political principle does not, indeed, oblige one to come down heavily on a friend's minor offences; rather, it allows one, once the main public

interest is secured, to use the balance, as it were, to help and support friends, and labour on their behalf. There are also favours which do not arouse resentment: to help a friend for preference in an election or to put him in the way of an honourable administrative appointment, or a mission of good will, such as conveying honorific messages to the emperor, or making an approach to another city for friendship and concord. If the task, however great and glorious, also involves much trouble, one should appoint oneself to do it first, and then choose a friend, as Diomedes did:*

> if you command me now to choose a friend,
> how could I not think of divine Odysseus?[1]

Odysseus then returns the compliment:

> These Thracian horses, sir, of which you ask,
> are lately come; brave Diomede slew their master,
> him and his twelve companions, all good men.[2]

Giving way to friends like this does as much credit to the giver of praise as to the recipient. Self-centredness, as Plato says,[3] shares a lodging with loneliness. Again, you should associate your friends with your honourable and generous actions, and teach the beneficiaries of these to praise and respect them. Dishonest or unreasonable requests are to be gently deflected, not harshly, and it should be pointed out, by way of softening the blow, that the request was unworthy of the asker's character and reputation. Epaminondas was a master of this art. When Pelopidas asked him to release the shopkeeper from prison, he refused; but when his mistress asked him, he complied. 'Favours like this', he explained, 'may be properly received by a mistress, but not by a general.' Cato, on the other hand, behaved in a heavy-handed, arrogant way, when his close friend and associate, the censor Catulus, asked pardon for a person convicted in Cato's quaestorship. 'It is a disgrace', said Cato, 'for you, whose duty it is to keep us young men in order, to be thrown out of the room by our servants.' He could perfectly well have denied the actual favour while dispensing with the harshness and roughness of his language; that would have made the point that he was not causing pain by his action deliberately, but only out of necessity, because of law and justice.

There are also honourable ways of giving financial help to friends in need through one's public position. Themistocles, after the battle,* saw a corpse wearing a gold collar and necklace. 'Pick that up,' he said, turning to a friend, 'you're not a 809
Themistocles.' Circumstances often provide the politician with such opportunities of helping friends. Not everyone is a Menemachus! Give one man a well-paid brief in a good cause; introduce another to a rich man who needs management services and legal protection; help another to get this contract or that profitable lease. Epaminondas once advised a friend to ask a rich man for a talent, and said he would himself advise the other to give it. The rich man came and asked why he had received the request. 'Because he is poor but honest,' said Epaminondas, 'and you are richer because you have robbed the city of so much.' Xenophon reports that Agesilaus also took pride in making his friends rich, though he himself was above money.[1]

[14] 'Every lark must have its crest,' says Simonides;[2] and every public career involves enmities and quarrels, and this too is a subject to which the politician must pay special attention. Many people approve of Themistocles and Aristides, who laid aside their enmity at the frontier, whenever they went abroad on a diplomatic mission or a campaign, and took it up again on their return. Some too think very well of the action of Cretines of Magnesia, a political rival of Hermias, who was an ambitious and pretentious person of no great capacity. Then came the war with Mithridates. Cretines saw the peril to the city, and urged Hermias to take office and deal with the situation; he himself would stand aside; but if Hermias wanted him to command, he should remove himself, lest their rivalry should ruin the city. Hermias liked this challenge. He declared Cretines the better soldier, and withdrew with his wife and children. Cretines escorted him to the frontier, and provided him, out of his own resources, with means more suitable to an exile than to a man in a besieged city. He then conducted the war admirably, and brought the city through, against all hope, from the very brink of disaster. If it is a noble and proud thing to say 'I love my children, but my country more,'[3] would it not be easier for everyone to say 'I hate that man, and I want to hurt him, but I love my country more'? It is surely a savage and barbarous attitude to refuse a reconciliation with an enemy for reasons for which it is right to abandon a friend! Phocion and Cato did better; allowing no personal hostility to enter into their political differences, they confined their unremitting championship of the expedient to public affairs; on the private level, they treated their political opponents with humanity and without rancour. One should never regard a fellow citizen as an enemy, unless some Aristion or Nabis or Catiline springs up to infest and plague the city. Performers who are simply giving the wrong note can be brought into tune by the musician, as it were, by gently loosening or tightening the strings—not attacking the offender angrily and rudely, but with an appeal to his better feelings, as in Homer's lines:

> Dear friend, I thought you wiser than the rest,[4]

and

> You know a better thought to tell than this.[5]

And if people say or do something good, you should not feel annoyed by honours given them, or spare fair words for fair deeds. This will ensure that blame is believed when it should be, and that we make them quarrel with vice by magnifying virtue, and comparing one course of conduct with the other as being
810 worthier and more appropriate for them. For my own part, I think that the politician should actually bear just witness on behalf of his opponents, defend them against prosecution by informers, and not give credence to charges which are alien to their general character. Nero, not long before he killed Thrasea, whom he both hated and feared, nevertheless, when someone accused Thrasea of an unjust judgement, said 'I only wish Thrasea was as fond of me as he is outstanding as a judge.' If you need to reprove a person whose defects of character make him prone to bad conduct, it is no bad thing to remind him of an enemy who has a better nature, and say 'So-and-so wouldn't have said or done that.' Some, again, should be reminded of their father's qualities, when they go astray: 'Tydeus begot a son unlike himself!'[1] Appius, contesting an election* against Scipio Africanus, exclaimed 'How you must be groaning in your grave, Paulus, to see your son attended by Philonicus the

publican as he canvasses for the censorship!' Such remarks both set the offender right and do honour to the critic. Nestor in Sophocles makes a statesmanlike reply to Ajax' abuse: 'I blame you not: you do well, but speak ill.'[2] And Cato, having quarrelled with Pompey over the violence which the latter had done to the city in collaboration with Caesar, later, when they went to war, recommended giving the supreme command to Pompey, on the ground that it takes the same abilities to put an end to great evils as to cause them. A mixture of praise and blame, frank but not rude, exciting not resentment but simply a sense of guilt and repentance, seems kindly and therapeutic. Abuse, on the other hand, is not at all seemly in a politician. Think of what Demosthenes said about Aeschines, or Aeschines about Demosthenes, or Hyperides about Demades: would Solon or Pericles or the Spartan Lycurgus or Pittacus of Lesbos have said such things? Yet it is only in his forensic pleading that Demosthenes employs abuse. The *Philippics* are entirely free of jest and rude humour, because such things shame the speaker more than the audience; they also muddle the issues and throw Council or Assembly into confusion. Phocion was quite right: he had stopped and given way to an abusive speaker, but came forward again when the man had at last finished, and said 'You have heard about the cavalry and the hoplites; it remains for me to tell you about the light infantry and the peltasts.' But, since many people find it hard to restrain themselves in these things, and abuse is often gagged by an apt retort, this retort should be brief, and not marked by anger or rancour but by good temper, inserting its sting with wit and humour. These requirements are best met by retorts that reverse the original remark. When a missile rebounds against the thrower, this happens, presumably, because the strength and solidity of the target deflects it back. Similarly, the word that has been spoken is likely to rebound against the insulter, because of the strength and intelligence of his victim. Callistratus reproached the Thebans with Oedipus' parricide, and the Argives with Orestes' matricide. Epaminondas' retort* was to say 'We threw the guilty out; you gave them asylum.'
When an Athenian said to the Spartan Antalcidas, 'We often 811
chased you away from the Cephissus', Antalcidas replied, 'We never chased you away from the Eurotas.' Demades yelled at

Phocion 'The Athenians will kill you'; Phocion answered 'They will, if they're mad; if they're sane, they'll kill you.' Domitius said to the orator Crassus, 'Didn't you weep when the moray died that you were keeping in your fish-pond?', and Crassus retorted, 'Didn't you have dry eyes when you buried your three wives?' These things have a certain use in life generally!

[15] As to political life, some, like Cato, plunge into every department, believing that the good citizen, so far as he can, should neglect no subject of concern or attention. They approve Epaminondas, who took trouble to perform the duties of telearch, to which office the Thebans had maliciously and insultingly appointed him. He argued that it is not only the office that proves the man but the man that proves the office, and he thus raised the telearchy to a position of splendour and dignity, whereas it had previously been nothing but a certain responsibility for the disposal of garbage in the streets and the diversion of watercourses. Visitors no doubt laugh at me when they see me (as they often do) engaged in such matters in public. Antisthenes' famous remark then comes to my aid. When someone expressed surprise that he was carrying some dried fish through the market-place himself, he replied 'Well, it's for myself.'[1] My position is the contrary of this. When they reproach me with personally supervising the checking of tiles and the delivery of cement or stones, I reply 'Well, I'm not building this for myself, but for the city.' In many other causes, of course, one would be mean and petty-minded to organize things for oneself and be one's own manager; but if it is in the public cause, and for the city's sake, one does not demean oneself—indeed, care and zeal are all the more impressive when they extend to details. Some people, however, (Critolaus the Peripatetic is one) hold Pericles' attitude to be grander and more dignified: he expected the city to employ him only on the most important and significant tasks, just as the *Salaminia* and the *Paralus*, the two state galleys, were sent to sea only on vital and important missions. One thinks of the ruler of the universe:

> God handles the large actions, but the small
> he leaves to Fortune,

as Euripides says.[2] Nor can I approve Theagenes' obsession with honour and victory. Victor of the entire festival circuit, and of many competitions besides, not only in the pancration, but in boxing and long-distance running, he was once present at a festival at the grave of a hero; everyone was given their portion of the feast, as the custom was, and then Theagenes jumped up and challenged them all at the pancration, because he would not let anyone else win while he was present. By this means, he collected 1,200 victory crowns, most of which might be considered mere rubbish. Well, people who strip for every possible political action are like that. They soon make the people tired of them, they are a bore and an object of envy if they succeed, and of malicious gloating if they fail, and all the admiration that was felt for them when they took over the job turns to mockery and ridicule:

> Metiochus commands the army,
> Metiochus the roads;
> Metiochus inspects the bread,
> Metiochus the flour;
> Metiochus cures all our ills;
> Metiochus be damned![3]

This Metiochus was a friend of Pericles who apparently used the influence which that connection gave him in a manner calculated to produce envy and disgust. There is a saying that the politician should treat the people as his lover, and create in them a longing for him in his absence. Scipio Africanus achieved this by staying a long time on his farm, thereby reducing the weight 812
of envy and giving a respite to those who felt oppressed by his reputation. Timesias of Clazomenae, an admirable public figure in most respects, remained unaware of the jealousy and dislike he had incurred by insisting on taking everything on himself, until the following incident happened. There were some boys playing the game of knocking a knuckle-bone out of a hole in the road, when Timesias passed by. They all declared the bone was still in the hole, except the boy who had knocked it out, and he said 'I wish I could knock out Timesias' brains as well as that bone's been knocked out!' Timesias overheard, and so realized how universal was the ill-feeling against him. He went home and told his wife, and then ordered her to pack up and follow

him. He marched straight from his own door out of town. Something of the same kind seems to have happened also to Themistocles, at the hands of the Athenians; but his response was only 'My dear friends, are you tired of having it so good?' Some of these reactions are commendable, others not. You must never be lacking, of course, in care and concern for all public matters; you must attend to everything and understand everything, and not just stay on the side—like the emergency anchor of a ship—waiting for desperate crises or disasters. But helmsmen do only some things with their own hands—there are other manœuvres where they sit at a distance and direct the ship by means of various instruments handled by other people. They make use of sailors, look-outs, and boatswains, and often call some of these to the stern and entrust them with the steering. It is like that with the politician: he should allow others to hold office, and invite them on to the platform in a kindly and generous spirit, not doing all the city's business by his own words, proposals, and actions, but having loyal and able helpers, and assigning each his task according to his ability. Pericles employed Menippus in his army commands, used Ephialtes to humiliate the Areopagus, passed the Megarian decree in Charinus' name, and sent Lampon to found the colony of Thurii. When power appears to be divided, not only does its extent arouse envy less, but the needs of the moment are better fulfilled. The division of the hand into fingers does not reduce its usefulness but makes it the instrument of our skills; and, similarly, the person who gives over a share of his political activity to others adds effectiveness to it by the very act of sharing. On the other hand, anyone whose insatiable appetite for power or prestige leads him to concentrate the whole political scene on himself, and force himself to attempt things for which he has no ability and no training—like Cleon trying to be a general, or Philopoemen an admiral or Hannibal an orator—has no excuse if he fails.* He is addressed in the words of Euripides:

> you are a carpenter, yet what you did
> was certainly not woodwork.[1]

You are an unconvincing speaker, yet you went as ambassador; you are lazy, yet you tried to be manager; you are not numerate,

yet you tried to be treasurer; you are old and weak, yet you took command of the army. Pericles divided his power with Cimon, himself ruling at home and Cimon manning the ships to fight the barbarian; the one had greater gifts for politics, the other for war. Men think well also of Eubulus of Anaphlystus, because, trusted and influential as he was, he nevertheless made no attempt to conduct foreign policy or to command in the field, but took charge of the finances and increased the state revenues, thereby doing the city a great deal of good. Iphicrates, on the other hand, was ridiculed for practising speeches at home in the presence of an audience; for even if he had been a good speaker 813
rather than a bad one, he ought to have been content with his military reputation and left the school to the sophists.*

[16] In a democracy, politicians are always the object of malice and censoriousness. Many useful measures, even if they do not produce party strife or vocal opposition, are suspected of being the product of conspiracy. This greatly discredits clubs and friendships. Real enmities and differences must, of course, not be allowed to remain. (There was a Chian demagogue actually called Demos who triumphed in a revolution but would not allow his followers to exile all their opponents: 'we must be careful not to start quarrelling with our friends,' he explained, 'after getting rid of our enemies altogether.' That was silly of him.) But when the public has suspicions about some important measure which will save the situation, we must not all come forward, as if by prior arrangement, to make the same proposal. Two or three of our friends should quietly separate themselves from us and oppose the item, and then later claim to be convinced and change their minds. They will carry the people with them, because it will be thought that they are guided by their sense of the expedient. In small matters of little consequence, on the other hand, it is a good idea to let one's friends have genuine differences of opinion, each with his own arguments, so that their consensus for good in matters of moment and significance does not appear to have been preconcerted.

[17] The statesman is the natural ruler of the city at all times, the king-bee in the hive. He must have this constantly in mind as he keeps his hold on public affairs. 'Powers' and elective offices are not to be pursued too often or too anxiously, for love of office is neither dignified nor popular. But neither are they to be rejected, if the people offers an office legally and invites you to accept it. Even offices which are beneath your position should be welcomed and made a source of pride. It is only fair that men honoured by great office should in turn lend their honour to lesser ones, and prove themselves modest enough to sacrifice some of the grandeur of such offices as the generalship at Athens, the presidency at Rhodes, or our post of boeotarch, and lend respectability and weight to positions of less importance. The object is to avoid being despised in the lesser offices, and to avoid being envied in the greater ones. When you enter into any office, you must, of course, bring to the front of your mind the thoughts of which Pericles reminded himself whenever he put on his general's cloak: 'Be careful, Pericles: you are in command of free men, of Greeks, of your fellow Athenians.' But there is another thing too which you must say to yourself: 'You are in command, but you are under command; you rule a city subject to proconsuls, to Caesar's procurators.* There are no "lances of the plains",[1] this is not ancient Sardis, or the historic power of Lydia.' Make your cloak more modest, look at the orator's platform from the standpoint of the governor's office, don't attach much pride to your crown, or trust in it: you can see his boots above your head! Take a hint from the actors, who put their own emotion and character and reputation into the play, but obey the prompter, and never go beyond the rhythms and measures of the power allowed by the superior authority. On our stage, failure doesn't just lead to hissing and hooting and catcalling: many have found themselves underneath 'the punishing axe, sharp severer of the neck',[2] like your friend Pardalas and his party, when they forgot the permitted limits. And there was the other man, a castaway on an island,

> a Pholegandrian now or Sicinetan,*
> 814 not an Athenian, now he's changed his country[1]

as Solon has it. When we see little children trying to put on their father's shoes or garlands for fun, we laugh. Now there are magistrates in our cities foolish enough to recommend the people to imitate the deeds and spirit and actions of their forefathers, which are quite out of proportion to their present times and circumstances. They rouse the mob like this; but their ridiculous performance has consequences for them which are not at all ridiculous, unless they are lucky enough to be completely despised. There are plenty of episodes in the history of the ancient Greeks which can be told in order to form the character and control the passions of the men of our own day. At Athens, it is not the history of wars which is now needed, but, for example, the vote of amnesty* following the usurpation of the Thirty, or the fine imposed on Phrynichus for producing a tragedy* about the capture of Miletus, or the story that the citizens wore garlands to celebrate Cassander's founding Thebes,* but ordered a purification of the Assembly on receipt of the news of the 'clubbing' at Argos,* in which the Argives massacred 1,500 of their own people. Or again, one might recall that, when they were searching houses at the time of the Harpalus scandal, they deliberately passed over the house of the newly married couple. These are ways in which we can still imitate our ancestors today. But Marathon and Eurymedon and Plataea, and all the historical instances that make the masses swell with false pride and flaunt themselves about nothing, are best left behind in the sophists' classrooms.

[**18**] It is not enough to keep oneself and one's city blameless in the eyes of our rulers: one should always have a friend among the really powerful people up there, as a secure prop for one's policy. The Romans themselves are very keen to support their friends' political interests. One can also reap a fine harvest from the friendship of the great, as did Polybius and Panaetius, who did great good to the prosperity of their native countries through Scipio's goodwill towards them. Think too of Arius: Octavian had him at his side as he entered Alexandria* as its captor, and conversed with none other of his friends. The Alexandrians expected a terrible fate, and came to plead their cause. Octavian answered that he wished to be reconciled with them, because of the greatness of their city, their foundation by Alexander, and 'thirdly,' he added, 'as a favour to my friend here'. Can there be any comparison between this favour and the lucrative procuratorships and governorships of provinces, in pursuit of which so many neglect affairs at home and grow old in other men's waiting-rooms? Perhaps we should adapt the lines of Euripides,*

and proclaim that, if it is ever right to lose sleep and frequent courts and submit to the familiarity of princes, 'It were best' to do so for one's country's sake, and 'otherwise' embrace and preserve friendships which are founded on fairness and equality.

[19] However, in ensuring that your country is obedient to the ruling power, there is no need to chain up your neck as well. Yet some do precisely this. They refer great matters and small alike to the governor, and so make our subject-status a reproach, or rather destroy the whole basis of our political life, reducing us to cowering, frightened impotence. Patients who never eat or take a bath without advice from the doctor are failing to use the gifts of nature to further their health; and likewise, those who submit every decision, meeting, piece of favour, or administrative action, to the judgement of the governor, are forcing our rulers to be our masters more than they themselves want. The
815 main cause of this is the greed and ambition of our leading men. Either they force lesser persons into exile by the damage they do to them, or they bring in the superior power because, in their disputes with one another, they cannot bear to take second place among their fellow citizens. In both cases, council, people, courts, and magistrates lose their power altogether. The proper course is to mollify ordinary citizens by treating them as equals, and the powerful by giving way to them in your turn; this will keep them all within the political community, and dissolve the difficulties. This is the statesman's cure for these hidden diseases, as we may call them. You should be readier yourself to lose a battle with your fellow citizens than to win by violence and the destruction of local rights; and you should plead with others too, and point out all the evils of contentiousness. And yet, as the world is, men take their quarrels, to their great shame and loss, to the advocate's door, and put them into their lawyer's hands, all in order to avoid making honourable and graceful concessions to their fellow citizens and fellow-tribesmen* at home, to their neighbours and their colleagues. If doctors cannot get rid of a disease altogether, they bring it out on the surface of the body; but if the statesman cannot keep his city entirely free of trouble, he will try to cure and control it by hiding the elements of disturbance and sedition within the city itself, so as not to need physicians or medicines from outside.

And, while his policy should concentrate on security and avoid the confusions and delusions of empty vanity, as we said, his disposition should have some pride about it, and

> that fighting spirit,
> unfearing, such as enters into men
> who fight the foe in their own land's defence[1]

and contend manfully with difficult circumstances and obstructive times. Don't raise a storm yourself, but don't run away when one blows up. Don't make perilous changes, but be sure to be at hand to help your city in trouble or in danger. Plain speaking is the emergency anchor, to be taken out of your store in great crises—like those which struck Pergamum in Nero's time,* or Rhodes more recently under Domitian, or Thessaly in the time of Augustus, when they burnt Petraeus alive. At such times 'you will not see' the true statesman 'sleeping'*[2] or taking cover or blaming others or putting himself out of the reach of danger. He accepts the mission, he puts out to sea, he not only begins by saying 'we, who killed him, have come: Apollo, avert the plague',[3] but accepts his share in the dangers, even if he has had no part personally in the people's offence. This is very noble; and not only is it noble, but admiration for the courage and spirit of a single individual has often been known to turn the edge of anger felt towards the whole community, and scatter the threatening cloud of terror and cruelty. This is what apparently happened to the Persian king in regard to the Spartans Boulis and Sperchis. Pompeius had similar feelings towards Sthennon,* when the latter said to him, as punishment was about to be meted out to the Mamertines for their revolt, that he would be wrong to punish many innocent people for the act of one guilty man: it was he himself, he said, who induced the city to revolt, persuading his friends, and compelling his enemies, to join. This confession so affected Pompeius that he spared the city, and treated Sthennon himself kindly. Sulla's friend, on the other hand, though just as good a man, died an honourable death
because he displayed his virtue to someone very different from 816
himself. After capturing Praeneste,* Sulla was going to massacre the whole population, sparing only this man because he was a friend. The man, however, declared that he didn't want to

owe his life to the murderer of his country. So he joined the rest, and was killed with them. Let us pray that such times do not come upon us, but if they do, expect a better outcome than this.

[20] Any office is a serious and sacred thing. The holder especially must respect it; and this respect lies in harmony and friendship with one's colleagues more than in any crowns or purple-edged cloaks. If people regard comradeship in the army or as students as a basis of friendship, but treat association with colleagues in the office of general or magistrate as a cause of enmity, they are bound to fall into one of three errors: if they think their colleagues are their equals, they are creating factions; if they think them their superiors, they are guilty of envy; if they think them below themselves, guilty of contempt. The right attitude is to serve your superior, advance your inferior, and honour your equal, remaining agreeable and friendly to all. These are not friends of the table or the cup, or indeed 'of the hearth', but friends by virtue of the popular vote, possessors, as it were, of a heritage of goodwill bequeathed by the fatherland. Scipio earned a bad reputation in Rome for failing to invite his colleague Mummius* to a banquet he held for his friends, to commemorate the consecration of the temple of Hercules. People expected them to show some signs of mutual respect and friendship on such an occasion, because of their office, even if they did not regard each other in general as friends. Now, if the omission of such a trivial courtesy raised a suspicion of haughtiness against a man so greatly admired on other grounds as Scipio, how can a man be thought fair and decent if he curtails a colleague's prestige, or is spiteful about generous actions, or so selfish as to take the credit for everything to himself and deprive his colleague? I remember that, as a young man, I was sent with a colleague on a mission to the proconsul. My colleague was left behind for some reason, and I had the interview alone and successfully concluded the business. When I returned home, and was about to make my final report, my father stood up and privately told me not to say 'I went' and 'I said', but 'we went' and 'we said', and in every way to associate my colleague with myself throughout the report. Not only is this fair and generous; it also removes from one's moment of glory anything that excites envy. This is why great men ascribe part of their success to destiny and fortune. Timoleon, for instance, who brought down the tyrannies in Sicily, built a temple to 'Automatia', or Chance. Python, admired and honoured at Athens for killing Cotys, said simply 'God did this, but he borrowed a hand from me.' King Theopompus of Sparta answered the man who said that Sparta was saved by her king's talent for government by saying that it was much more the result of the people's talent for obedience.

[21] These two qualities are interdependent. Most people, however, say and believe that the function of education in citizenship is to make us good subjects, because there are always more subjects than rulers in a city, and each of us, living in a democracy, holds office for a short time and is ruled for the rest of his life. Therefore (they say) the most honourable and useful thing to learn is obedience to those in government, even if they are inferior to oneself in influence and prestige. On the stage, a leading actor like Theodorus or Polus often appears as the attendant of the hired actor taking the third part, and addresses him in humble language, if it is he who wears the crown and carries the sceptre. So it is absurd, in real life, for the man of 817
wealth and standing to despise a poor, uneducated magistrate, and use his own position to insult and detract from the authority of the state, instead of using his influence (as he should) to bolster up and support the magistrate's office. In Sparta, the kings used to give way to the ephors, and any other Spartan they summoned would come running through the agora to show his fellow citizens his readiness to obey, taking pride in respecting the magistrates. How different from those ill-mannered and insensitive persons who flaunt their superfluous strength, as it were, by insulting umpires at the games, abusing producers at the Dionysia, and ridiculing generals and gymnasiarchs! These characters can have no knowledge or understanding of the fact that it is often more honourable to oneself to give respect than to receive it. It does greater credit to a man of great influence to be seen in attendance on a magistrate than to be attended or escorted by one. Indeed, the latter situation produces only envy and disgust, while the former brings the only true glory, that which comes from goodwill. By being seen at the magistrate's

door, or greeting him first, or giving him the middle place of honour when walking in public, you can improve the city's image without detracting from your own.

[22] It is democratic too to bear hard words and anger from a magistrate. One can say to oneself, with Diomedes, 'glory shall attend upon him',[1] or with Demosthenes, 'Now he is not only Demosthenes, but also a legislator, or a producer, or a crown-bearer.'[2] So put off revenge for the time being; we shall either attack him when his period of office is over, or at the very least profit from the disappearance of our anger while we are waiting!

[23] It is in zeal and forethought and concern for the common good that one needs to be always competing with every office-holder. If he is a good man, suggest the right measures, point them out to him, let him make use of a good idea and be praised for doing good to the community. If he is hesitant, procrastinating, or ill-disposed to the proposal, then you should come forward and address the people yourself, not stand aside or give up public concerns on the ground that it is wrong to interfere or run a second government beside his. The law always gives first place to the man who does right and recognizes the expedient. 'There was in the army one Xenophon, neither a general nor a captain',[3] but that man put himself in command and led the Greeks through to safety, thanks to his understanding of the need of the moment and his boldness in coming forward. And of all Philopoemen's achievements, the most outstanding was his initiative in going to rescue Messene,* with an enthusiastic band of volunteers but no official authority, when Nabis had seized the place and the Achaean general did not have the courage to send a relieving force. Such private enterprise, however, is not to be undertaken for trivial ends, but only in absolute necessity (as with Philopoemen) or for glory, as when Epaminondas illegally prolonged his tenure of office as boeotarch for four months,* in which time he invaded Laconia and established the situation at Messene. The point is that, if any accusation or complaint follows, we should have a plea of necessity to defend ourselves against the charge, and the greatness and splendour of the action as a justification of the risks taken.

[24] We read of a remark by the Thessalian monarch Jason,
818 who always used to say, when he was harassing people or taking

violent measures, 'One has to do wrong in small things if one wants to do right in great.' You see at once that this is the remark of a despot. A more citizen-like piece of advice would be to make small concessions in favour of the masses on condition of being able to oppose and prevent their errors in greater matters. Anyone who is always totally rigorous and extreme, never yielding or conceding anything, but consistently harsh and inexorable, gets the people into the habit of fractious opposition to his government. My advice is to 'let out the sheet a little when the waves rise high',[1] partly by relaxing and by joining in the popular amusements at sacrifices, games, and theatrical shows, for example; and partly by pretending to be blind and deaf to offences (as we do with our young people at home), so that the medicine of reproof and plain speaking does not lose its efficacy through too much use, but stays fresh and is still credible when the time comes to chide the masses and sting them hard over some serious question. Alexander was once told that his sister had had sexual relations with a handsome young man. Instead of showing anger, he merely observed that she too ought to be allowed some advantage from her royal position. This complaisance was wrong, and unworthy of an Alexander. Outrages like that should be thought of as the ruin of authority, not as a profit to be had from it. So far as possible, the politician will not let the people commit acts of outrage against fellow citizens—there will be no confiscation of property or distribution of public assets. He will resist, by all means of persuasion, instruction, and dire warning, the sort of desires that Cleon's friends nourished and encouraged, introducing thereby (as Plato has it) 'many a stinging drone'[2] into society. On the other hand, if the populace takes the opportunity of a traditional feast or festival of a god to propose some spectacle or modest distribution of funds, or some display of charity or generosity, then let them enjoy the fruits of their freedom and prosperity in this way. There are many examples of this in the careers of Pericles and Demetrius. Cimon beautified the agora by planting plane-trees and laying out walks. Cato, seeing the people stirred up by Caesar during the Catilinarian troubles and dangerously inclined to revolution, persuaded the Senate to vote distributions to the poor, and this gift halted the disturbances and ended the uprising. Doctors, after drawing off a large quantity of diseased blood, give the patient a little harmless food; and similarly, the politician, after removing some serious cause of disgrace or damage, quiets discontent and complaining by some small act of favour and generosity.

[25] It is also a good plan to divert interest to other useful ends. This was done by Demades, when he was in charge of the revenues of Athens. The Athenians were keen to send triremes to help the rebels against Alexander, and they ordered Demades to provide the moneys for this. 'You have the money', he replied, 'because I made it available for the Feast of Choes,* so that you could all have half a mina each. But if you prefer to spend it on this expedition, it is your own money: you decide how to use it.' They gave up the expedition so as not to lose their hand-out, and so Demades succeeded in removing a cause of dispute between Alexander and Athens. It often happens that one cannot prevent
819 an inexpedient move directly; some roundabout and circuitous method is then required. Phocion used such a device when ordered to invade Boeotia* at an inopportune time. He issued a proclamation ordering all men up to sixty to report for duty. The older men complained loudly, but Phocion had an answer: 'What's so dreadful about it? I shall be with you as general, and I'm eighty.' On this principle, we can put a stop to untimely embassies by recruiting numbers of unsuitable persons to them, to useless building-projects by asking for contributions, and to improper litigation by expecting the parties to attend in person and travel to the court. The proponents and advocates of such actions should be the first to be made to be involved in them; they will either opt out, and so be thought to destroy the proposal themselves, or else go along and take their share of the unpleasantness.

[26] When what is to be done is important and useful, but also involving much controversy and effort, try to choose your most powerful friends, and among these choose the best-tempered. They will help most, and hinder least; they will be sensible, but not aggressive. You need also to understand your own capacity, and so choose people who are more competent in things where you are not so strong, rather than people like yourself. Thus Diomedes passed over the brave* and chose the man of sense to go with him on the spying mission. When those involved pride themselves on different excellences and capabilities, their achievements are more in balance, and mutual rivalries do not arise. So, if you are not a competent speaker yourself, choose the practised orator as your colleague in the case or on the embassy, as Pelopidas chose Epaminondas. If you are high and mighty, and find it hard to be convincing to the mass of the people, like Callicratidas,* choose a conciliatory and gracious companion. If you are physically feeble and incapable of much exertion, choose a man of vigour and endurance, as Nicias chose Lamachus.* There is no reason to envy Geryon for his many legs and arms and hands and eyes, even if he did control them all with a single mind; politicians, if they are of one mind, can make not only bodies or resources, but circumstances, capacities, and virtues of all kinds contribute to a single purpose, and so all win fame by different means in the course of a single enterprise. They do not have to be like the Argonauts,* who, having left Heracles behind, were then obliged to go by way of the women's quarters and submit to charms and drugs in order to save themselves and steal the fleece.

In some temples, it is the custom to leave your gold outside when you go in; and iron is practically never taken into any temple. Now the speaker's platform is in effect the common shrine of Zeus of Good Counsel, Zeus of the City, Themis, and Justice: so, the moment you are there, strip off your love of riches and money—it is but rusty iron, a sickness of the soul—throw it away in the market-places, among the shopkeepers and money-lenders, and 'turn away yourself'.[1] A man who makes profit out of public life should be regarded as a thief who steals from temples, tombs, and friends, by treachery or by false witness—a faithless adviser, a perjured judge, and a corrupt official; there is no wickedness from which he is free. There is no need to elaborate.

[27] Love of honour, though grander than love of gain, is no less a plague in politics. It involves a higher degree of boldness, and is found in vigorous and energetic characters rather than in the inactive or unambitious. The tide of popular favour, sweeping it along on the crest of a wave of praise, often makes 820
it unmanageable and uncontrollable. Plato says[1] that young

people should be told in childhood that they ought not to wear gold on their persons or keep it as a possession, because they have their own gold in their souls. He was, I imagine, speaking enigmatically of the inherited virtue that comes into our natural endowment. We should restrain our love of honour on this principle. Let us say that we have our own honour within ourselves, pure, uncorrupted, untouched by malice or blame, and developing with our reasoned evaluation and observation of our own actions and policies. We do not need paintings or models or bronze images of our honours, for the fame of these belongs to others, not to us. It is not the man for whom the *Trumpeter* or the *Doryphorus** was made who gets the praise for it, but the artist. When Rome was filling up with statues, Cato forbade one to be made of him. 'I would rather people asked why there was not one of me', he said, 'than why there was.' Indeed, these things arouse envy. The mass of the people think that they owe a favour to those who have not received such rewards, whereas those who have are a burden to them, because they seem to demand these things as wages for services rendered. If a man sails beyond Syrtis* but is wrecked in the crossing, he has done nothing remarkable; and likewise, if a man keeps the treasury or the office of public contracts safe and secure, but comes to grief as chairman or president, he is shipwrecked on a high cliff, to be sure, but he's in the water all the same. The best man is the one who asks for none of these things, and indeed avoids and declines them. If it proves difficult to reject a favour or expression of goodwill on the part of an enthusiastic people, then, if we view the political race as one whose prizes are not silver or rich gifts but the crown that belongs to a truly sacred contest, we shall be content with an inscription or a tablet or a decree—or even a green branch, such as Epimenides* was given from the Acropolis for purifying Athens. Anaxagoras, in refusing the honours offered to him, asked that the day of his death should be a holiday for schoolchildren. The privilege given to the seven Persians who killed the Magi* and to their descendants was that of wearing their head-dress with the ends attached to the head in front; this had been the signal they displayed, it appears, when they went into action. There is something democratic even in an honour accepted by Pittacus: he was invited to take as much as he chose of the territory he had won for his fellow citizens, and he took only just so much as the area he could reach with a throw of his javelin. Publius the Roman* similarly took the land he could plough round in a single day–and he was lame. An honour should be a symbol of achievement, not a reward, if it is to abide, like these, for long time to come. Of the 300 statues erected to honour Demetrius of Phalerum, not one ever became rusty or encrusted with dirt, because they were all pulled down in his own lifetime. Demades' statues were actually recast as chamber-pots.* Many honours have ended in some such way, becoming objects of disgust not only because of the faults of the recipient, but because the gift was excessive. Inexpensiveness is the best and most secure preservative of an honour; ambitious, excessive, and oppressive honours, like top-heavy statues, are soon overturned.

[28] In this context, I use the word 'honours' for things to which the many (I quote Empedocles)

> give not the name they should, but I myself
> follow their custom.[2]

True honour, true favour, that dwells in the goodwill and disposition of those who remember, is something the statesman will never disdain. Nor will he disregard reputation by avoiding 821
'pleasing the neighbours', as Democritus advised.[1] Huntsmen and horse-breeders do not reject the friendly greeting of their dogs and the affection of their horses; it is both pleasant and useful to induce in the animals with which one lives and associates feelings like those which Lysimachus' dog displayed towards him, or Achilles' horses* to Patroclus, as Homer tells us.[2] I am sure bees would do better if they were as ready to be friendly and welcoming to bee-keepers as they are to sting and irritate them. As it is, we control our bees with smoke, and lead unruly horses or runaway dogs by the force of bit or collar; but to make a human being gentle and amenable to another human being of his own free will, nothing avails except confidence in one's goodwill and a reputation for honour and justice. Demosthenes was right to describe distrust as a city's greatest protection against tyrants,[3] for it is the part of ourselves with which we feel trust that is most vulnerable. Cassandra had no reputation, and that is why her prophecies did her people no good:

> God made me prophesy to no avail,
> and when men suffer and are deep in trouble
> they call me wise—till then, a madwoman.[4]

Popular confidence in Archytas and goodwill towards Battus, due to the reputation they bore, greatly benefited those who sought their advice. Indeed, the first and greatest benefit of a politician's reputation is the trust that gives him access to public life. The second benefit is that popular goodwill is a good man's weapon against slander and wickedness; like the mother in Homer who 'flicks flies off baby, as he sweetly sleeps',[5] this goodwill wards off malice, and puts the man of humble origin on equal terms with the nobleman, the poor with the rich, the private individual with the ruler. In a word, so long as sincerity and virtue are there too, this gives a fair and steady wind to waft you over the sea of politics.

Consider the contrary disposition, as seen in the following examples.

Dionysius' children and wife were raped and killed by the Italians, and their bodies burnt and the ashes thrown overboard and scattered in the sea. But when Menander, the good king of Bactria, was killed in war, the cities of his kingdom joined to perform the funeral ceremonies but quarrelled about the possession of his remains, finally agreeing to divide the ashes equally, each city to have its own memorial to him.

The citizens of Acragas, having rid themselves of Phalaris, voted that no one should henceforth wear a blue-grey cloak, because that was the colour worn by the tyrant's attendants. The Persians, on the other hand, still love hook-noses and think them the height of beauty, for no other reason than that King Cyrus had a hooked nose.

[29] Thus the love of cities and peoples for individuals on account of their virtue is the strongest and most divine love of all, while the spurious and insincere honours that come from theatrical performances, distributions of money, or gladiatorial shows are nothing but the meretricious flattery of the mob, conferring the smile of an ephemeral and insecure reputation on anyone who at any time gives it presents or grants it favours. It
822 has been well said that the first overthrow of democracy was

due to the man who first gave a bribe, for the many lose their power the moment they stoop to accept one. But the bribers should bear in mind that they are in fact overthrowing their own power when they buy reputation at a high price and thereby make the many strong and bold, because they come to think they have the power to confer or withhold something important.

[30] All this, however, gives no reason for being mean about the normal, expected donations, so long as your financial circumstances are adequate. The many think worse of a rich man who doesn't hand over some of his own money than of a poor man who steals from the public purse. They judge that the former despises and looks down upon them, whereas the latter is driven by necessity. So, first, make your contributions without expecting any return; they will dazzle and disarm the recipients all the more. Secondly, choose a moment which provides an attractive and honourable pretext, as when the cult of a god moves the whole community to piety. For it is when the many see those whom they honour and think great spending lavishly and readily in the service of god that there arises in their minds a powerful sense of the grandeur and awesomeness of the divine power. And so, just as Plato debarred his young men, while they were in training, from the use of the Lydian and Ionian musical modes, because the one excites our tendency to grief and lamentation and the other our proneness to excessive indulgence in pleasure,[1] so should you, if you can, drive out of your city all those expensive displays that arouse and nurture either brutal craving for blood or undisciplined vulgarity. If you can't do this, at any rate avoid them and resist popular demands for such shows; in their place, promote morally acceptable fields of expenditure, such as meet the needs of necessity or honour, or at least tend to pleasures and gratifications free of damaging or outrageous features.

[31] If your means are moderate and circumscribed, so as just to meet your needs with nothing to spare, there can be nothing mean or disgraceful in confessing your poverty and declining to take a part in the expensive displays of the well-to-do, rather than borrowing money and making a pitiful laughing-stock of yourself over your public service. Failure cannot be hidden, once people importune their friends or court the money-lenders;

when that happens, the expenditure is seen to bring disgrace and contempt rather than influence and reputation. It is always worth while remembering Phocion and Lamachus. Phocion, when the Athenians were noisily demanding a subvention at a sacrifice, answered 'I should be ashamed to give you a subvention and not pay Callicles here'—and he pointed at his money-lender—'what is his due.' Lamachus always put down a sum for his own boots and cloak in the accounts of his expenditure as general. And when Hermon sought to avoid office* by pleading poverty, the Thessalians voted him a gallon of wine a month and a bushel of flour from each of the four provinces. It is indeed no disgrace to confess poverty. Poor men are no less influential in cities than those who give banquets and subsidize choruses, so long as they have the freedom of speech and trust that virtue gives them. Of course, one must control oneself in these matters. The infantry must not go down to fight the cavalry in the plain, nor the poor man descend to racecourses and theatres and banqueting-tables to contend for prestige and power against the rich; he should compete instead with those who try to guide the
823 city by reason, relying on their virtue and spirit, wherein reside not only honour and dignity, but charm and attraction 'lovelier than Croesus' pieces of gold'.* The good man is not selfish or offensive, nor the temperate man self-satisfied, nor does he 'stalk by with looks that hurt the citizens'.[1] No; he is affable and equally approachable and accessible to all, he keeps open house as a refuge for all who need him, he displays his caring nature and humanity not only in practical services but in sympathy with the griefs and successes of others. He never makes himself offensive or overbearing by taking a crowd of servants to the baths, or by appropriating special seats at the theatre; nor does he mark himself out by invidious exhibitions of luxury and extravagance. On the contrary, in clothes, in life-style, in the education of his children and the care of his wife, he is just like everyone else; it is as though he wants to share the society and common humanity of the masses. Furthermore, he offers himself as a friendly counsellor, an unpaid advocate, and a kindly reconciler of wife to husband or friend to friend. He is not content simply to pass an hour or so a day in public work, on the platform or the rostrum, and then spend the rest of his life

collecting services and agencies for himself from every side 'as the north-easter tugs the clouds'.[2] No; his thoughts are all given over to the public interest, and he treats politics not, like most people, as an interruption of leisure or an imposed duty. In all these, and in other ways, he attracts and wins the hearts of the many, who come to see the enticements and seductions of other politicians as base metal compared with his caring wisdom. Demetrius' flatterers thought that no one else deserved the title of king; they therefore called Seleucus 'the elephant-master', Lysimachus 'the treasure-warden', Ptolemy 'the admiral', and Agathocles 'the governor of the island'. The many, similarly, even if at first they reject the wise and good man, come later to understand his real character and regard him as the only true, democratic politician or ruler; the rest they call chorus-managers, caterers, or gymnasium-wardens, and treat them accordingly. Again, at those famous dinners where Callias or Alcibiades spends the money,* it is Socrates who is listened to, Socrates to whom everybody turns; and, similarly, in healthy societies Ismenias gives the money, Lichas provides the dinners, Niceratus pays for the choruses—but it is Epaminondas or Aristides or Lysander who holds office, controls policy, and commands the army. In view of this, do not feel humiliated or dazzled by the reputations pressed upon the mob by theatres, canteens, and public halls; they do not survive long, they vanish with the gladiators and the scenery, and bring no real honour or dignity.

[32] People who have experience of keeping and breeding bees regard the hive that buzzes loudest and is fullest of disturbance as the healthiest and most flourishing; but the man to whom god has given the care of the rational, political hive will judge its happiness by the quiet and calm of the people. He will accept and imitate, so far as he can, most of Solon's principles; but he will be at a loss to think what induced that great man to decree that the citizen who attached himself to neither party in a
time of strife should be deprived of his rights. When the body is 824
sick, the change to health never begins with the afflicted organs; it happens only when the temperament of the healthy parts finds strength to expel the unnatural disorder of the rest. It is like that with a people involved in internal strife: if the dissension is not to be dangerous or terminal but is going to stop one day, there

must be a strong, persistent, and pervasive element which remains healthy and unaffected; this receives congenial reinforcement from the sane and wise, and will in time penetrate the diseased part. On the other hand, cities where total confusion reigns are utterly ruined, unless forcibly brought to their senses by disaster, through some external compulsion or chastisement. Nevertheless, it is wrong to sit idle in the midst of conflict, insensible and unaffected, singing the praises of one's own impassivity and happy, carefree life, and taking pleasure in the follies of others. Better to put on Theramenes' comfortable shoe,* talk to both sides, and join neither. You will not be thought an outsider for not joining in their wrongdoing, but a universal friend because you help them. Nor will you attract envy for not sharing their misfortunes, so long as you are seen to sympathize equally with everybody. But the best plan of all is to take precautions to forestall disorder. This is the greatest and noblest part of the art of statesmanship. Consider what the greatest political blessings are. They are peace, freedom, prosperity, populousness, and concord. For peace, our peoples have no need of politicians at present; every Greek war, every foreign war has passed away from us. As to freedom, the people have as much as the ruling power allows; and it is perhaps best that they should have no more. Fertility of the soil and a kindly climate, the birth of children 'like their parents'[1] and their safe rearing—these are things for which the man of sense will pray to the gods on his fellow citizens' behalf. There therefore remains for the statesman only one of these great objects, but it is second to none: to ensure perpetual concord and friendship among one's fellows, and the removal of all kinds of strife, dissension, and hostility. One must do as one does with the disputes of personal friends. First conciliate the party which feels most aggrieved, giving the impression of sharing its sense of injustice and indignation. Then try to calm it down by showing that those who give way actually show themselves superior to the violent and aggressive, not only in terms of moderation and decency, but in spirit and greatness of mind; small concessions win the biggest prize. Secondly, explain in clear terms, both to individuals and in public, the weakness of Greece, which brings one great advantage to the wise, the chance to live one's life in peace and concord. Fortune has left us no other prize to fight for. What power, what glory can the victor expect? What influence is this, that a short pronouncement from the proconsul suppresses or transfers to another? Even if you keep it, there is nothing there worth the trouble.

Fires rarely start in temples or public buildings. Most often, a neglected lamp or some rubbish catching alight in a house starts a conflagration which ends in widespread public damage. Likewise, it is not always public causes of dispute that kindle disorder in a city; most often, differences arising out of private 825
difficulties and offences throw the whole city into turmoil. The statesman must therefore take special care to cure or anticipate these problems, so as to ensure either that they do not arise at all, or that they soon give over, or at any rate that they do not extend to set the whole society on fire, but remain confined to the original disputants. He must bear in mind, and draw to the attention of others, the consideration that the neglect of small or private difficulties, and failure to treat or cure them in the early stages, make them the cause of great or public problems. For example, the greatest revolution in the history of Delphi* is said to have been occasioned by Crates. His daughter was about to marry Orsilaus, the son of Phamis; but when the mixing-bowl broke accidentally at the moment of the libation, the bridegroom took it as a bad omen and departed with his father, leaving his bride behind. A little time later, when they were at sacrifice, Crates planted one of the gold treasures of the temple on them, and had Orsilaus and his brother thrown over the cliff without trial. He also killed some of their friends and relatives, who were suppliants in the temple of Athena Pronaia.* After a number of such episodes, the Delphians killed Crates and his fellow-conspirators, and used their money, on which a curse had been pronounced, to rebuild the lower temples. Another instance comes from Syracuse. There were two young friends, one of whom, having been entrusted with the other's beloved while he was away, seduced the boy; whereupon the other, in revenge as it were, seduced his friend's wife. One of the old citizens appeared before the Council to urge that both youngsters should be banished before their enmity could affect the whole city. He failed to win his point; and the Syracusans began a period of

conflict which led to their overturning their excellent constitution, with disastrous consequences. You have another example nearer home, in the enmity of Pardalas and Tyrrhenus, which came near to ruining Sardis, plunging the city into war and rebellion for a trivial, private cause. The statesman must not disregard injuries which (as in the body) can spread quickly. He should take hold of them, grip them firmly, and go to the rescue. As Cato says, care makes great things small and small things as nothing. The best technique of persuasion in these matters is to make oneself an even-tempered conciliator in one's own private disputes—free from anger, confining oneself to the original charges, never introducing contentiousness or indignation or any other emotion which brings harshness or bitterness into unavoidable disagreements. We tie padded gloves round boxers' hands in the palaestra, so that the fight doesn't end in incurable injuries, but the punches are soft and painless. In trials and lawsuits against fellow citizens, however, it is better to fight with clean, bare accusations, and not do massive and incurable public damage by sharpening the arrows of your case, as it were, and poisoning them with slander, malice, and menaces. A man who deals with his own associates on these principles will win others to serve him; once private enmities are removed, public rivalries cost little, and bring no unpleasant or irremediable consequences.

VIII

HOW TO PROFIT FROM YOUR ENEMIES

This essay was placed by Byzantine editors among the pieces on friendship (4–7); but it is in fact a sequel and supplement to 'Rules for Politicians', and it deals mainly with relationships of friendship and enmity in public life. It is addressed to Cn. Cornelius Pulcher, a native of Epidaurus, who had a career of some note in Roman administration, and was at one time procurator in Achaea. Plutarch represents it as the written version of a spoken discourse based on a text out of Xenophon's *Oeconomicus*, but also as a response to the addressee's request for advice. He wants us to believe that he had been talking to students on the very subject on which his friend (and patron?) now asks for help.

[1] I observe, my dear Cornelius Pulcher, that you have chosen 86
the most peaceable style of politics, whereby you best combine service to the common good with inoffensiveness in your private dealings. But a country without wild beasts (though they say this of Crete*) has never been discovered, and there has never yet been a political career which did not excite malice, envy, and competitiveness, the very emotions that most breed enmities. If nothing else involves us in enmities, our friendships do, as Chilon the Wise knew when he asked the man who claimed to have no enemies whether he also had no friends! Many questions concerning enmities deserve the politician's consideration. In particular, he must pay real attention to Xenophon's remark that it is a mark of a man of sense to 'profit from his enemies'.[1] I have therefore collected the remarks that occurred to me in speaking of this the other day, and I send them to you, in almost the same words, leaving out, so far as possible, material contained in my *Rules for Politicians*, because I see that you often have that book in your hands.

[2] The men of early times, in their dealings with strange wild animals, were content to protect themselves from injury, and this was the aim of all their battles with the beasts. Later generations, however, learnt to make use of the animals and profit by them, feeding on their flesh, clothing themselves in

their hair, finding medical uses for their gall and rennet, making armour out of their hides. One may well fear that if the animals become extinct, human life will become brutish and savage. Similarly, while the mass of mankind are content to avoid injury from their enemies, men of sense, as Xenophon says, profit from their opponents. And we should believe this, and see if we can devise some art or method to ensure that those for whom life without enemies is impossible, derive this good from them. The farmer cannot domesticate every species of tree, nor the huntsman tame every animal. They have therefore looked for other ways to profit from the barren and the wild. Sea water is bad and undrinkable, but the sea nourishes fish, and is the means of passage and transport for travellers everywhere. When fire first appeared, the satyr wanted to kiss and cuddle it, till Prometheus said 'Old goat, you'll soon be sorry for your beard.'[2] It burns if you touch it, but it gives light and warmth and is a tool of every craft, if you learn to use it.

So consider your enemy. Ask yourself whether, damaging and unmanageable as he may be in other respects, he may yet
87 somehow present an opportunity or a usefulness of his own by which you can profit. The circumstances of life also are often unfriendly, repulsive, or contrary to us; but you can see that some people take advantage even of illness to lead a quiet life, while others are fortified and exercised by troubles. Some have used exile and loss of fortune as a passport to philosophical leisure, like Diogenes and Crates. Zeno, on hearing of the wreck of his ship and cargo, said 'Thank you, Fortune, for forcing me back to my old cloak!'* Healthy animals with strong stomachs can digest snakes and scorpions—some even feed on stones and shells, which the vigour and heat of their spirits convert into nourishment—while on the other hand sickly and delicate people suffer nausea when they try to take bread and wine. Similarly, fools ruin their friendships, while the wise make good use even of their enmities.

[3] To begin, then, it seems to me that the most damaging element in enmity can also be the most useful to those who address their minds to it. What is it? Your enemy is always wide awake, watching every move, looking for an opening, circling round and round. He doesn't merely see through oaks like Lynceus, or through bricks or stones; he sees through friends, servants, intimates, doing his utmost to ferret out your actions and probe and undermine your plans. Neglect and heedlessness often blind us to the illnesses and deaths of friends; but with our enemies, our curiosity all but extends to their dreams. An enemy notices illness, indebtedness, or marital difficulties sooner than the sufferer. In particular, he pursues and fastens on faults. As vultures swoop down to the smell of rotting carrion, but have no awareness of the clean and healthy body, so the diseased, worthless, and flawed features of a life attract an enemy. Hatred makes a rush at these, lays hold on them, and tears them to pieces. Is this useful? Yes, indeed; it is useful in helping us to live warily, to watch ourselves, to refrain from doing or saying anything without due heed and circumspection, and to preserve our lives from reproach by a strict regime. The caution that restrains emotions and concentrates thought in this way leads to the practice and adoption of a respectable and irreproachable style of life.

Cities chastened by wars with neighbours and incessant campaigning come to appreciate orderly government and political health; and similarly, individuals who have been forced, because of enmities, to maintain a sober vigilance in their lives, to guard against laziness and negligence, and to do all things to good purpose, slip imperceptibly by sheer habit into the way of avoiding mistakes and disciplining their character, even if reason has little hand in the process. Those who keep in mind the line 'how Priam and his children would rejoice!'*[1] are influenced by it, and diverted and deterred from the sort of actions enjoyed and ridiculed by enemies. We often see musicians give a relaxed performance, without enthusiasm and without precision, while they are playing on their own; but when there is a competition or contest against others, they pull themselves and their instruments together, test the strings, tune the instruments, and play their pipes with a great deal more care. Likewise, a
man who knows that his enemy competes with him in career and 88
reputation pays more attention to himself, watches his affairs more closely, and retunes his life. It is a feature of vice that we feel more ashamed of our sins before our enemies than before our friends. When it was being thought and said that Rome was

safe because Carthage had been destroyed and the Achaeans enslaved,* Scipio Nasica said 'No, it is now that we are in danger, because we have left ourselves no one to make us feel afraid or ashamed.'

[4] Take to heart also that wise and statesmanlike answer of Diogenes: 'How shall I defend myself against my enemy?' 'By becoming a good man.' It annoys people to see an enemy's horses winning, or his dogs praised. If they see his farm well cultivated, or his garden blooming, they groan aloud. Then what do you suppose will happen, if you show yourself as just and prudent and honest, famous for learning, pure in deed, modest in life,

> reaping in wisdom that deep-furrowed field
> wherein the harvest of good counsel grows?[1]

As Pindar says, 'men in defeat, their tongues are tied by dumbness'[2]—yet not completely, at least not all of them, but only those who see that they are surpassed by their enemies in diligence, honesty, magnanimity, humanity, and good deeds. This, to quote Demosthenes, 'halts your tongue, stops your mouth, throttles you and shuts you up'.[3]

> Be better than the wicked, for you can.[4]

If you want to give pain to the man who hates you, do not abuse him as a pervert, as a homosexual, as immoral, vulgar, and mean, but be a man yourself, be temperate, be sincere, be kind and just to those you deal with. If you feel moved to abuse a man, remove yourself as far as possible from the vices of which you accuse him. Delve into your heart, seek out the rotten parts, lest someone quotes at you the line of the tragic poet: 'Doctor to others, full of sores yourself.'[5] If you call a man uneducated, strengthen your own commitment to learning and study; if a coward, rouse your own manhood and courage; if he is to be called immoral and licentious, erase any hidden trace of indulgence from your own heart. Nothing is more shameful or painful than a slander that rebounds on the slanderer: reflected light hurts weak eyes more than direct light, and blame reflected by the truth hurts the blamer more than the blamed. A bad life attracts abuse, 'as the north-easter tugs the clouds'.[6]

[5] Whenever Plato encountered people who behaved badly, he would say to himself as he went away, 'Am I a little like that myself?' Anyone who abuses another's life and at once examines his own and corrects, redresses, and reforms it, will have had some benefit from his abuse, useless and foolish as that is, and is always held to be. People laugh if a bald man or a hunchback makes fun of another with the same deformity; indeed, as a general principle it is absurd to abuse or make fun of anything when the joke can be turned against yourself. Leon of Byzantium, when a hunchback was rude about his weak eyes, answered 'You are blaming me for something which is inherent in human life; and you carry your nemesis on your back.' So do not abuse an adulterer if you are a child-molester, or a profligate if you are a miser. Alcmaeon said to Adrastus,

> Of her who killed her husband,
> you are the brother[7]

and Adrastus replied by referring to a cause of shame which attached not to a relative but to Alcmacon himself:

> and you were your own mother's murderer.[7]

Domitius said to Crassus, 'Didn't you weep when the moray 89
you were keeping* in your pond died?' Crassus replied, 'Didn't you bury three wives without shedding a tear?' It is not wit that the would-be slanderer needs, nor a loud voice, nor a bold heart, but a character above slander and reproach. The god's injunction 'Know thyself'* applies to no one better than to the man who is about to blame another. It warns against the risk of being told what you don't like as a consequence of saying what you like. As Sophocles says, the man like that

> pouring out words in vain
> unwilling hears the things he willing said.[1]

[6] These are the uses and advantages that come from abusing an enemy. No less significant are those which come from suffering abuse and hard words at an enemy's hands. Antisthenes was right to say that, in order to be saved, a man needs genuine friends or fiery enemies:[2] the former deter wrongdoers by reproof, the latter by abuse. But friendship nowadays has a faint

voice for frank speaking; loud in flattery, it is dumb in reproof. We have therefore to depend on our enemies to learn the truth. As Telephus, finding no healer on his own side, submitted his wound to the touch of an enemy's spear,* so those who have no access to friendly reproof must necessarily endure the words of an enemy who hates them, if he is prepared to expose and correct the fault. It is the effect, not the intention, of the hard words that we have to consider. The would-be murderer of Prometheus of Thessaly* split a tumour with the stroke of his sword; the tumour burst, and the victim was rid of it and his life saved. Similarly, an angry or hostile criticism often cures some fault of character which has gone unnoticed or neglected. Yet most people, if subjected to abuse, ask not whether the accusation is true, but what other charges can be brought against their abuser. Like wrestlers, they do not wipe off the dust of the abuse, but smear each other, and roll on the ground together, covered in each other's dirt. But if an enemy speaks ill of you, and the charge sticks, the right thing is to get rid of it, even more than you would a stain on your coat which someone had pointed out; and if it is a false allegation, you should none the less find out what gave rise to the slander, and take precautions and be apprehensive of falling inadvertently into some error near or like that which is alleged. Lacedes, king of Argos, won a bad reputation for effeminacy because of his hair-style and his walk; Pompeius was believed to be an advanced sexual pervert because he used to scratch his head with one finger. Crassus was accused of having an affair with one of the Vestal Virgins because he was negotiating to buy a handsome estate from her, and often met her privately and courted her. Postumia's ready laughter* and forward conversation with men brought her so much under suspicion that she was prosecuted for immorality. She was indeed acquitted, but, in dismissing her, the pontifex Spurius Minucius warned her not to use talk that did not match the dignity of her life. Suspicion of treachery rubbed off on the innocent Themistocles because of his friendship with Pausanias and the fact that he had frequently written or sent messages to him.

[7] So, when untrue things are said, one should not despise and neglect them because they are false, but consider whether

anything in your words, actions, interests, or associates displays 90
some resemblance to what is alleged; and if it does, take care and avoid it. After all, if others learn useful lessons from their unfortunate circumstances—like Merope, who says that

> Fortune took the dearest things I have
> as fee, and made me wise[1]—

what is there to prevent one from benefiting from an enemy—a teacher who charges no fee—and learning things that were hidden from you? Enemies notice more than friends—'love is blind about its object', as Plato says[2]—whereas hatred is inquisitive and talkative. Hiero was once abused by an enemy for his bad breath: so when he went home he asked his wife why she hadn't told him about it. 'I thought all men smelt like that,' the chaste and innocent lady replied. So even obvious faults, plain to all, may be sooner learned from enemies than from friends and intimates.

[8] Apart from this, it is impossible to keep control of the tongue (and this is no small part of virtue) in a manner responsive and obedient to reason, unless one succeeds in subduing the worst emotions, like anger, by exercise, practice, and effort. 'A word slipped out against its will', 'the word escaped the fence of teeth', 'some words fly off on their own'—these are things that happen to untrained tempers which slide and slither out of control through weakness of reason, unstable judgement, and a habit of recklessness. A word is the lightest of things, but the punishment for it, from gods and men, is of the heaviest; so says our divine Plato. Silence, on the other hand, never has to answer for itself (Hippocrates says it never produces thirst, but this is only a part of the story), and in a situation of abuse it possesses a dignity worthy of Socrates—or indeed of Heracles, if it is true that he also 'heeded the hateful words less than a fly'.[3] Nothing can be more dignified or noble than holding your peace when your enemy abuses you, and 'swimming past' the man who rails at you, 'as past a treacherous rock';[4] nor indeed is there any more useful exercise. If you accustom yourself to bear an enemy's abuse in silence, you will find it easy to bear your wife's angry scolding, to endure the sharp words of friend or brother without complaint, and to submit calmly and unresentfully to being

thrashed or having things thrown at you by father or mother. Socrates endured Xanthippe's bad temper because he hoped to be comfortable with others if he accustomed himself to bear with her; but it is surely better to get your practice from the rudeness, anger, and ridicule of strangers and enemies, in order to habituate your temper to be quiet and not fret at abuse.

[9] Mildness and tolerance can thus be displayed in circumstances of enmity, and these conditions give an even better opportunity than friendship for the exhibition of sincerity, magnanimity, and goodness. It is less honourable to do good to a friend than it is shameful not to do it when he asks; with an enemy, it shows decency merely to forgo the chance of revenge when it presents itself. If a man sympathizes with an enemy's distress or helps him in need or shows practical concern for his children or relatives in their necessity, then not to admire his kindness or praise his goodness argues 'a dark heart forged of
91 iron or adamant'.[1] When Caesar ordered Pompey's demolished statues to be restored, Cicero commented 'You have put back Pompey's statues, and put your own on a firm base.' Do not grudge praise or honour to an enemy who is justly famous. Such praise earns greater praise for itself; moreover, should you subsequently find fault with him, you will be believed, because you will be seen to be disapproving the action, not disliking the man. Best of all, the man who accustoms himself to praise his enemies and not to feel aggrieved or look askance at their successes, will also set himself apart from any envy of the success or good fortune of friends or relatives. And what other exercise confers a greater benefit or a better disposition of mind than one which removes our tendency to envy and malice? There is a similarity too between war and enmity. In war, many necessary evils acquire the status of law and custom, and it is very difficult to escape from the damage they do. Enmity brings not only hatred but envy, jealousy, gloating over troubles, and lasting grievance; and it leaves these behind it. Furthermore, dishonesty, deceit, and treachery, all thought right and proper in relation to an enemy, become ineradicable once they have taken root; and people come to use them out of habit in relation to their friends, if they have not taken precautions against them in their dealings with enemies. Pythagoras, who wanted to use

animals to habituate us to refrain from greed and cruelty, used to intercede with bird-catchers and buy fishermen's catches and tell them to put them back in the sea, and in general sought to forbid the slaughter of domestic animals. If he was right, then surely it is a much bigger thing, in human disputes and quarrels, to control and reduce one's wicked, ignoble or dishonest emotions by being a noble, just, and honourable enemy, in such a way as to make sure of their quiescence and good behaviour in one's dealings with friends. Scaurus was an enemy of Domitius and prosecuted him. Before the trial began, one of Domitius' servants came to see him and offered to reveal a circumstance not known to him. Scaurus refused to listen,* apprehended the man, and sent him back to his master. When Cato was prosecuting Murena* for corrupt practices and was collecting his evidence, he was accompanied (as was the custom) by observers of his proceedings. They would often ask him if he was going to collect any material or do any business relevant to the prosecution today, and if he said no, they believed him and took the day off. This is a great testimony to Cato's character; but it is an even greater credit to us if, by habituating ourselves to deal justly even with our enemies, we can ensure that we never deal unjustly or dishonestly with our friends and intimates.

[10] 'Every lark', says Simonides, 'must have its crest.'[2] Every human being is born with competitiveness, jealousy, and envy, that 'comrade of the vain of heart', as Pindar has it.[3] It is surely a great boon, then, if we discharge these passions upon our enemies and divert the stream away from friends, companions, and family. That Chian politician, Demos, seems to have grasped this. When his party triumphed, he warned his friends against driving all their opponents into exile; they must leave 92
some, he said, 'so that we do not start quarrelling with our friends, because we have no enemies left'. For us too, expending such emotions on enemies will save our friends from trouble. It is not right for 'potter to be angry with potter' or 'poet with poet' (to quote Hesiod),[1] or to be envious of a neighbour or a cousin or a brother who is 'on the road to wealth' or enjoying some success. If there is no other way of ridding yourself of strife and envy and contention, make a habit of being indignant at your enemy's good fortune; sharpen and whet your

competitive instinct on him. Expert gardeners think that roses and violets do better if you plant garlic or onions nearby, because all the sharpness and strong odour of the soil passes into these. Similarly, the concentration of malice and spite on an enemy will make one kinder and more agreeable to successful friends. We must therefore compete with our enemies for honour, power, and honestly obtained riches; we should not simply feel hurt if they get the better of us, but observe carefully how they do it, and try to surpass them in diligence, industry, temperance, and concentration. Themistocles, remember, used to say that it was Miltiades' victory at Marathon that wouldn't let him sleep. If a man believes that it is good fortune that gives an enemy superiority in office or advocacy or politics, or influence with the rich and powerful, and his active ambition thus degenerates into spitefulness and despair, his envy of his rival is wholly negative and ineffectual. If, on the other hand, he is not blind to the good qualities of the man he hates, but casts a fair eye on his life and character, his words and actions, then he will discover that most of the things he envies come to their possessor by diligence and forethought and good actions. With this as his goal, he will develop honourable ambition, and eradicate his sleepy lethargy.

[11] And suppose that our enemies appear to acquire power in courts or political circles by disgraceful and ungentlemanly means—flattery, trickery, bribery, or corruption. This will give us more pleasure than distress, so long as we can contrast with them the liberality, purity, and innocence of our own lives. 'All the gold on earth and below earth is not equal in price to virtue,' says Plato.[2] Solon's remark also is something to keep always in mind: 'We'll never change our virtue for their wealth'[3]—no, nor for the applause of fêted multitudes, nor for honour and precedence in the houses of royal eunuchs and mistresses and governors. Nothing enviable or honourable comes out of evil. But (to quote Plato's words again) 'love is blind about its object',[4] and it is our enemies' improprieties that we notice most; so let us not allow our pleasure at their mistakes or our pain at their success be without some practical consequences: let us use both sentiments to help us to excel them by avoiding their errors, and equal them by imitating their strengths.

IX

CURIOSITY

This and the following two pieces represent the side of Plutarch's practical philosophy which consisted in diagnosing faults of character, and recommending habit-forming exercises and 'useful reflections' calculated to mend them. The Byzantine editors collected many of these together (27–40 in the corpus). *Polypragmosynē* is 'meddling in many matters', and it describes something which Greek society generally disliked. Plutarch narrows it to 'unhealthy concern for other people's troubles', and offers an analysis and a course of treatment, by self-examination and exercise. As with superstition, he does not dwell on the humorous side of the subject, for fear of making it seem trivial. He relates it to envy and malice, both bad 'diseases of the soul', but also notes its affinity with the good quality of an inquiring spirit. This essay seems (see Notes) to have been a favourite with Jeremy Taylor.

[1] If a house is airless, dark, cold, or unhealthy, it is probably 515
best to avoid it; but if familiarity makes you feel at home there, you can make it lighter, airier, and healthier by moving the lights or changing the staircase or opening up a door. Some people have benefited their native cities by this kind of change. My own home town, it is said, used to face west and receive the evening sun falling on it from Parnassus, until Chaeron relocated it to face the sunrise. Again, the scientist Empedocles is supposed to have banished pestilence from the land by blocking a gorge which allowed the unpleasant and unhealthy south wind to blow down on to the plain.[1] Similarly there are sickly and harmful passions that bring storm and darkness to the soul, and it is well to expel these or level them with the ground and give oneself light and air; but if this cannot be done, then one should at least contrive somehow to change the situation by giving them a new direction and reversing their effect.

Curiosity is a case in point. It is a passion for learning about other people's troubles. This is a disease intimately connected with envy and malice,

> Why, man of malice, are your eyes so sharp
> for others' ills, so blind towards your own?[2]

Turn curiosity round, direct it inwards; if you enjoy investigating evils, there is plenty for you to do at home: you will find plenty of mistakes in your life, morbid passions in your soul, and oversights in your duties

> as many as the drops in the Alizon
> or leaves upon the oak.[3]

As Xenophon says that the housekeeper should have separate places for the apparatus of sacrifice, for the dinner-service, for the farm equipment, and for the weapons,[4] so should you make separate compartments for your faults of envy, jealousy, cowardice, and meanness: review them and inspect them over and over again; block the doors and passages that lead to your neighbours against curiosity, open up the way to your own men's quarters, your women's quarters, your servants' daily arrangements. Here, curiosity and inquisitiveness have scope for useful and beneficial service rather than for unprofitable malice. Everyone should say to himself, 'Where did I go wrong, and what did I do? What duty was not done?*[5]

[2] The story goes that Lamia was blind as long as she was at
516 home and asleep, because she kept her eyes in a bucket and only put them in to see when she went out. People are like that in the real world too. Each one of us lets his officiousness serve as the eye of malice in regard to others, while we often fall over our own errors and weaknesses through ignorance, because we fail to provide ourselves with eyes and light to see them by. Curious people are therefore more useful to their enemies than they are to themselves; they search out, reveal, and expose what they ought to prevent or correct, but at the same time they are so excited by what goes on elsewhere that they fail to see their own failings. Odysseus could not even let himself talk to his mother* until he had asked the prophet the question he had come to Hades to ask; only then did he turn to her and inquire about the other women and ask who Tyro was, or who was 'fair Chloris', or why Epicaste died 'hanging a noose from the lofty rooftree'.[1] We are not like that. Easygoing and ignorant so far as our

own affairs are concerned, we neglect them in order to inquire into the families and genealogies of others. Our neighbour has a Syrian grandfather or a Thracian nurse; old so-and-so has a debt of three talents and hasn't paid the interest. We ask where so-and-so's wife has been, or what those two were arguing about in the corner. Socrates went round asking what was convincing in the doctrines of Pythagoras. Aristippus meeting Ischomachus at Olympia asked what there was in Socrates' conversation to make the young men so excited about him; and then when he had picked up a few seeds or specimens of the arguments, he became so deeply affected by them that he actually lost weight and became pale and thin, until he made the voyage to Athens, thirsty and parched for knowledge, drew from the fountain, and found out about the man himself, his talk, and his philosophy, the essence of which was the recognition of one's own faults and consequent liberation from them.

[3] Some people, however, cannot bear the horrid sight of their own lives. They cannot, as it were, turn the light of thought upon themselves. In them, the mind is burdened with ills of every kind. It fears and shudders at what lies within, and rushes outside to roam over strange ground, feeding and fattening its malice. Hens often go into corners in a house, though there is food enough set out for them, and scratch away 'where gleams a grain of barley in the muck'.[2] So too with curious people: they pass over publicly available material and information and things that no one stops them asking or is angry with them for asking, and instead pick out the hidden, secret problems of every household. I like the reply of the Egyptian to the questioner who asked what he was carrying, all wrapped up. 'That's just why it *is* wrapped up,' he said. And why should *you* be inquisitive about the thing that is hidden? If it had not been bad, it would not have been hidden.

It is bad manners to go into someone else's house without knocking at the door; nowadays there are doorkeepers, in olden times there was just a knocker on the door to give warning, so that the stranger should not find the mistress of the house or the unmarried daughter in a public room, or a slave being punished, or the maids screaming. But this is just what the curious man slips inside to see; he has no pleasure in viewing a decent,

well-ordered household, even if you invite him; what he likes is to reveal and publicize whatever is secured by keys and bars and outer doors. 'The winds we dislike most', says Ariston, 'are those that blow our clothes open.'[3] The curious man doesn't strip off his neighbours' coats and shirts, but their walls; he flings their doors open, and pierces right through 'the tender maid'[4] like a wind, investigating and informing on Bacchic
517 rites, dances, and nocturnal vigils.

[4] Cleon in the comedy has 'hands in Aetolia, but his heart's in Thieving'.*[1] So with our inquisitive friend: his mind is simultaneously in rich men's halls and poor men's hovels, in kings' courts and newly-weds' bedrooms. He investigates everything, foreigners and rulers not excluded, and not without danger to himself: if your curiosity about the stuff leads you to taste aconite, you will destroy your own senses before you have got the sense of it, and in the same way people who research into the troubles of the great destroy themselves before they get to know the facts.

People who despise the diffused light which the sun unstintingly bestows upon us all, and instead force themselves to venture to look impudently into his very orb and distinguish his light within their own eyes, are blinded in the attempt. I like the remark of the comic poet Philippides. When King Lysimachus once said to him 'Which of my possessions shall I give you?', he replied 'Anything, sire, except your secrets.' The pleasantest and fairest of royal possessions are on the outside—dinners, riches, festivals, benefactions; if there is anything secret, do not go near or disturb it. A king's joy is not hidden when he is happy, nor his laughter when he is amused, nor his provision for generosity and kindness. It is what is concealed that is to be feared: the grim, unsmiling unapproachableness, the hoarded anger superficially healed, the plotting of bitter revenge, the jealousy of a wife, the suspicions of a son, the distrust of a friend. Avoid this black and gathering storm-cloud; then you will not be caught unawares by the thunder and lightning, when the hidden emotions break out.

[5] So what escape? Distraction and diversion of curiosity, as I said. If possible, turn your mind to better, pleasanter things. Be curious about the phenomena of the sky, of earth and air and

sea. Were you born to be a spectator of little things or of great? If of great, be curious about the sun: where does it go down, and whence does it rise? Research into the changes of the moon, as you would into the changes of a man: where does she lose all that light, whence does she get it back again, how does she

> when new, come forth from darkness, and
> make beautiful her face and full her orb,
> and, when she shines her fairest, once again
> fade and decrease and so return to nothing?[2]

These are nature's secrets, but she is not angry with those who find them out.

Have you despaired of great subjects? Then use your curiosity on smaller ones: why are some plants always flourishing and green, proudly showing their wealth in all seasons, whereas others are like this only sometimes, and are sometimes left bare and beggared, having spent their store all at once, like a thriftless man? Why is the fruit of some trees long, some pointed, some round or spherical?

Maybe you will not feel any curiosity about these things, because there is no evil in them. Well, if inquisitiveness must always feed on evil, like a snake on poisonous weeds, let us lead it towards history, and set abundance and plenty of evils before it. Here are to be found 'men's tumbles, lives kicked over',[3] seductions of women, conspiracies of slaves, slander of friends, poisonings, malice, envy, shipwrecks of households, exiles of rulers: take your fill, enjoy yourself, you will cause your companions no pain or trouble.

[6] But curiosity, it seems, takes no pleasure in stale evils. It needs them fresh and warm, it likes to see new tragedies, and has no enthusiasm for the cheerful or the comic. Our curious 518
friend is a careless, inattentive listener if you tell him about a wedding or a sacrifice or an honorific send-off. He says he has heard most of it before, and tells the narrator to cut his story short and pass on. But sit beside him and tell about a girl seduced, or an adulterous wife, or a lawsuit being got up, or a quarrel between brothers, and he doesn't nod off or find business to do, but 'asks to hear more, and cups his ear to listen'.[1] The lines

> Ah me, the bad news to men's ears
> flies quicker than the good[2]

are true indeed of the curious.

As cupping-vessels* suck the worst out of the flesh, so the ears of the curious draw in the worst talk.

Better: as cities have gates of abomination or doom by which they cast out condemned prisoners, refuse, or scapegoats, no pure or holy thing ever going in or out that way, so too nothing good or polite treads a path through the ears of the curious, but only words of blood, bringing foul and abominable stories.

> The only song that comes into my house
> is song of wailing[3]

and this indeed is the 'one and only Muse and Siren' of the curious, the entertainment they most like to hear.

Curiosity is a passion for inquiring into what is hidden away so as not to be seen. Now, no one hides a good thing if he has it; people rather claim good things which they don't have. So the curious person, with his passion for inquiring into trouble, is liable to the vice of gloating,* the brother of envy and malice. Envy is pain at another's good: gloating is pleasure at another's hurt. Both derive from the savage, bestial passion of malice.

[7] Revealing our own troubles is so painful to us that many die sooner than show the doctor some private illness. Imagine Herophilus or Erasistratus or Asclepius himself, when he was a man, coming into a house with his drugs and instruments, and asking whether anyone had a fistula in the anus or any woman a cancer of the womb! Yet in medicine, curiosity spells salvation. Of course, everyone would have chased him away, because he had come to spy on the troubles of others uninvited and without waiting for the need. Curious people, however, seek out all this, and worse, not to cure but simply to uncover. They are rightly hated.

We grumble at customs officers and are indignant with them not when they pick out what we are bringing in quite openly, but when they rummage in others' bags and baggage in the search for hidden things. Yet the law allows them to do this, and it is their loss if they do not.* The curious, on the other hand, ruin and sacrifice their own affairs by their preoccupation with other people's. They rarely go to their estates, because they cannot bear the quiet and silence of the empty countryside; and if they ever do put in a rare and brief visit, they cast their eyes on their neighbours' vines rather than their own, and ask how many cattle the neighbour has lost, or how much of his wine has gone sour. They have soon had enough of this, and off they go again.

Your true farmer is not much pleased even to hear news that accidentally reaches him from town:

> And while he digs, he'll tell me 519
> the terms of the truce: that's what the wretched fellow
> concerns himself with, while he walks abroad.[1]

[8] The curious, by contrast, avoid country life—they think it stale and flat and undramatic—but they jostle one another in the bazaar and the agora and the harbour: 'Any news?' 'Weren't you in the agora this morning?' 'Of course I was.' 'Well, then: do you think there's been a political revolution in these three hours?'

And if anyone does have such a piece of news, the curious person gets off his horse, takes the man by the hand, kisses him, and stands there to listen. If his contact has nothing to report, he waxes angry. 'What! Haven't you been in the agora? Didn't you pass the Generals' office? Didn't you meet the people from Italy?'

The rulers of Locri* were wise indeed: they fined the man who asked 'What news?' when he came home from abroad.

Cooks pray for a good supply of meat, fishermen for a good catch; the curious pray for a good crop of trouble, masses of happenings, novelties, changes, so that there is always something for them to pursue and cut to pieces.

The lawgiver of Thurii* made a good regulation too: he forbade public satire of any citizen except adulterers and the curious. Adultery is in fact a sort of curiosity about other people's pleasures, an investigation and research into something kept under guard and outside common knowledge; curiosity, for its part, is intrusion into secrets, and the destruction and disclosure of them.

[9] While wordiness is sometimes incidental to great learning—which is why Pythagoras enjoined five years' silence on his students, calling it a 'word-stop'—evil-speaking is an inevitable consequence of inquisitiveness. What those people take trouble to collect from others, they take pleasure in revealing to a third party. Consequently, over and above the other troubles, they find that their disease is itself an obstacle to their desire. Everybody is on his guard with them, and conceals things from them. No one likes to do anything in the presence of such a person, or to say anything in his hearing. People put off deliberations and postpone discussions until he is out of the way. And should he appear while any secret matter is being debated or any serious action brought to a head, they take it away and hide it, just as people hide meat when a weasel runs by. Thus what is heard and seen freely by others often goes unheard and unseen just by these persons.

This is why the curious man enjoys no confidence. We entrust letters, documents, and seals to servants and strangers rather than to friends and close connections who are of this character. Bellerophon did not even break the seal of the letter he was carrying, though it was against himself. He kept his hands off the king's letter, just as he kept his hands off the king's wife. Curiosity and adultery are both manifestations of incontinence, and also of a terrible degree of stupidity and folly. It is surely the uttermost idiocy and madness to pass over all the women who are publicly available and common property, and force one's way into the one who is locked up, expensive and probably plain! But this is just what the curious do. They pass over so many beautiful spectacles and entertainments, lectures and lessons, and instead break into other people's letters, press their ears to their neighbours' walls, and whisper with servants and women, often to their own danger and disgrace.

[10] The most useful device for the curious to use to rid themselves of their failing is therefore recollection of previous knowledge.
520 Simonides used to say that, when he opened his boxes after an interval, he always found his fee-box full and his gratitude-box empty. Similarly, if you open your curiosity deposit after an interval, and see how full it is of useless, idle, unpleasant stuff, it will very likely disgust you with its nasty, rubbishy appearance. Anyone who was to go through the books of the ancients,

choosing the worst things in them and compile a book, as it were, of headless lines* in Homer, solecisms in the tragedians, indecencies and improprieties in Archilochus' attacks on women, in which he makes an example of himself, would surely deserve the curse in the tragedy 'Plague on you, picker of men's miseries!'[1] Quite apart from this curse, though, a store full of other people's mistakes is indecent and unprofitable, like the city which Philip founded and peopled with the most vicious and uncontrolled characters, and called it 'Roguestown'.* Now what the curious anthologize and collect is faults and errors and solecisms, not in lines and verses but in human lives. Their memories make a walking archive of troubles, thoroughly tasteless and disagreeable. At Rome, there are people who pay no attention to pictures and statues, or indeed to the beauty of the boys and girls for sale as slaves, but haunt the Monster Market, marking those without legs or with deformed arms or three eyes or sparrow heads, and asking if there happens to have been born some 'mixed brood or unformed monster'.[2] If you repeatedly bring yourself into contact with such sights, they will soon produce surfeit and nausea. And similarly, those who are inquisitive about failures, family disgraces, perversions, and wrongs in other people's houses, ought to remind themselves that what they knew before brought them no pleasure or benefit.

[11] However the most effective means of averting this condition is habituation. We should start at a distance from our object, and train and teach ourselves to acquire this self-control. It was habit also that allowed the disease to develop gradually until it became serious. We can learn how this happens by including some discussion of exercise. Let us begin with the smallest and most trivial things. What is difficult about not reading the inscriptions on the tombs by the side of the road? What is disagreeable about letting your eye pass over the graffiti on the walls as you go for your walk? You can put it to yourself that there is nothing of any use or pleasure in them. They just say someone 'remembers' someone 'for good', or that someone is someone's 'best friend', or some such nonsense. Reading them appears to do no harm, but in fact it does, without one's being aware of it, because it implants the practice of inquiring after things which are none of our business. Huntsmen do not let

dogs turn aside and pursue every scent, but pull them back with the lead and restrain them, keeping their sense of smell clean and pure for its proper function, so that the dog fastens on the spoor more energetically, 'with nostrils tracking their wild quarry's pads'.[3] This is precisely how one should check the excursions and divagations of the curious, whom every sight and sound distracts, and pull them back into useful courses. Cats and lions retract their claws when they walk, so as not to blunt their sharp points; similarly, we should remember that curiosity
521 possesses a sharp point and edge, namely the love of learning, and should not waste or blunt this on matters of no usefulness.

[12] Secondly, let us form the habit of not looking inside other people's doors as we pass by, or, as it were, gathering a handful of their domestic affairs in our curious eyes. We should bear in mind the remark of Xenocrates, that there is no difference between setting your feet in a house and setting your eyes in it. It is neither honest nor honourable, nor is the view pleasant: 'inside, sir, all is ugliness to see.'[1] Domestic interiors are mostly ugly: utensils lying around, maidservants sitting about, nothing interesting or pleasing. But there is a real ugliness, a vicious moral habit, in those sidelong looks and glancing shots that pervert the soul. When Diogenes saw the Olympic victor Dioxippus riding in his triumphal procession, unable to take his eyes off a pretty woman who was among the spectators, but constantly turning round and snatching a glimpse of her, he exclaimed 'Look! the little girl has thrown the champion!' Any sight will throw and distract the curious, once they have formed the habit and practice of letting their eyes wander everywhere. To my way of thinking, our senses ought not to go roving around like a badly trained maidservant,* but should make contact with the objects to which the mind dispatches them and report back quickly, then staying modestly at home with Reason, and listening to her. But what happens in reality is what Sophocles describes in the line: 'and then the Aenian's hard-mouthed horses bolted.'*[2] In other words, senses which have not received the correct training and exercise that we have described, often run out of control, drag the understanding along with them, and upset it in places where it should never go. It is untrue that Democritus deliberately destroyed his eyesight by looking fixedly at a red-hot mirror* and receiving the force of the reflection, so as to prevent his eyes from disturbing his understanding by summoning it so often to the outside world, instead of letting it stay at home and occupy itself with the intelligible, and (as it were) blocking up the windows on the street side. It certainly is very true that those who do excite their senses much make most use of their minds. Men have established shrines of the Muses away from cities, and have given night the name Euphrone*—'Friend of Thought'—because quiet and absence of distraction are important for research and inquiry.

[13] Nor is it difficult or troublesome to keep at a distance when people are berating and abusing one another in the market-place, or to sit quietly by when everyone is rushing to see something, or, if you really cannot control yourself, just to get up and go away. You will get no good from mixing with the curious, but you will be doing yourself a great service if you can divert and restrain your curiosity, so that it accustoms itself to obeying reason. After this, it would be a good idea to step up the exercise. Walk past a theatre where there is a good show on, decline your friends' invitation to join them to see a dance-show or a comedy, pay no attention when you hear shouting from the sports ground or the racecourse. Socrates recommended being wary of food that tempts one to eat when not hungry, and drink that tempts one when not thirsty. Similarly, we should be wary of and avoid sights and sounds which captivate or attract us when we have no need of them. Cyrus declined to see Panthea,
and when Araspas said that her beauty was worth seeing, he 522
replied, 'That is just why I must avoid her, for she might perhaps persuade me to go again when I had no time, and to look at her and sit beside her, at the sacrifice of much serious business.'[3] Likewise, Alexander did not go to see Darius' wife, who was said to be outstandingly beautiful, and, when he visited her old mother, did not stay to see the young and beautiful daughter. Yet when we let our eyes creep under a woman's litter or hang in suspense at her window, we imagine we are doing nothing wrong, though in fact we are letting our curiosity slide down a very slippery slope!

[14] It is good practice for justice to decline a just source of profit sometimes in order to habituate yourself to keep well

away from unjust ones, and for chastity to abstain from relations with your own wife so as never to be excited by anyone else's. Try to apply the same principle to curiosity. Be deaf or blind to some things that are your own concern. When someone wants to report some domestic matter to you, put him off. When things seem to be said about yourself, pay no heed. It was curiosity that brought Oedipus to utter disaster.* For it was while he was inquiring about himself, supposing himself to be a foreigner and not a Corinthian, that he fell in with Laius; then, when he had killed him, taken his wife and the kingdom with her, and thought himself blessed with fortune, he began to inquire about himself again; his wife tried to stop him, but he questioned the old man who knew the truth all the more eagerly, and brought every possible pressure to bear upon him. In the end, when the conversation begins to lead back by what it suggests, and the old man cries out 'Now I am at the dreadful point of telling', Oedipus is so inflamed by his passion, and yet in agony, that he answers 'And I, of hearing; but hear it now I must.'[4] There is a sort of bitter-sweet, uncontrollable titillation in curiosity, that makes itself bleed like a wound when it is scratched. A man who is cured of this disease, and is naturally of a mild disposition, may well say, if he has ignored some piece of bad news, 'How wise thou art, Forgetfulness of Ill!'[5]

[15] We must therefore accustom ourselves not to open a letter quickly or hastily when it is brought to us, as so many people do, biting through the strings with their teeth if their hands are too slow; nor to jump up and run to meet the messenger when he appears. If a friend says 'I've got some news for you,' what we *ought* to say is 'I would rather you had something useful or serviceable for me.' Once, when I was lecturing in Rome,* Rusticus, the man whom Domitian put to death out of jealousy of his reputation, was in the audience. During my lecture, a soldier came in and gave him a letter from the emperor. There was a silence, and I paused, so as to let him read the letter, but he declined to do so, nor did he open it until I had finished and the session had broken up. Everyone admired his gravity. But if you nourish your curiosity on permissible objects till it grows strong and violent, you will no longer be able to control it easily if familiarity leads it into forbidden areas.

People then open their friends' letters, intrude in secret conclaves, watch rituals which one is not supposed to see, walk over forbidden ground, and inquire into the words and affairs of kings.

[16] As to tyrants, who need to know everything, there is nothing that does more to make them oppressors than the race of men called their 'ears' or their 'reporters'. It was Darius the Bastard who was the first to employ Listeners, because he had no confidence in himself and suspected and feared everyone. Dionysius I and Dionysius II both infiltrated 'reporters' into the 523
Syracusan population, and when the revolution came, these were the first people the Syracusans caught and killed. The whole race of fake informers comes from the tribe and family of the curious; the only difference is that the informers confine themselves to uncovering evil designs or actions, whereas the curious also investigate their neighbours' involuntary mishaps and give publicity to these. The word *alitērios*, meaning 'sinner', is supposed to have been derived from a case of curiosity. At a time of severe famine at Athens, when those who had wheat did not make it generally available but milled it in secret at night in their houses, people went round listening for the sound of the mills, and were therefore called *alitērioi*, from *alein* 'to grind' and *tērein*, 'to watch for'. The word 'sycophant', meaning 'false informer', has a similar origin. When the export of figs (*sȳka*) was forbidden, those who informed against and disclosed (*phainein*) the exporters were called 'sycophants'. It is useful for the curious to bear these facts in mind too, so that they feel ashamed of the likeness of their pursuits to those of people who are the object of so much hatred and dislike.

X

TALKATIVENESS

This is another essay in therapy: diagnosis, description, treatment. *Adoleschia*—loquacity, talkativeness—is a hard word to translate, the more so because Plutarch uses it to cover two somewhat different faults: harmless but boring chatter, and indiscretion or 'dangerous talk'. In doing this, he enhances the seriousness of his theme. His 'talkative man'—unlike those sketched with humorous detail in Theophrastus' *Characters*—is a real menace. The essay was probably written after 'Curiosity'. It is much used by Jeremy Taylor in his sermons on 'The Good and Evil Tongue' (*Eniautos: Twenty-five Sermons*, xxii–xxiii).

[1] Talkativeness is a troublesome and difficult subject for
502 philosophical therapy. The medicine, which consists of words, involves listening, but the talkative listen to no one, because they are always chattering. The first undesirable consequence of the inability to be silent is inability to listen. This is self-induced deafness: the victims doubtless complain because nature has given them two ears but only one tongue.

If it was right for Euripides to say to the unintelligent listener

> I cannot fill a pot that does not hold,
> pouring wise words into an unwise head,[1]

it would be even more appropriate to say to a talkative man, 'I cannot fill one who doesn't accept what I say, pouring wise words into—or I should say "all over"—a man who talks to people who don't listen, and doesn't listen to people who talk.' If he listens for a moment, his loquacity being, as it were, at a low ebb, he soon returns the favour many times over. The portico at Olympia that returns many echoes of a single sound is called the Stoa of Seven Voices;* but if the smallest word strikes Talkativeness, she echoes it back without delay, 'touching the untouched lyre-strings of the heart'.[2] Maybe these people's ears are connected directly not with the mind but with the tongue, and this is why words stick in other people's heads but run out of theirs, and then off they go, empty of sense and full of sound, like so many empty pots.

[2] But, if we are determined to leave nothing untried, let us say to the talker, 'Be silent, child; there is much good in silence'[3]—and especially two things, listening and being listened to. Neither of these is the lot of the talkative; they lack the patience to get what they themselves desire. Most diseases of the mind—love of money, fame, or pleasure—at least attain what they covet; but the worst part of the fate of the talkative is that they long for listeners but never have them, because everyone takes to his heels. If a group sitting in a meeting-area, or walking under a colonnade, sees the talkative man coming, they soon give themselves the signal to decamp. When a sudden silence falls on the company, people say 'Hermes has come in';* likewise, when a talker appears at dinner or at a gathering of friends, 503
everybody stops talking, not wanting to give him an opening; and if he opens his mouth without being spoken to, then

> as when before the storm
> the North Wind lashes the sea-facing cliff,[1]

up they all get in anticipation of a rough sea and *mal-de-mer*. This man never has willing fellow-guests at dinner or companions on a journey by land or sea, but only conscripts; he is ever at your side, pulling at your coat or your beard, constantly nudging you in the ribs. 'Then feet are what we value most,'[2] as Archilochus says—and Aristotle too, for that matter, for he once found himself annoyed by one of these gentry and battered by a shower of extraordinary stories. 'Isn't that remarkable, Aristotle?' said the man. 'The remarkable thing', replied the philosopher, 'is that anyone who has a pair of feet stops for you.' Another man, after a long story, said to Aristotle, 'I've talked you down, philosopher,' 'No, you haven't,' he replied, 'I wasn't attending.' If the garrulous force their chatter upon you, the mind lets them deluge the ears outside, while within she opens up other thoughts and rehearses them to herself. Hence the talkative cannot find listeners to attend to or believe them. Men who are given to frequent sexual activity are said to have infertile seed; with the talkative, it is speech that has no consummation and no fruit.

[3] Yet there is no part of our bodies that nature has fenced around so securely as the tongue. She has set the teeth to guard it, so that if it ever fails to obey or curl up when reason within pulls on the 'shining reins',* we can check its disobedience by biting till it bleeds. 'Of mouths unbridled, misery is the end,'[3] says Euripides—'mouths', mark you, not treasuries or storehouses. And anyone who fancies that storehouses without doors, or purses without fastenings are no use to their owners, but at the same time has a mouth that has no lock or door on it but is always flowing outwards, like the Black Sea, must believe that the Word is of all things the least deserving of honour.

Hence they do not even win credence, which is what all speech aims at, since its proper goal is to induce belief in the hearer. The talkative are not believed even when they tell the truth. When wheat is kept in a jar, it increases in volume but deteriorates in quality; and similarly, when a story gets into the mouth of a talkative man, the amount of fiction increases, and the credibility goes down.

[4] Every modest, decent man shuns getting drunk: for while anger, as some say, is next-door neighbour to madness, drunkenness is her fellow lodger—or, to be more accurate, drunkenness *is* madness, shorter-lived but more reprehensible, because there is an element of voluntary choice in it. Now no charge is more generally made against drunkenness than that of uncontrolled and unregulated talk. 'Wine', says Homer

> sets even the wise man singing
> and makes him softly laugh and dance.[4]

And what is so very bad? Singing, laughing, dancing? Nothing at all so far; but then he 'lets out a word were better left unsaid'. And *that* is where the evil and the danger lie. It may be that Homer was trying to solve a problem discussed by philosophers, and makes a distinction between 'taking wine' and 'drunkenness', 'taking wine' producing relaxation; 'drunkenness' foolish talk. As the proverb has it, what is in the sober man's mind is on the drunkard's tongue. Bias said nothing at a drinking-party, and was ridiculed as a fool by a garrulous companion: his reply was, 'How could a fool manage to say nothing in his cups?' There

was a man once entertaining royal ambassadors at Athens who 504
was anxious to satisfy their interests by bringing them into company with the philosophers. Most of the guests talked freely enough, and made their contribution; only Zeno said nothing. The visitors turned to him politely and drank his health. 'Zeno,' they said, 'what shall we tell the king about you?' 'Tell him', he replied, 'simply that there is an old man at Athens who knows how to stay silent over his drink.' Silence is a profound, secret, sober thing; drunkenness is a talker: foolish, thoughtless, and therefore noisy. The philosophers' definition of drunkenness is actually 'babbling over wine'; it is not the drinking that is culpable, if silence accompanies it, but the foolish talk that turns the wine-taking into drunkenness.

So the drunkard babbles over his wine, but the talkative man babbles everywhere—in the agora, in the theatre, in the public walks, by day, by night. As a doctor he is worse than the disease, as a fellow passenger he is worse than the seasickness, his praise is more annoying than any blame. We enjoy the company of a wicked man who has wit more than that of a virtuous man who is talkative. Nestor in Sophocles spoke with understanding of character when he sought to calm the angry Ajax with words, saying 'I blame you not; you do well, but speak ill.'[1] We do not feel like that towards the talkative. Their untimely words ruin any pleasure their actions give.

[5] Lysias once wrote a speech for a litigant,* and handed it to him. The client read it several times, and then came to see Lysias, and said despondently that he had thought the speech marvellous when he first read it, but on the second and third reading it came to seem utterly flat and ineffectual. Lysias laughed. 'Well,' he said, 'you're not going to read it more than once to the jury, are you?' Just think of Lysias' persuasiveness and charm! Him indeed do I proclaim

> recipient of the Muses' favour,
> the Muses with their violet hair.[2]

And the truest remark made about Homer is that he is uniquely able to prevail over our human capacity for boredom, for he is always fresh and youthful in his charm. But when he says about himself that he hates 'to tell again tales that are plainly told',[3] he is trying avoid the sense of satiety that threatens all our speech, by leading the hearer from one story to another and relieving his feeling of fullness by novelty. Our talkative friends, on the other hand, grate on our ears with their repetitiousness, as though they were scratching through a reused papyrus.

[6] So let us first remind them that, just as wine was invented for pleasure and good fellowship, but becomes a source of disgust and rudeness when people are forced to drink it neat in quantity, so it is with speech. Talking is the most pleasant and humane of our common activities, yet those who use it badly or thoughtlessly render it inhuman and antisocial. They pain those they think to please, they are ridiculed by those whose admiration they seek, they are disliked by those by whom they want to be loved. If the man who uses Aphrodite's magic belt* to drive away and alienate his company is no friend of hers, then the man who uses speech to cause pain or dislike is no friend of the Muses or of the art of the word.

[7] Most passions and diseases are either dangerous or loathsome or ridiculous. Talkativeness is all three of these. These people are mocked for their hackneyed stories, hated for their
505 bad news, and imperilled because they cannot keep a secret. Anacharsis, having had dinner with Solon, was observed lying down with his left hand on his genitals and his right hand over his mouth; he thought it was the tongue that needed the firmer curb, and he was right. It would be hard to list as many individuals ruined through sexual license as cities and empires destroyed by the disclosure of secrets. There was Sulla besieging Athens;* he had not much time to spare, for 'other labours pressed upon him',[1] with Mithridates seizing Asia, and Marius' party once again in control of Rome. Then his agents overheard some older men in a barber's shop saying that Seven Bronzes* wasn't guarded, and that the city might be taken on that side. They reported this to Sulla, who brought his forces up around midnight and led the army into the city. He practically razed it, and filled it with murder and corpses. The Ceramicus was awash with blood. And his anger with the Athenians was due to their words rather than their deeds; they had abused him and Metella, jumping up on the walls and shouting 'Sulla is a mulberry, sprinkled all with flour!'[2] By such foolish nonsense they drew

upon themselves 'a heavier penalty for the lightest of things'—that is, 'words'—as Plato puts it.[3]

Again, it was a single individual's loose talk that prevented Rome from getting rid of Nero* and becoming a free republic. All the preparations had been made. There was one night to go before the tyrant was to be killed. The intended assassin was on his way to the theatre when he saw a prisoner at the gate about to be taken before Nero, and lamenting his fate. The conspirator went up to him and whispered in his ear: 'Pray to get through today, and tomorrow you will thank me.' The man grasped the hint, and reflected, no doubt, that

> a fool is he who leaves what's safe in hand
> to chase the uncertain.[4]

So he chose the surer road to safety rather than the more honourable. He reported the words to Nero, and the man was instantly arrested. Torture, fire, whip followed: the conspirator denied in the face of necessity what he had unnecessarily revealed.

[8] The philosopher Zeno,* fearful lest his body should disclose some secret under torture against his will, bit through his tongue and spat it in the tyrant's face.

Leaena* is another person whose self-control was deservedly rewarded. She was a courtesan in the circle of Harmodius and Aristogiton, and took part in the conspiracy against the tyrants in spirit, as a woman can; for she too had shared the revels round that fair mixing-bowl of love and was initiated in the god's secrets. When they failed and were put to death, she refused at her interrogation to name those conspirators who were still unknown, but endured to the end, showing that the men had done nothing unworthy of themselves in loving such a woman. The Athenians set up a bronze lioness (*leaina*) without a tongue at the gate of the acropolis. The courage of the beast symbolizes the woman's invincible spirit; the absence of the tongue represents her silence and secrecy.

There has never been as much good done by uttering a word as has often been done by suppressing one. What is not said may be said one day; what has once been said can never be suppressed. It is spilt and gone out into the world. Hence, no doubt, we have human teachers of speech, and gods to teach us silence, for we learn silence in initiations and mysteries.

506 Homer makes Odysseus the most eloquent of men, but also the most silent—and his son and his wife and his nurse also. The nurse says: 'I will hold firm as stubborn oak or iron.'[1] And Odysseus himself, sitting beside Penelope,

> inwardly pitied his sad, grieving wife,
> but his eyes were fixed and hard as horn or iron
> unmoving under the eyelids.[2]

So completely was every part of his body under control. In him, reason held everything in obedience and subordination; it told the eyes not to weep, the tongue not to speak, the heart not to tremble or 'growl':[3] 'his heart was still, obedient, and endured',[4] because his reason permeated even his irrational movements and made breath and blood obedient and amenable to its commands. Most of his companions had the same qualities. One cannot conceive a higher level of self-control and trust than that which they showed when they were dragged along the ground by the Cyclops and yet never betrayed Odysseus or revealed the fire-hardened weapon that had been got ready to attack the giant's eye. They would rather have been eaten alive than give away a secret.

So it was a good move of Pittacus, when the king of Egypt* sent him an animal for sacrifice and told him to select 'the best meat and the worst', to take the tongue and send it, because it was the instrument both of the greatest good and the greatest ill.

[9] Ino in Euripides, speaking frankly about herself, says she knows how 'to speak where safe, be silent where it's needed'.[5] Those who have enjoyed a truly noble and royal education learn to be silent before they learn to talk.

King Antigonus was once asked by his son when they were going to strike camp. 'What!' he replied, 'Are you afraid of being the only man who won't hear the trumpet?' Did he then not want to entrust a secret to one to whom he was leaving his kingdom? No; he was giving the prince a lesson in self-control and caution in such matters.

Old Metellus, when asked a similar question on campaign, replied 'If I thought my shirt knew that, I should take it off and put it on the fire.'

Eumenes, hearing that Craterus was advancing, told none of his friends but falsely put it about that it was Neoptolemus, because the soldiers despised him but admired Craterus' reputation and appreciated his courage. So no one except Eumenes knew who the enemy general was. They fought and won the battle, and killed Craterus, not knowing until they recognized the body. Silence planned that battle, silence hid that formidable adversary. Eumenes' friends had to admire rather than criticize him for not giving them warning.* And if one does find fault, better to complain when you owe your life to not being trusted, than to bring accusations when you have been ruined because someone trusted you.

[10] Yet who really leaves himself free to blame a man who fails to keep a secret? If it should have remained unknown, it was wrong to tell anybody in the first place. If you let the secret out of your own hands and try to keep it in another's, you have sacrificed your own reliability to take refuge in another's. Then, if he is like you, you are lost, and you deserve it; if he is a better man, you are saved unexpectedly, because you have found someone more reliable than yourself in your own interest. 'But he was my friend.' Well, he too will have a friend to trust, as I trust him, and that friend will have another; and so the tale proliferates and multiplies in a chain of broken confidences.

As the Monad does not go beyond its own definition but 507
remains One once for all (which is why it is called 'Monad'), whereas the Dyad is an indefinite principle of diversity* (for it immediately loses its identity by turning into plurality by the process of doubling), so a word that rests with its first possessor remains truly secret, but once it passes to another, it becomes common talk. Homer speaks of 'winged words': it is hard to catch a creature with wings once you let it out of your hands, and impossible to grasp and control a word that you have let slip from your lips; it 'arches its swift wings'[1] and is off, spreading from one group of people to another.

If a ship is caught by the wind, sailors steady it and reduce speed by means of cables and anchors; but once a word has left port, there is no roadstead or anchorage for it; it is carried away with a great roar, and in its wreck it sinks the speaker in a deep and frightful sea of danger.

From one small torch, all Ida's forests burn;
tell one your secret, all the people know.[2]

[11] The Roman Senate once spent many days debating a secret plan. It was a dark and dubious matter. A woman—a good woman, but still a woman—kept pestering her husband, begging to be told the secret, with pledges of silence, curses on herself if she broke faith, and tears of complaint that she was not trusted. The Roman husband* wanted to show her her folly. 'You win, wife,' he said, 'let me tell you: it is a most terrible and extraordinary business. We have had a report from the augurs that a lark has been seen flying with a gold helmet and spear. So we are considering whether this is a good or a bad sign, and discussing the problem with the augurs. But don't tell anyone.' So off he went to the forum; and his wife seized the first of her maids who happened to come in to her, and beat her breast and tore her hair. 'Alas, alas!' she cried, 'My husband and my country! What is to become of us?' She was willing the maid to ask what had happened; and so she did. The lady then repeated the whole tale, and added the refrain that every gossip adds, 'Don't tell anybody, keep it to yourself.' The maid had scarcely left her mistress before she told it to a fellow servant whom she found with time on her hands. This girl in turn told her lover, who happened to come by. The story rolled on its way down to the forum, where it arrived before its inventor. 'Have you just come from home?' said one of his friends. 'Yes, just now.' 'Then you haven't heard?' 'Is there any news?' 'A lark has been seen flying with a gold helmet and spear, and the magistrates are going to consult the Senate about it.' The senator laughed. 'Well done, wife,' he said, 'that was quick! The story got to the forum before me!' When he met the magistrates, he was able to put them out of their anxiety; but he had a mind to punish his wife. So, when he got home, he said to her, 'Wife, you have ruined me. It is known that the secret got out from my house. I shall have to go into exile because of your loose tongue.' She tried to deny it. 'Weren't there three hundred of you who heard it?' she asked. 'Three hundred!' said he; 'I made it up myself, because you were so insistent, and I wanted to try an experiment.'

Well, that senator put his wife to the test safely and sensibly. He didn't pour his wine or oil into the broken pot, only water. It was otherwise with Augustus' friend Fabius.* He had heard the 508
old emperor lamenting the losses in his family: two of his grandsons were dead, the surviving one, Postumus, was exiled because of some scandal, and he was having perforce to bring back his wife's son as his successor, though he felt sorry for his grandchild and wanted to recall him. Fabius reported this to his own wife, and she to Livia. Livia bitterly attacked Augustus: why, if he had decided on that, had he not long ago sent for his grandson, instead of leading her into a position of enmity and hostility to the desired successor. Fabius then went in to see Augustus in the morning, as usual. 'Good day, Caesar,' he said. 'Goodbye, Fabius,' replied the emperor. Fabius took the hint and went home. He sent for his wife and said to her, 'Caesar knows that I didn't keep his secret. I am therefore going to do away with myself.' 'And rightly so,' replied his wife, 'because, though you have lived with me so long, you did not recognize or guard against my loose tongue. But let me do it first.' And she seized the sword and killed herself before her husband took his own life.

[12] So it was an apt rejoinder of the comic poet Philippides, when King Lysimachus showed him a favour and asked 'What shall I give you out of what I have?' 'Anything you choose, sire,' replied the poet, 'except your secrets.'

There is another vice that accompanies talkativeness and is no less serious: curiosity. Talkative people want to hear much, so as to have much to say. They go around trying to ferret out and uncover information, especially what is secret or hidden, because they want to put together a cargo, as it were, for the benefit of their foolish talk; and then, like children with pieces of ice, they will neither hold it nor let go. To put it more accurately, they take secrets like snakes into their bosom, are unable to hold them, and end by being devoured by them. Needlefish* and vipers are said to burst when they produce their young; and emerging secrets destroy these leaky souls in just the same way.

Seleucus the Victorious, having lost his whole army and power in the battle against the Galatians, tore off his crown and fled on horseback with three or four companions, wandering a long time through a trackless wilderness. At last, tired and hungry, he came to a farm, met the owner, and asked for bread and water. The farmer provided it, and generously entertained his visitor with whatever he had on the farm; in the course of this, he recognized the king's face. Overjoyed at the lucky encounter, he was unable to restrain himself, or go along with the king's wish to keep his identity secret. He accompanied him back to the road, and, as he parted from him, said 'Goodbye, King Seleucus.' The king extended his right hand, and drew the man towards him as though to embrace him. At the same time, he signed to one of his companions to cut off the fellow's head with his sword: 'and as he talked, his head rolled in the dust.'[1] Yet if he had kept silent a little while, he would surely have earned a greater reward for his discretion than for his hospitality, when Seleucus' fortunes improved and he became a great monarch.

Nevertheless, the farmer had some excuse for his loose talk, in his expectations and his goodwill.

[13] Most careless talkers, however, destroy themselves without so much as a cause. For example: there was talk once in a barber's shop about the unbreakable strength of Dionysius' tyranny. The barber laughed. 'Fancy you saying that', he said,
509 'about Dionysius! I have my razor at his throat every few days.' Dionysius got to hear of this, and crucified the man. Barbers are, of course, a very talkative race, because the bigger talkers flock to their shop and sit with them, so they naturally catch the habit. King Archelaus, when a talkative barber was putting the sheet around him and asking him how he should cut his hair, wittily replied 'In silence.' And it was a barber who was the first to bring the news of the great Athenian disaster in Sicily.* He heard it at Piraeus, from the servant of one of those who had escaped, and he left his shop and ran to the city 'lest someone won the glory' of bringing the news, and he 'come second'. There was naturally a panic. The people gathered in the Assembly and began to investigate the source of the story. The barber was produced and questioned. He did not even know his informant's name, but referred to an unknown, anonymous person as his source. Angry cries erupted from the crowd: 'Torture the villain, put him on the rack! He's made it all up! Who else heard it? Who believed it?' The wheel was brought in, the man

stretched on it. At that moment, in came messengers with the report of the disaster, survivors of the actual battle. Everyone departed, each to mourn his own loss, leaving the poor barber strapped to the wheel. It was evening before he was released; and he proceeded to ask the executioner whether they heard how Nicias the general had died! How unconquerable and incorrigible a vice is habitual talkativeness!

[14] Bearers of bad news arouse disgust and dislike in their audience, just as people who drink bitter or malodorous drugs find even the cups from which they drink disgusting. Sophocles raised the question very neatly:

> 'Is it in the ears you're hurt, or in the mind?'
> 'Why try to fix my hurt and where it lies?'
> 'I hurt your ears; the doer hurts your heart.'[1]

In fact, however, tellers as well as doers give pain, but there is no check or control on a running tongue.

The temple of Athena of the Bronze Shrine* at Sparta was found to have been robbed, and there was an empty jar inside. The crowd that gathered couldn't make it out. One man ventured an opinion: 'If you please,' he said, 'I'll tell what I think about this jar. I suspect that the robbers drank hemlock before embarking on such a risky enterprise, and also brought wine with them, so that, if they got away successfully, they could drink the wine to counteract the effect of the poison, and go their ways safely; whereas, if they were caught, they would find an easy and painless death from the drug before they could be tortured.' Such a complicated and ingenious theory seemed to those present to indicate knowledge rather than mere conjecture. They surrounded the speaker and fired questions at him from every side. 'Who are you?' 'Who knows you?' 'How do you know these things?' Thus interrogated, he finally confessed to being one of the robbers.

Were not the murderers of Ibycus* caught in the same way? They were sitting in the theatre when some cranes flew overhead, and they laughed and whispered to one another 'There go the avengers of Ibycus!' Their neighbours in the theatre overheard, and, since Ibycus had disappeared some time before and there was a search being made, took note of the words and

reported them to the authorities. The criminals were thus convicted and taken off to execution—punished not by the cranes,
510 but by their own loose talk, which was, as it were, the avenging Fury that forced them to reveal the murder.

In the same way that diseased or painful organs in the body exercise an attraction on adjacent parts, so the careless talker's tongue, inflamed and throbbing, gathers mysteries and secrets to itself. That is why it must be fenced in; reason has always to be there as a barrier to restrain the floodwater and the landslip of the tongue. Without this, we shall be found stupider than geese, which (so they say) hold big stones in their beaks as a sort of stopper or curb to silence their cries as they cross the Taurus on their way from Cilicia, because there are a lot of eagles in the area; they make the crossing stealthily by night.*

[15] If we ask 'Who's the very worst and vilest?'[1] the answer must be the traitor Euthycrates,* who 'roofed his house with Macedonian timber', according to Demosthenes;[2] Philocrates received a large sum in gold and 'bought women and fish with it'; Euphorbus and Philagrus, who betrayed Eretria, were given estates by the Persian king. But the man with a loose tongue is a traitor, unrewarded and self-proclaimed; he does not betray horses or forts, but publicizes the secrets of lawsuits, party disputes, and political manœuvres. No one thanks him for it; he is grateful if anyone listens. What is said about the indiscriminate giver, who pours out his substance in favours to all and sundry—'no, you're not kind; you're sick, you enjoy the giving'[3]—applies equally well to the random talker: 'you're no friend if you tell me this, you've no good feelings; you're sick, you enjoy your silly prattle.'

[16] These remarks are not meant as a denunciation of talkativeness, but as therapy. We overcome morbid conditions by judgement and exercise. Judgement comes first. No one acquires the habit of avoiding and erasing from his personality a characteristic for which he does not feel disgust; and we feel disgust for a condition when we rationally observe the damage and shame that result from it. Thus we observe, in the case of the talkative, that they annoy when they wish to ingratiate, are ridiculed when they think themselves admired, spend their resources without profit, wrong their friends and benefit their enemies, and ruin themselves. The first treatment and medicine for the disease is rational evaluation of its disgraceful and painful consequences.

[17] But one must also make a second evaluation—that of the opposite state. We need to learn, remember, and have at our fingertips the praises of secrecy and the solemnity, holiness, and mysterious quality of silence. Concise and laconic speakers, and those who compress much meaning into few words, are more admired and approved, and believed to be wiser, than those who run out of control. Plato praises such people, comparing them to skilful javelin-throwers, because their speech is close-textured, dense, and concentrated.[4] Lycurgus prepared and toughened the minds of his fellow citizens to produce this sort of forcefulness by constraining them to silence in childhood. As the Celtiberians put a hard edge on their iron by burying it in the ground and then cleaning off the earthy dross, so the Spartans' words have no outer dross, but are sharpened and tempered for action by the removal of all superfluity. Their capacity for epigram and
the apt and pointed repartee derives from their habit of silence. 511
Talkative people need to remind themselves of the charm and power in sayings of this kind. For example: 'Lacedaemonians to Philip: Dionysius at Corinth'.* Or again: when Philip wrote 'If I invade Laconia, I shall eliminate you,' they replied, 'If.' When King Demetrius angrily complained that the Lacedaemonians had only sent one ambassador to him, the envoy, nothing daunted, replied 'One to one.' Brevity is admired also in ancient sayings. The Amphictyons did not inscribe the *Iliad* or the *Odyssey* or even Pindar's *Paeans* on the temple of Pythian Apollo, but 'Know Thyself', 'Nothing too much', and 'Give a guarantee, and be ruined'. They admired the compact simplicity of these expressions, which contain in a short space thoughts that have been well hammered out. And is not the god himself a lover of conciseness and brevity in his oracles? Is he not called Loxias because he is more afraid of long-windedness than of obscurity? Are not people who express their meaning by symbols without words particularly admired and praised? Take Heraclitus: his countrymen asked him to give an opinion on concord, and what he did was to mount the platform, take a cup of cold water, sprinkle some barley-groats on it, stir it with a

sprig of pennyroyal, drink it—and go away. This performance was to show that what maintains cities in peace and concord is to be content with ordinary things and not crave expensive luxuries.

Scilurus, king of Scythia, who had eighty sons, asked on his deathbed for a bundle of sticks. He first told his sons to break them as they were, in a bundle; when they failed, he took the sticks one by one and easily broke them all. He thereby demonstrated that harmony and concord were strong and indestructible, while separation made for weakness and impermanence.

[18] These and similar stories, repeated and gone over in the mind, may well stop a man taking pleasure in idle talk. But what most puts me to shame, when I reflect on the importance of attending to one's words and keeping control of one's purpose, is the story of the slave. The orator Pupius Piso, wishing to avoid being unnecessarily disturbed, ordered his slaves to answer his questions but not add anything to their answers. He then wanted to give a welcome to Clodius, who was holding office, and gave instructions that he should be invited to dinner. He set up a splendid feast. The time came, the other guests arrived, Clodius was expected. Piso kept sending the slave who was responsible for invitations to see if he was coming. Evening came; Clodius was despaired of. 'Did you invite him?' Piso asked his slave. 'Yes.' 'Then why didn't he come?' 'Because he declined.' 'Then why didn't you tell me?' 'Because you didn't ask.' Such is the way of the Roman slave! The Athenian on the other hand, as he goes on digging, will tell his master 'the terms on which the treaty has been made'.[1] Such is the force of habit; and that is what we must now discuss.

[19] One cannot restrain a talkative person by, as it were, putting a bit in his mouth. The illness must be controlled by habit. First, let him accustom himself to say nothing when there are questions asked in company, until everyone else has declined to reply: 'to counsel well is not to run a race', says Sophocles,[2] and the same goes for speaking and answering. In a race, the victory goes to the first to reach the goal; in discussion, if someone else gives an adequate answer, the right thing to do is to
512 approve and agree, so as to be thought a well-disposed person; if not, it becomes perfectly unobjectionable, and indeed timely, to correct ignorance and supply missing considerations. Let us

especially guard against answering out of turn, when the question has been put to someone else. It is probably *never* right to thrust aside the person to whom a point has been put and volunteer an answer oneself. That will give the impression of criticizing both parties—the one for being unable to satisfy the demand made on him, the other for not knowing who to ask. But this kind of rashness and pushiness is particularly rude in the case of answers to inquiries. The person who jumps in to answer before the person who is addressed implies 'Why do you ask *him*? What does *he* know about it? While I'm here, there's no point in asking anyone else.' But we often ask questions not because we need the answer but because we wish to encourage someone to talk and be friendly, and are anxious to bring them into the conversation. This is what Socrates does to Theaetetus and Charmides.* Jumping in with an answer, and so catching the ear and the attention of a person for oneself, is exactly like rushing up to someone and kissing him when he wants to be kissed by someone different, or making someone look towards you whose eyes are turned on another person altogether. Even if the person asked refuses to answer, the right thing is to wait, accommodate oneself to the questioner's wishes, and deal with the situation modestly and quietly, treating it is an invitation intended for someone else. Those to whom questions are put are very properly forgiven if they stumble in their answers, but the man who puts himself forward of his own accord and anticipates the answer is not popular even if he gets it right, and if he makes a mistake he is an object of ridicule and malicious delight.

[20] A second exercise involves questions asked of ourselves. This is a point wherein the talkative man must be particularly careful. He must first avoid the trap of giving a serious answer to people who challenge him merely to ridicule or insult him. There are people who invent questions unnecessarily, simply for fun and diversion, and pose them to provoke the talkative to their usual nonsense. One must watch out for this, and not plunge into a speech as though grateful for the chance, but consider the character and purpose of the questioner. If he clearly has a genuine desire to learn, one should form the habit of pausing and leaving an interval between question and answer, for the questioner to add anything and to give oneself time to consider one's answer. Avoid overrunning the question, burying it under a heap of words, giving a whole string of answers in your enthusiasm while (as often happens) the question is still being framed. The Pythian priestess, of course, sometimes gives instant oracles, before being asked, because the god whom she serves 'hears the unspeaking and understands the dumb',[3] but ordinary people who want to give right answers must first wait to know the questioner's intention and purpose exactly, so as to avoid exemplifying the proverb about 'asking for buckets'.* In any case, this violent appetite for talking must be resisted, so as not to make people think that you have a sort of pressure building up behind the tongue waiting to be released by the question. Socrates used to control his thirst by not allowing himself to drink after exercise until he had drawn and poured away the first jugful. This was to accustom the irrational part of his soul to wait for the moment approved by reason.

513 [21] Now there are three kinds of answers to questions: the barely adequate, the kind, and the superfluous. If anyone asks 'Is Socrates at home?' the unwilling, unenthusiastic answer is 'Not at home'—or just plain 'No', if one wants to be laconic; the Spartans themselves wrote a big 'No' on the paper in answer to Philip's letter inquiring whether they would admit him into the city. The kind answer would be 'Not at home, but at the bank', or, if you want to give rather better measure, 'waiting for some foreign friends there'. The superfluous, talkative answer, if you happen to have read Antimachus of Colophon,* goes: 'Not at home, but at the bank, waiting for some Ionian friends, recommended to him by Alcibiades, who wants to return from exile, and that's why he has made Tissaphernes change sides.' Then we will get the whole of the eighth book of Thucydides,* drowning the poor man, all the way down to the capture of Miletus and Alcibiades' second exile.

The right thing to do, then, is to keep one's talkativeness in check and tread closely in the footsteps of the question, making the questioner's need the measure by which to circumscribe your answer.

Carneades, when not yet famous, was having a philosophical conversation in the gymnasium, when the official in charge sent to tell him to lower his voice (which was very loud). 'Give me the measure to keep to,' said Carneades. 'It's the man you're arguing with,' replied the official, and it was a good reply. The questioner's wish is the respondent's regulator.

[22] Again: as Socrates recommended the avoidance of food and drink which encourage one to eat or drink when not hungry or thirsty, so should the talkative man fear and resist the sort of talk that he most enjoys or in which he indulges to excess. Military men, for example, are fond of telling war-stories. Homer represents Nestor like this, as often retelling his own brilliant deeds. Men who have succeeded at law or been unexpectedly fortunate in dealing with emperors and governors suffer from the consequential disease of often recalling and relating the way in which they obtained the audience, were introduced, spoke, argued, refuted opponents or prosecutors, and won praise. Happiness is a good deal more talkative than the sleeplessness of which the comic poet tells us;[1] it often revives and renews itself by its tales. This makes people ready to slip into such talk at any excuse. Not only do we all 'put our hands where the pain is'; pleasure has the power of attracting the voice and guiding the tongue, in its desire to linger on the happy memory. Lovers spend most of their time discussing things that remind them of those they love. Even if they don't speak to human hearers, they address inanimate objects on the subject:

> O darling bed!

or

> O blessed lamp, Bacchis made you her god;
> greatest of gods, if such you seem to her!

Of course, the talkative make no distinction between one subject of conversation and another; but all the same, an individual 514
who has a particular liking for certain themes should take special precautions and back away from these as far as possible, since the pleasure of them is liable to lead on into further prolixity. The same applies to subjects of which people think they have some superior experience or capacity. Self-love and vanity make such people

> devote the greater part of every day
> to those pursuits where they surpass themselves,[1]

the great reader to recondite learning, the grammarian to the technicalities of language, the much-travelled wanderer to tales of foreign lands. This too is to be guarded against: talkativeness always has the temptation to stray, like an animal, to familiar pastures. The boy Cyrus* behaved remarkably in challenging his contemporaries not to competitions at which he was better, but to those where he was less experienced than they, in order not to hurt them by his success but to profit by learning from them. Our talkative friend does just the opposite. He thrusts aside any discussion from which he might learn or discover something he doesn't know. He cannot pay the small price of being silent. Round and round he goes, forcing the conversation into the well-trodden paths of his old, old, story. I had a friend who happened to have read two or three books of Ephorus.* He wore everybody out, and broke up every dinner-party, with his story of the battle of Leuctra and what happened thereafter. We nicknamed him Epaminondas.

[23] But this is the least of evils. One ought really to divert talkativeness into these harmless paths. Loquaciousness on scholarly subjects is not so disagreeable. Such people, however, should acquire the habit of writing or private discussion.* The Stoic Antipater, unable and unwilling to confront Carneades' voluble attack on the Stoics directly, filled books with written arguments against him, and came to be called 'the shouting pen'. Now it may be that this sort of noisy shadow-boxing with a written text might keep the talkative away from the people at large and gradually make them less of a burden to others, just as dogs become less savage to men if they can vent their bad temper on sticks and stones. But it will always be best for the talkative to consort with their elders and betters, because they will get into the habit of being silent, out of respect for these people's opinion. All this habit-forming must be closely combined and associated with attention and reflection. Whenever we are about to speak, and the words come into our mouths, we must say to ourselves: 'What is this remark that is forcing itself upon me? What is my tongue panting to do? What good comes of saying this? What harm of saying nothing?' The words are not a sort of oppressive weight of which you can be relieved. Even when they have been said, they are still there. Human beings talk:

either for their own advantage, because they need something; or to help the listener; or, thirdly, to give pleasure to one another, using words as salt, as it were, to improve the flavour of whatever pursuit or activity they are engaged in. But if what is said is neither useful to the speaker nor necessary to the listener, and there is no pleasure or charm in it, why is it said? There is a pointlessness and fruitlessness in words just as much as in actions.

Finally, and above all, we must keep fresh in our minds the saying of Simonides, that he often repented of speaking but 515
never of being silent. We must remember also that exercise conquers all, and is stronger than all things. Men can even, by effort and attention, and with much labour and pain, rid themselves of a hiccup or a cough. Silence, says Hippocrates, does not produce thirst; neither does it produce pain or distress.

XI

BASHFULNESS

Dysōpia, whose diagnosis and cure are the subject of this essay, means something like 'being put out of countenance'. English equivalents are hard to find: 'bashfulness', 'naughty bashfulness', 'compliance', 'false shame', 'misplaced embarrassment', 'undue scrupulousness', have all been tried by translators. In any case, it is, as Plutarch observes, a fault associated with the virtue of modesty; it leads to disaster when its victims find themselves unable to say 'no' to anything or to resist pressure or moral blackmail. Plutarch's discussion is unique in the ancient moralists. The actual word *dysōpia* was thought unclassical, and purists found fault with Plutarch for using it.

528 **[1]** Some of the natural products of the earth are wild and unfertile and, as they grow, do damage to cultivated plants and seeds; yet farmers regard them as signs not of a poor soil, but of one that is strong and rich. Similarly, some psychological conditions, though not good in themselves, form a sort of growth that occurs in a nature which is good and generally capable of improvement by reason. Among these I count what is called bashfulness. It is not a bad sign, but it can be a cause of evil. Shame often produces the same errors as shamelessness, except that it is accompanied by pain and grief at the error, instead of pleasure. A shameless man feels no pain in disgrace, whereas one who is easily abashed suffers even from the appearance of disgrace. Bashfulness is an excess of shame. This is why it is called by the name, *dysōpia*, meaning 'being put out of countenance', because in this condition, the face somehow displays confusion and debility at the same time as the mind. As we define dejection as a distress that makes us lower our eyes, so we use the term that means 'being put out of countenance' for a sense of shame which inhibits you from looking people who make demands on you straight in the eye. This is why the orator said that the shameless man 'had whores in his eyes, not pupils';*[1] the easily abashed, on the other hand, show their softness and effeminacy in their eyes, euphemistically using the word 'shame' to describe their defeat at the hands of the shameless.

Cato used to say that he preferred young men who blush to those who are pale. He was right to rub in the lesson that blame is to be more feared than hard work, and suspicion than danger; but one should also try to eliminate excessive sensibility and neurotic anxiety about blame. It is common to find men just as 529
afraid of ill words as of ill treatment, and therefore abandoning honourable causes out of cowardice, because they cannot bear the loss of face.

[2] This weakness must not pass uncriticized; but neither should we approve its unbending and unblinking opposite:

> next there appeared,* where'er he made a rush,
> bold Anaxarchus, stubborn as a dog.[1]

What we should try to contrive is a reasonable mixture of the two extremes, avoiding both the shamelessness that never backs down, and the weakness that gives way too much. The cure is difficult, the curtailment of such excesses is not without risk. If a farmer is clearing away some worthless weeds, he either wields the spade without sparing and digs out the roots, or calls fire to his aid and burns the weeds out; whereas when he approaches a vine or an apple or an olive that needs pruning, he goes to work with a careful hand, anxious not to damage healthy growth. Similarly, if a philosopher is trying to eradicate from a young man's soul the mean and obstinate growth of envy, or a premature love of money* or intemperate love of pleasure, he draws blood, he presses hard, he makes a deep cut and scar. On the other hand, when he brings a word of chastisement to bear on a delicate and tender part of the personality, like that which is subject to bashfulness and confusion, he takes care not to cut out shame inadvertently at the same time. When nurses wipe dirt off children, they sometimes rub the flesh raw and cause pain. We must not cut young people's bashfulness right down to the quick and make them hardened and insensitive. People who demolish houses next door to temples leave contiguous buildings standing and shore them up. Similarly, we should attack bashfulness with caution, taking care not to pull down with it the neighbouring qualities of modesty, moderation, and civilized behaviour, under cover of which it insinuates itself, flattering its victim with the idea that he is a humane, civilized, sociable being, not at all inflexible or self-willed. The Stoics therefore actually made a distinction between shame (*aischūnē*) and bashfulness on the one hand, and modesty (*aidōs*) on the other. Their object was to prevent a confusion of terms from providing an excuse for damaging behaviour. But I trust they will permit us to use the words without quibbling—indeed, in Homer's sense, when he speaks of modesty (*aidōs*) that 'does men much harm, and also good'.[2] He was right to put the harm first: modesty only becomes useful when reason has eliminated its excesses and left it in moderation.

[3] The victim of a grave case of bashfulness must first be convinced that his condition is damaging, that nothing damaging is honourable, and that it is wrong to be seduced by praise into taking pleasure in being called 'smart' and 'nice' rather than grave and great and just, or, like Pegasus in Euripides, who 'crouched, yielding more, the more his rider wished',[3] to surrender and humiliate oneself before importunate demands, because one is afraid of being called hard and stubborn. They say that the asp sent by Isis to curl round the head of the cruel Egyptian Bocchoris cast its shadow upon him, to make him give just decisions. Bashfulness, on the other hand, bears down on the unmanly and unvigorous, who have not the strength to say no or speak out against anything; it perverts their judgements, it muzzles their advice, it forces them to do many things that they
530 would rather not. It is always the most brutal who dominate such persons, because their shamelessness beats down their victims' modesty. Bashfulness is like a low-lying, soft piece of ground; it cannot repel or turn away an attack, and is accessible to the most disgraceful feelings and actions. It is a bad protector of childhood, as Brutus pointed out when he said, of a man who never said no to a proposal, that he cannot have made good use of his youth. It is a bad protector also of marriage, and of the women's quarters, as the penitent adulteress* in Sophocles says to her lover: 'You persuaded me, you coaxed me.'[1] Bashfulness is the first seducer, and opens the door to immorality. It betrays the whole place to the attacker—unsecured, unlocked, a downhill run. Offers of money, of course, capture women of bad character; persuasion and exploiting their bashfulness often bring the virtuous to surrender. I say nothing of the financial problems

incident to bashfulness: lending to people you don't trust, standing surety for people you don't want to guarantee, approving the old saying 'Give a guarantee, and be ruined', but not having the will to act on it.

[4] It would be difficult to count the victims whom this affliction has ruined. When Creon said to Medea

> Better for me to be your enemy now,
> than soften towards you and be sorry later,[2]

he gave good advice to others, but himself gave way to his embarrassment, granted her request for a day's stay of execution, and thereby destroyed his whole house. There have been cases also of persons who suspected assassination or poison, but were deflected from their doubts in this way. This is how Dion met his death. He was not unaware of Callippus' conspiracy, but was ashamed to take precautions against such a close friend. The case of Antipater,* the son of Cassander, is similar. After entertaining Demetrius to dinner, he was invited back the following day, and felt ashamed to distrust the man who had trusted him. So he went along, and after the dinner he was murdered. Again: Polyperchon agreed, for a fee of a hundred talents, to kill Heracles, Alexander's son by Barsine, and accordingly invited him to dinner. The boy was suspicious and afraid, and excused himself on grounds of illness. Polyperchon then went to see him. 'Young man,' he said, 'you should model yourself on your father's easy ways and good companionship, unless of course you are afraid that I am in a plot against you.' The lad felt ashamed, and went along. His hospitable hosts strangled him. So Hesiod's remark is not (as some say) absurd or foolish, but actually wise: 'Ask friends to dinner, leave your foes alone.'[3] Do not show embarrassment before your enemy, and do not make up to him if he appears to trust you. If you invite him, you will be invited back; if you give him a meal, you will get one from him, and your sense of shame will have led you to sacrifice the keen edge of the distrust which guarded you.

[5] This disease, then, is the cause of many evils. We must try to rid ourselves of it by exercises. We can begin—as with other things we practise—with little incidents which are not too hard to stare in the face. Suppose someone proposes your health at

dinner, when you have already drunk enough. Do not be bashful, or force yourself; put your cup down. Or suppose again someone suggests a game of dice at dinner. Do not be bashful, do not be frightened of ridicule. Do as Xenophanes did, when Lasus of Hermione called him a coward for not being willing to play dice with him: admit that you are a coward and have no stomach for shameful doings. Again: you have met a talkative character, who holds on and sticks firmly to you. Do not be bashful: cut him short and get on with your business. This kind
531 of avoidance and rejection, which gives practice in resisting bashfulness at the cost of slight offence, forms the habits needed for greater exploits. It is worth remembering a remark of Demosthenes. When the Athenians were eager to help Harpalus and were arming themselves against Alexander, Philoxenus, Alexander's admiral, suddenly put in an appearance. The Athenians were appalled, and too frightened to speak in the Assembly. Only Demosthenes spoke up. 'If people cannot look at the lamp,' he said, 'what will they do when they see the sun?' What will *you* do at some important moment, when the emperor makes a request, or your people try to put pressure on you, if you cannot so much as reject the cup when a friend toasts you, or extricate yourself from the grip of a chatterer, but let him walk all over you with his drivel, because you haven't the courage to say 'See you later, I'm busy just now'?

[6] There is value also in small-scale exercises and practice in not being embarrassed where praise is involved. Suppose a friend's harpist gives a bad performance at dinner, or an actor bought at great expense murders Menander, and yet the audience applauds and admires. It is surely not difficult or awkward just to listen quietly and not utter insincere words of praise in the face of the evidence. If you cannot control yourself in this, what will you do when a friend reads out a poor poem or delivers a silly and ridiculously written speech? Presumably you will praise him, and join the flatterers in their applause. How then will you be able to reprove your friend when he goes wrong in business? How will you set him right when he behaves badly in the matter of an office or a marriage or a political move? I cannot myself approve Pericles' answer to the friend who asked him to bear false witness and swear to it: 'I am your

friend', he said, 'as far as the altar.' He had already gone too near. A man who has long accustomed himself not to praise an orator or applaud a singer, or join in a laugh at an inept joke against his better judgement, will not let anyone go so far or say 'Take an oath for me, give false witness, pronounce a wrong verdict' to a man who has proved himself immune to pressure in those lesser matters.

[7] The same sort of resistance should be made to demands for money. Good habits may be formed in unimportant cases, where excuses are easy. Archelaus, king of Macedon, was asked for a gold cup at dinner by a man whose one idea of the good life was acquisition. He told the slave to give the cup to Euripides, and then turned to the man who had asked for it. 'You', he said, 'are the right person to ask and not to get it; he is the right person to get it, without so much as asking.' Excellent: this was to make judgement, not possible embarrassment, the decisive factor in giving and granting favours. We do not all do so well: we often pass over decent men who are our friends and confer our gifts on forward and importunate askers. It is not that we want to give, only that we are unable to refuse. Old Antigonus, likewise, was frequently annoyed by the importunities of Bion, until he finally said 'Give Violence and Necessity* their talent.' Yet Antigonus was of all kings the most skilful and urbane in shaking off this kind of approach. When a Cynic asked for a drachma, he replied 'That's not a sum for a king to give'; and when the man retorted 'Then give me a talent', he came back with 'That's not a sum for a Cynic to receive.' Diogenes used to go round begging from the statues in the Ceramicus, and when people wondered what he was doing, he used to say he was practising being refused. What we have to do is to practise first in small matters, and train ourselves to refuse small improper requests, so that we shall have funds to help those who 532
make proper ones. As Demosthenes put it, no one 'having spent what he has on what he ought not, will find the means for what he ought in what he has not.'[1] And the disgrace is many times worse when it is extravagance in superfluities that leads to lack of means for a good cause.

[8] But it is not only in regard to money that bashfulness is a poor and foolish manager. It deprives us of the benefit of our

reason in greater matters also. When we are ill, we fail to call in the expert because we are embarrassed not to ask a medical friend. As teachers for our children, we choose not the best, but those who apply to us. In court, we often fail to let an effective and experienced advocate speak for us, because we want to show favour to a friend's or relative's son by letting him show off his rhetorical education. Finally, we even see many so-called philosophers professing Epicureanism or Stoicism not for choice or after ripe consideration, but in order to attach themselves to friends or relatives who exploit their embarrassment. Let us therefore train ourselves for these circumstances also before we get near them, using the small incidents of everyday life, accustoming ourselves not to choose a barber or a laundry because of any personal embarrassment, not to lodge in a bad hotel where there is a better one because the hotel-keeper has often been polite to us, but always to choose the better alternative (even if it is only slightly better) for the sake of establishing a habit. The Pythagoreans always took care never to cross the left leg over the right, or choose an even number rather than an odd, if the choice was otherwise indifferent. One should also make a habit, when celebrating a sacrifice or a marriage or otherwise receiving guests, of not inviting persons who have saluted us or hastened to meet us, so much as good men who wish us well. A man who has practised these exercises and formed these habits will be hard to victimize, indeed unassailable, in matters of greater moment.

[9] So much, then, for exercises. I turn next to useful reflections. The first is that which teaches and reminds us that all affections and maladies are accompanied by the very evils that we think to avoid by their means: bad reputation accompanies love of reputation, pain goes with love of pleasure, hard labour with softness, defeat and condemnation with the will to win. It is the fate of bashfulness that, in endeavouring to avoid the smoke of disrepute, it falls into the fire of real disgrace. Ashamed to oppose those who rudely try to embarrass us, people later come to be put to shame by just reproach. Fearful of trivial censure, they often submit to admitted disgrace. Too embarrassed to refuse a friend's request for money, they are subsequently proved not to have the wherewithal, and cut a sorry figure. Hav-

ing agreed to help someone in a lawsuit, they are outfaced by the opposition, and run away to hide. Bashfulness has often locked a man into an unprofitable contract for a daughter's or sister's marriage, and then makes him change his mind and break his word.

[10] Someone once said as a joke that the inhabitants of Asia were the slaves of one man simply because they could not pronounce the single syllable 'no'. Victims of bashfulness, however, can avoid many a strange and unwanted act of subservience simply by raising an eyebrow or looking at the ground without saying a word. Euripides says that silence is 'an answer to the wise',[2] but we seem rather to need it with the foolish, for the intelligent can be wooed with words. Indeed, one should also have at hand a supply of the sayings of the good and great, for use with those who seek to cause embarrassment. A good example is Phocion's answer to Antipater—'You cannot have me both as a friend and as a flatterer'—or his words to the Athen- 533
ians, who asked him for a money contribution at a festival, and gave him a handclap: 'I am ashamed to pay you, and not repay *him*'—and he pointed to the moneylender Callicles. As Thucydides says, 'there is no disgrace in admitting poverty, but there is disgrace in doing nothing practical to avoid it'.[1] But the man who, in his foolish weakness, is too embarrassed to say to the insistent asker 'There's no white silver in my cave, good sir',[2] and later renounces the undertaking he was (as it were) pledged to, is 'bound fast in chains forged not of bronze but shame'.[3] Persaeus, lending money to a friend, none the less insisted on a formal agreement made in public through a bank. He was doubtless mindful of Hesiod's words 'And with your brother—laugh, but bring a witness.'[4] The friend was amazed and asked Persaeus whether it had to be done so legally. 'Yes, it has,' he replied, 'so that I can get the money back by friendly arrangement, instead of having to claim it legally.' Many who have dispensed with guarantees at first, because they were embarrassed about it, end by going to law in an atmosphere of enmity.

[11] Again, Plato gave Helicon of Cyzicus a letter of recommendation to Dionysius, in which he praised Helicon as a fair-minded and reasonable man, but added at the end of the letter, 'I write this about a human being, a creature naturally liable to change.'[5] Xenocrates, austere as he was, was moved by bashfulness to recommend an unsatisfactory person to Polyperchon, as the event showed. The Macedonian welcomed the man, and asked if he needed anything. The man asked for a talent. Polyperchon gave it, but wrote to Xenocrates advising him in future to be more careful about his recommendations. Xenocrates at least acted in ignorance; but we often write letters and give money in full knowledge of the unworthiness of the recipients, thereby damaging ourselves; nor indeed is there any pleasure in it, as there is in doing favours to a mistress or a flatterer, but only the disgust and indignation that we feel at the impudence that subverts and overthrows our reason. There are no circumstances more appropriate than a confrontation with those who try to embarrass us, in which to quote 'I know indeed what evils I shall do'[6] by giving false witness or a corrupt judgement or a wrong vote or a loan to a non-payer.

[12] That is why bashfulness, more than any other condition, leads to repentance—not postponed, but instantaneous. We grumble as we give, we are ashamed as we bear witness, we lose face as we collaborate, we are found out when we fail to oblige. Being too feeble to resist, we often make impossible promises to our insistent claimants—recommendations at court, or introductions to great men—because we neither want nor have the guts to say 'The emperor doesn't know me, go to someone else.' Even after quarrelling with Agesilaus, Lysander was supposed to have great influence with him because of his reputation; yet he was not ashamed to excuse himself to claimants for favour, and tell them to apply elsewhere, and try people who had more influence with the king than he had. There is no disgrace in not being omnipotent. What is both disgraceful and very painful is to undertake such tasks and be put under pressure to do so, when you have no power or no natural ability to fulfil them.

[13] Look at it in another way. It is right to meet reasonable and appropriate demands with enthusiasm, willingly, and with-
534 out any sense of embarrassment. As to unsuitable or damaging requests, keep in mind the story of Zeno. He met a young man of his acquaintance walking quietly along by the wall, and discovered that he was trying to avoid a friend who was pressing

him to give false evidence. 'You fool,' said Zeno, 'what are you saying? Can it be that this foolish and wicked man is not afraid or ashamed before you, while you haven't the courage to stand up to him in a just cause?' The poet who wrote 'Against the wicked, wickedness is never a useless sword'[1] teaches a bad lesson if he is telling us to defend ourselves against vice by copying it. But to use one's own freedom from embarrassment to brush off immodest and unabashed importunities, or one's own sense of shame to avoid granting shameful favours to the shameless—that is something wise men can rightly and properly do.

[14] And here is a further point. There is no difficulty in resisting the obscure, humble, and worthless among those who seek to impose upon us. Some evade their attacks simply by a laugh or a joke. For example, Theocritus found two people at the bath wanting to borrow his strigil; one was a stranger, the other a known thief. He got out of it by saying, 'I don't know *you*—and I do know *you*.' Lysimache, the priestess of Athena Polias* at Athens, had an answer for the mule-drivers who had brought the sacrifices, when they asked her for a drink: 'I fear this too may become a tradition,' she said. Antigonus also had an answer for the cowardly and unmanly son of a brave officer, when the boy asked for promotion: 'My promotions, my lad,' he said, 'are for doing good work, not having a good father.'

[15] But it is different when the pressure comes from a person of power or prestige. Such people are particularly hard to put off or shake off when they make requests about legal decisions or votes. What young Cato did to Catulus* may well seem neither convenient nor necessary. Catulus stood in very high regard at Rome, and at the time held the office of censor, while Cato had charge of the public treasury. Catulus approached Cato to request a remission for someone who had been fined, and became very insistent in his attempt to force Cato to oblige him. Cato became angry. 'It is a disgrace, Catulus,' he cried, 'for you, a censor, to be thrown out of my office by my staff, because you will not leave of your own accord.' Catulus was ashamed, and departed angrily. More moderate and reasonable, perhaps, are the responses of Agesilaus and Themistocles. Agesilaus, asked by his father to decide a case contrary to law, replied 'But it was from you, father, that I first learnt to obey the laws; so it's on your instructions that I am now doing nothing against them.' Themistocles' answer to Simonides' request for an improper favour runs like this: 'You wouldn't be a good poet if you sang without regard to the tune, and I shouldn't be a good magistrate if I gave a judgement without regard to the law.'

[16] Yet, as Plato says,[2] it is not because of discord between foot and lyre that city quarrels with city and friend with friend, suffering terrible things at each others' hands, but because their management of law and justice is out of tune. Nevertheless, there are some people who maintain perfect accuracy in song and writing and metre, but expect others to pay no heed to such standards in office, in court, or in public affairs. So we must deal with them on this same principle. Suppose an orator approaches you when you are acting as judge, or a popular politician when you are on the Council: grant him his wish, on condition that he makes a solecism in his proemium or a barbarism in his narrative. He won't want to do so, because it *seems* disgraceful; some people, as we know, won't even tolerate a clash between vowel and vowel* in their speeches! Again, sup-
535 pose a famous and distinguished man tries to put pressure on you. Tell him to dance or pull a face as he crosses the square! If he refuses, then it's your turn to speak, and ask which is really disgraceful—to make mistakes in grammar and pull an ugly face, or to disregard the law and break one's oath, and improperly give preference to the bad over the good. Nicostratus of Argos is another example in point. Archidamus once tried to bribe him to betray Cromnus, offering him a large sum of money, and marriage to any lady in Sparta he chose. He replied that Archidamus could surely not be a descendant of Heracles, since Heracles went round killing wicked men, whereas Archidamus was making good men wicked. Similarly, we can say to a person who claims to be a gentleman, if he tries to put pressure on us and embarrass us, that what he is doing is inappropriate to, and unworthy of, his family and his character.

[17] Turn now to the less reputable. The point to consider is, for example, whether you can shame the miser into lending you a talent without an agreement, or the vain man into giving up his right of precedence, or the office-hunter his candidature, if he seems likely to be successful. It would indeed be terrible if these characters were to stand fast, firm and steady in their morbid passions, while we, who wish and claim to be lovers of honour and justice, are not masters of ourselves, but allow our good qualities to be subverted and sacrificed. If our intimidators act as they do for the sake of power or reputation, it is absurd for us to make fools of ourselves and hear bad things spoken of us, in the course of honouring and raising others in the world. We should be like dishonest umpires at the games, or those who confer offices or crowns or glory improperly on others by public vote, thereby losing their own honour and reputation. And if we see that the pressure put upon us is motivated by love of money, does it not spring to mind that it is monstrous to sacrifice one's own virtue and good name to make someone else's purse heavier? These thoughts do indeed occur to many, and they are not unaware that they are doing wrong. They are like guests forced to drink huge bumpers of wine, who, with much difficulty, much groaning, and much distortion of countenance, finally succeed in fulfilling their assignment.

[18] Flabbiness of character is like the sort of physical temperament that is unduly susceptible to heat and cold. These people dither and go limp under the influence of the praise bestowed on them by those who exploit their weakness, while they have a neurotic terror of the reproaches and contempt of the disappointed. Both kinds of attack should be resisted. There is no call to yield either to intimidation or to flattery. Thucydides knew that envy is an inevitable concomitant of power: 'it is a wise adviser', he says, 'who incurs envy only for really important causes.'[1] Our position is different. We find it hard to escape envy, but impossible to escape blame or to avoid displeasing some of our acquaintances. Wise policy with us therefore will be to accept the hostility of the foolish rather than that of those who justifiably reproach us if we do unjust services to the others. Praise from people who want to put pressure on us is false coin; we must guard against it, and not behave like pigs, by letting anyone wreak his will on us in return for a scratch and a tickle, and grovelling under his feet. People who surrender their ears to flatterers are no better than people who let others trip them up by the legs. Indeed, they take a worse tumble.

536 Either they give up opposition to, and punishment of, the wicked in order to be thought kind, merciful, and sympathetic; or else they are persuaded by their flatterers to undertake unnecessary and dangerous quarrels and prosecutions, by being dubbed the only 'real men', the only persons 'immune to flattery', the only 'mouths' and 'voices' of free speech! Bion compared such people to jars, which are easily carried by the 'ears'. The sophist Alexinus, they say, once made derogatory remarks, on the public walk, about Stilpo of Megara. One of the company remarked, 'But Stilpo was praising you the other day.' 'Of course he was,' said Alexinus, 'he's an excellent fellow.' Menedemus, on the other hand, hearing that Alexinus often praised him, remarked 'But I always criticize Alexinus; so he must be a bad man, either because he praises a bad man, or because he is criticized by a good man.' Such was Menedemus' invincible immunity to this kind of attack; such too was his grasp of the precept delivered by Heracles in Antisthenes, who tells his children never to thank anyone for praising them.[1] This is equivalent to telling them not to be bashful and not to respond to flattery in kind. Pindar's remark to the man who claimed to praise him everywhere is a sufficient retort: 'I return your favour; I make you tell the truth!'

[19] Victims of bashfulness have particular need of a remedy that is, in fact, of service in all emotional disorders. When they are forced by their foible to do something wrong contrary to their better judgement, and have failed to resist the pressure, the best thing for them to do is to fix the event in their memory and rehearse and retain in their minds as long as possible the symptoms of the pain and the remorse. Wayfarers who have stumbled over rocks, or pilots who have been wrecked on a headland, continue to fear and take precautions against these and similar perils as long as they remember what happened to them. Similarly, those who constantly set before themselves, in pain and remorse, the shameful and damaging effects of this bashfulness, will take a hold on themselves when like circumstances recur, and will not easily let themselves be led astray.

XII

AGAINST BORROWING MONEY

This vivid, rhetorical, even satirical piece—its variety and vivacity recall Roman satire—is unusual in style for Plutarch. It addresses a social evil based on individual moral weakness; so it is not so much an attack on an economic system as a plea to the individual for self-amendment. There are two main themes: the evil of indebtedness, and its cure. The book was popular with later moralists: St Basil and St Gregory of Nyssa both have sermons against moneylenders which draw heavily on it.

[1] Plato, in the *Laws*, forbids people to draw from their neigh- 827
bour's water-supply unless they have first dug down to the clay and proved their own land to be waterless.[1] The clay, being dense and sticky, holds water and does not let it through. However, he adds, those who cannot find water of their own should take it from another; the law (he says) comes to the aid of the needy. Then should there not also be a law about money, to prevent borrowing from others and drawing on other people's supply unless a man has first reviewed his own resources and assembled, drop by drop, as it were, what is necessary for his needs? As things are, however, luxury, easy living, and extravagance prevent men from making use of what they have, and induce them to take money from others at high rates of interest when they have no need. There is a nice proof of this: people do not lend to the needy, but only to those who want to secure a certain prosperity, while the creditor produces witnesses and guarantors whose evidence that he has means is to be trusted, whereas if he really does have means he ought not to be borrowing.

[2] Why do you count your banker as your financial agent?
Borrow from your own table;* you have cups, dishes, silver 828
bowls. Pledge these to meet your debts. Colias or Tenedos* will supply your table with earthenware: it's cleaner than silver, and it doesn't have that horrid rusty smell of usury that tarnishes your extravagance day in, day out; and it won't remind you of the first day of the month, the holy day that the moneylenders make so ominous and hateful. Not even Zeus the Possessor can

rescue people who pledge their goods instead of selling them. Ashamed to take a price, they nevertheless feel no shame at paying interest on their own money! The famous Pericles made the ornaments of Athena, forty talents' weight of fine gold, detachable from the statue, 'so that if we use them for the war, we can restore no less afterwards'.* Being in debt is like being besieged: let us not admit a garrison from our enemy the moneylender, or watch our property given away into slavery. Rather than that, let us strip the superfluities from table, bed, carriage, life-style; let us keep ourselves free—we will restore it all if fortune smiles on us.

[3] The women of Rome* gave their valuables as a first offering to Pythian Apollo; that is how the golden bowl came to be sent to Delphi. The women of Carthage cut their hair and used it to string the catapults and engines to save their country. Yet we are ashamed to be self-sufficient, and enslave ourselves to bills and mortgages, when we ought to be drawing in our horns and sticking to the necessities, and building a temple of liberty for our wives and children out of the break-up and sale of our useless and superfluous goods. Artemis of Ephesus grants sanctuary and security from creditors to debtors who seek asylum in her temple; but the sanctuary of Economy, safe and inviolate, stands open everywhere to the prudent, and offers them a wide field of happy and honourable leisure. The Pythia told the Athenians in the Persian War that the god was giving them a wooden wall; they abandoned their land and city and property and houses, and took refuge in the ships to fight for freedom. God gives us too a wooden table, an earthenware bowl, and a coarse cloak, if we are ready to live as free men.

'Wait not for horses to ride',* nor for chariots, ornamented and silvered, which usury soon catches up and passes in the race. Choose an ordinary ass or horse to escape your enemy, your tyrant, the moneylender; he is not asking for earth and water,* like the king of Persia, but he's got his hands on your liberty, he's cancelling your rights as a citizen. If you don't pay, he persecutes you; if you have the money, he won't take it; if you want to sell, he beats you down; if you won't sell, he puts on the pressure; if you go to law, he works on the judge; if you swear you can't attend, he takes steps to compel you; if you go to visit him, he shuts you out; if you stay at home, he camps on your doorstep and batters on the door.

[4] What good did Solon do to the Athenians when he abolished debts on the security of the person? They are still slaves to every liquidator—or rather, not to the principals, which would not be so bad, but to rude, savage, barbarous slaves, like the fiery torturers and executioners who Plato says are put in charge of the wicked in Hades. These people make the market-place a true 'place of the wicked'[1] for the miserable debtors. They feed
on them like vultures, they gnaw them 'deep plunging in the 829
flesh'[2]. Others they treat like Tantalus, standing over them and barring them from tasting their own produce when they bring in the vintage or the harvest. Darius sent Datis and Artaphernes to Athens with chains and bonds for the prisoners; these men bring chests full of contracts and bills to Greece—fetters indeed—and drive through the cities on their way, not sowing a kindly crop, like Triptolemus, but planting roots of debt, painful, prolific, and ineradicable, that encircle and invade our cities, crushing and strangling. Hares—so they say—can bear and rear young and conceive again at the same time; but the debts administered by these barbarous scoundrels breed before they conceive: they demand repayment the moment they offer the loan; when they put the money down, they take it away again, and lend what they take in return for providing the loan.

[5] The Messenians say,

> Pylos there is before Pylos, and Pylos there is yet another;[1]

and so we can say to the moneylenders,

> interest there is before interest, and interest there is yet another!

And then these dare to laugh at the physicists who claim that 'nothing can be created out of nothing'! With these people, interest is created* out of something which has no being or substance any more. They think it a disgrace to be a tax-contractor, though this is perfectly legal, while they are themselves illegally collecting taxes—or, to be more accurate, cancelling debts in the act of making the loan, since the man who receives less than is written in his contract is having part of the debt to him cancelled.

Yet the Persians* think lying the second worst sin, and indebtedness the first, because debtors usually also have to lie;

but creditors lie and deceive even more in their own day-books, where they write that they are paying so much to so-and-so, when in fact they are paying less. Moreover, their lies are occasioned not by necessity but by greed, not by poverty but by insatiable desires, 'the end of which bringeth no joy' or use, but only ruin to the victims. These people do not farm the lands of which they rob their debtors, nor occupy the houses from which they have thrown them out, nor eat at their tables, nor wear their clothes. Scarcely is the first victim ruined, before he is used as bait in the hunt for a second. The devastation spreads like fire, growing by the ruin and destruction of those who come in its way, consuming one after another. And the moneylender who fans the flames and feeds them to produce all these sufferers gets nothing in return but the pleasure of reading from time to time how many people he has sold up or driven out, and where the money comes from that rolls along and accumulates in his books.

[6] Now don't think I am saying this because I have declared war on the moneylenders: 'my cattle and horses they have never taken.'[2] No, I only want to show those who borrow readily what disgrace and indignity there is in the business, and that borrowing is a sign of extreme foolishness and weakness. Are you in funds? Don't borrow: you have no need. Are you out of funds? Don't borrow; you won't be able to pay.

Let us look at these two alternatives.

Cato said to an old man who was behaving badly, 'Sir, why do you pile the disgrace of crime on top of all the evils of old age?'
830 And so I say to *you*, 'Don't pile the hopelessness of borrowing and owing money on top of all the evils of poverty. Don't rob poverty of the only point in which she is preferable to wealth—her freedom from anxieties.' That will end in the situation that the proverb makes fun of: 'I can't carry the goat, so give me the ox to carry.' You can't carry poverty, so you give yourself the moneylender to carry, and that's a burden that even a rich man finds hard to bear. 'Then how shall I keep myself alive?' You ask that, when you've got hands and feet and a voice, and you're a human being, capable of loving and being loved, giving pleasure and being grateful? You can make a living as a schoolteacher, a tutor, a porter, a sailor, a supercargo. None of

these possibilities is any more disgraceful or disagreeable than hearing someone tell you to 'Pay up!'

[7] The famous Rutilius once went up to Musonius in Rome.

'Musonius,' he said, 'Zeus the Saviour, whom you seek to imitate, does not borrow.'

'Neither does he lend,' replied Musonius with a smile. For Rutilius, who was reproving him for borrowing, was himself the lender. This is real Stoic vanity; why bring in Zeus the Saviour when ordinary life teaches the lesson well enough? Swallows do not borrow, ants do not borrow, though nature has given them no hands, no reason, no skills. Man's superior intellect and ingenuity enable him to keep horses, dogs, partridges, jackdaws: why make yourself stupider than a jackdaw and dumber than a partridge and more cowardly than a dog, by not allowing yourself to be helped by a fellow human being in return for attendance, amusement, protection, or defence? 'Many things doth the sea provide, many the land.'

'And Micylus I saw',* says Crates,

> carding his wool, his wife at the work beside him,
> escaping starvation, in times of dire high prices.[1]

King Antigonus, seeing Cleanthes at Athens after a long interval, said to him, 'Are you still working at the mill, Cleanthes?' 'Yes, Sire,' he replied, 'I work at the mill in order not to have to give up Zeno and philosophy.' Think of that man's spirit! The hand that ground the grain and kneaded the flour went from mill and kneading-trough to write about gods and moon and stars and sun! Yet we think such work fit for slaves! And so borrow money to stay 'free', and flatter a crew of slaves, escort them around, give them dinner, pay them presents and tribute—not because we are poor (no one gives credit to a poor man) but because we are extravagant. If we were content with the necessities of life, there would no more be a race of moneylenders than there is of Centaurs or Gorgons. Luxury created the moneylenders, just as it created goldsmiths and silversmiths, perfumers and dyers. It's not for the price of bread and wine that we are in debt, but for farms, slaves, mules, and dining-rooms and tables; it's because we make lavish donations to our cities, performing prestigious but fruitless and thankless acts of generosity. Once enmeshed, however, the debtor is caught for all time. Like the horse that has acepted the curb, he merely exchanges one rider for another. He has no escape to the pastures and the meadows, but wanders like Empedocles' *daimones*, chased from heaven by god:

> the mighty Aether chases them to the sea,
> sea spits them forth upon the shores of earth,
> earth drives them to the sun's unwearying beams,
> and these to Aether's whirlpools once again.
> 831 Each seizes them in turn—[2]

usurer or financier, one from Corinth, one from Patrae, one from Athens, until the victim is smashed and shredded into little pieces under their onslaught. If you fall in the mud, you must either get up or lie there; if you turn and roll over, you gather much more dirt on your wet and slippery limbs; and so it is here. By changing creditors and transferring debts, people merely bring fresh demands for interest upon themselves, and are more and more weighed down. It's like a bilious patient who declines treatment, but goes on vomiting the prescribed amount and then producing more and more bile next time. Debtors too refuse to be purged, but vomit up their interest with pain and griping at each season of the year, only to endure nausea and headache again as soon as a fresh accumulation assails them, whereas what they ought to do to become sound and free is to rid themselves of it altogether.

[8] I am speaking now to the richer and more comfortable among you, those who say 'Am I to do without slaves and hearth and home?' It is as though a man swollen with dropsy were to say to his doctor 'Am I to be thin and empty?' Why not, to recover your health? Do without slaves, so as not to be a slave. Do without property, so as not to be the property of someone else. Let me tell you the story of the two vultures. One was vomiting, and said he was bringing up guts. 'So what?' said the other, 'they're not your own guts, they belonged to the corpse we've just been tearing up.' A debtor, you see, doesn't sell his own farm or his own house, but his creditor's, whom he has legally made the owner. 'Yes, but my father left me the farm.' Your father also gave you freedom and citizen's rights, and you ought to take more account of these. Your father produced your foot and your hand too, but, if they are septic, you pay the surgeon who amputates them. Calypso clothed Odysseus 'in sweet-smelling raiment',[1] fragrant of her immortal flesh, as a gift and memento of her love; but when he capsized and sank and had difficulty in getting to the surface, the soaked clothes were a heavy weight, and he stripped them off, and tied a scarf under his bare chest, as he 'looked to the land and swam'. Once saved, he was not short either of clothing or of food. Well, don't debtors face a storm when the creditor appears in due season and cries 'Pay up!'?

> So speaking, he gathers the clouds, and stirs the sea;
> east, south, and vicious west, the winds blow all together,[2]

as interest piles on interest. The drowning debtor grasps at the weight that drags him down, unable to swim to safety. Down he is thrust into the depths, and disappears, taking with him the friends who were his guarantors. Crates of Thebes, with no claims made against him and no debts owing, but merely weary of the anxieties and distractions of managing his affairs, gave away assets worth eight talents, took up his cloak and wallet, and escaped, by way of poverty, to philosophy. Anaxagoras left his farm to be grazed by sheep. But why use these philosophers as examples, when even Philoxenus the lyric poet can teach the same lesson? He was given an estate and a living and a house, assuring him affluence, in a Sicilian colony, but when he saw the luxury, ease, and lack of culture of the area, he exclaimed, 'These good things aren't going to finish me—I'm going to finish them', and handed the estate over to others and took
the boat home. But debtors perservere, and endure all demands, 832
impositions, slavery, liquidation. Like Phineus, they feed the winged Harpies, who carry off their food and tear it up, buying in the corn before it is harvested, selling the oil before the olives are off the tree. 'I take the wine for so much,' says the man, and gives a credit for the price: and the bunches are still hanging on the vine, waiting for Arcturus to rise.*

XIII

EROTICUS

In this dialogue, Plutarch's son Autobulus is made to report, at second hand, an event which took place in the early days of his parents' marriage. Plutarch and his wife, Timoxena, were at Thespiae, at the shrine of Eros, where they had come to fulfil a vow of his wife's. The town was convulsed by a scandal: a young man named Bacchon, very beautiful and with many male lovers, is being courted by the rich widow Ismenodora, and she ends by kidnapping him, though not (it seems) against his will, since marriage soon ensues. The general conversation consists of a discussion of the relative merits of heterosexual and homosexual love, interrupted from time to time by reports of what is going on in the town, which is some distance away from the shrine of the Muses, where the disputants are gathered. The characters are ingeniously drawn. Pisias, a chief defender of homosexuality, is abrupt and violent. Anthemion and Daphnaeus, supporters of marriage, are more sympathetically represented. Soclarus, a close friend of Plutarch is worldly-wise and prudent. The young Plutarch himself is very like the somewhat garrulous mature Plutarch we know from the books. The main theme is important to Plutarch and the society in which he moved. The prominence of homosexual relations in the dialogues of Plato and the Athenian society they reflect had given currency to an association between philosophy and homosexuality, which Plutarch is anxious to disown. The general Roman disapproval of homosexuality will have strengthened his desire to distance himself from the Platonic picture. Nevertheless, his view of *eros* is essentially Platonic, inasmuch as he sees in it a power capable of exalting and leading us from the sensible world to higher realities; but what can be said in this regard, as well as what can be said of the dangers and damage of love, applies equally to all its forms. Conjugal love wins the day; and it is significant that Pisias ends as a willing guest at Bacchon's wedding.

The combination of narrative and argument recalls 'Socrates' *Daimonion*'; but theme and story here have a more obvious link. The text is unfortunately not well preserved, and there are considerable gaps.

748 [1] FLAVIANUS

Are you saying, Autobulus, that it was on Helicon that the discussion about Eros was held which you either wrote out or committed to memory by repeatedly asking your father about it, and are now going to relate to us, at our special request?

AUTOBULUS

Yes, Flavianus, it was on Helicon, at the shrine of the Muses,* when the Thespians were celebrating the Erotidia. They hold a lavish and splendid festival every four years in honour of Eros, just as they do of the Muses.

FLAVIANUS

Then do you know what all of us who have come to listen to you would like to ask?

AUTOBULUS

No, but I shall if you people tell me. 749

FLAVIANUS

For this once, strip your narrative bare of all those poets' meads and shady groves and rambling ivy and smilax, of everything in fact that descriptions of such places tempt writers to insert, when they feel like appropriating Plato's Ilissus*[1] and the famous *agnus castus* and the gently sloping sward, with more enthusiasm than good taste.

AUTOBULUS

My dear Flavianus, what need has this story of any such introduction? Even the occasion which triggered off the discussion cries out for dramatic presentation and the stage. And everything else about it is pure drama. Let us simply pray to the Mother of the Muses* to grant me her favour and her presence and help me preserve the story.

[2] It happened before I was born. My father had lately married my mother, and there had been some difference or dispute between their parents, which led him to come to sacrifice to Eros. He brought my mother with him to the festival, for it was her vow and sacrifice. He had his usual friends from home with him, and at Thespiae he met Daphnaeus, the son of Archidamus, who was in love with Lysandra, the daughter of Simon, and the most hopeful suitor for her hand. There were also Soclarus of

Tithora, the son of Aristion, two foreigners—Protogenes of Tarsus and Zeuxippus of Sparta—and many distinguished Boeotians. They seem to have spent two or three days quietly in the town, having philosophical discussions in the wrestling-schools and theatres. Then, to avoid a painful musical competition, which was surrounded by intrigue and partisanship, most of them decamped from the enemy territory, as it were, and took up position on Helicon at the shrine of the Muses. They were joined there next morning by two men of note, Anthemion and Pisias. Both were related to Bacchon, the famous 'beauty', and bore a certain animosity towards each other because of their affection for him. The cause of this difficulty was Ismenodora, a wealthy lady of Thespiae, of high birth and exemplary life. Though young and beautiful, she had been a widow for some time, without a breath of scandal. Bacchon's mother was one of her close friends, and she therefore sought to arrange a marriage for him with one of her own relations. However, by seeing much of the young man and often talking with him, she came to be attracted by him herself. She heard much good of him, and she spoke much good of him; and, seeing that he was surrounded by a horde of noble lovers, began to fall in love with him, and formed the design not of having any clandestine relationship, but of marrying and living with him openly for the rest of her life. This was thought most extraordinary. Bacchon's mother viewed the position and pride of Ismenodora's family with disquiet. It was altogether above the young man's station. Some of his hunting-companions also alarmed him by talking of the disparity of age, and their jokes proved a more potent discouragement of the marriage than the serious objections of others. A young man of student age was naturally shy of setting up house with a widow. However, he paid no attention to any of them, except Pisias and Anthemion, to whom he gave the privilege of advising him on what he should do for the best. Anthemion was his older cousin, and Pisias the most serious-minded of his lovers. Pisias therefore opposed the marriage, and chided Anthemion with handing the young man over to Ismenodora. Anthemion, in return, accused Pisias of improper conduct; for all his moral principles, he said, he was doing as bad lovers do, seeking to deprive his friend of family, marriage, and great prosperity, in order to keep him fresh and unsullied, to strip for him in the wrestling-school as long as possible.

[3] Not wishing their mutual irritation to develop into serious 750
anger, these two chose my father and his friends to arbitrate and judge between them. That was why they had all come. Among the friends, there was—as it were by arrangement—one partisan of Anthemion, Daphnaeus, and one of Pisias, Protogenes. The latter launched into a general attack on Ismenodora, which made Daphnaeus indignant.

'Good heavens!' he cried, 'What can we *not* expect, when Protogenes is here to make war on love. Why, all his life, work, and play, has been devoted to love.

> Forgetting his own words,
> Forgetting his own country[1]

was something that happened to Laius after five days' absence, but *his* love was a slow, pedestrian creature compared with yours, which "arches swift wings"[2] and flies beyond the sea from Cilicia to Athens, looking out for beautiful young men, and travelling around with them.'

[4] Now this, more or less, was what had made Protogenes go on his travels. So there was a general burst of laughter.

'Do you really think', Protogenes replied, 'that I am at war with love, and not fighting his battles against the immorality and violence that invade the noblest and holiest words with disgraceful actions and emotions?'

'You mean that marriage and the union of man and woman are disgraceful?' said Daphnaeus, 'yet there is no holier union and never has been.'

'Lawgivers,' replied Protogenes, 'are right to glorify and commend such unions to the masses, because they are necessary for procreation. But true love has nothing whatever to do with the women's quarters. Indeed, I cannot admit that those of you who have feelings for women or girls are in love at all. Flies are not in love with milk, or bees with honeycombs, and provision-merchants don't fatten calves and poultry in the dark because they have kindly feelings towards them. No; just as nature directs our appetite towards bread and meat in moderation, just so far as to satisfy us, whereas the excess, that produces emotional disorder, is called gluttony or gormandising, so men and women have a natural need of the pleasure they derive from each other, but are mistaken in attaching the word 'love' to the impulse that drives them to it, when it becomes vehement, powerful, and difficult to control. Love lays hold of the young, well-endowed soul and proceeds by way of friendship to the goal of virtue; but the best that can result from the desire for women is that we reap some pleasure and enjoyment in youth and beauty. This is the burden of Aristippus' remark, when he answered the man who complained that Lais did not like him by saying that he didn't think his wine or his fish liked him, though he enjoyed both. Pleasure and enjoyment are the end of desire; but if love loses the expectation of liking, it gives up its patient courting of the brilliant flower of youth, if there is no proper return in affection and virtue. You must remember the married man in the tragedy, who says to his wife:

> You hate me, do you? I am happy to be hated,
> and turn my loss of standing to my profit.[3]

'A man who endures a bad, unaffectionate wife not for gain but for pure sexual satisfaction is no more a true lover than that character in the play. It reminds one of the joke made by the comic poet Philippides against the orator Stratocles: "as she turns away, you can just kiss her head."[4] If this feeling is to be called love, it is an effeminate one and a spurious one; it belongs to the women's quarters as bastards do to Cynosarges.* Or again—and here is a better parallel—we are told there is one genuine mountain-eagle, called by Homer 'black' or 'the
751 hunter',[5] and other kinds of bastard eagles, which catch fish and slow-flying birds in the marshes, and utter a plaintive, hungry cry when they are unsuccessful. So too there is only one genuine love, that of boys, and it is not 'dripping with desire', as Anacreon says of the love of girls, nor 'drenched in perfume and bejewelled'.[1] You will find it, sincere and free of coquetry, in philosophers' class-rooms and in gymnasia and wrestling-schools. It pursues the young, and gives a clear, exhilarating call to virtue to those who merit its attentions. The other kind—the compliant, home-keeping love that dwells in women's laps and beds, always pursuing comfort and softened by pleasures that have no manliness in them, no friendship and no warm pas-

sion—is something to be put down, as Solon put it down. He forbade slaves to make love to boys or 'rub down',* but did not forbid them intercourse with women. Affection is a fine and noble thing, pleasure is common and ignoble. There is nothing gentlemanly or smart in loving slave-boys. That love is just a love of intercourse, like the love of women.'

[5] Protogenes would have liked to go on, but Daphnaeus interrupted him.

'I am so glad you mentioned Solon,' he said, 'and we can certainly use him as a standard of the lover:

> as long as he loves boys in the glorious flower of their youth,
> yearning for their thighs and the sweetness of their mouths.[2]

You can add Aeschylus too:

> ungrateful for my showers of kisses,
> you honoured not my reverence for your thighs.[3]

Some people ridicule these passages as suggesting that lovers should look at the thighs and the loins like priests or diviners at a sacrifice. My view is that this is a major point in favour of the women. For if unnatural intercourse between males does nothing to destroy or damage the lover's affectionate feeling, it is even more likely that the love between men and women, being natural, should advance through favour (*charis*) to affection. "Favour", Protogenes, is the name the ancients gave to the yielding of the female to the male. Thus Pindar says that Hephaestus was born of Hera "without favour".[4] Sappho addresses a girl not yet ripe for marriage in the words:

> you seemed to me a little, favourless child.[5]

And Heracles is asked by someone:

> Did you exact
> favour by violence, or by courting her?[6]

'But the "favour" of boys, which, if they are reluctant, depends on violent rape, and, if they are willing, signifies that they surrender themselves unnaturally, out of softness and effeminacy, to be "covered", as Plato puts it, "and impregnated like animals"[7]—that so-called "favour" is favourless, indecent, and loveless. And so, as I see it, Solon wrote the lines we just quoted when he was young and "bursting with seed", to use a phrase of Plato;[8] when he was old, he wrote differently:

> Dear to me now are the works of the goddess of Cyprus,
> of Dionysus too, and of the Muses;
> for they give joy to men.[9]

He had escaped by this time from the squalls and storms of love for boys, and brought his life into the calm waters of marriage and philosophy. If we look at the reality of it all, Protogenes, the experience of love is the same whether it is directed at boys or at women. But if you want to make a distinction, for the sake of argument, then the effects of this love of boys may not look so good; it will seem to have come into the world late and out of season, clandestine and illegitimate, and to drive out the genuine, older love. It was only the other day, really, that it penetrated the gymnasia, after young men began to strip and be seen naked, and surreptitiously proceeded to touch and embrace them. Later still,
752 it gradually grew its wings, in the wrestling-schools, and now it has become insufferable, insulting and reviling the married love that helps our mortal race to immortality and rekindles the dying fires of our life through new births. It denies pleasure, for it is ashamed and afraid to confess it; but it needs a plausible pretext for approaching the young and handsome, and it finds that pretext in friendship and virtue. So it exposes itself to the dust, takes cold baths, raises its eyebrows,* says it's studying philosophy, behaving indeed with perfect propriety to outward view because of the law. In the silence of the night, however, "sweet is the ripe fruit when the guard has left his post!"[1] Now if, as Protogenes alleges, Aphrodite plays no part in associations with boys, how can Eros be there without her? His duty, which the gods assigned to him, is to serve and attend her, and enjoy just so much honour and power as she determines. If, on the other hand, Eros can exist without Aphrodite—as there can be drunkenness without wine, from drinks made from figs or barley—the excitement it causes is barren and unconsummated, quickly turning to satiety and disgust.'

[6] All through this speech, Pisias was clearly irritated and getting stirred up against Daphnaeus. So when the latter paused for a moment, he rushed in.

'Heracles!' he cried, 'what irresponsible audacity! These people admit that they are hitched on to the female of the species by their sexual organ, just like dogs: and then they propose to move Eros out of the gymnasia and the walks and all his clean, open occupations in the sunshine, and imprison him among the brothels and the hairdressers and the potions and sorceries of a set of immoral women. Decent women ought never to fall in love or respond to it.'

My father told me that, at this point, he also put in his word against Protogenes.

' "Such talk", he began, "gives weapons to the Argive host."[2] It makes me an advocate for Daphnaeus' view to hear Pisias exaggerate so, and treat marriage as a loveless partnership with no divine affection in it, whereas in fact we know that, when the persuasion and favour of love has gone, a partnership can hardly be held together by the yoke and curb of shame and fear.'

'That argument doesn't much interest me,' said Pisias, 'I can see what is happening to Daphnaeus. It's like what happens to bronze, which melts and liquefies far more easily if melted bronze is poured on it than if you put it in the fire. Similarly, it's not Lysandra's beauty that is Daphnaeus' burden. It is that he has long been close to a person who has so long been on fire, and so has caught it himself. Clearly, he will melt down too, if he doesn't make a quick escape to join us. But I see I am giving offence to the jury myself, which is just what Anthemion would like; so I will stop.'

'Good,' said Anthemion, 'I am glad; but you ought to have spoken to the point from the beginning.'

[7] 'Well,' said Pisias, 'my opinion—which I preface by proclaiming for my own part a lack of love for the whole sex—is that the young man ought to be wary of the lady's wealth. We don't want to find that, by exposing him to such grandeur and state, we have inadvertently made him vanish, as tin vanishes in making bronze. It would be creditable if a young boy marrying a woman of no consequence and plain life was able to prevail over her, in the way wine prevails over water in the mixture. This lady, however, is accustomed to command and dominate. Otherwise, she wouldn't have rejected so many offers of honour, family, and wealth, to woo a lad still in a boy's tunic and in

need of a servant to take him to school. This is why wise men deliberately give up their wives' excessive fortunes, clipping their wings as it were. Money makes for luxury, vanity, levity, and inconstancy, and the women often fly away. If they do stay, it is better to be bound by fetters of gold, as in Ethiopia,* than by a wife's wealth.'

753 'Don't you also mean', interjected Protogenes, 'that we are absurdly and ridiculously inverting the advice of Hesiod. He writes:

> Not much under thirty, not much over thirty:
> that is the time to marry. For the woman,
> let her be four years from maturity,
> then in the fifth year let her go and marry.[1]

But we should be marrying an immature lad to a woman older than he is by as much as the bridegroom should be older than the bride. It would be like cultivating figs or dates.* "But she is very much in love with him." Who stops her from going to his house with a party of friends, serenading him from the doorstep, hanging garlands on his picture, or fighting her rivals, no holds barred? These are the things lovers do. Let her stop raising her eyebrows and playing the haughty beauty. Let her look the lover's part. If she is modest and bashful, let her sit decently at home waiting for serious suitors. If a woman proclaims her love, a man can at any rate run away in disgust. One certainly shouldn't let this sort of wantonness inadvertently turn into a foundation for marriage.'

[9] When Protogenes stopped, my father spoke up. 'You see, Anthemion,' he said, 'that they are opening up the subject again. They are forcing an answer out of those of us who freely admit to being devotees of married love.'

'By all means', said Anthemion, 'let us have a full defence of her love, and say something in defence of her wealth too, for that's what Pisias mainly uses to alarm us.'

'Anything could be made an accusation against a woman', my father began, 'if we are to reject Ismenodora on the grounds of her love and her wealth. "She is rich and grand." Yes; but what of her youth and beauty? What of her distinguished birth and her fame? Don't "respectable" women display a horrid, intolerable severity and superciliousness, and don't people call them

"avenging Furies", and say they are angry with their husbands *because* they are respectable? But does it follow that one should therefore take a wife off the streets, some Habrotonon from Thrace or some Bacchis from Miletus, omitting the legal ceremony and simply paying the money and scattering the nuts?* No. Many men have been shamefully enslaved by women like that. And Samian flute-girls and dancing-girls, an Aristonica, an Oenanthe with her tambourine, an Agathoclea, have trodden on kings' crowns. The Syrian Semiramis was a servant and concubine of a palace slave. Yet when the Great King Ninus met her and fell in love with her, she had such mastery and contempt of him that she asked him to let her sit on the throne, wearing the crown and doing the king's business for a day; and when he agreed and ordered everyone to obey her and do her bidding as they would do his own, the first commands she issued were moderate—she wanted to see how the guards would respond—but when she found they had no hesitations, and no inclination to oppose her, she ordered them to arrest Ninus, put him in chains, and finally kill him. This done, she reigned as queen of Asia for many years, and in great splendour. And wasn't Belestiche, whose temple and shrine they have at Alexandria, with the inscription to "Aphrodite Belestiche", put up by the king who loved her, only a barbarian woman bought in the market? And the woman who shares the shrine of Eros* in our city, and has her statue in gold at Delphi amid kings and queens—what dowry did she bring to win her lovers? But, as those lovers slipped into becoming the prey of women by their own weakness and feebleness, so, on the other hand, there have been poor and undistinguished men whose connection with wealthy and brilliant women has not ruined them or broken their spirit, but enabled them to live their days as the honoured and dominant 754
partners in an affectionate relationship. But the man who restricts and constrains his wife—like the thin man who makes his ring smaller for fear it will slip off—is behaving like those breeders of mules who cut off mares' manes and take them to a pond or river, where (it is said) they see the ugly reflection of their deformity, lose their high spirit, and submit to be covered by asses. To think more of a woman's wealth than of her virtue or breeding shows lack of ambition and of generosity; but if the

wealth is combined with virtue and breeding, it is sheer folly to run away from it. Antigonus wrote to the commander of the garrison of Munychia,* who had fortified the place, ordering him not only to make the collar strong, but to make the dog lean. He meant that he was to reduce the Athenians' resources. On the other hand, the husband of a rich or beautiful woman does not do right to do this or to make his wife poor or ugly. He should rather make himself independent and equal to her by his self-control, wisdom, and refusal to be overawed by any of her advantages. He will tip the scale in his favour by the weight of his personality, which achieves control and guidance which is both honourable and practical. The right age for marriage is that which makes it possible for the couple to have children. Now I understand that this lady is in her prime'—he smiled at Pisias—'and no older than her rivals. Certainly she hasn't got grey hair like some who are hanging around Bacchon now! If there is deemed to be no disparity of age in *their* case, why shouldn't the lady take better care of the boy than a young woman would? Young people find it harder to come together as one. It takes time and effort for them to drop their high spirit and aggressiveness. At first, they toss about and fight against the yoke, and if love has entered into them, its high wind, as it were, shakes and breaks up the pilotless ship of their marriage even more, because they are unable to rule and unwilling to be ruled. Yet the nurse rules the child, the teacher the boy, the gymnasiarch the ephebus, the lover the youth, and the law and the general the grown man.* No one is free of rule, no one is independent. So what is wrong with an older woman of sense governing a young man? Her better sense helps him, her love is pleasant and agreeable to him. As Boeotians', my father went on, 'we ought to respect Heracles* and not be offended by disparities of age in marriage. We know that Heracles gave his own wife, Megara, when she was 33, to Iolaus, who was only 16.'

[10] During this conversation, according to my father, one of Pisias' friends arrived. He had ridden at full speed from Thespiae, and he had an extraordinary tale of daring to tell. Ismenodora, it seems, believed that Bacchon himself was not averse to the marriage, but was in awe of those who wished to deter him. She therefore resolved that she would not give him up. She sent

for those of her male friends who were young and strong and sympathetic to her love, and laid her plans with them and with her women friends. She waited for the hour when Bacchon was in the habit of presenting himself at her house, with perfect correctness, on his way from the wrestling-school. On this particular day, he had two or three friends with him, and he was freshly anointed.* She met him at the door and touched his chlamys, while her friends prettily kidnapped the pretty boy, chlamys and cloak* and all, and took him into the house with them, and shut the door. Once indoors, the women pulled off the chlamys and dressed him in a bridegroom's himation. The servants ran hither 755
and thither, putting garlands of olive and bay on Ismenodora's door and also on Bacchon's. The girl piper walked along the street playing. Citizens and visitors either laughed or waxed indignant and tried to move the gymnasiarchs to action; they keep a tight hold on the ephebi, and have a sharp eye for what they get up to. By now, nobody was paying any attention to the competitors. The spectators had all deserted the theatre, and were arguing and brawling with one another on Ismenodora's doorstep.

Pisias' friend galloped up like a messenger in a battle, and excitedly blurted out the gist of this story—'Ismenodora has kidnapped Bacchon!' Zeuxippus' reaction, according to my father, was to laugh, and quote his favourite Euripides:

> Proud of your wealth, my lady, keep your thoughts
> within the limits of our mortal lot.[1]

Pisias, however, jumped up and shouted 'Good God! What is to be the end of this liberty that is turning the city upside down! Independence is proving the road to anarchy!* But it's absurd to complain about the destruction of law and justice; female rule is an offence against nature herself! Lemnos is nothing to this.* Let's go,' he cried, 'let's go, let's give up the gymnasium and the Council House to the women, since the city has been totally emasculated!' He led the way, and Protogenes tried to keep with him, sharing his indignation, but at the same time endeavouring to calm him down.

'It's certainly a bold stroke,' remarked Anthemion, 'and it does remind one of Lemnos. But—since we're by ourselves now—it looks like the action of a woman really in love.'

Soclarus gave a gentle smile. 'Do you really think', he said 'that this is a genuine, violent kidnapping? Don't you think it's an excuse and a trick invented by this sensible young man, who has escaped his lovers' embraces and deserted into the arms of a rich and beautiful woman?'

'Don't say that, Soclarus,' said Anthemion, 'you mustn't have such suspicions of Bacchon. Even if he hadn't been simple and straightforward by nature, he wouldn't have kept such a plan secret from me. He tells me everything, and knows that I am enthusiastically on Ismenodora's side in all this. But it is love, not anger as Heraclitus says, that is "hard to fight, for it buys what it will, even at the price of soul"[2]—and money, and reputation. Is there a more impeccably behaved person in town than Ismenodora? When did any disreputable story or suspicion of evil touch her family? Some divine force has possessed her, some power superior to human reason.'

[12] Pemptides laughed. 'Well,' he said, 'there is even a physical disease that is called "sacred",* so there's nothing paradoxical about calling the greatest and most manic passion of the mind sacred or divine. I once saw two neighbours in Egypt arguing about a snake that had crawled into the road. Both called it the Good Daimon, and each wanted it for himself. You people are like that. I see some of you claiming Eros for the men's apartments, and others for the women, as the supreme divine blessing. It didn't surprise me, therefore, that a passion possessing such power and honour should be exalted and glorified by the very people who ought to be expelling or restraining it wherever it occurs. So hitherto I have held my peace, because I could see that the dispute was a private rather than a public one.
756 But now that we have got rid of Pisias, I should very much like to hear from you what observation it was that made the first people who said this declare Eros to be a god.'

[13] Just as my father was beginning to speak to this, in response to Pemptides' remarks, another messenger arrived from Thespiae. Ismenodora had sent for Anthemion. The disturbances were increasing, and the gymnasiarchs could not agree: one of them was for demanding the return of Bacchon, the other was for not interfering. Anthemion therefore got up and went on his way. My father then addressed Pemptides.

'It seems to me', he said, 'that you have touched a very large and dangerous subject. It would be more accurate to say that you are disturbing the undisturbed foundation of our belief in the gods, by demanding rational demonstrations for every point. The ancient faith of our fathers suffices; no clearer evidences can be conceived or found, "whatever cleverness keen minds discover".[1] It is this that gives a firm, common basis for piety. But if the secure recognition of it is once disturbed or shaken by one individual, then it becomes doubtful and suspect to all. You know, no doubt, that Euripides faced an uproar when he began his *Melanippe* with the lines:

> Zeus, whosoe'er he be—I know him only
> from hearsay,

but then was allotted a fresh chorus (he had confidence in the play because of its grand and magnificent style) and changed the beginning into the version we now read:

> Zeus, as the tale is truly told.[2]

Now what is the difference between making our belief in Zeus ambiguous and obscure by our words, and doing the same for Athena or Eros? This is not the first occasion Eros has demanded an altar and a sacrifice. He is no intruder from foreign superstitions—an Attes or an Adonaios—creeping in surreptitiously to reap honours he has no right to, through the agency of hermaphrodites or women,* and exposing himself to prosecution for false registration and illegitimacy as a god! When you read in Empedocles, my friend, that

> Friendship among them there is, and in length and in breadth she is
> equal;
> her you must see with the mind, not sit there confused by the vision,[3]

you have to realize that this means Eros. He is known to us not by our eyes but by our belief, and is among our most ancient gods. If you ask for evidence for every one of these, if you lay your hands on every temple and put every altar to some sophisticated test, you won't be able to exempt any god from malicious prosecution and examination under torture. "I go not far away":*

Do you not see how great is Aphrodite?
She sows and gives that Love, whose children we
who dwell on earth are, every one of us.[4]

Empedocles called her "life-giver",[5] Sophocles "fruitful":[6] both very proper and appropriate epithets. Yet this great wonder is Aphrodite's work, and Eros' secondary activity, when he is with her; for if he is absent, the thing is unenviable, "unhonoured, unbefriended".[7] Loveless intercourse, like hunger and thirst, ends in brute satisfaction, and comes to no good. It is thanks to Eros that the goddess takes the satiety out of the pleasure, and induces affection and union. Parmenides makes Eros the oldest of Aphrodite's works, when he writes in his cosmogony:

First of all gods she fashioned Eros.[8]

But Hesiod, in my opinion, makes a better scientific point when he calls Eros the oldest of all things,[9] so that everything comes into being through his agency. So if we eject Eros from his customary honours, neither will those of Aphrodite stay as they are.
757 Nor is it possible to say that people abuse Eros without attacking Aphrodite also. We hear on the stage both that

Eros is idle, born for idle men[1]

and that

Cypris, my children, is not only Cypris,*
but there are many names she bears as well:
for she is Hades, violence undying,
and raving madness.[2]

No other god altogether escapes attack at the hands of abusive ignorance. Think of all the honours given to Ares, who stands, as you might say, diametrically opposed to Eros, if we imagine them both on a bronze model;* and think of the abuse levelled at him also:

He's blind, is Ares, ladies, he can't see;
he roots up trouble with his big pig's snout.[3]

Homer calls him "murderous" and "two-faced".[4] Chrysippus' explanation of the name involves a criticism and a condemnation: he says "Ares" means "Anaires", "The Destroyer",[5] and gives support to those who believe that the pugnacious, quarrelsome, and aggressive element in us is "Ares". Others again will say that Aphrodite is desire, Hermes speech, the Muses arts, and Athena wisdom. You can see the abyss of atheism that opens under our feet if we classify the gods as various passions, capacities, or virtues.'

'Yes, I do see,' said Pemptides, 'but it's no more impious to identify gods with passions than to think passions are gods.'

'Well then,' said my father, 'do you think Ares is a god or a passion of ours?'

Pemptides answered that he believed Ares to be a god who controlled our virile and aggressive qualities.

'In that case,' cried my father, 'battle, war, and enmity have their god, but affection, community, and concord have none! There is a god (is there?), an Enualios or a Stratios,* to supervise and oversee killing and being killed, armour and weapons and sieges and plunder! But for marriage, for the love that leads to unity and society, we have no god to sponsor or supervise or guide or help? Hunters of buck, hare, and deer have the goddess Agrotera* to encourage them and join in their hunting-cries; trappers who catch wolves and bears in pits and nets pray to Aristaeus

> Who first set snares to trap the beasts of the wild.[6]

'Heracles, according to Aeschylus, summoned yet another god to his aid when he was about to raise his bow to shoot the bird: "Apollo Agreus, guide my shafts aright!"[7] Yet when a man tries to capture the best prey of all, affection, there is, according to you, no god or *daimon* to guide or aid his efforts!

'Now I happen to believe, my dear Daphnaeus, that man is as fair and splendid a plant as any oak or olive or what Homer grandly calls the *hemeris*, the cultivated vine; for the impulse of growth in man discloses youth and beauty of mind as well as of body'.

[15] 'For heaven's sake,' said Daphnaeus, 'who denies *that*?'

'All those', replied my father, 'who think that it is proper for gods to have care of ploughing and sowing and planting—there are dryads (aren't there?)

> whose lifespan is the trees[8]

and there's Dionysus, who

> with joy makes grow the garth of trees,
> the holy gleam of autumn,[9]

to quote Pindar—but at the same time maintain that the education and development of lads and boys as they are formed and fashioned is no business of any god or *daimon*—in fact, that there is no power whose concern it is that the developing human
758 being should grow straight in virtue and not have its innate nobility bent or distorted by lack of care or by bad surroundings. Surely, even to *say* this is a mark of dreadful ingratitude. We enjoy the kindness of god: it extends universally and it never abandons us in our necessities, even though some of those necessities end in ways more inevitable than good. Our birth, for example, is not a pretty thing—it is an affair of blood and pain—but it has its divine overseers, Ilithyia and Locheia:* yet it might be better not to be born than to be born bad, and have no good guardian or protector. In illness too, man is not deserted by the god to whom that service and power have been allotted. Nor even does god abandon us in death; for there too is one to convey us hence and help us at our end, putting us to bed and giving our souls guidance, like the god who says*

> Night did not bear me to be the lyre's master,
> or a prophet, or a doctor, but the help of souls.[1]

These aspects of life contain much unpleasantness. On the other hand, one cannot think of a holier work or a contest or competition more appropriate to the oversight and arbitration of a god than the lover's care and pursuit of the young and beautiful. Here is nothing ugly, nothing forced, only persuasion and grace making "labour sweet, and toil toil-free"[2] and leading to a virtue and an affection that cannot reach its goal without god, and has no god as guide and master save only the companion of the Muses, of the Graces, and of Aphrodite—that is, Eros. It is he who joins the greatest pleasure to the greatest beauty,

> sowing a sweet harvest
> in a man's heart's desire,[3]

as Melanippides puts it. Or what do we say, Zeuxippus?'

[16] 'Precisely that,' he replied, 'for the opposite is patently absurd.'

'There is another absurdity, too,' said my father. 'The ancients distinguished four types of friendship: that of nature, that of hospitality, that of companionship, and that of love. The first three have their patron gods, Zeus Philios, Zeus Xenios, Zeus Homognios, Zeus Patroos. Is it not absurd that the friendship of love alone, as though ill-starred, should be left godless and masterless, though of all things it most needs care and guidance?'

'There is certainly a great irrationality in that,' said Zeuxippus.

'However,' went on my father, 'Plato's words may apply to our argument,* even if it tries to escape them. The madness that rises from body to soul, through the circulation of a harmful exhalation caused by some unhappy mixture or combination of elements, is a harsh, awkward, morbid affection. But there is another kind of madness, not unconnected with the divine, and not home-bred. This is an inspiring visitation from outside us, a diversion of rational thought, and it originates from, and is set in motion by, a higher power. Its general name is "ENthusiasm"; for just as what is full of *pneuma*, "breath", is called *EMpnoun*, and what is full of *phronēsis*, "wisdom", is called *EMphron*, so this mental disturbance is called "ENthusiasm", because it has *in* (EN) it a power that comes from *theos*, that is from "god". Prophetic "enthusiasm" thus comes from the inspiration and possession of Apollo, Bacchic from that of Dionysus; "Dance with the Corybants," says Sophocles,[4] for the rituals of Pan and of the Great Mother have much in common with those of Bacchus. The "third madness"[5] comes from the Muses. It seizes the "tender untrodden soul",[6] and fans the spark of poetry and music. As for the madness of battle, we all know to which god its frenzy belongs, and by whom it is inspired when it

> arms Ares the choirless, the lyreless,
> the bringer of tears,
> and the people shout for war.[7]

'There remains one further type of alienation and aberration 759
in man, Daphnaeus. It is not obscure or passive, and I should like to ask Pemptides a question about it . . . "What god

brandishes the fruitful thyrsus"[1] of affectionate enthusiasm for brave boys and honest women, the keenest and warmest enthusiasm of all? Observe: when the soldier lays down his arms, he rests from the madness of war,

> and happily
> his servants lift the armour from his shoulders,[2]

and there he sits, an unwarlike spectator of the others. Again, musicians can sedate these Bacchic and Corybantic gambols by abandoning the trochaic rhythm and the Phrygian mode. Even the Pythian priestess, once she leaves her tripod and her inspiration, is at peace and at rest. But the madness of love is different. Once it seizes a man and sets him on fire, no Muse or "soothing charm",[3] no change of place can give him rest. Lovers love when they are present, and yearn when they are away. They pursue their loves by day, they lie on their doorsteps at night. They call for them when sober, they sing their praises when drunk. The imaginings of poets, it has been said, are waking dreams, because they are so vivid. This is much more true of the imaginings of lovers, who talk and embrace and chide just as though the beloved was there. Sight seems to paint all our other imaginings in water, so soon do they fade and go out of mind; but the visual imagination of the lover is painted, as it were, in encaustic, and leaves on the memory likenesses that move and live and last forever. The Roman Cato said that the lover's soul dwelt in the soul of the loved one: <but it is truer to say that the loved one dwells in the lover>—his form, his character, his life, and his actions. These enable the love to go a long way in a little time, like the man who finds, in the Cynic phrase, a "stiff short-cut to virtue". For the mind <attains virtue and> affection, with the god's help, by travelling on the waves of emotion. In a word: the enthusiasm of lovers is divinely controlled, and the god whose oversight and guidance it enjoys is he whose feast and sacrifice we are now celebrating.

'However, we generally honour a god for his power and the benefit he confers, on the same principle as we regard royalty and virtue as the two divinest of human blessings. So let us now ask whether Eros cedes power to any other god. But "great and strong is the victory that Cypris wins",[4] as Sophocles says, and

great too is the force of Ares, and, in a sense, we can see the force of all the other gods divided between these two. For the force that attracts us towards beauty, and the force that makes us resist ugliness, are both in our souls from the beginning, as Plato <suggests when he distinguishes the> parts <of the soul>.[5] Let us remind ourselves to begin with that, if we set love on one side, Aphrodite's business is on sale for one drachma. Nobody puts up with effort or danger for the sake of sex, unless he is in love. To say nothing of Phryne, my friend, people often pass by a Lais or a Gnathainion who "kindles at eve"[6] her lamp's bright glow to welcome or invite you in. But the "sudden rising of the wind"[7] of love and desire instantly makes it worth all the fabled treasures of Tantalus and his kingdom. So weak and transient is the charm of Aphrodite, if Eros is not there to blow upon it. There is an even clearer testimony in the fact that many men share sexual favours with others, making available not only their mistresses but also their wives. Why, sir, the famous Roman Gabba,* when entertaining Maecenas to dinner, 760
observed that he was flirting with his wife after they had exchanged signals. So he put his head on one side and pretended to be asleep. At that moment, however, one of the slaves stole up to the table and removed some of the wine. "Damn you," said Gabba, opening his eyes, "don't you know I'm only asleep to Maecenas?" This is perhaps not particularly shocking; Gabba was a professional humorist. Not so Nicostratus, the rival of Phayllus in the politics of Argos. King Philip was visiting the town, and Phayllus had some expectation of securing some power or office for himself by arranging for the king to have an affair with his beautiful wife. Nicostratus and his friends became aware of this, and kept watch outside the house. But Phayllus dressed his wife up in military boots, cloak, and Macedonian hat, and so smuggled her out disguised as one of the king's young attendants. But of all the <homosexual> lovers there are or ever have been, can you think of one who would have acted as procurer for his beloved, even in return for being honoured like Zeus? I imagine not: after all, tyrants who have no political dissent or opposition to contend with, nevertheless have many rivals for the love of the young and beautiful. You know how Aristogiton at Athens, Antileon at Metapontum, and

Melanippus at Acragas had no quarrel with the tyrants of those cities, though they could see that they were ruining and vandalizing everything, until they made attempts on the young men they loved. Then to defend what to them was sacred and inviolate, they did not spare themselves. Alexander is said to have written to Theodorus, the brother of Proteas:* "Send me the girl musician for ten talents, unless you are in love with her." And when another of his companions, Antipatrides, came to visit him with a girl harpist, Alexander felt attracted by the girl and asked Antipatrides whether he was in love with her. "Indeed I am," said Antipatrides. "Then may you come to a bad end!" said Alexander; but he kept away from the girl.

[17] 'Again,' my father continued, 'think of Eros' power in war! He is no idler,[1] as Euripides said, nor does he avoid service or "pass his nights on girls' soft cheeks".[2] A man inspired by Eros has no need of Ares to fight his enemies; with his own god to help him, he

> will pass through fire and sea
> and on the winds of heaven[3]

wherever his beloved bids him go. In Sophocles, when Niobe's children die under the hail of arrows, the only person any of them calls in aid is a lover: "O, put <your arms> around me!"[4] And you know, no doubt, how Cleomachus of Pharsalus came to die in battle.'

'No we don't,' said Pemptides, 'but we should like to hear.'

'It is a story worth telling,' said my father. 'He had come to aid the Chalcidians against Eretria at the height of the Thessalian war.* The Chalcidians were thought to be strong in infantry, but found it very difficult to repulse the enemy horse. The allies therefore asked Cleomachus, a splendidly courageous man, to lead the attack on the cavalry. He asked the boy he loved, who was with him, whether he too would like to see the battle. The boy said he would, embraced Cleomachus with affection, and put on his helmet. Cleomachus, in great spirits, collected the bravest of the Thessalians and rode forth with them in brave array. He fell upon the enemy, and broke and routed their cavalry. The infantry then fled, and the Chalcidians
761 won a notable victory. Cleomachus, however, was killed. They

show his tomb in the agora at Chalcis, and the great column still stands upon it. And so, having previously been disapproving of homosexual love, they came afterwards to admire and honour it more than other peoples. Aristotle,* however, alleges that Cleomachus died in different circumstances, after defeating the Eretrians; and that the lover embraced by his beloved was one of the Chalcidians from Thrace sent to aid the Chalcidians of Euboea. This, he says, is the origin of the popular Chalcidian song:

> Lads of grace and noble fathers,
> do not grudge the brave your beauty;
> valour and limb-loosing Eros
> blossom in the towns of Chalcis.[1]

According to the poet Dionysius in his *Aitia*,*[2] the lover's name was Anton, and the boy's Philistus. And in your native Thebes, Pemptides, used not lovers to present their beloved with a suit of armour when they were enrolled as adults? It was a lover called Pammenes who reformed the organization of hoplites in battle. He argued that Homer knew nothing about love, because he grouped the Achaeans in tribes and brotherhoods, not lover beside lover, so that "shield should press shield and helmet helmet",[3] Eros being the only invincible general. Men desert tribesmen, kinsmen, parents, and children; but no enemy can drive a way between an impassioned lover and his beloved. These will exhibit their love of danger and disregard for their own safety even when there is no call for it. Theron the Thessalian, for instance, laid his left hand against the wall, drew his sword, and cut off the thumb, and challenged his rival to do the same. Another, who fell on his face in battle, asked the enemy soldier who was about to strike him, to wait a moment for him to turn over, so that his beloved should not see him wounded in the back. And it is not only the most warlike nations who are most devoted to love—the Boeotians and Spartans and Cretans—but ancient heroes too: Meleager, Achilles, Cimon, and Epaminondas; the last-named loved two young men, Asopichus and Cephisodorus. The latter died with him at Mantinea and is buried near him, while Asopichus, a most fearsome warrior, was at last confronted and struck down by Eucnamus of Amphissa, who came to be worshipped as a hero in Phocis. Heracles' many loves defy enumeration; but lovers still worship and honour Iolaus, whom they believe to have been his favourite, and exact oaths and pledges from the beloved at his tomb. Heracles is said also to have used his medical skill* to save Alcestis, when her life was despaired of, out of kindness to Admetus, who loved his wife and had himself been loved by Heracles. Indeed, the myth relates that Apollo also was Admetus' lover and "worked as his serf a long year through".[4] I am glad I remembered Alcestis. Women have nothing to do with Ares; but possession by Eros can lead them to dare and die beyond their nature. If myth can ever be regarded as valid evidence, the stories of Alcestis, Protesilaus, and Orpheus' wife Eurydice demonstrate that Eros is the only god whom Hades obeys. Towards all others, as Sophocles tells us,

> he knows no fairness and no favour,
> but loves bare judgement only,[5]

whereas he feels respect for lovers, and to them alone proves neither implacable nor invincible. It is a fine thing indeed, my friend, to take part in the mysteries of Eleusis; but in my judgement the celebrants and initiates of Eros have a better doom in
762 Hades. I neither believe myths nor altogether disbelieve them. They say well, and by some divine chance touch on the truth, when they assert that lovers have a way of ascending from Hades to the light. How it happens, the myths do not know; they failed to find the path that Plato with his philosophy was the first human to behold. Yet there are some slight, faint trickles of the truth scattered around in Egyptian mythology, though it needs a clever tracker to detect them, and one who can see great things in small.

'So let us pass over this, and proceed now from the topic of Eros' strength to that of his kindness and favour to men. I do not ask whether he does great good to those who are loved (that is obvious to us all) but whether he does greater good to the lovers themselves. Euripides, though he was well acquainted with love, speaks admiringly of its smallest manifestation when he writes: "Love makes a poet of the unmusical."[1] For he also makes a sensible person of the lazy-minded, and a brave man (as we have seen) of the coward, as we make soft wood strong by heating it in the fire. Every lover becomes liberal, amenable, and generous, even if he was mean before; his avarice and meanness melt like iron in the fire. He enjoys giving presents to the beloved, and he doesn't enjoy receiving them himself. I am sure you know the story of Alcibiades. When Anytus, the son of Anthemion, was his lover, and was giving a splendid and extravagant dinner to his friends, Alcibiades burst in after dinner, drunk, and removed half the drinking-service on the table. The guests were indignant. "That lad's insulting you with his arrogance," they said. "No," said Anytus, "he's being kind; he left me half the service, when he might have taken it all." '

[18] Zeuxippus was delighted with this story. 'Marvellous!' he cried, 'It almost ends my family feud with Anytus* on behalf of Socrates and philosophy to learn that he was such a noble and obliging lover!'

'Well,' said my father, 'doesn't love make the glum and sullen fonder of mankind and better company? "Better the house to behold when the fire is alight",[2] and brighter the man, it seems, in the warmth of love. The common perception of these things is paradoxical. If people see a blaze in a house at night, they marvel and think it a divine sign; but when they see a small, mean, and ignoble mind suddenly filled with pride, freedom, generosity, charm, and self-sacrifice, they do not feel obliged to use Telemachus' words:* "Truly, there is a god within."[3] And another thing, Daphnaeus—by all the Graces, it's miraculous! The lover who scorns almost everyone, comrades and kinsfolk, laws and magistrates and kings, fearing nothing, admiring nothing, owing service to no one, but ready to face "the lightning's spear", as Pindar has it,[4] nevertheless, on merely catching a glimpse of his beloved,

> shrinks like a cock that bows its craven wing,
> his boldness broken, his heart's pride smashed to pieces.[5]

'Here, in the home of the Muses, is the right place to speak of Sappho. The Romans say that Cacus, the son of Vulcan, poured a stream of fire and flame from his mouth; similarly, Sappho's words are truly mixed with fire. Her songs reflect the warmth of the heart, as (in the words of Philoxenus) "she medicines love with the sweet Muses' voice".[6] Now, Daphnaeus—unless

Lysandra has made you forgetful of your former loves—remind
763 us of the passage in which beautiful Sappho* tells how, the moment she sets eyes on the girl she loves, her voice dries up, her body burns, and she is overcome by pallor and distraction and dizziness.'[7]

Daphnaeus thereupon repeated the famous lines, and my father then resumed his speech.

'In heaven's name,' he said, 'Isn't this a plain case of possession by the god, a real daemonic storm in the soul? Does the Pythia sitting on her tripod have an experience the equal of this? Do the pipes and drums and all the rituals of the Great Mother send her votaries into such ecstasy? Yet many see the same body and the same beauty, but only the lover is so gripped. Why? I don't understand Menander, or find him helpful, when he says:

> The illness is the soul's own crucial moment;
> the victim's wounded by his destined blow.[8]

In fact, it is the god who causes it. He strikes one, and passes another by.

'Now there is something I ought to have said at the beginning; but now that it has "come to my lips", to quote Aeschylus,[9] I cannot forbear to mention it. It is extremely important. Our belief in most things that do not impinge on our minds through the sense rests on myth, law, or reason. For our belief in the gods, however, we have other teachers and guides: first, poets; secondly, lawgivers; thirdly, philosophers. These all posit the existence of the gods, though they differ very much about their number, order, substance, and power. The gods of the philosophers are

> from ills and age exempt,
> knowing no pain, and safe
> from Acheron's roaring tide.[10]

They do not admit Strife or Prayers,* as the poets do, or allow that Terror and Fear can be gods or children of Ares. They have many points of disagreement with the lawgivers. Xenophanes, for example, told the Egyptians not to honour Osiris as a god if they believed him to be mortal,[11] and not to mourn for him if they believed him to be a god. On the other hand, the poets and lawgivers can't bear to hear the philosophers—and can't understand them either—when they treat ideas, numbers, monads, and spirits (*pneumata*) as gods. There are indeed great differences and anomalies in all these beliefs. Yet, just as there were once three factions at Athens, the Coast, the Mountain, and the Plain, which long quarrelled but finally united to give all their votes to Solon, who incontestably held the prize for virtue, to be their mediator, ruler, and lawgiver, so the three factions in theology, despite having such differences of opinion, despite voting in so many different ways and finding it so hard to accept one another's gods, all agree firmly in one thing: Eros is on the list of gods according to the best poets and lawgivers and philosophers. "They praise him mightily with single voice", as Alcaeus says the Mitylenaeans chose Pittacus to be tyrant.[12] Eros, our king and ruler and governor, is brought down from Helicon to the Academy by Hesiod and Plato and Solon, with a crown on his head; he rides, splendidly adorned, in a great procession of chariots of friendship and fellowship. The compulsion he imposes is not like that described by Euripides, "bound with fetters not of bronze",[13] cold, heavy, put on us in our need by shame; no, this affection takes wing and flies upwards to the fairest and divinest of realities. But others have spoken of this better than I can.'

[19] 'You see, don't you,' said Soclarus, when my father had finished, 'that this is the second time you have come to this same point, and then somehow wrenched yourself away—not 764
paying your debt, if I may say what I think, to a sacred discourse? You mentioned Plato and the Egyptians together, just now, apparently reluctantly, and then passed on; and now you are doing the same again. Now as to what was "so plainly spoke"[1] by Plato, or rather what the Muses said through Plato's mouth, "you would not tell us even though we ask";[2] but the hint you gave about the agreement between Plato and the Egyptian myth about Eros, *that* you absolutely must disclose and reveal to us. We shall be content even to hear a little about such a mighty matter.' The others associated themselves with this request, and my father explained that the Egyptians, like the Greeks, distinguish two Erotes—Popular Eros and Heavenly Eros—but believe that the sun is a third Eros. They also identify Aphrodite <with the moon> and hold her in great honour. 'But

we Greeks', he continued, 'see that there is a great affinity between Eros and the sun. Neither of them is fire (as some believe), but each is a sweet, fruitful source of light and heat. The sun gives our bodies food and light and growth, and Eros does the same for our souls. And just as the sun is warmer when it emerges from clouds and after a mist, so Eros is sweeter and keener when lovers are reconciled after anger and jealousy. Again, as some tell us that the sun is repeatedly kindled and extinguished, so they say the same of mortal, unstable Eros. And just as a body which is in poor condition cannot bear the sun without pain, so an untrained soul cannot bear Eros. Both become distraught and ill in similar ways, and they blame the god's power, not their own weakness. The difference (one may say) is that the sun displays beauty and ugliness equally to the eye, whereas Eros is a light only for beauty and makes lovers look and turn only to this, neglecting all else. And in identifying Aphrodite not with the earth but with the moon, the Egyptians have grasped a certain point of likeness. For the moon is of earth, but she is also of heaven; she is the place where mortal and immortal join, but in herself she is faint and dim unless the sun shines upon her. So it is with Aphrodite when Eros is absent. So it is reasonable to think of the moon as *like* Aphrodite, and the sun as *like* Eros more than like any other god, but not that they are absolutely the same. Soul is not the same as body but different, just as the sun is visible and Eros intelligible. If it is not thought too contentious a point, one might add that the sun actually has the opposite effect from Eros, because it diverts the mind from the intelligible to the sensible, fascinating it by the grace and brilliance of sight, and persuading it to seek even for truth within and around itself, and not anywhere else.

> We are cursed with unhappy love
> for whatever this is that glitters on earth,[3]

as Euripides says,

> and all through ignorance
> of any life beyond,

or, to be more accurate, through our forgetfulness of those things of which Eros is recollection. When we wake to bright

light, all sleeping visions flee from the soul; and similarly when we are born into this world, changing our condition, the sun seems to dumbfound our memories and drug our minds, as pleasure and wonder make us forget the other side. Yet the soul's waking vision is in truth yonder, and relates to that other world; here, she can but welcome and marvel at the divine beauty in dreams: "There poured around her sweet, beguiling dreams",[4] making her believe that all beauty and honour is here on earth, unless she finds some chaste, divine Eros to heal and save her. . . . He comes <here> in bodily form and guides her to- 765
wards truth . . . and from Hades to the Plain of Truth, where massive, pure, and undeceptive beauty lies; and when we long to embrace and be with that beauty after so long, Eros bears us up and directs our way, our kindly mystagogue in this our mystery. But when we are sent on earth again, he no longer consorts with the soul on its own, but only through the body. And, as geometers put tangible and visible models of spheres, cubes, and dodecahedrons before children, because they are not yet capable of being initiated on their own into the intelligible forms of incorporeal and impassive being, similarly the Eros of heaven contrives beautiful mirror-images of the beautiful for us; yet they are mortal images of the divine, changeable images of the unalterable, sensible images of the intelligible. He displays them, brilliant with the bloom of youth, in shapes and colours and forms, and uses them to stir our memory, which at first is but feebly kindled. Hence some people, through the ill-advised efforts of friends and relatives who try to suppress the passion forcibly and irrationally, have no benefit from it. They either fill themselves with smoke and confusion, or else plunge into dark and lawless pleasures and waste away in disgrace. Others, however, through sober reason and modesty, take the frenzy out of the fire, and leave the soul with brilliance and light and warmth. And this warmth does not, as some say, produce an oscillation that generates sperm,* nor a slippage of atoms rubbing against one another in lubricious titillation, but a wonderful, fertile expansion, like that of a growing plant, opening the way of obedience and affection. Ere long, such persons pass beyond the body of the beloved, and enter in and make contact with his character. Their eyes are opened, and they see, and talk together

and do things together often, if they find a pattern or image of the beautiful in each other's mind. If not, they let him be and turn to others, just as bees leave alone many blooming flowers that contain no honey. But where they find a trace of the divine, some seductive effluence or likeness, they are possessed by pleasure and wonder. They cherish it, and memory's light is happily renewed in the awareness of that truly desirable, blessed, and uniquely dear object of all men's love.

[20] 'Most of what the poets write and sing in their merry songs to the god hardly seems serious, but they have said a few significant things, whether through their own thought and reason or because the god has helped them to touch upon the truth. One such passage is about the birth of Eros:

> most terrible of gods,
> whom lovely-sandalled Iris bore
> to Zephyr of the golden hair.[1]

Or perhaps scholars have persuaded you that this imagery merely refers to the diversity and colourfulness of the passion of love?'

'Why, what else could it refer to?' said Daphnaeus.

'Let me tell you,' said my father. 'The phenomena compel us to give this account of it. When we see a rainbow, our vision experiences refraction. When it encounters a damp, smooth, and not very dense cloud, it makes contact with the sun by refraction, and, sensing its brilliance and light, produces in us the impression that the appearance is in the cloud. Such too is love's contrivance and device for the rightly endowed and appreciative spirit: it produces a refraction of memory from the appearances called beautiful here on earth to that truly divine, lovely, blessed, and marvellous beauty. Yet most people, pursuing and fondling its image as it appears in the mirror, so to speak, of boys or women, achieve nothing more substantial than
766 a mixture of pleasure and pain. This is what seems to be meant by the delusion and hallucination of Ixion, who chased an illusory desire in the unreality of the clouds, as children long to catch the rainbow in their hands, because the look of it charms them. Your well-endowed lover of the right character is not like this. He experiences refraction with respect to the divine, intel-

ligible beauty, and when he encounters the beauty of a visible body, he uses it as an instrument of memory, as it were, and welcomes and appreciates it; and the more he consorts with it and rejoices in it, the more is his mind set on fire. Such lovers do not sit idly here in their bodily lives, longing for, and marvelling at, this common light; nor yet, when they pass over yonder after death do they turn back here again, like runaways, to haunt the doors and bedrooms of the newly wed, like the nightmarish fantasies* of men and women who love pleasure and the body, and have no right to be called devotees of Eros.

'The true devotee, when he passes yonder and consorts with the beautiful in the manner there permitted, takes wing, is inspired, and spends his time dancing in those high places with his own god, accompanying him until such time as he comes again to the meadows of Aphrodite and the moon, falls asleep there, and begins a new cycle of birth. But this is to go well beyond our present subject,' my father went on. 'Like other gods, however, Eros, as Euripides tells us, can "take pleasure in the honours men may give";[1] and he can also sometimes react in the opposite way! Very kind to those who give him a proper welcome, he can be severe on the obstinate. Zeus Xenios is no quicker to avenge the wrongs of strangers and suppliants, Zeus Genethlios no quicker to execute the curses of parents, than Eros is to hear the complaints of wronged lovers, and punish the ill-mannered and the arrogant. Need I remind you of Euxynthetus and Leucocomas?* Or of the Peeper, as they still call her, in Cyprus? But you may never have heard of the punishment meted out to Gorgo in Crete. It was not unlike what happened to the Peeper,* except that the Peeper was turned to stone when she peeped out and saw her lover carried to his grave. Gorgo was loved by an excellent man, of a good family, named Asandros: he had fallen from his high estate into a humble and lowly way of life, but nevertheless set a high value on himself, and asked Gorgo (he was her kinsman) in marriage, though she was rich and therefore in contention among many suitors. He naturally had many rivals, but he won over all the girl's guardians and relations [*There is evidently a lengthy passage lost here. In it, not only was the story of Gorgo completed, but the whole party left Helicon to go back to Thespiae, and Zeuxippus (on the* *way?) expounded the view that love was responsible for many evils, and indeed was an obstacle to friendship and virtue. Plutarch answered this, it seems, by showing that such an attack would apply to homosexual and conjugal love equally. He is still speaking to this point where our text resumes*].

[21] 'The causes and modes of generation of love, as described, are not peculiar to one kind. They are common to both. If images intrude upon the lover, as they pervade him, and stir and titillate the body into producing sperm, by joining the sliding movements of other atomic configurations, cannot this be provoked as much by women as by boys? And those beautiful and holy recollections, as we call them, that point to the true divine, Olympian beauty—recollections which give the soul its wings—what is there to prevent their being provoked not only by boys and youths but by girls and women, when a pure and well-ordered personality is revealed by grace and bloom of form (a well-shaped shoe reveals a shapely foot, as Ariston[2] says), or when people who are clever at perceiving such things detect the clear, straight tracks of a splendid soul in beautiful forms and pure bodies? If we think that the libertine who was asked whether "he leant towards the female or the male", and replied, "wherever beauty lies, I'm ambidextrous",[2] gave an answer that matched his desires, then surely the honourable lover of beauty
767 will direct his love to beauty and a fair endowment of nature, not to differences of sex. The horse-lover feels as pleased with Podargus' temper as with "Agamemnon's Aithe".* The hunter's pleasure is not confined to dogs; he breeds Cretan and Laconian bitches too. So should not the lover of human beauty be even-handed between the sexes? Does he think there are differences between men and women in the matter of love as there are in the matter of clothes? . . . Youth, we are told, is "the bloom of virtue".* It is surely absurd to deny "bloom" to the female, or to claim that she gives no sign of a natural tendency to virtue. Aeschylus was right:

> I cannot miss the woman's burning eye
> who once has tasted man.[1]

Can it be, then, that the signs of a forward, wanton, and corrupt disposition are visible in a woman's face, while there is no light upon the countenance of the modest and well-conducted? Or is it that there are indeed many such signs, but they have no attraction and do not stimulate love? Neither possibility is either plausible or true.

'So all these points, we have now shown, apply equally to both kinds of love. Both have the same battle to fight. Next, Daphnaeus, let us face the actual arguments that Zeuxippus has just rehearsed. He identifies love with an unstable desire leading the soul into incontinence. It is not that he believes this himself. He has merely heard it often from sundry disagreeable and unlovely persons. Some of these, attracted by a dowry, however small, proceed to take the money and plunge their miserable wives into housekeeping and petty calculations; they quarrel daily, but keep them in hand. Others, who desire children more than a wife, behave like cicadas,* which deposit their seed on squills or what you will, and hastily impregnate any female they come upon, gather the harvest, and let the marriage go—or, if it holds, they do not give a thought to loving or being loved, which they regard as quite unimportant. In my view, though, the fact that the verb *stergein*, "to love", differs by only one letter from *stegein*, "to protect", itself expresses the mutual goodwill that time and familiarity inevitably produce. When Eros lights upon a man and inspires him, the first consequence is that he takes the words "mine" and "not mine"* in the sense they are given in Plato's *Republic*; for the saying "friends' things are common property"[2] is not universally true, but only of persons who, though physically separate, force their souls together and melt into one, neither wishing to be two separate persons nor believing that they are. Secondly, self-control, which is specially needed in marriage, is of two kinds. It may come from without and be subject to law; in that case, the compulsions of shame and fear play a larger part in it than free will. It does "the work of many curbs and many rudders",[3] and is indeed always available to married couples. Eros, however, possesses within himself such a store of order, control, and faith that, even if he chances to lay hands on an intemperate soul, he turns it away from other lovers, knocks its audacity out of it, breaks its pride and indiscipline, gives it modesty, silence, quiet, and decency, and finally brings it into obedience to a single master. You have doubtless heard how the much-celebrated and much-loved Lais fired all Greece with desire, and the two seas fought over her.* Well, when Eros took hold of her, in the shape of love for Hippolochus of Thessaly, she

> left the crags of Acrocorinth
> which the grey-green waters lap,[4]

secretly abandoned her other lovers, and went soberly away <to Thessaly> leaving all her colleagues behind. In Thessaly, then, the women were so jealous of her beauty that they took her into
768 a temple of Aphrodite and stoned her to death. This seems to be the origin of the so-called temple of "Aphrodite the Murderess". We know of slave girls avoiding the sexual advances of their owners, and of private citizens scorning those of queens, when Eros is master of the soul. It is like what happens in Rome when a dictator is appointed and the other magistrates lay down their offices; those whom Eros comes to master are independent of all other lords and rulers, they go unfettered like temple slaves. A good woman in love with her lawful husband would rather be embraced by bears and serpents than be touched by, or go to bed with, any other man.

[22] 'You people who are Eros' neighbours* and devotees must know many examples of this. But I should not like to pass over the story of Camma,* the Galatian. This beautiful woman was married to the tetrarch Sinatus; but the powerful Sinorix fell in love with her and killed her husband, because he was unable to rape or seduce her while Sinatus was alive. Camma's refuge, her consolation in her bereavement, was a position she had inherited as priestess of Artemis. She now spent most of her time in the temple of the goddess, receiving no visitors, though many kings and potentates wooed her. Sinorix, however, did attempt to discuss marriage with her. She did not avoid the question, or blame him for the past. She admitted that he had acted not out of a wicked heart, but out of affection and desire for her. He trusted her, and came and formally asked her in marriage. She met him, greeted him, and led him to the altar of the goddess. There she poured a libation of wine and honey from a cup. She had poisoned it. She drank half herself, and gave Sinorix the rest. When she saw he had drunk it, she gave a loud cry and

spoke her dead husband's name. "Dearest husband," she cried, "I have lived in pain till this day without you. Receive me now and be glad. I have avenged you on this wicked man, and I rejoice to have had a part in your life, and in his death." Sinorix was carried off on a stretcher, and soon expired. Camma lived through the day and the following night, and is said to have died in brave and happy mood.

[23] 'There have been many such happenings, both in Greece and in other lands. How then can one bear the abuse of Aphrodite, that alleges that her presence in company with Eros prevents the development of affection? The intercourse of man with man—immorality or assault, it would be better named—is well described in the line "Hybris does this, not Cypris".*[1] This is why we regard men who take pleasure in passive submission as practising the lowest kind of vice, and allow them no loyalty or modesty or affection. Sophocles was right:

> men joy to lose such friends as these; or if
> they have them, then their wish is to escape.[2]

Persons who, without being evil by nature, are tricked or forced into giving themselves or making themselves available, continue to suspect and loath those who were responsible for their plight, and avenge themselves on them bitterly if occasion offers. Thus Crateas killed his former lover Archelaus, and Pytholaus killed Alexander of Pherae. Periander, tyrant of Ambracia, actually asked his favourite whether he was pregnant yet. The young man was incensed, and killed him. Yet for married couples, sexual relations are a foundation of affection, a 769
communion, as it were, in a great mystery. The pleasure may be momentary, but the honour, grace, and mutual love and trust arising therefrom day by day proves the Delphians right when they gave Aphrodite the name Harma—"Harmony"—and Homer right when he used the word *philotes*—"loving friendship"—of this association. It proves also that Solon was a very experienced legislator in marital matters, because he laid down that a man should have intercourse with his wife not less than three times a month—not for pleasure, of course, but because he wished the marriage, whatever difficulties it encountered from time to time, to be renewed by this expression of fondness, as

cities periodically renew their peace-treaties with each other. "There is much badness and much madness in the love of women", yes, but is there not more in the love of boys? "I saw a kindred spirit, and I fell." "A beardless, tender, beautiful young boy." "To die embracing, and be so recorded."[1] This is *paedomania*, boy-madness; the other is *gynaecomania*, woman-madness. Neither is love.

'So it is absurd to think that women have no share in virtue. Why speak of their temperance, intelligence, loyalty, and justice, when manliness, boldness, and greatness of spirit are manifest in so many? It is outrageous to praise their nature in other respects and then criticize it as ill-adapted for one thing only, affection. They are affectionate towards children and husbands, they have a fund of loving care, abounding in persuasion and charm, a fertile soil for affection to grow. Poetry makes the educative element in literature more effective, and the damaging element harder to guard against, by adding the embellishments of song, metre, and rhythm to words. It is so also with women. Nature endows them with charms for the eye, persuasiveness of tongue, and seductiveness of form; she therefore contributes both to the deceptive delights of the wanton and to the conjugal affection and kindliness of the chaste. Xenocrates, who was a grand fellow and a great man, but rather austere of character, was recommended by Plato to "sacrifice to the Graces". A good and chaste woman might equally well be recommended to sacrifice to Eros, and pray that he should be a kindly household presence in her marriage and give her feminine charm, lest her husband should turn elsewhere and be made to say, like the man in the comedy, "Wretched am I that wrong so good a lady!"[2] In marriage, it is more important to love than to be loved. It helps us to rid ourselves of so many mistakes—indeed, from all the errors that corrupt and destroy marriages.

[24] 'Do not be afraid, my dear Zeuxippus, of the initial sharp pain. It is not a wound or a bite. Even if there is a wound, there is perhaps nothing very terrible in grafting oneself, as it were, on to a good woman. The first step in a conception is also a lesion; there is no union unless the parties to it suffer mutually. Likewise, mathematics worries children, and philosophy worries students, at the beginning of the course; but the pain does not

last for ever. Nor does it with lovers. Love induces a sort of effervescence and turbulence at first, as when two liquids are mixed, but it settles down and clears and produces a perfectly stable result. This integration of lovers is indeed what scientists call "total integration";* the combining of persons who live together otherwise is more like Epicurus's "contacts" and "nexuses", subject to collisions and repulsions, but not resulting in the kind of unity that Eros sets up within a conjugal union. No mutual pleasures are greater, no mutual services more constant, 770
no form of affection is more enviable and estimable for its sheer beauty than

> when man and wife in harmony of mind
> keep house together.[1]

And the law too helps Eros, to assure society's increase . . .

'Nature also shows that even the gods need Eros. That is why the poets say that "earth is in love with rain", and heaven with earth,* and the scientists tell us that the sun is in love with the moon and joins with him, and conception follows. And must not Earth, mother of men and origin of all animals and plants, die and be snuffed out one day, when the great love and desire of the god abandons her material substance, and when she ceases to yearn for and pursue the impulse and motion that she derives from this? But let us not seem to wander too far afield, or to talk utter nonsense. Let us get back to the love of boys. They say you can disrupt that affection like cutting an egg with a hair. Lovers, they tell us, are like tribes of nomads, spending the spring where the grass grows and the flowers, and then moving camp, like an army leaving enemy territory. The sophist Bion's saying is cruder than this: he called a boy's first beard "Harmodius and Aristogiton",* because it freed his lovers from the tyranny of his beauty. But that would not be true of genuine lovers. Euripides' remark is very neat: embracing and kissing Agathon, who was by then beginning to have a beard, he observed that "in the beautiful, even the autumn is beautiful".[2] <The love of women, indeed> has no autumn. It flourishes on grey hairs and wrinkles, it endures to the burial and the tomb. There are few instances of permanent relationships of love with boys but innumerable with women, preserving a community of loyalty and ardour in every circumstance. I should like to relate one such episode, which occurred in our own time, in the reign of Vespasian.

[25] 'Civilis, the man who raised the rebellion in Gaul,* had many collaborators. One was a young noble called Sabinus, distinguished among the Gauls for his riches and his reputation. Their great attempt failed, and they awaited punishment. Some killed themselves, some were captured while trying to escape. Sabinus' circumstances would have made it easy for him to vanish into exile in some barbarian country. But he had married an excellent wife, whom the Gauls called Empona, though in Greek we might well call her Herois. He could neither leave her nor take her with him. Now he had on his estate an underground treasure-chamber, of which only two of his freedmen knew. He sent the other servants away, pretending to be about to take poison, but then took the two faithful freedmen with him down into the underground room. He also sent his freedman Martialis to his wife, to inform her that he had died of poison, and that the house and his body had alike gone up in flames. His intention was to use his wife's genuine grief as proof of his supposed death. And so it fell out. She threw herself on the ground, with tears and lamentations, and passed three days and three nights without food. Sabinus, when he heard this, was afraid that she might put an end to her life. He therefore ordered Martialis to inform her secretly that he was alive and hidden, but at the same time to bid her persist in her mourning for a time, and
771 endeavour to make her performance as convincing as possible. She acted her tragic part as a bereaved wife in a manner fit for the stage; but her longing to see her husband made her visit him at night, and then return to her home. No one else knew that she was more or less living with her husband in the other world for more than seven months. In this period, she disguised Sabinus with new clothes, shortened his hair, made him wear a hood, and took him, quite unrecognized, to Rome. Some hope of a pardon had been given her; but she was unsuccessful, and returned home, once more to live most of the time with her husband underground, visiting the town and seen by her friends at intervals. The most extraordinary thing was that the women with whom she went to the baths never knew she was pregnant.

The ointment which women use to tint their hair blonde contains a fat which makes flesh and produces a swelling of the body, amounting to a sort of general dilation or expansion. By applying this all over and in great quantity, she succeeded in concealing the growing fullness of her belly. She endured the pains of labour without aid, going down to her husband as a lioness goes to her den, and she reared the two male cubs in secret. Of these sons, one fell in Egypt, the other, whose name is Sabinus, was here with us in Delphi only the other day.* Caesar did in the end have her executed; but he paid the penalty, for his whole family was destroyed within a short time. No action of his reign was grimmer, or more likely to cause gods and *daimones* to turn away from him. Her bold words both lessened the spectators' pity for her, and angered Vespasian. When she had no more hope of life, she bade him change places with her; for, as she said, she had "enjoyed life more in the darkness underground than he did on his throne". '

[26] According to my father, this marked the end of their talk about Eros. They were now near Thespiae. Diogenes, a friend of Pisias, could be seen approaching at something more than walking pace. Before he could reach them, Soclarus called out, 'No messenger of war, I see, Diogenes!' 'Don't say such things,' cried Diogenes, 'there's a wedding, and you must make haste; the sacrifice is held up for you.' Everyone was delighted, though Zeuxippus asked whether Pisias was still angry. 'Not at all,' replied Diogenes, 'he was the first to give way to Ismenodora; he is pleased to wear a garland and a white cloak and is ready to lead the procession through the agora to the temple.' 'Well, let's go,' said my father, 'let's go. We can have a laugh against him and also pay our respects to the god, who is evidently pleased, and graces the event with his presence and favour.'

XIV

ADVICE ON MARRIAGE

'The subject is delightful, the form even more so,' wrote Daniel Wyttenbach, Plutarch's greatest editor. This carefully written composition is a wedding-present for two young friends. A Flavius Pollianus of Tithorea is known from an inscription, and is probably the bridegroom. The 'precepts' (*parangelmata*) are not without order: there are associative connections, and the end of the work clearly recalls the beginning in the emphasis laid on the philosophical education of both husband and wife (Introd. p. xxi). Many of the 'precepts' too are in the form of 'similitudes' (*homoiōmata*), a rhetorical device which Plutarch uses throughout his writing, but which is here developed with peculiar formality and elegance. Jeremy Taylor's sermons on 'The Marriage Ring' (*Eniautos: Twenty-five Sermons*, xvii–xviii) make abundant use of this material.

For Pollianus and Eurydice

138 After the traditional ordinance, which the priestess of Demeter laid upon you when you were shut up in your wedding-chamber together, it may be that words* (*logos*) also will touch you and contribute to your wedding in a way that is both useful and in harmony with the law. In music, there was a tune for the pipe called 'The Rampant Stallion',* designed, it seems, to urge the stallion to cover the mare. In philosophy too there are many fine subjects of discourse, but none more important than this discourse of marriage, whereby philosophy charms those who come together to share their lives, and makes them gentle and amenable to each other. I have therefore put together in the form of some brief similitudes, so that they are the more easily remembered, the main points of the teaching you have often heard in the course of your education in philosophy. These I send as a gift to you both, praying that the Muses may assist Aphrodite in her work; for it is less their duty to tune lyre or zither than it is to ensure the tunefulness of marriage and home by discourse, harmony, and philosophy. The ancients set Hermes at Aphrodite's side, knowing that the pleasure of marriage needed his word more than anything, and with them they set persuasion and the Graces, that married couples might have

their desire from each other by persuasion, not in conflict or quarrelsomeness.

[1] Solon ordered that the bride should eat some quince before retiring to bed with the bridegroom. He meant to suggest (I suppose) that the first favour of lip and voice should be harmonious and sweet.

[2] In Boeotia, when they veil the bride, they give her a garland of asparagus.* This is a plant that gives the sweetest fruit from the sharpest thorn, just as the bride will give a life of calm and sweetness to the man who does not shrink from, or feel distaste for, the first harsh and disagreeable impressions. Men who cannot put up with a young girl's first quarrels are like people who leave the ripe bunch to others because the unripe grape was tart. Many newly married girls also show distaste for their bridegrooms because of the first experience; they are like people who put up with the bee's sting but let the honeycomb go.

[3] It is especially at the start that married couples should beware of differences and disputes. They should observe that jointed articles* are easily broken at first by quite trivial accidents, whereas once the joints have become firm with use they can hardly be parted by fire or steel.

[4] As fire is easily kindled in chaff or tinder or rabbit fur, but also easily extinguished unless it takes hold of some other material capable of protecting and feeding it, so one must realize that the love of the newly married, blazing up quickly out of physical attraction, is not persistent or secure unless it settles in the character, lays hold of the mind, and acquires a life of its own.

[5] Poisoned bait catches fish quickly and easily, but makes 139
them nasty and inedible. Similarly, women who contrive potions and charms to entice men and win them over by pleasure find they have unreliable, foolish, and spoilt partners in life. Circe had no profit from the victims of her potions, for she could not use them for anything when they became pigs or asses; it was Odysseus, the man of sense, who consorted wisely with her, whom she loved so much.

[6] Women who prefer to dominate fools rather than obey men of sense are like people who would rather guide the blind on the road than follow the sighted man who knows the way.

[7] Women do not believe that Pasiphae fell in love with a bull when she lived with a king. Yet they see some women finding strict and moral husbands a burden, and preferring to go with men who have the intemperate, pleasure-loving natures of dogs or goats.

[8] Persons whose weakness or feebleness does not allow them to leap on to a horse teach the horse to kneel and lower itself. Similarly, some men who take rich or highly born wives do not improve themselves, but diminish their wives; they think they will rule them better if they are brought low. But, as with the horse, it is the curb you need to use, paying attention to the greatness and prestige of the lady.

[9] We see the moon bright and conspicuous when she is far from the sun; when near, she vanishes and is hidden. A good woman, on the other hand, should be seen most when she is with her husband, and stay at home and be hidden when he is away.

[10] Herodotus was wrong to say that a woman doffs her modesty when she doffs her clothes.[1] The opposite is true: a good woman wears modesty in place of clothes, and the sign of great love is great modesty towards each other.

[11] When two notes are struck together, the melody belongs to the lower note. Similarly, every action performed in a good household is done by the agreement of the partners, but displays the leadership and decision of the husband.

[12] The sun beat the north wind! The wind blew hard and tried to strip off the man's cloak; but he gripped it tight and held the folds together. After the wind, the sun was warm; and the man, feeling first warm and then hot, took off not only his cloak but his shirt. This is how most women behave. When their husbands take away their luxuries and extravagances, they fight and quarrel; but if they are persuaded by reason, they lay them aside without complaint and behave with moderation.

[13] Cato expelled from the Senate the man who kissed his wife in their daughter's presence. That was perhaps somewhat extreme; but if it is disgraceful (as indeed it is) to kiss and embrace in the presence of others, is it not more disgraceful to quarrel and abuse each other before others, or to treat your love and affection for your wife as a secret, while exposing your frank reproaches and fault-finding to the open light of day?

[14] There is no usefulness in a mirror ornamented with gold and jewels, unless it shows a likeness. Similarly, there is no profit in a rich wife, unless she makes her life and character resemble and harmonize with her husband's. If a mirror shows a scowling image of a happy face, or a cheery, grinning image of an angry sullen face, it is faulty and worthless. And so, if a wife puts on a glum look when her husband wants to be playful and affectionate, or if she laughs and jokes when he is serious, she is a poor wife, and has no sense of occasion; she proves herself in the first case disagreeable, in the second insensitive. Mathe-
maticians tell us that lines and surfaces do not move on their 140
own, but only in conjunction with bodies. Similarly, a wife should have no feelings of her own, but share her husband's seriousness and sport, his anxiety and his laughter.

[15] Husbands who do not like to see their wives eating with them thereby teach them to stuff themselves in private. Similarly, men who do not converse cheerfully with their wives or share their play and laughter thereby teach them to seek private pleasures without them.

[16] When Persian kings dine, their legal wives sit beside them and share the feast. But if they want to amuse themselves or get drunk, they send their wives away, and summon the singing-girls and the concubines. And they are quite right not to share their drunken orgies with their wives. So, if a private citizen, intemperate and tasteless in his pleasures, commits an offence with a mistress or a maidservant, his wife ought not to be angry or annoyed, but reflect that it is his respect for her that makes her husband share his intemperance or violent behaviour with another woman.

[17] Kings who love music produce many musicians, scholarly kings scholars, athletic kings athletes. Similarly, a husband who loves the body produces a wife who adorns her person; a lover of pleasure, one who is free and immoral; and a lover of goodness and honour a chaste and sober wife.

[18] A Spartan girl, when asked if she had yet come to her husband, replied, 'No, but he has come to me.' This is how the true housewife should be; she does not avoid or show displeasure with such things, if her husband takes the initiative, but neither does she take the initiative herself; the latter would be forward and more like a mistress than a wife, the former shows arrogance and lack of affection.

[19] A wife ought not to have friends of her own, but use her husband's as their common stock. And the first and most important of our friends are the gods. A married woman should therefore worship and recognize the gods whom her husband holds dear, and these alone. The door must be closed to strange cults and foreign superstitions. No god takes pleasure in cult performed furtively and in secret by a woman.

[20] Plato says that the happy and blessed city is one in which the words 'mine' and 'not mine' are least to be heard,[1] because the citizens treat everything of importance, so far as possible, as their common property. Even more firmly should these words be banished from a marriage. Doctors tell us that an injury on the left side refers the sensation to the right. Similarly, it is good for a wife to share her husband's feelings, and a husband his wife's, so that, just as ropes gain strength from the twisting of the strands, so their communion may be the better preserved by their joint efforts, through mutual exchanges of goodwill. Nature joins you together in your bodies, so that she may take a part of each, and by mixing them together give you a child that belongs to you both, such that neither of you can say what is his or her own, and what the other's. Community of resources also is particularly appropriate for the married; they should pour everything into one fund, mix it all together, and not think of one part as belonging to one and another to the other, but of the whole as their own, and none of it anyone else's. We call our mixed drink 'wine', though there is more water than wine in it; similarly, the property and the house should be called the husband's even if the wife contributes the greater part.

[21] Helen loved wealth, Paris loved pleasure. Odysseus was wise, Penelope was prudent. The latter pair had a happy and enviable marriage; the marriage of the others brought an Iliad of
141 disaster on Greeks and barbarians.

[22] The Roman who was reproached by his friends* for divorcing his chaste, rich, and beautiful wife, replied by holding up his shoe. 'This shoe', he said, 'is new and beautiful, but no one knows where it pinches me.' A wife should not rely on her dowry, her birth, or her beauty, but ensure by her conversation,

manners, and behaviour, which are the points that most touch a husband, that there is nothing in their daily life harsh or hurtful, but only painless and harmonious affection. Doctors are more alarmed by fevers that come from obscure and gradually developing causes than they are by those that have an obvious and conspicuous origin. Similarly, repeated, trivial daily annoyances that go unnoticed cause more damage and disruption to the joint life of husband and wife.

[23] King Philip loved a Thessalian lady, who was charged with giving him a love potion. Queen Olympias was anxious to get the woman into her power. But when she appeared, and was seen to be beautiful, and conversed very properly and intelligently with the queen, Olympias said, 'We can forget the accusations; you have your charms in yourself.' Thus a lawful, wedded wife is invincible, if she has everything in herself—dowry, birth, potions, Aphrodite's magic belt—and wins goodwill by her character and virtue.

[24] It was Olympias again who, when a young courtier married a beautiful woman with a bad reputation, observed 'He has no sense, or he would not have married with his eyes.' Indeed, one must not marry with the eyes, nor yet with the fingers,* as those do who calculate how much money their intended will bring, not how she will turn out as a companion in life.

[25] Socrates' advice to young men who looked at themselves in the mirror, if they were ugly, was to compensate for their looks by virtue; if they were handsome, not to mar their beauty by vice. So when the housewife has her mirror in her hand, she should say to herself, if she is plain, 'But what does it matter if I am chaste?' and if she is handsome, 'But what does it matter if I am also chaste?' For it is an honour to the plain woman to be loved for her character, and to the beauty to be loved also for her character.

[26] The tyrant of Sicily* sent expensive cloaks and necklaces to Lysander's daughters. Lysander refused them, saying 'these ornaments will disfigure me more than they will adorn my daughters.' Sophocles anticipated Lysander's thought:

> there's no adornment here to see, you wretch,
> but unadornment, and your heart's blind folly.[1]

'Adornment', said Crates, 'is what adorns'; and what adorns a woman is what makes her better ordered*—not gold nor emerald nor scarlet, but whatever gives an impression of dignity, discipline, and modesty.

[27] In the sacrifice to Hera, as goddess of marriage, they do not consecrate the gall-bladder with the rest of the victim, but take it out and throw it away by the altar. The inventor of this practice thereby intimates enigmatically that there should never be any gall or anger in a marriage. The sharpness of the housewife, like that of wine, should be profitable and pleasant—not bitter and poisonous, like aloes.

[28] Plato advised Xenocrates, who was a man of excellent character but of rather too grave a manner, that he should sacrifice to the Graces. So also the chaste wife needs graces in handling her husband, so as to enjoy living with him and not 'feel
142 angry because she is chaste', as Metrodorus said. A woman of simple tastes should not neglect cleanliness, nor one who loves her husband neglect expressions of affection. Bad temper makes a woman's good behaviour disagreeable, and dirtiness does the same for simplicity.

[29] A wife who is afraid to laugh and joke with her husband, for fear of seeming bold and forward, is no different from one who uses no oil for fear of seeming to have perfumed her head, or does not wash for fear of seeming to use make-up. We note that poets and orators who avoid vulgar, cheap affectations of language cultivate the art of influencing and affecting their audiences by subject, arrangement, and character. Thus the mistress of the house also, because she is right to avoid and reject all meretricious and ostentatious display, has none the less to cultivate the art of handling her husband by charms of character and daily life, training him in good ways with pleasure. If she is naturally stern, austere, and without charm, her husband must be indulgent. When Antipater ordered Phocion to do something that was neither honourable nor decent, Phocion replied 'You cannot have me both as a friend and as a flatterer.' Similarly, the husband of a modest and austere wife must reflect, 'I cannot have her both as a wife and as a mistress.'

[30] According to the old custom, Egyptian women did not wear shoes; this was so that they should spend all day at home.

With most women, if you take away their gilded shoes and bracelets and anklets, their purple dresses and their pearls, they too will stay at home.

[31] Theano once exposed her hand as she was arranging her cloak. 'What a beautiful arm,' said someone. 'But not public property,' she replied. Not only the arms but the words of a modest woman must never be public property. She should be shy with her speech as with her body, and guard it against strangers. Feelings, character, and disposition can all be seen in a woman's talk.

[32] Phidias' statue of Aphrodite* at Elis has her foot resting on a tortoise, to symbolize homekeeping and silence. A wife should speak only to her husband or through her husband, and should not feel aggrieved if, like a piper, she makes nobler music through another's tongue.

[33] Rich men and kings who honour philosophers adorn both themselves and their beneficiaries; but philosophers courting the rich do nothing to increase the reputation of these people, but merely diminish their own. It is the same with wives. If they submit to their husbands, they are praised. If they try to rule them, they cut a worse figure than their subjects. But the husband should rule the wife, not as a master rules a slave, but as the soul rules the body, sharing her feelings and growing together with her in affection. That is the just way. One can care for one's body without being a slave to its pleasures and desires; and one can rule a wife while giving her enjoyment and kindness.

[34] Philosophers distinguish three classes of bodies: those made up of separate units, like a fleet or an army; those made of units connected together, like a house or a ship; and those which have a natural unity, such as animals have. A marriage between lovers has this natural unity; a marriage for money or children is made of units connected together; a marriage based simply on the pleasure of sleeping together is made of separate units, and should be called cohabitation rather than a shared life.

Scientists tell us that liquids mix completely: so should the
bodies, resources, friends, and connections of a married couple. 143
The Roman lawgiver* forbade married couples to give or receive presents from each other. This was not to stop them sharing, but to make them think everything their common property.

[35] In the African city of Leptis, the custom is for the bride, the day after her marriage, to send a message to her husband's mother, asking for a pot. The mother-in-law refuses, and says she does not have one. This is to ensure that the bride knows from the start the stepmotherliness of a mother-in-law, and so is not angry or upset if something worse follows later. Recognizing this, the wife must seek to palliate the cause. This is a mother's jealous rivalry for her son's love. The only way to cure this is to secure the husband's love privately, but not attempt to loosen or weaken his love for his mother.

[36] Mothers seem to prefer sons because sons can help them, while fathers prefer daughters because daughters need their help. It may perhaps be that it is out of respect for each other that each parent wants to be seen to welcome and love that which is close to the other. This perhaps matters little: what is good is for a wife to be seen to honour her husband's parents more than her own, and refer to them if she is hurt, keeping her own parents in ignorance. To be seen to trust makes you trusted; to be seen to love makes you loved.

[37] Cyrus' Greek troops* were ordered by their generals to receive the enemy attack in silence if the enemy advanced shouting, and to shout if the enemy was silent. Sensible wives keep quiet when their husbands shout in anger, but speak and try to calm them down if their anger is silent.

[38] Euripides was right to condemn the use of the lyre over our wine.[1] Music should be invoked to ease anger or grief rather than to give further relaxation at times of pleasure. So you should reflect that it is wrong to sleep together for pleasure while sleeping apart when you are angry or have a difference; for that is especially the time to call in Aphrodite, who is the best doctor for such troubles. Homer teaches this lesson, when he makes Hera say:

> I'll end this endless quarrel,
> letting him come to me in love to bed.[2]

[39] A wife must always and everywhere avoid offending her husband, and a husband his wife. It is particularly important to be careful about this in sleeping together. The woman in labour, much distressed, said to those who were helping her to bed,

'How can the bed cure what I got in bed?' Yet disputes and quarrels bred in bed cannot easily be resolved at any other time or place.

[40] Hermione is thought to have said a true word when she said 'Visits of evil women ruined me.'[3] But the ruin does not happen just like that, but when a difference or jealous quarrel with a husband opens not only doors but also ears to women of that kind. The wise wife will close her ears, and guard against whispers, so as not to heap fire on fire. She will keep in mind the story of Philip. He was being incited to anger by friends who pointed out that the Greeks had done well at his hands but spoke ill of him in return. 'And what will happen', he replied 'if we treat them badly?' So when scandalmongering women say 'Your husband is hurting you, though you love him and are faithful,' the answer is 'And what will happen if I start to hate 144
and wrong him?'

[41] A man saw a runaway slave, after a long search. He gave chase, and the slave ran into a mill.* 'And where else would I have rather found you?' said the master. So let a jealous woman, writing a notice of divorce and extremely angry, say to herself 'And where would my rival be better pleased to see me? What would she rather find me doing than grieving and quarrelling with my husband, and deliberately throwing away my household and my marriage?'

[42] The Athenians have three Sacred Ploughings: one at Sciron, a memorial to the earliest sowing of a field; one at Raria; and one under the Acropolis, called the 'Ox-Yoking'. But holiest of all is the sowing and ploughing in marriage for the procreation of children. Sophocles well called Aphrodite 'fruitful Cytherea'. Husband and wife must go about this piously, keeping themselves pure of any unholy or lawless intercourse with others, or not sowing where they do not wish the crop to grow, and where they are ashamed if the fruit comes, and seek to hide it.

[43] When the orator Gorgias read out a speech at Olympia* to the Greeks on the subject of concord, Melanthius commented: 'Does this man advise us on concord when he can't persuade three individuals in his private life—himself, his wife, and the maid—to agree together?' Gorgias is supposed to have been in love with the maid, and his wife to have been jealous. A man who proposes to produce harmony in the city or in the market-place or among his own friends, must have harmony at home. Wives' sins are more often overlooked than sins against wives.

[44] Cats, we are told, are disturbed and maddened by the smell of perfume. Now if it were the case that women were made wild and distraught in the same way, it would be a dreadful thing if men did not abstain from using perfume, but let their wives suffer for the sake of their own momentary pleasure. But what does drive women mad is not their husbands' use of perfume, but their association with other women. It is therefore wrong to cause such pain and disturbance to wives for the sake of a little pleasure. Better to treat a wife as we treat bees, which are believed to become angry and pugnacious towards those who have just had sexual relations with a woman,* and so keep yourself pure and clean of intercourse with others when you go to your wife's bed.

[45] One does not wear bright clothes when approaching elephants, or red clothes with bulls: these animals are put into a rage by these colours in particular. Tigers, on the other hand, are (we are told) sent into a complete frenzy by the beating of drums around them, and tear themselves to pieces. Now some men cannot bear scarlet or purple clothes, and others hate drums and cymbals. What is wrong, then, in women therefore avoiding these things, and not irritating or angering their husbands, but consorting with them quietly and patiently?

[46] A woman said to Philip, when he tried to lay hands on her against her will, 'Let go: every woman is the same when the lamp is taken away.' This was a good rejoinder to a vicious adulterer; but for a married woman, it is precisely when the lamp has been removed that she needs to be different from ordinary women; when her body is not seen, her chastity, her faithfulness, her discipline, and her affection must be apparent to her husband.

[47] Plato advised old men to be particularly respectful of the young, so that the young should respect them in turn.[1] Where the old are shameless, he says, there is no modesty or reverence in the young. A husband should keep this in mind, and respect

no one more than he does his wife. The bedroom will be her
school of discipline or immorality. A husband who enjoys pleas- 145
ures which he prohibits in his wife is like a man who tells his wife to fight the enemy to whom he has himself surrendered.

[48] Eurydice, I would have you read what Timoxena* wrote to Aristylla about the love of ornament, and try to memorize it. As for you, Pollianus, do not think that your wife will avoid extravagance and expense if she sees that you do not despise it in other matters, but take pleasure yourself in gilt cups, painted rooms, or elaborate collars for your horses and mules. If extravagance is abroad in the men's quarters, it cannot be driven out of the women's. You are old enough now to study philosophy; use its demonstrations and arguments to improve your character, conversing and associating with those who can help you. Gather whatever is valuable from every quarter, like a bee; carry it yourself to your wife, share it with her, discuss it with her, making the best arguments her friends and familiars. You are her 'father'[1] and her 'lady mother' and her 'brother'; but it is just as honourable to hear a wife say 'Husband, you are my guide and philosopher, my teacher of the noblest and divinest lessons.' Such studies, in the first place, keep women away from absurd behaviour: a woman who understands mathematics will be ashamed to dance; if she hears the magic of Plato's or Xenophon's words, she will not let the magic of witchcraft into her life. If a witch undertakes to pull down the moon, she will laugh at the ignorance and folly of women who believe such things, for she will know something of astronomy, and will have heard of Aglaonice, the daughter of Hegetor the Thessalian, who understood about full-moon eclipses and could forecast the time when the moon is caught in the shadow, and so deceived the other women into believing that she was bringing the moon down by her own efforts.

No woman can make a child without the part played by a man; the shapeless, fleshy masses formed in the womb as a result of corruption are called 'moles'. One must take precautions against such developments in women's minds also. If they do not receive the seeds of good words or share their husband's education, they conceive many strange and evil schemes and feelings on their own. Familiarize yourself, Eurydice, in

particular with the sayings of good and wise men. Always have on your lips the remarks you learnt with me as a girl. That will please your husband and earn you the admiration of other women, because you will be so splendidly and grandly adorned at no expense. This rich woman's pearls, this foreigner's silks, cannot be acquired or worn save at a great price; but the ornaments that adorned Theano and Cleobulina, and Gorgo the wife of Leonidas, and Timoclea the sister of Theagenes, and Claudia of old, and Cornelia the daughter of Scipio, and all the other marvellous famous women—these can be worn as jewellery at no expense, and they will give you a life of honour and happi-
146 ness. If Sappho was proud enough of her beautiful songs to write to a rich lady,

> When you are dead, there shall you lie,
> and there will be no memory
> of you, who have no share
> in roses that the Muses bear,[1]

will *you* not be able to have proud and splendid thoughts of yourself, if you have a share not in the roses, but actually in the fruit the Muses bear, and which they lavish upon those who admire education and philosophy?

XV

A CONSOLATION TO HIS WIFE

As the details of Plutarch's life are uncertain, the date of this piece is not known. The daughter who has died was younger than four sons, two of whom had already died. It would appear, since no mention is made of the possibility of more children, that Plutarch's wife is now too old. The letter (Plutarch is away from home) is both moving and illuminating: the ideals it suggests—rejection of superstition, philosophical calm and understanding—are very much those put forward in 'Advice on Marriage'. The text is very defective towards the end, but the general sense is clear. Plutarch's Platonizing views of reincarnation and the eventual escape of the soul from the cycle of birth and death naturally provide topics of consolation for the death of a child. Plutarch ends by giving a comforting interpretation of the practice of withholding funeral rites from children, though this probably had a quite different origin, in the belief that those who die prematurely (*aoroi*) have no rest in death.

Plutarch to his wife, greetings 608

[1] The messenger you sent to tell me of the child's death must have missed me on his way to Athens; I only heard of it from my niece* when I got to Tanagra. I imagine the funeral is now over, and hope it has been done in the way that will make for least pain for you both now and in the future. If there is anything you wished to do but refrained from doing, waiting for my decision, but which you think will make things easier to bear, pray do it, without extravagance or superstition, for which I know you have no inclination.

[2] Only, my dear wife, at this sad moment, keep yourself, and me, calm. I know, I can get the measure of what has happened; but if I see you grieving to excess, that will hurt me more than the loss. But I am no 'child of oak or rock':* you know that, you have shared with me the upbringing of all our children, all reared at home by ourselves, and you know that this child was beloved by me above all, because she was the daughter you wanted after four sons and she gave me the opportunity to give her your name. There is a special savour in our affection for

children of that age; it lies in the purity of the pleasure they give, the freedom from any crossness or complaint. She herself too had great natural goodness and gentleness of temper: her response to affection and her generosity both gave pleasure and enabled us to perceive the human kindness in her nature. She would ask her nurse to feed not only other babies but the objects and toys that she liked playing with, and would generously invite them, as it were, to her table, offering the good things she had and sharing her greatest pleasures with those who delighted her.

[3] But I cannot see, my dear wife, why this and other such things should have given us pleasure while she was alive but are now to pain and trouble us when they cross our minds. On the other hand, I am also afraid of throwing out the memory with the grief, as Clymene in Euripides, who says

> I hate the crooked bow of cornel wood,
> and wish all sports away![1]

because she is frightened of remembering her son, her grief being inseparable from his memory. But our daughter was the sweetest thing to fondle, to watch, and to hear; and we ought to let the thought of her also dwell in our minds and lives, for there is much more joy in it than sorrow—if, that is, we can expect benefit ourselves in time of need from the consolation we have often given others, and are not to lie down under it, repaying all these pleasures with grief many times as great.

[4] Those who were with you tell me, with admiration, that you did not put on mourning, or allow yourself and the servants to disfigure yourselves; nor were there any ostentatious or lavish funeral-preparations: everything was done decently and silently, and in the presence of close friends. It did not surprise
609 me that you, who have never tricked yourself out for theatres or processions and have always believed that expense was useless in pleasures, should also have maintained the same simplicity and modesty in time of sorrow. It is not only 'in Bacchic revels'[1] that a good woman should avoid corruption; she should also realize that the distress and emotional disturbance of mourning stands in need of control, not in order to resist feelings of affection (as is often thought), but to resist licence. We

freely indulge our affection in desiring, honouring, and remembering the dead; but the insatiable craving for lamentation that leads to wailing and beating the breast is no less disgraceful than incontinence in pleasure, but is excused, apparently, by the fact that the disgrace is attended not by joy but by pain and bitterness. What is more irrational than to eliminate excesses in laughter and rejoicing, but open the floodgates of tears and lamentation, which all come from the same source? Or for men to resist women in matters of perfumes and purples, but allow mourning hair-styles, black-dyed clothing, and sitting or lying in unseemly or uncomfortable vigils? Or (worst of all) to oppose and obstruct them if they punish maidservants excessively or unjustly but freely let them punish themselves brutally and cruelly in sadness and misfortune that calls rather for comfort and kindness?

[5] You and I, my dear wife, have never needed that first conflict, nor, I believe, shall we need the other. Every philosopher who has been in our company has been amazed by the simplicity of your person and the unpretentiousness of your life. Every citizen in our temples, at our sacrifices, in our theatres, finds your simplicity a sight to behold. You have already displayed your stability in situations like the present at the loss of your eldest child, and again when our beautiful Chaeron left us. I remember that some stranger had travelled up from the sea with me when the news of the child's death arrived, and entered our house with the others. When they saw such complete peace and quiet, as they subsequently told others too, they could not believe anything dreadful had happened, and thought the report must have been false; so soberly had you ordered the household at a time which gave so much licence for disorder. Yet you had nursed Chaeron at your own breast, and endured surgery when your nipple was bruised. This indeed was noble and loving.

[6] Most mothers, though, take their children in their arms like toys when they have been cleaned and made pretty by others, and then, if they die, dissolve into vain, ungrateful grief, not out of affection (which is a good and reasoned thing) but because a large admixture of vanity in a small quantity of natural emotion makes the act of grieving wild, insane, and difficult to sedate. Aesop* seems to have been well aware of this. He says that when Zeus was distributing honours among the gods,

Grief came and asked for his. Zeus granted the request, but only among men who chose and wished to honour Grief. And this is what happens in the early stages: everyone invites Grief in. But when he is established, and become a member of the family, he does not go away, however much they wish it. One should resist him at the door and not abandon the fort through mourning-
610 clothes or hair-style or anything like that: these things, encountered daily and causing embarrassment as they do, produce a mean, narrow, timid frame of mind that sees no way out and finds no appeasement; surrounded and occupied with all this, because of Grief, the mind knows no laughter, no light, no kindly table. Neglect of the body follows, and distaste for unguents and baths and the other routines of life. What should happen is quite the contrary: the soul should be helped in her trouble by the strengthening body. The sharp edge of the pain is dulled, and its tightness loosened, dissipated by the body's calm like the waves in fair weather; whereas, if squalidness and unkemptness result from a mean style of life, and the body cannot send up to the mind any message of comfort or goodness but only the bitter and unpleasant exhalation, as it were, of pain and sorrow, it is not easy to recover, even if you wish to. Such are the consequences of this kind of ill treatment of the mind.

[7] The most fearful danger of all, however, is one that I shall not fear in you: the 'entrance of bad women',*[1] the cries and wailing with which they polish and sharpen the edge of pain and never let others reduce it, nor allow it to fade away on its own. I know the fight you fought lately to help Theon's sister, confronting the women who visited her with their howling and shrieking, truly 'heaping fire on fire'. When people see their friends' houses burning, they try to put the fire out with what speed and means they have; but when minds are ablaze, they bring fresh fuel to the flames. If a man has ophthalmia, they do not let all and sundry put their hands on him, nobody touches the inflamed eye; but a mourner sits there exposed to every passer-by to excite his flux and exacerbate his illness, which a little tickling and disturbance will scratch open into a horrible disfigurement.

[8] I know you will guard against this. Try, however, to take yourself away in thought to the time before we had this child,

when we had no complaint against the future: compare the present time with that, for our circumstances are once again the same. If we treat the time before she was born as one of which we have less cause to complain, we shall appear to regret her birth. The intervening two years are indeed not to be expunged from the memory, but counted as pleasure because of the charm and enjoyment they gave us; we should not treat a small blessing as a great evil, nor be ungrateful for what is given because fortune did not add thereto what we hoped for. Fair words about the gods, and uncomplaining serenity towards fortune always bear a good, sweet harvest. And in circumstances like these, he who most draws on the good things in his memory, and turns his thoughts to the bright and shining path of his life and away from darkness and troubles, either extinguishes his pain altogether or makes it dim and faint by the admixture of its opposite. Perfume always pleases the sense of smell, but it also has a medicinal value against bad smells; and similarly the thought of good things in bad times actually serves as a necessary aid to those who do not avoid the memory of good things or find fault with fortune for everything and in every way. It would be wrong for us to bring a false charge against our life, if it is like a book with 611
a single erasure but is otherwise perfectly clean and without blemish.

[9] You have often been told that happiness depends on right thinking, which results in a stable frame of mind, and that the vicissitudes of fortune do not mean a great decline or any catastrophic landslide in one's life. But if we too, like common folk, must needs be guided by external circumstances, count the strokes of fortune and make ordinary people the judges of our happiness; do not heed the present tears and lamentations of your visitors—they come from a bad custom and everyone encounters them—but think instead how much you are envied by these same women for your children, your household, and your way of life. It is absurd that others should be willing to prefer your fortune, even including the present bereavement, which so distresses us, while you, who really have it, grumble and complain, and cannot perceive in the very sharpness of your pain what delight there is in what is left to us. It would be absurd to behave like those who pick out the 'headless' or 'short-tailed'

lines* in Homer while paying no heed to all his marvellous poems, and count up maliciously and pedantically all the bad things in life while only forming an inarticulate, confused impression of the good. That is what misers do, who accumulate and then make no use of their accumulations but cry and moan when they are all lost. If you feel pity for her, because she died unmarried and childless, you can make yourself easier once again by reflecting that you have had a full share of these things: they are not the sort of blessings that are important to those who are deprived of them but trivial to those who do have them. She has come to painlessness; she does not need to cause us pain. What ill have we from her, if she now knows no pain? Deprivation even of great blessings loses its painfulness when the need is there no more. Your Timoxena is deprived of little things, for little things are all she knew and all she took delight in. How can she be said to be deprived of things her senses and her mind never conceived?

[10] You hear others say—many are convinced by them—that there is no evil or pain anywhere for the one who 'suffered dissolution'.* But I know that the traditional doctrines and the mystic tokens of the rites of Dionysus, known to us who share them, prevent you from believing this. You should think of the soul as immortal, and as like a captive bird. If it is reared a long time in the body and domesticated in this life by all its affairs and by long habit, then it comes back again into the world and does not cease from its involvement in passions and accidents in its successive births. Do not imagine that old age is abused and reviled for its wrinkles and grey hair and physical weakness; the worst of it is that it makes the soul stale in its recollection of the world beyond and anxious to hold on to this world, and so cramps and oppresses it, so that it retains the form that it was given in the body when it shared its fortunes. But a soul which <does not stay here long> in captivity leaps up towards its natural home . . . If you put out a fire and then rekindle it at once, it is soon fanned to flame and quickly takes hold . . . <And so those souls fare best whose fortune it is> 'soonest to pass the gate of Hades' house',[1] before they have acquired a deep love of this world and are drugged, as it were, into a state of softness
612 and fusion with the body.

[11] The truth about these things is made even clearer by our ancient, traditional laws and customs. People do not pour libations over dead infants, nor do they perform any other of the normal rites of the dead for them. Infants have no part in earth or earthly things. Nor do people tarry at the burial or the tomb or the wake, or sit a long time beside the body. The law forbids this in the case of small children, holding it wrong <to show grief thus> towards those who have passed to a better and holier land and lot. But as disbelief is harder than belief in these things, let us fulfil our outward observances as the law directs, but keep our inner health even more pure and undefiled and chaste.

XVI

VIRTUES IN WOMEN

This book consists of a series of stories illustrating the exercise of courage and other virtues by remarkable women. It is addressed to Flavia Clea, daughter of Memmia Eurydice (who just *might* be the bride addressed in xv); Clea was a Delphic priestess, and is also the addressee of Plutarch's *Isis and Osiris* (23). The occasion is the death of Leontis, who must be a lady of unusual achievements; and the book is a kind of consolation. A Leontis is known from inscriptions of the period, but it is often difficult to identify individuals known in this way with persons mentioned in the literary texts, and it is best to admit our ignorance of the circumstances that occasioned this collection. In any case, it gives good proof of Plutarch's narrative skill, so well displayed in the *Lives*; and it may serve as a specimen of a genre not otherwise represented in this selection, namely the collection of separate stories or discussions (cf. 18, 46, 59, 67), a familiar feature of late Greek literature.

There are twenty-seven stories, about half of which relate to events outside the Greek world. Plutarch deliberately omits well-known, central themes of Greek history. The stories are divided into 'public' and 'private' actions, the former stressing women's power of collective action, especially in war, the latter their individual endurance, chastity, intelligence, or cunning. It is difficult to see many associative links, though there is clearly some artistry in the arrangement, and a great deal of artistry in the actual narratives. Some stories are also found in the *Stratagems* of Polyaenus, who clearly used Plutarch. Plutarch himself may have known earlier similar collections; but there can be little doubt that most of the material comes from his own reading.

For a detailed commentary, see P. A. Stadter, *Plutarch's Historical Methods*, (Harvard UP, 1965).

242 On women's virtue, my dear Clea, my view is quite different from Thucydides'.[1] He declares that the best woman is the one who is least talked about abroad, for praise or for blame; and he believes that a good woman's name, like her body, should be kept under lock and key, and not allowed out. In my eyes, Gorgias does better,[2] when he advises that a woman's reputation should be more widely known than her beauty. Best of all, though, to my mind, is the Roman custom* of granting appro-

priate public praise after death to women as well as to men. And so, when our good Leontis died, you and I had much talk, talk rich in philosophical consolation; and now, in accordance with your wish, I have written up for you what was left over from our discussion, making the point that virtue is the same in man and
in woman. The historical facts in all this are intended to demon- 243
strate the point, they are not compiled for entertainment. But if the quality of an example adds pleasure to its lesson, the discussion does not shun charms that may contribute to the proof, nor does it feel any embarrassment in

> joining Graces with Muses,
> fairest of teams,

as Euripides says,[1] thereby anchoring credibility to the mind's love of beauty.

After all, had we been arguing that painting was the same, whether by men or by women, by producing pictures by women comparable to those left by Apelles, Zeuxis, or Nicomachus, no one could have found fault with us, surely, on the ground that we were aiming at charm and pleasure rather than at reasoned persuasion. Again, if, in endeavouring to prove poetry and prophecy no different in men and in women, we set Sappho's lyrics against Anacreon's, or the Sibyl's prophecies against those of Bacis, is there any real ground for criticizing the argument, because it brings the hearer to conviction in a happy and agreeable frame of mind? Surely not. And indeed, there is no way of understanding the similarities and differences between virtue in women and virtue in men, other than by comparing life with life, action with action, as works of a great craft,* and studying them to see if Semiramis' ambition has the same character and pattern as Sesostris', if Tanaquil's intelligence is the same as that of King Servius, Porcia's spirit the same as Brutus', or Timoclea's the same as Pelopidas', in their most significant common qualities and effects. Virtues do, of course, acquire differences—peculiar colours, as it were—because of the nature of the persons, and are assimilated to their underlying habits, physical temperaments, diet, and way of life. Achilles was brave in a different way from Ajax. Odysseus' wisdom was not like Nestor's. Cato and Agesilaus were not just in the same way. Irene did not show her love* for her husband in the way Alcestis did. Cornelia was not ambitious in the same way as Olympias. But let us not, on this account, construct many different courages and wisdoms and justices. We have only to ensure that individual dissimilarities do not disqualify any instance of virtue from its rightful recognition.

I propose to omit stories which are famous, and of which I conceive you already have information and knowledge from your reading. The only exceptions will be if any significant details have escaped the earlier reporters of these commonly treated and widely publicized incidents.

Women have done many notable deeds, both collectively and as individuals. A few of their collective achievements make the best beginning.

[1] The Trojan Women

Of those who fled from Troy after its capture, the largest party encountered storms; inexperienced in sailing and ignorant of the sea, they were carried away to Italy, and found shelter in the anchorage and harbour of the Tiber, where they managed to find refuge. The men wandered around the country, lacking guides; the women were struck by the thought that, for people of sense, any settlement on land was preferable to any possible wandering and voyaging. People who had lost their country (they reasoned) must create one for themselves. They therefore joined forces and burnt the ships, a lady called Rhome* (it is said) being the prime mover. This done, they went to meet their menfolk, who were hastening to the sea to their rescue. Fearful of the men's anger, they embraced and kissed their husbands or relatives, and by this display of affection succeeded in softening
244 their hearts. (This is why Roman women still preserve the custom of greeting their relatives with a kiss.) The Trojans evidently grasped the necessities of the situation, and, finding the natives friendly and welcoming, were content with what their women had done and settled there alongside the Latini.

[2] The Phocian Women

The story of the Phocian women has found no famous historian. Yet it is as notable as any instance of virtue in women, and it is attested by the great ceremonies which the Phocians perform to this day at Hyampolis, and by ancient decrees. Details of these events are given in my 'Life of Daiphantus'. The incident involving the women is as follows.

There was war without truce between the Thessalians and the Phocians. The latter had killed all the Thessalian governors and rulers in the Phocian towns on a single day. The Thessalians then put out the eyes of 150 Phocian hostages, and invaded the country by way of Locris with all their forces, determined to spare no adult male and to enslave the women and children. Daiphantus, son of Bathyllus, with his two colleagues, persuaded the Phocians to sally forth and do battle with the Thessalians, first assembling the women and children from the whole of Phocis in one place. They were to construct a barricade of piled timber around them, and leave a guard with orders, should news of defeat reach them, to set the timber alight and burn the people inside. This proposal was generally agreed by a vote; but one speaker stood up and urged that it was proper that the women also should consent; if they did not, the plan should be abandoned and no compulsion applied. Word of this debate reached the women, and they held a meeting of their own and voted for the same proposition. They also awarded a garland of honour to Daiphantus, for making the best plan for Phocis. The children also (so it is said) held a meeting and passed the same motion. This done, the Phocians fought the Thessalians at Cleonae by Hyampolis, and won the day. The Greeks called this decree 'The Phocians' Despair'; but to this day they celebrate the Elaphebolia* at Hyampolis in honour of Artemis as the greatest of all festivals, to commemorate this victory.

[3] The Chian Women

The Chians colonized Leuconia as a result of the following incident. A Chian notable was getting married, but as the bride was being taken home in a carriage, King Hippoclus, who was a friend of the bridegroom and was present among the guests, jumped on to the carriage, amid much drunken laughter, not intending any violence, but in fun, and in the ordinary way of such occasions. The bridegroom's friends nevertheless killed him. Indications of divine anger* against the Chians ensued;

and the god ordered them to put the murderers of Hippoclus to death. They said they had all killed Hippoclus; whereupon the god ordered them all to leave the city, since they all shared the pollution. Accordingly, they despatched those responsible for the murder or in any way consenting to it—a large and influential group—as colonists to Leuconia, which they had formerly occupied with Erythraean help, after taking it from the Coronaeans. Later, however, there was a war between them and the Erythraeans, who were at that time the most powerful people in Ionia. Unable to withstand the Erythraean attack on Leuconia, the Chians agreed to abandon the place under a truce, each taking
245 out nothing but a cloak and a himation. The women, however, denounced them as cowards for thus proposing to pass through the enemy lines stripped of their arms. The men replied that they were bound by their oath; whereupon the women told them not to leave their weapons behind, but to tell the enemy that, to a man of spirit, his spear is his 'cloak' and his shield is his 'himation.' The men did as they were told, spoke out boldly to the Erythraeans, and displayed their weapons. The Erythraeans were terrified at this show of daring; no one came forward or barred the way, they were happy to be rid of them. So the Chians were saved because their women taught them to be brave.

The women of Chios performed an equally notable deed of valour in a much later age, when Philip, son of Demetrius, was besieging the city.* He had issued a brutal and arrogant proclamation, urging the slaves to defect to him, with the promise of being granted freedom and marrying their mistresses. He proposed, in fact, to settle them down with their masters' wives. The women's anger was fierce and terrible. Joining forces with the slaves—who were equally indignant and went along with them—they proceeded to mount the walls, carrying supplies of stones and missiles, and encouraging and scolding the fighting men, until their defence and the hail of the missiles finally drove Philip away. Not a single slave defected.

[4] The Argive Women

Of actions performed by women collectively, none is more famous than the struggle of Argos against Cleomenes, in which the poetess Telesilla was the leading spirit. She came (we are told) from a distinguished family. Being of a sickly disposition, she was sent to the oracle to ask advice about her health. She was instructed to 'serve the Muses'. She accepted the god's advice, and devoted herself to the study of song and melody. Soon she was cured of her illness, and the women came to admire her greatly for her poetry.

Now when King Cleomenes of Sparta, having killed many Argives in battle*—though not 7,777, as some tell the tale—advanced against the city, the young women were possessed by a supernatural daring and impulse to defend their country against the enemy. Telesilla was their leader. They took up arms, stood on the battlements, and manned the whole circuit of the walls. The enemy were amazed. Cleomenes was repulsed with great loss, while the other king, Demaratus (according to Socrates) penetrated into the town and occupied the Pamphyliacum,* before being expelled. So the city survived. The women who fell in the battle were buried on the Argive Road, while the survivors were allowed to commemorate their exploits by erecting a statue of Enyalius. Some say the battle was fought on the seventh of the month now called Fourth, but in ancient times called Hermaeus by the Argives. Others say it was at the new moon, the day on which they still celebrate the Hybristica, when women are dressed in men's tunics and men in women's dresses and veils. To correct the loss of population, they united the women not with the slaves, as Herodotus says,[1] but with the best of the people living around (*perioeci*), whom they made citizens. The women, however, seemed to despise and neglect these husbands in bed, because they thought them below themselves. Hence the law which orders married women to wear beards when they go to bed with their husbands.

[5] The Persian Women

Cyrus, after inducing the Persians to rebel against King Astya- 246
ges and the Medes, was defeated in battle. The Persians fled into the city,* with the enemy almost entering at their heels; but outside the city the women met them, lifting their skirts to expose themselves. 'Where are you running,' they cried, 'you great cowards! You can't take refuge *here*, where you came from!' Shamed by the sight and by the words, the Persian men

reproached themselves, turned back, engaged the enemy anew, and routed him. From this event came a law, enacted by Cyrus, that every woman should receive a piece of gold every time the king entered the city. Ochus,* who was (apart from his other failings) the most miserly of the Persian kings, is said always to have skirted round the city and never entered it, thereby depriving the women of their present. Alexander, on the other hand, entered the city twice, and gave a double gift to women who were pregnant.

[6] The Celtic Women

Before they crossed the Alps and settled in the area of Italy they now occupy,* the Celts suffered from terrible, unending dissensions which broke out into civil war. The women, however, stood between the opposing weapons, seized them, and arbitrated between the rival causes so faultlessly and decisively that a marvellous harmony came to reign universally among their households and their cities. From that day forth, the Celts continued to take counsel with their women on matters of peace and war, and relied on their arbitration to settle disputes with their allies. In their treaty with Hannibal,* for example, they included the provision that if the Celts brought a complaint against the Carthaginians, the Carthaginian governors and commanders in Spain should be judges of it; but if the Carthaginians had complaints against the Celts, these should be submitted to the Celtic women.

[7] The Melian Women

The Melians, needing an extension of territory, appointed a young and handsome man named Nymphaeus to lead the colony. The god ordered them to set sail and settle 'wheresoever they lost their conveyors'. They struck the coast of Caria and disembarked, and the ships were destroyed in a storm. The Carian inhabitants of Cryassus, either out of pity for their plight or for fear of their daring, invited them to settle among them, and gave them a part of their territory. Later, however, when they saw how greatly the Melian settlement developed in a short time, they conspired to destroy them. A great feast and festival was to be the occasion. Now there was a Carian girl called

Caphene, who was in love with Nymphaeus, unknown to the others. She could not bear to see Nymphaeus killed as a consequence of this plan, and she revealed her countrymen's intention to him. So when the Cryassians arrived with the invitation, Nymphaeus replied that it was not the Greek custom to go to dinner without ladies. The Carians thereupon invited them to bring theirs with them. Nymphaeus then explained the situation to the Melians, and instructed the men to go unarmed, wearing the himation, and the women to carry swords in the folds of their dress and each sit next to her husband. In the course of the dinner, the Carians were given the agreed signal. The Greeks saw that the moment had come; the women opened their dresses, the men grabbed the swords, attacked the barbarians, and killed them all. They then took possession of the territory, demolished the existing city, and founded another, which they called New Cryassus. Caphene married Nymphaeus, and 247
received all the honour and gratitude due to her services. We should admire both the silence of the women, and their courage, and the fact that not one among so many betrayed the cause through cowardice, even involuntarily.

[8] The Tyrrhenian Women

The Tyrrhenians who occupied Lemnos and Imbros and kidnapped the Athenian women from Brauron, had children by them, whom the Athenians expelled from the islands as 'semi-barbarians'. These made a landfall at Taenarum and proved useful to the Spartans in the helot war. For this, they obtained citizenship and rights of marriage, but were not deemed worthy of holding office or being in the Council. They incurred the suspicion of meeting together for revolutionary purposes, and of intending to subvert the established regime. The Lacedaemonians therefore arrested them and held them in prison under strict guard, while seeking to convict them on clear and certain evidence. The wives of the prisoners, however, went to the prison, and, by dint of much begging and pleading, were allowed in by the guards, so far as to greet and speak to their husbands. Once inside, they told their husbands to exchange clothes with them quickly, leave them their own clothes, and themselves put on the women's things, cover their faces, and just walk out. This done, the women waited, prepared for any danger; and the guards fell for the trick, and let the men through in the belief that they were women. The men then occupied Taygetus, and roused the helots to rebellion and welcomed them into their own ranks. This terrified the Spartans, who sent emissaries and came to terms. The men were to take their wives back, accept money and ships, and depart: if they found land and a city elsewhere, they were to be regarded as colonists and kin of the Lacedaemonians. The Pelasgians followed up this proposal. They chose three Spartans—Pollis, Delphus, and Crataidas—as their leaders. Some of them settled in Melos, but the majority, under Pollis, set sail for Crete, to test the truth of an oracle; for it had been prophesied that they were to cease from their wanderings and found a city 'when they lost the goddess and the anchor'. Landing on what is called the Chersonese of Crete, they were troubled at night by panic noises; in their terror, they leapt back on board ship, in no order, leaving behind on land a statue of Artemis, an ancestral possession which they had taken from Brauron to Lemnos, and thence carried everywhere with them. The panic subsiding, they searched for it on the voyage, and Pollis noticed at the same time that the fluke was missing from the anchor; it had presumably been torn away, unnoticed, when the anchor was dragged over underwater rocks. He therefore pronounced the oracle fulfilled, and gave the signal to put back to land. He occupied the area and, after defeating the opposing forces in several battles, he founded Lyctus, and brought other cities under his control. And this is why these peoples believe that they are related to the Athenians on their mothers' side, while being also colonists of Sparta.

[9] The Women of Lycia*

What is said to have happened in Lycia seems fabulous, but there is a tradition which lends it support.

Amisodarus, so the story goes, whom the Lycians call Isaras, came from the Lycian colony at Zelea with pirate-ships commanded by a warlike, but savage and brutal, chief called Chi-
248 marrhus. His ship bore a lion as a figurehead on its prow, and a snake at the stern. He did great damage to the Lycians; it became impossible to sail the sea or be safe in the coastal cities.

Bellerophon chased this pirate away on Pegasus, and killed him, and also drove out the Amazons; but he did not receive his reward for these services. Indeed, Iobates was extremely unfair to him, and Bellerophon therefore waded into the sea and prayed to Poseidon to make Iobates' land barren and fruitless. Having called down this curse, he was walking away, when a wave rose and inundated the land. It was a grim sight: the towering sea followed Bellerophon inland and covered the plain. The men begged him to stop it, but they begged in vain; only when the women went to meet him with their skirts pulled up did he turn back in embarrassment; and the wave, they say, turned back with him.

Some writers, anxious to minimize the fabulous features of this story, deny that Bellerophon induced the flood by his curse. They say that the richest part of the plain lies below sea level, and Bellerophon broke through a dyke parallel to the shore which kept the sea out. Then, when the sea rushed in and flooded the plain, the men's prayers did not avail with him, but the women, gathering round him, moved him to shame and put an end to his anger.

Others again say that the so-called Chimaera was a mountain facing the sun, producing fierce, reflected heat in summer, the diffusion of which over the plain caused the crops to dry up. Bellerophon then, realizing what was happening, cut through the smoothest part of the cliff, which gave off the reflected heat most of all. He got no thanks for this, and in his anger attacked the Lycians, only to be begged off by the women.

The explanation given by Nymphis in Book IV of his work on Heraclea is the least fabulous. He says that Bellerophon killed a wild boar which had ravaged flocks and crops in the territory of Xanthus. Again, he got no reward; so he called upon Poseidon to curse the Xanthians, and the entire plain exuded salt, and was totally ruined, the soil becoming bitter. Finally, however, out of respect for the women, he appealed to Poseidon to give up his anger. This is how the Xanthians came to adopt the practice of taking their names from their mothers, not from their fathers.

[10] The Women of Salmantica

Hannibal, son of Barca, before leading his army against the Romans, attacked the great Iberian city of Salmantica. At first,

the besieged were terrified and agreed to do his bidding, handing over 300 talents of silver and 300 hostages. When he raised the siege, however, they changed their minds and fulfilled none of their agreements. Hannibal returned and ordered his soldiers to attack the city, with permission to sack and plunder. In dismay, the barbarians came to terms. The free men were to march out with one garment each, leaving behind arms, property, slaves, and the whole city. The women conceived the idea that the enemy would search each man as he went out, but not lay hands on women. They therefore took swords and hid them on their persons, and joined the men as refugees. When all had gone out, Hannibal held them in a suburb under the guard of a unit of Masaesylians. The rest of the army made an undisciplined rush into the city and sacked it. The Masaesylians could
249 not bear to watch as all the booty was taken out, and, instead of attending to their guard-duties, they became angry and began to leave their post, in order to share in the good things. This was the moment when the women called out to the men and passed the swords over to them—though some women actually attacked the guards on their own, and one seized a spear from the interpreter Banon and struck him with it; however, he was wearing a breastplate. The men either struck down or routed the rest of the guards, and joined the women to make a mass breakout. When Hannibal heard, he gave chase. Those he caught, he put to death; but others reached the mountains, and found safety for the time being, though they later sent their submission and were brought back to the city by him, pardoned, and treated with humanity.

[11] The Milesian Women

A strange and dreadful disorder once afflicted the young girls of Miletus. The cause was unknown; the best conjecture was that the air had acquired some toxic and manic quality, and thus produced some mental change and derangement in the girls. They were all suddenly seized by a desire for death and an insane impulse to hang themselves. Many did so unobserved; pleas and tears of parents, encouraging words of friends, all had no effect. They outwitted every trick and device of their guardians in order to make away with themselves. The problem seemed supernatural, and beyond human aid, until a proposition was made, on the motion of an intelligent man, that girls who hanged themselves should be carried naked through the market-place to their burial. The passing of this proposal not only checked, but finally put an end to the girls' desire for death. There is indeed powerful evidence of natural goodness and virtue in this anxiety to avoid disgrace, and in the fact that these women, who had no fear of the most frightening things, death and pain, were nevertheless incapable of enduring the thought of disgrace, or standing up to the shame which was to come to them after death.

[12] The Cian Women

It used to be the custom of the maidens of Cius to go together to the public temples, and to pass their days together. Their suitors would watch them playing and dancing. In the evening, they would go, in turn, to one another's houses, and wait on one another's parents and brothers, even washing their feet. Several suitors often fell in love with the same girl, but their love was so disciplined and controlled that, as soon as she was betrothed to one of them, the rest stopped courting her. The good discipline of these women is summed up in the fact that no case of adultery or seduction before betrothal has been recorded in Cius for 700 years.

[13] The Women of Phocis

When the Phocian tyrants were in occupation of Delphi, and the Thebans were waging the so-called Sacred War* against them, the women votaries of Dionysus, the Thyiades* as they are called, arrived unobserved at night in Amphissa, at the end of their frenzied wanderings. Exhausted, and still not returned to their senses, they threw themselves down here and there in the agora, and fell asleep. The women of Amphissa, afraid that the Thyiades might be roughly handled, because Amphissa was an ally of Phocis and there were many of the tyrants' soldiers in the town, all ran out into the agora and stood in a circle around the sleeping women, not speaking, and not approaching them closely. When the Thyiades at last got up, the Amphissian women individually took care of them, fed them, and finally, having secured their husbands' consent, escorted them safely to the frontier.

250 [14] Valeria and Cloelia*

Tarquin the Proud, the seventh king of Rome starting from Romulus, lost his throne through his own arrogance and the virtue of Lucretia, a lady married to a man of distinction related to the royal family. Lucretia was raped by one of Tarquin's sons, whom she had received as a guest; and, after telling her friends and relations what had happened, she killed herself on the spot. Expelled from his kingdom, Tarquin then fought many wars, endeavouring to recover his power, and finally induced the Etruscan ruler Porsena to advance on Rome with a large force. At Rome, a famine coincided with the war; and the Romans, hearing that Porsena was a good and just man as well as a brave soldier, sought to have him as a judge in their dispute with Tarquin. But Tarquin was obstinate. Porsena, he said, would not be a fair judge unless he remained a firm ally. So Porsena abandoned him, and made arrangements to depart as a friend of the Romans, merely recovering prisoners and such territory as the Romans had taken from the Etruscans. Ten boys and ten girls (including Valeria, the daughter of the consul Publicola) were surrendered to him as hostages, and he immediately ceased his warlike preparations, though the agreement was not concluded.

The girls went down to the river, on the plea of going to wash, some way away from the camp. On the suggestion of one of them, named Cloelia, they tied their dresses around their heads, risked swimming against the fast current and the deep eddies, and with great effort and difficulty, by hanging on to one another, succeeded in making the crossing. Some say that Cloelia secured a horse and rode it at a walk through the river, guiding and encouraging and helping the others as they swam. I shall explain later what led to this belief. When the Romans saw the girls were safe, they applauded their courage and daring, but were not pleased at their return; nor could they bear being found less trustworthy in keeping their word than the one man Porsena. They therefore ordered the girls to go back, and sent an escort with them. Having crossed the river, the party was ambushed by Tarquin, who very nearly got the girls into his power; but Valeria, Publicola's daughter, escaped with three servants to Porsena's camp, and the others were rescued by the timely arrival of Porsena's son Arruns. When they were brought before Porsena, he asked them who had incited and initiated their plan. Fearing for Cloelia, the rest said nothing; but Cloelia spoke up: 'I did,' she said. Porsena was delighted with her courage. He had a horse brought forward, beautifully caparisoned, presented it to Cloelia, and sent them all on their way, after treating them with kindness and humanity. This is the evidence that many writers use for the belief that Cloelia rode through the river; others deny this, and say that it was because Porsena regarded her strength and daring as above that of a woman that he thought it right to make her a present appropriate to a warrior. In any case, there was an equestrian statue of a woman on the Sacred Way, which some say is Cloelia, and others Valeria.

[15] Micca and Megisto*

Aristotimus, who established himself as tyrant of Elis, owed his strength to King Antigonus, and used his power harshly and unreasonably. His was a brutal nature, and fear made him the slave 251
of the miscellaneous barbarians who guarded his person and his authority, whom he allowed to commit many acts of violence and savagery against citizens. Philodemus' misfortunes are an example. This man had a beautiful daughter, called Micca, with whom one of the tyrant's mercenary captains, Lucius by name,* attempted to have a relationship. It was lust, not love. He sent for the girl; and her parents bowed to necessity and ordered her to go to him. But she was a noble and high-spirited woman, and begged her father, clinging to him and kneeling at his feet, to let her die rather than lose her virginity in so shameful and unlawful a way. Some time passed; and then Lucius, in his drunken passion, got up in anger in the middle of his drinking-bout, and came in person; he found Micca with her head on her father's knees, and ordered her to go with him. She refused; he stripped off her dress and whipped her, naked. She bore the pain without a murmur; but her father and mother, finding tears and pleas of no avail, cried out to call gods and men to witness the dreadful outrage they were suffering. The barbarian, now in a frenzy of

anger and drink, butchered the girl, as she lay there, with her face in her father's lap.

Even these events failed to move the tyrant. He continued to murder many, and exile even more. Eight hundred men, it is said, took refuge with the Aetolians, begging them to rescue their wives and small children from the tyrant. After a while, Aristotimus himself issued a proclamation that any women who so wished could go to their husbands, taking with them as much of their personal possessions as they chose. When he saw that they had all gladly accepted the terms (there were over 600 of them in all) he ordered them to travel all together on a certain day, when he would himself ensure their safe conduct. When the day arrived, they assembled at the gate, their belongings ready packed, their children carried in their arms or on the carriages, and waited for one another. Suddenly, a body of the tyrant's men bore down upon them, shouting at them from a distance to stay where they were. When they came up with them, they ordered the women to turn back, turned the teams and carriages round, and drove them into and through the women, quite mercilessly, not letting them follow or stay or help their dying children, who were being killed by falling out of the carriages or under them. The mercenaries drove the women like cattle with shouts and whips, and they fell under one another's feet, until all were herded into the prison, and the property all taken off to Aristotimus. These events greatly angered the Eleans. The 'Sixteen'—a group of holy women engaged in the worship of Dionysus—collected garlands and branches of supplication from the god's store, and confronted Aristotimus in the agora. His bodyguard made way for them out of respect, and they first stood before the tyrant in silence, piously holding out their branches of supplication. But when it became clear that they were petitioning him on behalf of the imprisoned women, and seeking to stay his wrath, he was furious with his bodyguard and shouted at them for letting these people pass, and made them drive them out of the agora by pushing and beating. He also fined each of the Sixteen two talents.

It was after this that a conspiracy against the tyrant was set afoot by Hellanicus, a man of whom Aristotimus took little notice, because he thought him unlikely to take any action,

he being an old man now and having lost his two sons. Meanwhile, the exiles crossed over from Aetolia and occupied a fort in Elis 252
called Amymone, which was well-placed to be a base of operations. Here they received the reinforcement of many citizens who were fleeing from Elis. Aristotimus took fright. He visited the women in prison, and, thinking terror a better way of gaining his ends than kindness, ordered them to write to their husbands and tell them to leave the country. Otherwise, he threatened, he would massacre them all, first torturing them and killing their children. He stood over them for some time, urging them to say if they would obey. All except one made no answer; they simply looked at one another without speaking, and made signs to assure one another that they were not frightened or dismayed by the threat. The one exception was Megisto, wife of Timoleon. Her husband and her own character gave her the status of a leader. She refused to stand up in the presence of the tyrant or let the others do so, but answered him from where she was sitting. 'If you were a man of sense,' she said, 'you would not be talking to wives about their husbands; you would have sent word to them, for they are our masters, and you would have found better words than those with which you tricked us. But if you despair of persuading them yourself, and are trying to use us to outwit them, do not expect to deceive us a second time; and I pray that they will not be so ill-advised as to abandon the cause of their country's freedom in order to spare a set of women and children. The evil of losing us, whom they do not have now, is less than the good of rescuing our fellow-citizens from your cruelty and violence.' Megisto's words were more than Aristotimus could bear. He gave orders for her child to be fetched, intending to kill it before her eyes. The servants accordingly went to look for the child, who was in the middle of a crowd of children playing and wrestling together. The mother called him by name. 'Come here, child,' she cried, 'be freed from a bitter tyranny before you can realize and understand it. It is harder for me to see you wrongfully enslaved than wrongfully killed.' At this, Aristotimus drew his sword against Megisto herself, and angrily bore down upon her. However, one of his associates, by name Cyllon, who was believed to be loyal but in fact detested him and was privy to Hellanicus' conspiracy, stood in

his way and made him turn aside, pleading with him and telling him that what he was doing was ignoble and womanish, not the act of a real leader who understood affairs. So Aristotimus finally saw sense and left the scene.

He was also vouchsafed an ominous sign. He was in bed with his wife in the middle of the day; and as their dinner was being prepared, an eagle was seen, high up, circling over the house; then, apparently taking deliberate aim, it dropped a large stone on to the roof over the bedroom where Aristotimus was lying. At the same moment, there was a loud noise from above, and shouting outside from people who had seen the bird. Aristotimus was terrified; when he discovered what had happened, he summoned a diviner, whom he regularly consulted in the agora, asking him anxious questions about the sign. The diviner encouraged him by explaining that Zeus was rousing him and was coming to his aid; but to citizens whom he trusted, the man gave another account, namely that retribution was hanging over the tyrant's head, and all but on the point of falling on him. Hellanicus and his fellow conspirators accordingly decided not to wait longer, but to attack next day.

That night, Hellanicus dreamt that one of his dead sons stood over him and said, 'Father, why are you asleep? Tomorrow you
253 must be in command of the city.' Emboldened by this dream, he
proceeded to hearten his friends, while Aristotimus, hearing that Craterus was encamped at Olympia with a large force, coming to his rescue, felt confident enough to go into the agora with Cyllon, unaccompanied by bodyguards. Hellanicus saw that the moment had come. He did not, however, give the signal agreed between himself and the would-be assassins; he simply stretched out his arms and cried in a loud voice, 'Brave friends, why wait? Here's a fine theatre to perform in, in the very heart of our country!' Cyllon was the first to draw sword, and cut down one of Aristotimus' attendants. Thrasybulus and Lampis bore down on him on the other side; and, though Aristotimus escaped to the temple of Zeus, they killed him there, threw the corpse out in the agora, and summoned the citizens to declare their freedom. The conspirators were not much ahead of their womenfolk: the women ran out, with shrieks of joy, and surrounded the men, festooning them with garlands and ribbons.

The mob next converged on the tyrant's house. His wife shut the bedroom door and hanged herself. His two young and beautiful daughters, both of marriageable age, were seized and dragged out. The mob had made up its mind to kill them, and to torture and mutilate them first; but Megisto and the other women confronted the crowd, and shouted at them: it was a shocking thing, they said, if they claimed to be a democracy and yet had the audacity to commit the same sort of outrages as tyrants. Many in the crowd respected the dignity of the woman who spoke so freely and shed such tears; and it was resolved to forgo the outrage to the girls' persons and let them die by their own hand. So they returned to the house and ordered them to die without delay. Myro, the elder of the two, unfastened her belt and made it into a noose. She then embraced her sister and bade her watch carefully and do exactly what she saw her doing. 'We must avoid making a disgraceful end,' she said, 'or one discreditable to ourselves.' The younger sister asked to be allowed to die first, and tried to take hold of the belt. 'Never before', said Myro, 'have I refused you anything you asked; so take this favour too, and I will bear what is harder than death, the sight of you, my darling, dying before me.' She then showed her sister how to fasten the noose round her neck, and, when she saw she was dead, took the body down and covered it up. Then she asked Megisto to take care of her own body, and not let her be laid out in an indecent attitude in death. No one who was there, however bitter and hostile to the tyrant, failed to weep and feel pity for the noble character of these girls.

These examples of the innumerable deeds performed by women acting collectively should suffice us. I shall now proceed to instances of individual virtue, putting them down just as they occur to me. I do not think our present purpose makes a chronological arrangement necessary.

[16] Pieria*

Some of the Ionian settlers in Miletus, having quarrelled with the sons of Neileus,* retired to Myus and settled there. They suffered much at the hands of the Milesians, who went to war with them because of their defection. This was not, however, a war that allowed no diplomatic or other intercourse. Indeed, the women continued to travel from Myus to Miletus at certain festivals.

Now there was a prominent citizen of Myus named Pythes, who had a wife called Iapygia and a daughter called Pieria. There was a feast and sacrifice to Artemis held by the Milesians,
254 and called the Nelea; and Pythes sent his wife and daughter there, because they wanted to take part in the festival. And Phrygius, the most influential of the sons of Neileus,* fell in love with Pieria, and wondered what he could do that would give her most pleasure. 'If you were to arrange for me to come here often', she replied, 'and with many companions.' Phrygius saw that she was asking for peace and friendship for her fellow citizens; and accordingly he put an end to the war. So Pieria enjoyed fame and honour in both cities; and even to this day the women of Miletus pray that their husbands may love them as well as Phrygius loved Pieria.

[17] Polycrite

Naxos and Miletus went to war* with each other because of Neaera, the wife of Hypsicreon of Miletus. She fell in love with Promedon of Naxos, and made advances to him. He was a friend of Hypsicreon, but consorted with the loving Neaera, and, because she was afraid of her husband, took her away to Naxos and placed her as a suppliant in the temple of Hestia. The Naxians refused to surrender her, as a favour to Promedon, though they made her status as a suppliant the ground of their refusal. War followed. Many Ionians, and particularly the Erythraeans, fought on the Milesian side, and the war was long and disastrous; and then, as it had started through a woman's bad conduct, so it ended through a woman's virtue.

The Erythraean commander Diognetus had charge of a fort, well placed and well equipped as a base against the city of Naxos. He took much Naxian plunder, and captured some free women and girls. With one of these, Polycrite, he fell in love, and he kept her not as a prisoner but as his lawful wife. On one occasion, when there was a feast in the Milesian camp and they were all drinking and enjoying themselves together, Polycrite asked Diognetus whether there was anything to prevent her sending pieces of cake to her brothers. He gave permission and told her to do so. She then enclosed a lead tablet in a cake, instructing the bearer to tell her brothers that they alone were to eat what she sent. They duly discovered the tablet, and read Polycrite's message, which was to tell them to attack the enemy in the night, because all precautions had been forgotten in the drinking that accompanied the festival. They reported this to the generals, and urged them to go out with them. The fort was captured, and many killed. Polycrite begged her countrymen to spare Diognetus' life, and so saved him. But when she found her fellow citizens meeting her at the gate, welcoming her with joy and with garlands and applauding her action, she was unable to bear the shock of joy, but fell down and died just by the gate. And there she is buried, and it is called the Tomb of Malice, as though Polycrite had been deprived of the enjoyment of her honours by the jealousy of some malicious Fate.

Such is the account given by the Naxian historians. Aristotle, however, says it was not because she was a captive but in some other circumstances that Diognetus saw and fell in love with Polycrite, and was ready to offer or do anything for her. She replied that she would come to him on one condition only, and for this, the philosopher tells us, she exacted an oath. Diognetus swore the oath, and Polycrite then asked to be given Delium—that was the name of the fort—or else she would not come to him. His passion for her and the force of his oath combined to make him give up the place and surrender it to Polycrite, who then passed it to her countrymen. This put Naxos and Miletus once again on equal terms, and the Naxians made peace on the conditions they wanted.

[18] Lampsace 255

In the family of the Codridae from Phocaea there were two brothers, Phoxus and Blepsus. Phoxus, according to Charon of Lampsacus, was the first man to throw himself off the Leucadian Rocks* into the sea. He was a man of power and regal standing, but it was private business that took him on a voyage to Parium. There he became a friend and guest of Mandron, king of the Bebryces of Pityoessa, and aided these people in war, when they were troubled by their neighbours. On Phoxus' departure, Mandron showed him much kindness and promised to give him a share in the city and territory, if he chose to bring Phocaean settlers to reinforce Pityoessa. Phoxus persuaded his countrymen, and sent his own brother with the settlers. Mandron did his part, as expected; but as the Phocaeans began to acquire great profit and plunder from the neighbouring barbarians, they were first resented, and then feared, by the Bebryces, who were therefore anxious to get rid of them. They were unable to persuade Mandron, who was an honourable man and fair in his dealings with the Greeks, but in his absence they made a plan to destroy the Phocaeans by treachery. However, Mandron's unmarried daughter Lampsace had prior knowledge of the plan, and first tried to dissuade her friends and relations from it, pointing out that they were embarking on an immoral and impious course in killing benefactors and allies who were now also their fellow citizens. Failing to convince them of this, she then secretly revealed the plan to the Greeks, and warned them to be on their guard. The Greeks prepared a sacrifice and banquet, and invited the Pityoessenes out to a suburb of the city. They then divided into two parties: one group seized the walls, the others killed the people. With the city thus in their hands, they sent for Mandron, inviting him to share the kingdom with their own leaders. And when Lampsace fell ill and died, they buried her with great magnificence in the city, and called it Lampsacus after her. Mandron, anxious to avoid suspicion of treachery, declined to take part in the settlement, but asked to be allowed to take the wives and children of the dead. The Phocaeans readily agreed to this, and sent them away unharmed. To Lampsace, they originally gave heroic honours, but later voted to sacrifice to her as a goddess,* and this they continue to do.

[19] Aretaphila

Aretaphila of Cyrene does not belong to early history, but to the age of Mithridates.* Yet she displayed virtue and capacity for action that rival any of the heroines.* She was the daughter of Aeglanor and wife of Phaedimus, both men of note. She was beautiful and had the reputation of being remarkable for her good sense and well-endowed with political skills. But it was the misfortunes of her country that made her famous.

Nicocrates, who had risen to be tyrant of Cyrene, murdered many of the citizens, among them Melanippus, priest of Apollo, whom he slew with his own hand and then held the priesthood himself, and Phaedimus, Aretaphila's husband, after whose death he married her, against her will. Among innumerable other violations of law and custom, he posted guards at the gates, who mutilated the bodies being taken out for burial, by prodding them with swords and putting burning torches to them, to make sure that no citizen escaped, disguised as a corpse.

Aretaphila had troubles at home that were hard to bear. It is true that the tyrant, thanks to his love for her, let her enjoy to the full the fruits of his power. He was completely under her sway; 256
she alone had some measure of control over this brutal and merciless man. But the unjust sufferings of her country pained her more than her own. Citizen after citizen was murdered, and there was no prospect of help from any quarter. The exiles were weak, terrified, and scattered. Aretaphila therefore put herself forward as her country's sole hope. She admired the famous and heroic deeds of Thebe of Pherae, but she had none of the loyal allies and kinsmen with whom circumstances provided that great lady. Poison was the method she decided on, to do her husband's business; but in the course of preparing, providing, and testing many potent mixtures, she was discovered and denounced. Proofs of guilt were produced; and Nicocrates' mother, Calbia, a bloodthirsty and ruthless woman, thought that Aretaphila must be tortured and put to death without delay. Nicocrates' love, however, infected his anger with hesitation and weakness, while Aretaphila herself met the accusation with a vigorous defence of her conduct, which gave some justification for his feelings. When she found herself convicted by the evidence, and saw that she could no longer deny the preparation of poison, she confessed, but alleged that what she had made was not a lethal compound. 'I am fighting for big stakes, husband,' she said, 'your affection for me and the reputation and influence which I enjoy through you and which make many wicked women envious of me. It was fear of their poisons and plots that made me resolve to plot in my turn. Maybe it was a foolish and feminine thing to do; but it doesn't warrant death—unless you deem love-potions and a trifle of magic grounds for

killing a woman who wants to be loved more than you wish to love her.' Despite this defence, Nicocrates decided to question her under torture. Calbia stood by, relentless and ruthless, as he examined her. But Aretaphila never yielded; and Calbia, reluctantly, gave up the struggle first. Thus Nicocrates let his wife go, and repented of having tortured her. Before long, he was back with her, his passion driving him, and lived with her, trying always to recover her affection by honours and generous gifts. But the woman who had conquered torture and pain was not one to yield to charm. To her passion for honour was now added the will to win, and she was soon planning new moves. She had a daughter of marriageable age, and very good-looking. She put this girl, as a bait, in the way of the tyrant's brother, a young man easily tempted by pleasures. It is widely believed that Aretaphila used spells and potions to conquer and corrupt the boy's better judgement in favour of the girl. Anyway, Laander (that was his name) was trapped, and obtained his brother's consent to the marriage. Then the girl, instructed by her mother, began to urge and persuade him to liberate the city; under a tyranny (she said) he was not even a free man himself, and had no power to contract or protect a marriage. At the same time, his friends, hoping to do Aretaphila a favour, were instilling into his mind suspicions and calumnies regarding his brother. Thus, when he realized that Aretaphila's plans and desires were the same as his wife's, he undertook the operation. He suborned his servant Daphnis, and used his hand to assassinate Nicocrates. From then on, however, he paid no attention to Aretaphila, but soon proved by his actions that he was a fratricide, but no tyrannicide.* His rule was thoughtless and impulsive. Aretaphila,
257 however, retained some respect and influence with him; he did not dislike her, and she was not openly hostile, but went quietly on with her arrangements. First of all, she provoked a war with the Libyans, inducing a chieftain named Anabus to raid the country and threaten the city. She then discredited Laander's friends and generals in his own eyes, by saying that they were reluctant to fight, and only wanted peace and quiet—which indeed (she said) was what his own situation as tyrant demanded, if he wished to keep firm control over his people. She undertook to arrange a truce herself, and bring Anabus to talks with him, if

that was his wish, before the war did irretrievable harm. Laander told her to proceed; and she first had conversations herself with the Libyan, in which she promised him a great reward if he would seize the tyrant when he came to negotiate with him. The Libyan agreed. Laander felt apprehensive; but, as Aretaphila promised to be present herself, he was ashamed not to go, and set out for the meeting unarmed and without an escort. Coming to the place, and seeing Anabus, he again became troubled, and wanted to wait for his bodyguard. Aretaphila, now at his side, one moment tried to give him heart, and the next reproached him for his cowardice. He still hesitated, until finally she seized him boldly and confidently by the hand, dragged him into the barbarian's presence, and handed him over. He was instantly seized, carried off, and kept under guard by the Libyan until Aretaphila's friends arrived with other citizens bringing her the money. Almost everyone had come out in answer to the summons the moment they heard the news. When they saw Aretaphila, however, they almost forgot their anger against the tyrant and felt his punishment to be a mere side-show; the first pleasure of freedom was to greet her with tears of joy, and fall at her feet as though she was a statue of a goddess. Wave upon wave of people came forward; and it was evening before they got possession of Laander and returned to the city. Only when they had done with honouring and praising Aretaphila to their hearts' content did they turn their attention to the tyrant and his family. They burnt Calbia alive, and sewed Laander up in a leather sack and dropped him in the sea. They also invited Aretaphila to join the leading citizens in the government of the city. But she had played out the many acts of her complex drama to the final prize-giving, and as soon as she saw the city free, she retired into the women's quarters, and, rejecting any possibility of intervention, spent the rest of her days quietly at her loom, among her friends and relations.

[20] Camma*

Sinatus and Sinorix were the most powerful of the tetrarchs in Galatia, and were related to each other in some degree. Sinatus took as his wife a maiden called Camma, of conspicuous beauty and youthful charm, but admired even more for her virtue. Not

only was she chaste and loyal to her husband, but intelligent, high-minded, and beloved by her inferiors for her kindness and generosity. It added to her distinction that she was priestess of Artemis,* whom the Galatians worship with special piety, and could be seen magnificently attired at sacrifices and processions. Sinorix fell in love with her. Unable to win her by persuasion or force while her husband was alive, he did a dreadful deed: he treacherously murdered Sinatus. Before long, he was courting Camma, who passed her days in the temple and bore
258 Sinorix' wicked act not in any pitiful or abject spirit, but with an anger tempered by intelligence and ready to bide its time. Sinorix was insistent in his wooing, and had no lack of plausible words: he was a better man than Sinatus, he claimed, and had killed him for no criminal reason, but out of love for Camma herself. To begin with, she declined his advances, but not too abruptly; and gradually she began to give the impression of softening towards him. Her relatives and friends also, concerned to serve and placate the all-powerful Sinorix, were at hand to persuade and put pressure upon her. Finally she gave way, and sent for him. Their consent and pledge to each other, she said, must be given in the presence of the goddess. He came. She received him kindly, led him up to the altar, and poured a libation from a cup. She drank some of it herself, and offered him the rest. It was a honey drink,* and it was poisoned. When she saw he had drunk it, she shouted for joy and did obeisance to the goddess. 'O honoured Power,' she cried, 'I call you to witness that it was for this day that I survived Sinatus' murder, having nothing to enjoy in life but the hope of justice, and, having this, I go down to join my husband. As for you, impious villain, let your family make ready your tomb instead of a bridal chamber for your wedding!' The Galatian heard her. He was already conscious of the poison working and affecting his body. He got into a carriage, to try the effect of movement and shaking; but he soon got out again, and moved over to a litter. He died that evening. Camma survived the night, and died happy and cheerful, knowing that Sinorix had met his end.

Galatia also provides the examples of Stratonice, wife of Deiotarus,* and Chiomara, wife of Ortiagon, both of whom deserve to be commemorated.

[21] Stratonice

Stratonice knew that her husband wished for legitimate children to provide for the succession to the kingdom. Being unfertile herself, she persuaded him to have a child by another woman and let it be passed off as hers. Deiotarus was greatly impressed by her idea, and put the whole matter into her hands. She found a beautiful girl among the prisoners of war, by name Electra, and introduced her to Deiotarus. The children born of this union she brought up with affection and in princely state, as though they had been her own.

[22] Chiomara

Chiomara, wife of Ortiagon, was taken prisoner with the other women when the Romans under Gnaeus* defeated the Galatians of Asia. The centurion who captured her used his good luck in soldierly fashion, and raped her. He was a man with no control over his feelings in regard either to pleasure or to money; but it was his love of money that got the better of him, so that when a large sum was agreed in return for the woman, he brought her to exchange for ransom. There was a river between the two parties. When the Galatians had crossed and handed the money over to the man, and received Chiomara in return, she made a sign to one of them to strike the Roman, as he was affectionately taking leave of her. The man understood, and cut off the Roman's head, which Chiomara picked up and took away with her in the folds of her dress. When she rejoined her husband, she threw the head down at his feet. 'Wife,' he said, surprised, 'it is honourable to keep one's word.' 'Yes,' she replied, 'but it is more honourable that there should be only one man living who has had me in bed.' Polybius says he conversed with this lady at Sardis, and admired her spirit and her understanding.

[23] The Woman of Pergamum* 259

When Mithridates summoned the sixty Galatian noblemen to Pergamum, as friends, and then treated them with the arrogance of a despot, they were all indignant, and one of them, Eporedorix, a man of great physical strength and exceptional courage, who was tetrarch of the Tosiopi,* undertook to grab Mithridates as he sat on the platform in the gymnasium dispensing justice, and push him down, platform and all, into the ravine. But on the day, Mithridates, as it chanced, did not go up to the gymnasium, but sent for the Galatians to his own house. Eporedorix urged them to be bold, and, when they were all there together, to fall on Mithridates from all sides, and tear him limb from limb. Mithridates was not unaware of these thoughts. Information had reached him, and his reaction was to hand over the Galatians, one by one, to be put to death. Then, however, he thought of a particularly handsome young man among them, and pity for him made him change his mind. He was very distressed, thinking that the youth must have been among the first to die; but he none the less sent orders for his release, in case he should still be alive. The young man's name was Bepolitanus. He had an extraordinary stroke of luck; for when he was arrested, he was wearing a beautiful, expensive coat, which the executioner was anxious to preserve clean and not bloodstained; and while he was carefully taking it off the young man's back, he saw the king's messengers running towards him, shouting the young man's name. And so avarice, the ruin of so many, paradoxically saved Bepolitanus' life. Eporedorix, however, was executed, and his body cast out unburied. None of his friends dared go near it. Only a woman of Pergamum, whom the Galatian had known as a prostitute, dared take the risk of burying him and wrapping up the corpse. The guards saw her, arrested her, and took her to the king. Mithridates is said to have been attracted by her beauty, for she seemed a simple young girl; more likely, he recognized that it was a matter of love, and so was moved to agree that she should take up and bury the body, using clothes and ornaments from the young man's property.

[24] Timoclea

Theagenes of Thebes, who had the same patriotic views as Epaminondas and Pelopidas and the other notables of the city, fell at Chaeronea,* in the common ruin of Greece, at the very moment of routing and pursuing his opponents. He was the man who, when asked 'How far are you going to pursue them?'

replied 'All the way to Macedonia.' He was survived by a sister, who herself gave proof that his greatness and distinction came from a family tradition of valour. She, however, gained some profit from her deeds, and so endured more easily the share of the common misfortunes that fell upon her.

When Alexander had defeated the Thebans, and his soldiers were sacking various areas of the city, Timoclea's house fell into the hands of a man of violent and thoughtless temper, without any decency or good feeling. He was the commanding officer of a company of Thracians, and he bore the same name as the king, though he in no way resembled him. He had no respect for the lady's family or her way of life, and, after dinner, when he had drunk enough, he summoned her to his bed. Nor was that the end of it: he asked after any gold or silver she might have kept hidden, accompanying his demands by threats or by promises to make her his wife. She seized the opportunity he gave. 'I wish I had died', she exclaimed, 'before this night, so as at least to keep my body safe from insult, though everything
else was lost! But as things have gone, if I must regard you as 260
guardian, master and husband to me, because Fortune has done this, I will not deprive you of what is your own. I see I am now whatever you wish me to be. I had my jewellery, I had silver drinking-cups, and I had some gold and some coin. When the city fell, I told the maids to gather it all up, and I threw it, or rather hid it for security, down a dry well. Not many people know this well; there is a cover over it, and dense bushes all around. Take it, and good luck with it. It shall be token and proof to you of the prosperity and splendour of my family.' The Macedonian did not wait till morning. He made straight for the spot, Timoclea guiding him. Ordering the garden door to be shut, so that no one should notice, he went down the well in his shirt. His guide was 'loathly Clotho', the avenging fate sent by Timoclea, who stood waiting at the top. When she could tell by his voice that he had reached the bottom, she and her servants all brought a lot of big stones and rolled them down on to him, until they battered and smothered him to death. When the Macedonians got to know, they recovered the body. Orders had already gone out that they were not to kill any of the Thebans, and so they merely seized her, took her to the king, and reported

her daring deed. Alexander saw the pride and nobility in her steady gaze and stately walk, and he began by asking who she was. Her reply was undaunted and confident. 'My brother was Theagenes, who fell at Chaeronea, commanding the troops and fighting against you for the liberty of Greece, in order that we should not suffer like this. But since we have suffered in ways our family does not deserve, we do not seek to escape death. It is surely better not to survive to endure another such night, unless you forbid it.' The more humane of those present wept for her; Alexander felt no pity for the woman—her deed was too great for forgiveness—but he admired her courage and the words with which she had cut him to the quick. He ordered his officers to take every precaution to prevent such violence being offered to a house of note again; and he released Timoclea and all of her family who could be found.

[25] Eryxo*

Arcesilaus, the son of Battus the Fortunate, was a very different person from his father. Even in his father's lifetime, he built a defensive stockade around his house, and was fined by his father a talent for doing so. After Battus' death, he proved a tyrant rather than a king, owing partly to his own cruel nature (he was called 'the Cruel'), and partly to his wicked friend Laarchus. This man, who was himself scheming for the tyranny, engaged in expelling or murdering the leading men in Cyrene, shifting the responsibility for this on to Arcesilaus, whom he finally killed by means of a drink containing sea-hare,* which led to painful wasting disease. He then assumed power, claiming to hold it on behalf of Arcesilaus' son Battus. The boy was held of no account—he was only a child, and he was lame—but many people paid court to his mother, an honourable and humane woman, who had many powerful connections. Laarchus also courted and wooed her; he proposed to marry her, and adopt Battus as a son and make him his colleague on the throne. Eryxo (that was the lady's name) sought the advice of her brothers, and invited Laarchus to meet them; she herself, she said,
261 welcomed the marriage. But when he did meet them, they deliberately misled him and put him off. Eryxo then sent her maid to him with the message that her brothers were at present

against the marriage, but would cease their objections and give their consent once the union was consummated. So, if he pleased, he should come to her at night: the beginning once made, the rest would go well. Laarchus was delighted. Excited by her willingness, he agreed to go to her any time she chose. All this Eryxo was doing in collusion with her eldest brother, Polyarchus. A time for the meeting was fixed, and Polyarchus was secretly introduced into his sister's bedroom, together with two young men, armed with swords, who were anxious to avenge their father, whom Laarchus had recently put to death. On receiving Eryxo's summons, Laarchus went into the room without a bodyguard. The young men attacked him, and he died under the blows of their swords. They threw his body out over the wall, and brought out Battus to proclaim him king on the terms that his father had enjoyed. Polyarchus thus restored the original constitution to Cyrene.

But there was in the town a force of soldiers belonging to Amasis, the king of Egypt. Laarchus had relied upon these, and his power to terrorize the citizens had rested largely upon them. They sent a message to Amasis, denouncing Polyarchus and Eryxo. Amasis was angry, and contemplated going to war against Cyrene. But it happened that his mother had died, and the messengers arrived while he was occupied in conducting the funeral. Polyarchus accordingly decided to go and make his own defence. Eryxo would not be left behind, but insisted on accompanying him and sharing the risks. Nor would their old mother, Critola, stay behind. She was a greatly respected lady, sister of Battus the Fortunate. When they reached Egypt, their action won general admiration. Amasis strongly approved Eryxo's goodness and courage. After honouring both Polyarchus and the two ladies with gifts and service appropriate to royalty, he sent them home to Cyrene.

[26] Xenocrite

No less admiration is due to Xenocrite of Cumae, for her actions in regard to the tyrant Aristodemus, whom some believe to have been called *Malakos*, in the sense of 'the Soft'. But this is a wrong interpretation; he was indeed called *Malakos* by the barbarians, but it means 'child', and the name was given

because he was only a boy when he distinguished himself in the wars with the barbarians, along with his contemporaries, all still wearing their hair long—and called *koronistai*,* presumably because of this; nor was it only his daring and his strong arm that brought him this reputation, but also his extraordinary intelligence and foresight. Advanced by his admiring countrymen to the highest offices, he was sent to lead a force helping the Romans against the Etruscans, who were then trying to restore Tarquin the Proud to his kingdom. In this long campaign, he so ingratiated himself with the citizens serving in the army, playing the demagogue rather than the general, that he was able to persuade them to join him in attacking the Council and driving out the powerful aristocracy. Once established as tyrant in consequence of these events, he surpassed himself in offences against free women and boys. He taught the boys, it is recorded, to wear their hair long and use gold jewellery, while he made the girls cut their hair short round the neck, and wear young
262 men's cloaks over short tunics. His great love was for Xenocrite, the daughter of an exile, whom he made no attempt to recall or to secure his consent; he assumed the girl was happy to be with him, because the citizens envied and congratulated her. In fact, however, this had no effect on Xenocrite herself; she was distressed to be living with a man to whom she had not been formally given or betrothed, and she was no less desirous of her country's liberty than any of those whom the tyrant detested. At this period, Aristodemus was constructing a ditch to encircle the whole territory. There was no need for this, and no practical use in it. He merely wanted to exhaust the citizens by constant labour and activity. Everyone was under orders to carry out a certain quantity of earth. <There was a woman who>, when she saw Aristodemus coming, always turned aside and hid her face in her dress. When he had gone by, the young men would ask her, as a joke, why she was so modest in Aristodemus' presence, but never with any other man. Her reply was deadly serious. 'Aristodemus,' she said, 'is the only MAN in Cumae.' The remark hurt them all, and stung the brave, for very shame, into making a bid for freedom. It is said that when Xenocrite heard the story, she said she would rather be carrying earth for her father, if he was there, than enjoying luxury and power with

Aristodemus. These events encouraged the conspiracy against Aristodemus which was led by Thymoteles. Xenocrite gave them safe access, and made sure Aristodemus was unarmed and unguarded. They easily got in and killed him. And so the city of Cumae was freed by the virtue of two women, one providing the concept and the impulse to action, the other helping to bring the matter to completion. Xenocrite was offered great honours and gifts, but declined them all, except to be allowed to bury Aristodemus' body. They granted her this, and elected her priestess of Demeter, thinking that the honour would be as pleasing to the goddess as it was appropriate to the woman.

[27] Pythes' Wife*

The wife of Pythes, in Xerxes' time, is also said to have been both wise and good. Pythes himself had discovered a gold-mine, and had an absolutely insatiable craving for the wealth he derived from it. He spent his time there himself, and forced all the citizens to go down on the same terms and dig or carry or wash out the gold. They had no other work or activity whatsoever. Many died, and all were weary; and their wives came to plead for them to the door of Pythes' wife. She told them to go away but not despair. She then took it upon herself to summon the goldsmiths whom she trusted most, and shut them up together, with instructions to make gold loaves, cakes, and fruits of all kind, especially the kinds of food and relish that she knew Pythes liked best. This was all completed by the time Pythes returned home from a journey abroad. He asked for his dinner, and his wife set before him a golden table, with nothing edible on it, but everything in gold. At first Pythes was delighted with the models, but when he had had enough of looking at them, he asked for something to eat. She brought him whatever he wanted—made of gold. He began to be angry, and cried out that he was hungry. 'Well,' she said, 'you have given us plenty of
this stuff, but nothing else. Every trade and skill has disap- 263
peared, no one farms the land, we leave behind the crops and plants and nourishment that the earth gives, and go on digging and seeking useless things, wearing out ourselves and our countrymen.' Pythes was moved. He did not, however, give up the whole of his mining-enterprise, but assigned only one-fifth

of the population to this work, diverting the rest to farming and other crafts.

When Xerxes marched against Greece, Pythes gave him the most generous hospitality and gifts, and asked the king in return to release one of his numerous sons from the army, and leave him at home to care for him in his old age. Xerxes was furious. He killed the son whose release Pythes had requested, cut his body in two, and made the army march between the two halves. The other sons he took with him, and they were all killed in the battles. Pythes, in his despair, now had the common experience of bad and foolish men. He feared death and hated life. He wanted not to be alive, but he had not the will to abandon life. Now there was a great dyke in the city, and a river, called the Pythopolites, flowing through it. Pythes constructed a monument on the dyke, and diverted the river so as to flow through the dyke right by the tomb. This done, he himself descended into the monument, and committed the government of the city to his wife, with orders not to go near him, but to send his dinner in a boat every day, until such time as the boat passed the tomb with the dinner untouched; then she was to stop, because he would be dead. And that is how he spent the rest of his days, while his wife managed the government well, and gave the people relief from their troubles.

XVII

GRYLLUS

The alternative title—'That Brute Beasts (*aloga*) Have Reason (*logos*)'—indicates the subject. Plutarch imagines Odysseus asking Circe to let him persuade one of her captive animals to be changed back to human form. A pig is produced for him to interview: its name is Gryllus (suggesting the verb *grulizo*, 'I grunt', but in fact a genuine Greek name, borne for example by a son of Xenophon) and it was evidently acquainted with Odysseus, having seen him long ago in Crete; it was not (as is often said) one of Odysseus' own companions. The shape of the debate is given by the conventional list of four cardinal virtues, and the extant part of the dialogue covers courage, temperance, and wisdom, in all of which Gryllus shows animals to be superior to men. This idea that animals are in some ways our betters is not uncommon in Greek thought; it occurs in Plutarch in *Love of Offspring* (32) and *The Intelligence of Animals* (63). See in general G. Boas, *The Happy Beast* (Baltimore, 1933), 35 ff.

[1] 985

ODYSSEUS Well, Circe, I think I understand that, and I shall remember it. But I should very much like to hear from you whether you have any Greeks among the men you have turned into wolves and lions.

CIRCE Darling Odysseus, many; but why do you ask?

ODYSSEUS Because I think it would do me much honour in the eyes of the Greeks if, by your favour, I could restore them to human form, and not let them grow old in their unnatural animal bodies, eking out such a pitiful and disgraceful existence.

CIRCE The man's foolish enough to think it's honourable for him to be the ruin not only of himself and his companions, but of people who have nothing to do with him at all!

ODYSSEUS This is a fresh potion you're making to drug me, Circe—words this time. You really do make an animal of me, if I am to agree with you that it is ruin for an animal to become human.

CIRCE Well, haven't you done something even odder to yourself? You refuse a life with me, exempt from death and old

age, and you're in a hurry to get back to that mortal wife* of yours—she must be an old woman by now—however many difficulties there are in the way. Do you expect to become
986 more famous and renowned than you are, if you pursue an unsubstantial image of the good, and not the real thing?

ODYSSEUS Have it as you will, Circe. Why do we keep quarrelling over the same thing? Just free these men, and give them to me as a favour.

CIRCE By Hecate,* it's not so simple! These are no ordinary people. Ask them first if they want it; if they say no, my brave friend, argue with them and persuade them; if you don't persuade them and they win the argument, you must just be satisfied with having made the wrong decision about yourself and your friends.

ODYSSEUS Dear lady, why do you laugh at me? How can they take part in the give-and-take of argument, so long as they are donkeys or pigs or lions?

CIRCE My dear, ambitious friend, just take heart. I will produce them for you, and they shall understand you and debate with you. Or rather, one will be enough to discuss with you on behalf of them all. Here you are! Talk to this one.

ODYSSEUS What shall I call him, Circe? Who was he as a man?

CIRCE Does that matter? Call him Gryllus, if you like. And I'll remove myself, so that you don't think he says things to please me, contrary to his own judgement.

[2] GRYLLUS Good morning, Odysseus.

ODYSSEUS Good morning, Gryllus.

GRYLLUS What is it you want to ask me?

ODYSSEUS I know that you were all humans, and I feel very sorry for you in your present plight; but naturally I feel particularly concerned for the Greeks among you who have had this bad luck. So I have asked Circe to release any of you who wishes it, restore him to his original shape, and let him go home with me.

GRYLLUS Stop, Odysseus! Say no more. We all despise you. There was no substance in the idea that you were so clever and supposed to be so superior to other men in wisdom. Why, you were even afraid of the change from bad to good. You didn't think carefully. Just as children are frightened of doctor's medicine and of their lessons, which change them from being sickly and stupid to being healthy and intelligent, so you rejected the chance of becoming a different being. You are living with Circe in constant fear and apprehension that she may turn you into a pig or a wolf without your being aware of it. At the same time, you try to persuade us, who are living a most comfortable life, to abandon all this, to abandon the lady who does it all for us, and to take ship with you, having first been turned back into men—the unluckiest species of all.

ODYSSEUS It sounds to me, Gryllus, as if it wasn't only your body that was destroyed by that potion, but your mind as well. You are full of totally absurd and perverted notions. Has the pleasure of habit magically bound you to this body? Or is it some swinish pleasure that magicked you into it?

GRYLLUS Neither, O king of the Cephallenians;* but if you are willing to debate rather than just abuse one, we shall soon persuade you, from our experience of both lives, that we are right to prefer our present existence to our former.

ODYSSEUS And I'm anxious to hear you.

[3] GRYLLUS And I to speak. Let us begin with the virtues on which we see you pride yourselves so much, as being so superior to animals in justice, wisdom, courage, and the rest. Now answer me, wise man. I heard you telling Circe about the land of the Cyclopes;* how, without being ploughed or planted, it is so generous and excellent that it bears all crops spontaneously. Do you rate this higher than your own rugged 987
Ithaca,* the land of goats, which barely yields a small, sparing, valueless return for all the farmers' labour? Don't be angry with me, and don't give an insincere answer out of patriotism.

ODYSSEUS No, I mustn't lie. I love and adore my country and its soil more, but I rate the other highly and I admire it.

GRYLLUS So we are to say that the wisest of men believes it right to praise and approve one thing but choose and love another? I assume that your answer also applies to matters of the soul, for the principle is the same as with land: the soul that produces virtue without labour, like a crop growing spontaneously, is the better.

ODYSSEUS Let me grant you that.

GRYLLUS So you are now admitting that the soul of animals has a better natural capacity for virtue and is more perfect; for it produces and develops naturally the virtue appropriate to each kind, without discipline or instruction, just like the soil that needs no sowing or ploughing.

ODYSSEUS And what virtue *do* animals possess. Gryllus?

[4] GRYLLUS What do they *not* possess, and in greater degree than the wisest of men?

Consider courage, first, if you will. You take great pride in this, and show no reticence about being called 'bold' or 'sacker of cities'. Yet what you did, you insufferable man, was to use tricks and wiles to cheat men who knew only a simple, noble form of warfare and had no experience of deceit and lies; and then you give your villainy the name of the one virtue that least admits villainy! Animals, on the other hand, as you see, contend with one another, and with you men in ways which are free of guile and artfulness, and defend themselves with open, naked bravery and genuine valour. With no law to compel them, and no fear of prosecution for avoidance of service, they instinctively reject defeat and persevere to the very end to preserve their invincible record. If they are physically overcome, they are not defeated, and their spirit never fails; they die fighting. In many of them, as they die, their courage and spirit somehow retreat and concentrate in some one part of the body, and continue to resist the killer, writhing and rebelling, until their fire, as it were, is wholly extinguished and destroyed. There is no pleading, no begging for mercy, no admission of defeat. Lion never cows before lion, nor horse before horse, out of unmanliness as man does before man, when he accepts to be cowed in slavery, in a state whose very name implies cowardice. As for those which men subdue by snare or trap, the adults reject food, endure thirst, and induce and welcome death in preference to servitude; while their chicks or cubs, easily led and malleable at that tender age, are offered various delicate

beguilements and cajolements to drug them into submission. They taste pleasures and styles of life foreign to their nature, and are gradually subdued into weakness, till they come to accept and tolerate what is called domestication, and is really a sort of emasculation of their vigour. There is evidence enough in this that animals are naturally courageous. In man, on the other hand, endurance is actually unnatural, as you can see, my friend, from various considerations. In the animals, for instance, the sexes are both equally capable of courage; the female no less than the male has strength to endure necessary hardships and fight battles for her children. You will have heard of the wild sow of Crommyon,* a female, that
gave Theseus so much trouble. And the Sphinx, sitting up on 988
Phicion and concocting her puzzles and riddles, would not have had much profit from her wisdom if she had not also had the strength and courage to prevail over the Cadmeans. In the same part of the world, we are told, dwelt the Teumessian vixen,* a 'horrid thing', and, nearby, the female serpent that fought a duel with Apollo for the Delphic oracle. Your king,* again, took the mare Aithe from the Sicyonians as a price for excusing him from service; it was a prudent arrangement to prefer a brave and high-spirited mare to a cowardly male human. You have observed yourself, with leopards and lions, that the females are not a scrap inferior to the males in spirit and courage. Yet your own wife, while you are at war, sits at home by the fire, making not as much resistance as a swallow to the attackers of herself and her household! And she is a Spartan!* I don't have to mention the ladies of Caria or Maeonia!* It is surely plain from this that male human beings have no natural manliness; otherwise, the female too would have her share of courage. You all, therefore, practice a form of courage that depends on force of law; it is not willing or voluntary, but the slave of custom, censure, alien doctrines, and vacillating reason. You endure hardship and danger, not because you have the courage to face them, but because you are more frightened of something else. In your crew, the man who gets there first stands to the light oar. He does not think it beneath him; he fears and avoids the heavier one. Similarly, a man who puts up with a beating to avoid a wound in battle,

or resists an enemy to avoid death or torture, is not brave in respect of what he endures; he is simply a coward about the alternative. So human courage can be seen to be intelligent cowardice, and human boldness nothing but the fear that understands how to avoid one evil by incurring another. To take a general point: if you think yourselves superior to animals in courage, why do your poets call the bravest warriors 'wolf hearts',[1] 'lion spirits', or 'strong as the boar'? No one calls a lion 'man-hearted' or a boar 'strong as a man'. I imagine that, just as they call fast runners 'fleet as the wind' and beautiful men 'godlike', by hyperbole, so they make these comparisons between good fighting-men and the creatures that are their superiors. The explanation is that anger is, as it were, the way to temper or hone the edge of courage.* Animals employ it undiluted, so to speak, when they fight, whereas *you* mix it with reason, like wine with water, so that it steps aside from danger, and fails in the moment of need. Some of you actually allege that anger is not to be used in battle, but set aside in favour of sober thought. This may be right from the point of view of safety and survival, but it is a disgraceful attitude in terms of valour and self-defence. It is surely ridiculous for you, on the other hand, to blame nature for not giving you stings or talons or teeth to defend yourselves, but at the same time to remove or restrain your soul's natural weapon.

[5] ODYSSEUS My word, Gryllus, you *have* become a clever sophist! Even in your swinish state, that's a most vigorous treatment of the problem that you've given me. Why didn't you go straight on to temperance?

GRYLLUS Because I thought you would first want to discuss what had been said so far. But no doubt you are anxious to hear about temperance, because you are the husband of the most chaste and temperate of wives, and you imagine yourself to have given proof of the same virtue by rejecting Circe's advances. But in this you are no better an example of continence than any of the animals. They have no desire to have sexual relations with their superiors, but find their loves
989 and pleasures with their own kind. So there's nothing to be

surprised at. The he-goat of Mendes,* so they say, is penned up with many beautiful women, but has no eagerness to copulate with them; he is more interested in she-goats. Similarly, you enjoy the sexual pleasures you are accustomed to, but, as man, have no desire to sleep with a goddess. As for Penelope's chastity, countless crows will croak their ridicule of it, and think nothing of it: if the male crow dies, the female remains a widow for nine whole generations of men. So your lovely Penelope is nine times less chaste than any old crow you care to find!

[6] But, since you see that I am a trained sophist, let me give my speech some organization. First I define temperance, then I classify desires. Temperance is a restraint and ordering of our desires, removing the superfluous and extraneous, and controlling the occasion and the degree of those that are necessary. There are obviously countless differences in desires. Those directed to food and drink have a natural, and also a necessary, element. Those of sex, which are initiated by nature but are not indispensable for a satisfactory life, are called 'natural but not necessary'. There remains the category of desires which are neither necessary nor natural, but introduced from outside, under the influence of vain ideas, because of your lack of discrimination. These, by their very number, come near to obliterating all your natural desires. They are like an immigrant mob forcing its way in the community against the native citizens. Animals are very different. Their souls are inaccessible to, and uncontaminated by, invading passions. Their lives are passed far away, as it were, from the sea of vain ideas;* and, though they fall short of elegance and luxury, they preserve most religiously both their temperance and the control of their resident desires, which are neither numerous nor alien. Like you, I was once dazzled by gold—I thought there was nothing remotely like it that one could own—and by silver and ivory. The man who had most of these seemed to me blessed and beloved of god. It didn't matter that he was a Phrygian or a Carian viler than Dolon and more unfortunate than Priam. With my desires fixated on this, I could find no joy or pleasure in my easy and comfortable circumstances. I grumbled at life, and felt I had been left

behind, deprived of its greatest blessings. I remember seeing you in Crete,* dressed for a great occasion in that cloak of yours; and it wasn't your wisdom or your virtue that I envied. No, it was the delicate workmanship of the fine tunic and the softness and beauty of the purple cloak that caught my gaze and my desire. And there was that gold clasp too, with the toy on it, a marvellous work of the jeweller's art. I was fascinated, and followed you around, as the women did. But now I am freed and purged of these vain follies and ideas; I pay no more attention to gold and silver than to any other stone I tread on; in fact I would just as soon lie down and rest in some deep, soft mud as on your coverlets and carpets. None of these 'imported' desires finds a home in *our* souls. For the most part, our life is based on the necessary desires and pleasures; if we indulge in the natural but unnecessary ones, we do so without excess or indiscipline.

990 [7] Let us take these last first. The pleasure relating to fragrant objects, the exhalations from which give the sense of smell its proper stimulation, is not only cheap and simple but contributes a practical service in identifying food. The tongue is, and is said to be, the indicator of sweet and piquant and acid, whenever flavours are diffused in contact with the organ of taste; but smell is an indicator of the quality of the substance *before* its flavour reaches us. It is much more perceptive than a king's official taster! It admits appropriate fare, and rejects the inappropriate, not allowing it to come into contact with, or give pain to, the taste; the bad quality is detected and condemned before any harm is done. Moreover, smell is never a trouble to us, as it is to you humans, when it impels you to blend and combine incense and cinnamon, nard and malobathrum* and the Arabian reed,* with the aid of that formidable adulterating art of the druggist which is called 'perfumery', and to pay vast sums for an unmanly, girlish, and totally useless form of indulgence. None the less, the sense of smell has corrupted not only all women, but now most men. They will not go to bed with their own wives unless the ladies reek of perfume and powder when they come to them. Yet the sow attracts the boar, and the she-goat and other animals their mates, by their own particular smells.

They are redolent of pure dew and the grasses of the meadow, and come together at their meeting in mutual affection. The females do not flirt or put up a show of deceit and trickery and denial to hide their desire. Nor do the males, under the stimulus of lust, purchase the work of procreation with money or labour or servitude. Instead, they pursue Aphrodite in season, with no guile and no wage to offer. She rouses the animals' desires in the summer, as she does the growth of plants, and quickly damps it down again. The female never admits the male once she has conceived, nor does he make the attempt. So small and weak is the regard we give to pleasure; for us, nature is all. Hence, so far at least, the desires of animals have not led to intercourse between male and male, or female and female. Yet that is common enough with you, even among the high and virtuous, to say nothing of the worthless among you. Agememnon travelled all through Boeotia in pursuit of the elusive Argynnus, falsely blamed the sea and the winds, and finally beautifully dipped his beautiful person into Lake Copais, there to quench his love and be rid of his desire. Heracles, likewise, pursued a beardless friend,* got left behind by the heroes, and deserted his ship. Again, one of you humans secretly wrote the words 'Achilles is beautiful' on the rotunda (*tholos*) of Apollo Ptoos, though Achilles was already a father; and I am told the inscription is still there. But if a cock mounts a cock, because there is no hen to hand, he is burnt alive: some prophet or portent-watcher is bound to declare it a dreadful event. You see how sure men are that chastity and abstention from unnatural pleasure are qualities characteristic of animals rather than of themselves! Even with the aid of the law, however, nature cannot keep your incontinence within bounds. It is carried along on the tide of desire, and brings about the most dreadful outrage, disorder, and confusion of nature in your sexual behaviour. There have been men who assault goats and sows
and mares, and women frantic for male animals. Such unions 991
give rise to your Minotaurs and Aegipans,* and perhaps your Sphinxes and your Centaurs. It has been known for a dog to eat man, or a bird to taste of him, when starving; but no animal has ever tried to consort sexually with a human being.

991 It is man who behaves violently and improperly towards these and many other animals.

[8] Vile and incontinent as men are in these respects, they are even more inferior to animals where the necessary desires are involved. These are the desires of food and drink. *We* always link need with pleasure; *you* pursue pleasure more than the natural requirement of nourishment. You are therefore plagued by many long illnesses, which are decanted into the body, as it were, from one source only, surfeit, and fill you with all kinds of gases very hard to get rid of. Now every animal species has its single natural food—grass for some, a certain sort of root or grain for others. Those that are carnivorous pay no attention to other kinds of food, and do not rob their weaker brethren of their nourishment; lion and wolf leave stag and sheep to browse as nature inclines them. Man, on the other hand, is led by his greediness to seek pleasure everywhere. He tries and tastes everything. Not knowing what is proper and peculiar to him, he has become the one and only omnivorous creature. His original use of flesh was not due to any lack of means or resources. He can always harvest or pluck the produce of plant and seed in season, one after the other, in such abundance that he need not labour. It is luxury and distaste for the merely necessary that leads him to look for an impure and unsuitable diet, and massacre animals with more savagery than the fiercest wild beast does. Blood and flesh and carrion are the natural fare of kites, wolves, and snakes; for man, they are no more than a tasty relish. Man makes use of every kind of creature; he does not, like us animals, abstain from most kinds and make war only on a few for food; there is nothing, practically speaking, that flies or swims or walks that escapes your supposedly civilized and hospitable tables.

[9] Well, then. It's only to give your food an interesting taste that you use these creatures, is it? Did <nature give you reason simply to live in luxury through killing others?>

[*Supplement is uncertain. There is perhaps more missing. We now pass to a new cardinal virtue, 'wisdom' or 'intelligence'.*]

Animals' intelligence gives no scope for any idle or useless skill. Instead, it provides us with the skills we need, without importing them from outside or making us pay to learn or painfully stick scraps of knowledge together in a long course of study. Our skills come naturally and instinctively from our intelligence itself. We are told that every Egyptian is a doctor. Well, every animal has not only its own skill of healing, but its own skills of feeding, self-defence, hunting, and music, so far as its nature demands. Who taught us to go to the river for crabs when we are ill? Who taught tortoises to eat origanum after making a meal of viper? Who taught the Cretan goats to look for dittany when they are shot, so as to expel the dart by eating the herb? If you say, truly enough, that nature is their teacher, you are attributing animal intelligence to the highest and wisest source. If you decline to call it 'reason' or 'intelligence', you had better look for a higher and more honourable name, since the power it displays in action is of a higher
and more wonderful order <than human intelligence>. It is 992
certainly not deprived of understanding and education; but it is self-instructed and self-sufficient, dispensing with the process of gathering learning from others, not out of weakness but by the very strength and perfection of its natural excellence. Animals to which men, for their sport or comfort, give instruction or training, are intelligent enough to grasp what they are taught even if it goes counter to their physical nature. I say nothing of puppies learning to follow tracks, or horses to walk to music, or crows taught to talk, or dogs to jump through revolving hoops. Horses and steers in the theatre learn and memorize to perfection the routines of lying down, dancing, holding a difficult pose, and performing movements not easy even for men. And this is simply a demonstration of their capacity to learn; there is no practical use in it.

If you doubt that we can learn skills, let me point out that we teach them. Partridges accustom their chicks to hide, when they are trying to escape, by turning on their backs and holding a piece of earth over themselves in their claws. And you can see how the adult storks are at hand to help their young on the roofs in their first attempts at flight. Nightingales teach their chicks to sing; those which are captured young and brought up by humans never sing as well—they have left school too soon, as it were.

[*A lacuna seems likely here.*]

Since I have been in this body, I have come to be amazed at the arguments by which the sophists used to persuade me that every creature save man is without reason or intelligence.

[10] ODYSSEUS So you've changed, have you, Gryllus, and come to think that sheep and asses are reasoning creatures?

GRYLLUS These are the very creatures which give the best proof that animal nature does have its share of reason and understanding. For, just as one tree is no more or less inanimate than the next, but all have the same degree of insensibility (none of them having a soul), so one animal could not be thought slower in mind or less ready to learn than another unless they *all* possessed reason and understanding, though to different degrees. Consider the point, then, that it is the ingenuity and sharpness of some that brings the stupidity and sluggishness of others into relief; for example, compare the ass and the sheep with the fox or the wolf or the bee. It's like comparing Polyphemus with you, or that Corinthian Homer* with your grandfather, Autolycus. There is less difference, I fancy, in intelligence, thought, and memory between one animal and another than between one man and another.

ODYSSEUS But, Gryllus, it's surely a very terrible and extreme position to allow reason to exist in creatures which have no concept of god.

GRYLLUS Then are we to say, Odysseus, that a clever and remarkable person like yourself could not have been descended from Sisyphus?*

[*Sisyphus despised the gods. Many scholars think there is a lot of the dialogue missing; and this seems to be so, since not only do we have no sequel to this incipient discussion of theology, but the fourth cardinal virtue, justice, has not been treated at all.*]

NOTES

These notes are intended to be used in conjunction with the Glossary of Proper Names and the List of Quotations.

1. Superstition

164 *atoms and void*: i.e. the Epicurean doctrine, which Plutarch usually treats more harshly, taking it to lead to a denial of providence and consequently a faulty moral life.

165 *earthquakes in Gaul*: for Aristotle (*Nicomachean Ethics* 3. 7. 1115^b27), the Gauls' failure to fear earthquakes illustrates foolish insensitivity to danger; but Plutarch's point is rather that earthquakes do not occur in Gaul, nor lightning-strikes in Ethiopia (for this belief, see, e.g. Arrian, *Meteora* fr. 4 Roos, in *Scripta minora et fragmenta* (Leipzig, 1968)).

voices and silence: I have omitted the word for 'dreams', which follows here in the text; Plutarch is going on to discuss the terrors of the superstitious man's sleep.

166 *smear you all over*: covering the body with mud or lime or sulphur was a commonly practised ritual of purification.

'*Death . . . mankind*': a quotation from a famous passage of Demosthenes (*De corona* 97).

167 *Heracles in his madness*: the madness of Heracles, inflicted by Hera, and his killing of his children in his delusion, are the subject of Euripides' *Heracles*.

168 '*use him as a peg*': i.e. hang charms (amulets) on him.

the war with Sparta: the First Messenian War, traditionally dated *c*. 735–715 BC, around which many legends grew.

dog's-tooth grass: Greek *agrōstis*, perhaps *Cynodon dactylon*; in any case an invasive weed whose presence signified desolation.

169 *Nicias*: in the Sicilian campaign of 413 BC, Nicias disastrously postponed the intended withdrawal of the army on account of an eclipse of the moon (Plutarch, *Nicias* 23).

Glaucus . . . nigh: a quotation from Archilochus.

The Jews: the story probably refers to the capture of Jerusalem by Pompey in 63 BC, but there are other possibilities—Ptolemy I in 320 BC, Antony in 38 BC, Titus in AD 70.

170 *Whether hasting . . . killer*: the text of this hymn to Hecate (Artemis) is very uncertain. The translation follows Wilamowitz' reconstruction (U. von Wilamonitz-Moellendorf, *Griechisches Lesebuch*, Text, Zweiter Halbband (Berlin, 1906), 336).

'*let me get his liver . . . and eat it*': Hecuba so speaks of Achilles, when she seeks to dissuade Priam from going to see him to beg for Hector's body (*Iliad* 24. 212).

the goddess of Syria: Atargatis, much worshipped throughout the Greek world in Plutarch's time, and sometimes identified with Hera.

Hermolaus . . . Chaereas: all these were assassins who conspired against and killed their masters.

171 '*craftsmen of day and night*': from Plato (*Timaeus* 40c).

Empedocles: the point of the lines is that, on the theory of transmigration of souls, the animal being sacrificed may well be the sacrificer's son.

sacrificed their children: Phoenician and Carthaginian infant-sacrifice is well-attested, as well as being the object of Jewish and Greek abhorrence. In the precinct of Tanit at Carthage have been found thousands of urns with the cremated remains of small children.

II. Oracles in Decline

409 *Navel*: an ancient stone in the Temple of Apollo was called the Omphalos (Navel), and believed to mark the mid-point of the earth.

410 "*sharp*": Greek *thoēn*; the word usually means 'swift', but its meaning in Homer was a subject of dispute in antiquity.

pints and quarts of water: time was measured by the water-clock, and as this could be used to measure the duration of the sunset as well as that of the sun's daily course, the apparent diameter of the sun could be calculated from these two measurements.

the plinth: this refers to a type of sundial.

411 *Syene*: Assouan, on the tropic of Cancer, where the sun is directly overhead at the summer solstice. The argument is that, if the years really were shorter, the tropic would be closer to the equator, and we should need to go even further south to encounter this phenomenon.

fires that never go out: a perpetual fire was maintained in many temples (e.g. Apollo Lykeios at Argos), and perpetually burning lamps were also common (e.g. Athena Polias at Athens, Hera at Argos). The most famous perpetual fire is that maintained by the Vestal Virgins at Rome (Vesta = Hestia = Hearth).

at the time of the Persian Wars: the text of much of this passage is defective. The story is told by Herodotus (8. 133–6), but Plutarch's account is rather different.

412 *"Palm" ... "Olive"*: according to the usual legend, Leto gave birth to Apollo and Artemis on Delos, resting in her labour against a palm-tree and an olive-tree.

the Delians: expelled from their home by the Athenians in 422 BC, but restored shortly afterwards, when peace was made with Sparta.

the Cnidian Meeting-House: the *leschē* dedicated by the people of Cnidos was famous for the paintings of Polygnotus, depicting the fall of Troy and Odysseus' descent into Hades.

the verb ballō: the future tense of *ballō* ('I throw') is *balō*.

"worse" ... "best": like English and Latin, Greek uses words of different roots to express the comparative and superlative of 'good' and 'bad'.

413 *Planetiades*: the nickname means 'wanderer's son', and is appropriate for the vagrant Cynic philosopher, who has no fixed abode.

shame and nemesis: 'Decency and Moral Disapproval will go to join the family of the immortals, abandoning mankind' (*Theogony and Works and Days* 197, tr. M. L. West (World's Classics, Oxford, 1988)).

I, being pretty well his closest friend: i.e. Lamprias, who is the narrator, though the text does not tell us this till Ammonius addresses him by name, just below, see [8].

a Pythian truce: around the great festivals (Olympian, Pythian, Isthmian, and Nemean games) there was supposed to be a cessation of all hostilities, so that people could come and go safely. So here the Cynic is asked to honour his surroundings by observing a 'Pythian truce' towards his enemy.

414 *the terrible dragon*: Python, whom Apollo killed with his arrows.

employed nine heralds: so in *Iliad* 2. 96.

ventriloquists: Eurycles was known from Aristophanes and Plato. The word *pythōn* (presumably from the dragon's name) is used of a spirit of prophecy present in a girl at Acts 16: 16.

415 *Hesiod*: see *Theogony and Works and Days*, pp. 40–1 (World's Classics). Plutarch wrote a commentary on *Works and Days*, and these interpretations probably reflect this work.

the Naiad: perhaps the wife of Chiron the Centaur, if (as seems likely) this passage comes from Hesiod's 'Precepts of Chiron'.

"*youth*" *or* "*eld*": Plutarch prefers the reading *hēbōntos* in Hesiod, but knows a variant reading *gērōntos*.

the generation of the soul: Plato, *Timaeus* 35A–C. We possess Plutarch's treatise (68) on the interpretation of this doctrine.

final conflagration: the Stoic *ekpyrōsis*, the fire which periodically destroys the entire universe, giving room for its renewal.

416 *the impossibilities . . . exaggerated view*: a very difficult and uncertain sentence.

chthonic: i.e. belonging to the Underworld.

the unity and community of the whole: Cleombrotus' argument lays stress on the idea that the universe must be a complete system, with no gaps in nature.

417 *eating of raw meat and tearing of flesh*: a feature of Dionysiac orgiastic worship, horribly portrayed in the closing scene of Euripides' *Bacchae*.

"*frenzies . . . turning*": from a dithyramb of Pindar (2. 13), i.e. a poem relating to Dionysus.

human sacrifices: this was a remote horror in Greek folk-memory, the sacrifice of Iphigenia at Aulis by her father Agamemnon being the most famous mythological instance.

for a girl: Iole, daughter of King Eurytus. The story is told in Sophocles' *Trachiniae*.

Molus: the festival was at Cnossus. This Molus is the son of Deucalion and father of Meriones, the companion of Idomeneus in the Trojan War. Cleombrotus makes the 'nymph' a sort of *daimon*: cf. the passage of Hesiod quoted above (415).

"*holy Apollo*": Apollo, having killed the Cyclopes in revenge for Zeus's killing Asclepius, was punished by being sent to serve King Admetus of Pherae as a herdsman (see Euripides' *Alcestis*), though it seems from this passage that in Sophocles' treatment of the legend he did more servile labour still, working at the mill.

418 *The hut*: the 'Threshing Floor', a circular area which the Sacred Way crosses just below the temple of Apollo, was the scene of this periodical ritual (*septērion*), usually taken to celebrate the killing of the dragon Python, and Apollo's flight to Tempe (so Plutarch, *Greek Questions* (= 18), 293c).

a boy: the text is corrupt, and may have named the group or clan concerned: Labyadai or Aiolidai.

whose parents are both living: *pueri patrimi et matrimi*, children who have not been diminished by the loss of a parent, are a potent force for good fortune, and appear in many Greek and Roman cult practices.

because . . . pollutions: the etymologies are forced and implausible.

the profane and uninitiated: presumably Epicureans or others whose views are regarded as impious.

the poems of Empedocles: according to Empedocles (B115), the spirits of sinners and perjurers are *daimones* and pass from one form of mortal life to another, from element to element, always abhorred and never at rest; 'and of these', he goes on, 'I too am one, an exile from god and a wanderer, trusting in frenzied Strife'.

419 "*idols*": *eidōla*, Democritus' term for the atomic images or effluences, given off by objects, which impinge on our senses.

I heard a story: the tale has been very famous. The Christian Eusebius (*Praeparatio Evangelica* 5. 17) interpreted it as an account of the death of all demons (i.e. pagan gods) when conquered by Christ. Rabelais (*Pantagruel*, IV. 28), who draws heavily on this dialogue, put forward the view that it is the death of Christ himself—'le bon Pan, le grand Pasteur'—which is meant.

Echinades . . . Paxi . . . Palodes: the distances involved are considerable, and make one wonder about the plausibility of the story. It is about 80 miles from the Echinades to Paxi, and 20 miles or so further north to Palodes (Butrinto), which is opposite the northern end of Corfu.

Demetrius . . . Britain: this Demetrius is almost certainly the dedicator of the York inscription to 'Ocean and Tethys' and 'the gods of the governor's *praetorium*'. His exploration (of the Western

Isles?), if Plutarch is not anachronistic in regard to the dramatic date, will be early in Agricola's governorship (AD 77–84).

violent storms of winds: for this widespread belief, cf. Pepys' fear (*Diary*, 19 Oct. 1663) that a storm of wind may mean the death of some great person. Rabelais (*Pantagruel* IV. 27), with Plutarch in mind, tells of strange phenomena preceding the death of his patron, the Sieur de Langey.

420 *where Cronus lay asleep*: the story is told at greater length in *The Face in the Moon* (60), 941A ff., where the isle of Cronus is said to be five days' sail west of Britain, and about 600 miles from 'the continent which encircles the great sea', which is inhabited by Greeks, and lies on the other side of an 'earthy' stretch of water, hard to row through. This fuller version probably antedates our dialogue, in which Plutarch alludes to it.

And yet, if one asserts . . . impossible or unreal: this passage contains a number of uncertainties of text and interpretation.

421 *a most melodious Doric*: the holy man thus addresses the Spartan Cleombrotus in his own dialect.

Typhon . . . Uranus: Typhon plotted against Osiris, found the chest in which his body was contained, and dismembered and scattered the corpse (see Plutarch's own version of this Egyptian myth in 'Isis and Osiris' (23)). Cronus the Titan, in Greek myth, castrated his father, Uranus, with the sickle given him by his mother, Gaia.

Arsalus, Dryus and Trosobius: a triad of gods worshipped in Lycia.

Dius . . . Hermaeus: most Greek proper names are honorific or of good omen, and indicate victory, success, political attitudes, or (as with these names) connection with a god: 'Dius' is from 'Zeus'.

422 *settled for a single world*: Plato, *Timaeus* 55C–D. Much of the complex argument which follows is based on *Timaeus*.

Plain of Truth: this phrase is taken from the myth in Plato, *Phaedrus* 248B, where the 'plain' of truth is the 'meadow' where grows the pasturage for the soul's noblest part, the intellect.

"*in a row*": the Greek *kata stoicheion* might also mean 'by element', and the phrase is as obscure to us as to Lamprias.

the Three Gods: Zeus, Poseidon, and Hades. In Homer (*Iliad* 15. 187 ff.), Hades has 'the misty darkness', Zeus the heaven, Poseidon the sea, and earth and Olympus are common to all.

424 *Aristotle's theory*: as known to us from *De caelo* 1. 8 (276^a18 ff.).

425 *its own earth and sea*: the Greek *gē* means both 'earth' (as opposed to heaven or the planets) and 'land' (as opposed to sea), and this makes translation difficult in this passage.

a moon in it anywhere: if this reading is correct (some read 'in the centre'), the point is that a world is only a world if it has each part (e.g. its moon) in the right place. 'Brains in heels' and 'heart in temples' are proverbial absurdities.

"*Zens*": *Zēn* is an alternative word for Zeus, and happens to be a homonym of the verb *zēn*, 'to live'.

their infinite cosmic cycles: on the Stoic view, the universe is periodically destroyed and reborn, so that new gods come into being, though the universal *logos* (which they would also call Zeus) is eternal.

426 *ruler-bees*: the ancients believed the 'ruler' of the hive was a 'king' rather than a 'queen'. Cf. VII, 813.

the sons of Tyndareus: Castor and Pollux, the 'great Twin Brethren', believed to be responsible for the phenomenon called St Elmo's Fire, an electrical discharge that sometimes appears around the masts and rigging of ships in storms, and was thought a good omen.

Homer's Zeus does not divert his gaze: in *Iliad* 13. 2, Zeus leaves the Trojans to fight, and himself 'turns his shining eyes', 'looking from afar on the land of the horse-riding Thracians, the Mysians, closefighters, and the noble Horse-milkers, who live on milk'.

nor inward upon himself (as some have thought): this again is directed against Aristotle, who held (*Metaphysics* 1074^b) that God could only 'think' himself, because all other objects of thought were inferior, and similarly (*Eudemian Ethics* 1245^b15) that he does not need friends. (This last point is addressed by Plutarch's earlier argument (423 above), that if God is good, he must have a field in which to exercise his social virtues.)

the famous E: this is the subject of another of Plutarch's 'Pythian dialogues' (24). An object resembling a capital E was an ancient dedication in the temple of Apollo, and its significance was much discussed. E is the fifth letter of the Greek alphabet, and was used as the numeral five; EI (which could be written E in archaic script) means 'if', but also 'thou art'. All these ideas are canvassed in the dialogue.

triangular number: a number which is the sum of a series of numbers beginning with one and increasing by one: e.g. 1 + 2 + 3 + 4 = 10.

perfect number: i.e. a number 'equal to its own parts', i.e. (according to one common definition) the sum of its factors, as 6 = 1 + 2 + 3.

427 *five equiangular and equilateral solids*: the four named below, *plus* the cube, of which (as is later pointed out) Lamprias takes no account. Nothing is known of Theodorus of Soli, whose exposition is said to have been followed. *Timaeus* 55 ff. is again the basic Platonic text.

428 "*half-triangle*": i.e. half of an equilateral triangle.

the categories of Being, Sameness, Otherness, Motion, and Rest: here (as in the dialogue 'On the E at Delphi', 391B), Plutarch links the doctrine of the Five Solids from the *Timaeus* with that of the Five Categories from *Sophist* 254B–256D.

the One and the Indefinite Dyad: this summary of 'Platonic' doctrine seems to be based on Aristotle's account of his master's teaching (e.g. in *Metaphysics* 1. 6). The two principles correspond both to the formal and material causes and, in some sense, to good and evil.

429 "*fiving*": Greek *pempazein*, from *pente*, 'five'.

the most beautiful right-angled triangle: that with a hypotenuse of 5, and the other sides 3 and 4.

five parts of the soul: the first two are Aristotelian additions to the Platonic three (appetitive, spirited, rational), so that this enumeration represents a tradition in which Aristotelian and Platonic doctrines were combined.

five children at a birth: so also Aristotle (*Hist. An.* 584^{b}33), who reports a case of a woman who had four sets of quintuplets.

Rhea: according to Plutarch's *Isis and Osiris* (355D), Rhea (= Egyptian Nut) had five children (Osiris, Aroueris, Typhon, Isis, Nephthys) by three different consorts.

430 *the planets*: the four 'planetary orbits' not named here are those of the Moon, Jupiter, Saturn, and Mars. Venus and Mercury (which are nearer to the sun than the Earth is) were regarded as having the same orbit round the earth as the sun.

the fifth structure: the dodecahedron (*Timaeus* 55C). All this 'hymn to the number Five' may be compared with Sir Thomas Browne's speculation in 'The Garden of Cyrus'.

431 *the teaching of the Academy*: Lamprias means the post-Platonic Academy, under Carneades and others, which turned away from dogma to a sceptical emphasis on the ability to argue both sides of a case.

some visitors at Lebadea: perhaps a reference to another (lost) dialogue rather than to any real (or fictitious) occasion.

432 "*the hearing . . . blind*": the Greek word for 'deaf' also means 'dumb', and the word for 'blind' may also mean 'invisible'.

distancing, or ecstasy: Greek *ekstasis* literally means 'standing outside' or 'away from' something (e.g. oneself).

"*enthusiasm*": 'having a god within one', in other words 'possession by a god': see below, XIII. 758.

433 "*spirit*": Greek *pneuma*, here conceived as a physical phenomenon, a 'breath' or 'wind'.

434 *ribbons of stone*: asbestos is meant.

the great earthquake here: in 373 BC.

"*black*": the implication is that the god of the oracle wishes to be regarded as a chthonic, not an Olympian, deity.

435 *Plato . . . Anaxagoras*: the reference is to the account of Socrates' intellectual development which Plato puts into his mouth, *Phaedo* 97B.

436 *mixing-bowl*: according to Herodotus (1. 25), Alyattes, king of Lydia, dedicated a silver bowl and an iron stand for it; this latter object survived in Plutarch's time, though the silver bowl had been melted down by the Phocians during their occupation of Delphi in the 4th century BC.

Polygnotus: the inscription is thought to be by Simonides (*Anth. Pal.* 9. 700).

"*Zeus, the beginning . . . Zeus*": a line of an Orphic hymn.

437 *hosioi*: 'holy ones', a college of five who worked with the priests and prophets at Delphi.

III. Why Are Delphic Oracles No Longer Given in Verse?

394 *the dragon's teeth*: Jason, in his quest for the Golden Fleece, was ordered by Aeetes to plough a field with two savage bulls, and to sow the teeth of a dragon; from these sprang up a crop of armed men, whom Jason killed while they were fighting one another.

the Corycian cave . . . Lycorea: the cave, two or three hours' climb from Delphi, was sacred to Pan and the nymphs. The site of Lycorea (supposed to be older than Delphi itself) is uncertain.

395 *the Admirals*: a group of statues commemorating the Spartan victory over the Athenians at Aegospotami (405 BC).

Corinthian bronze: a high-quality bronze, the manufacture of which is variously described. The story of the accidental fusing of metals in a fire is usually connected with the sack of Corinth by the Romans in 146 BC.

396 *Aegon, king of Argos*: Aegon was chosen as king when an oracle had told the Argives that an eagle would show them their king, and an eagle then swooped down on Aegon's house.

397 *she was cast out . . . together with Ruin*: the poet Sarapion here refines on *Iliad* 19. 126, where Zeus, angry at being cheated by Hera, takes Ruin (*Atē*) by the head and throws her out of heaven for ever.

the Spartan Hiero: the name is uncertain, and may be an erroneous repetition of the name of Hiero of Syracuse; in that case, the real name cannot be recovered.

the palm-tree: this had been dedicated after the Athenian victory over the Persians at the River Eurymedon (468 BC.).

398 *the oracles of the Sibyl*: 'Sibyls' were inspired prophetesses, associated with various places. The 'first' was said to have lived at Erythrae or (as Plutarch says here) at Delphi. The most famous is the Sibyl of Cumae in Italy, from whose cave Virgil's Aeneas descends to the Underworld. Many 'Sibylline oracles' were current in Plutarch's time. The passage Sarapion quotes is very like one preserved by Phlegon of Tralles, a near contemporary (*F. Gr. Hist.* 257 F 37). The large extant collection of such oracles is partly Jewish and partly Christian in origin.

sacred animals: i.e. animals to be sacrificed, whose organs (especially the liver) would give signs of the future, according to the rules of extispicy.

Cumae and Dicaearchia: the eruptions of Vesuvius in AD 79 (Dicaearchia is Pozzuoli (Puteoli)). Plutarch mentions this oracle again (41, 566E).

399 *the oracle about the island*: an island (Thera) appeared in the crater of Santorini in 198/7 BC, after the defeat of the Carthaginians in the Second Punic War (which ended 202 BC) and shortly

before the Roman victory over the Macedonians at Cynoscephalae (197 BC). Plutarch seems a little vague about the chronology.

"*war against all nations at once*": this probably refers to the war against the slave-rebellion led by Spartacus (73–71 BC), since slaves were a heterogeneous and cosmopolitan mass. 'Five hundred years' takes us back to a time in the sixth century BC, before Roman contacts with Delphi; it may be a supposed 'Sibylline oracle' that Plutarch has in mind.

Essential Thoughts: *Kuriai Doxai*, a set of easily memorized sentences summarizing the main tenets of Epicureanism.

400 *a child sitting on a lotus flower*: Horus. In *Isis and Osiris* 355A, Plutarch seems to accept the view that Philinus here ridicules: 'they do not think the sun comes up out of the lotus as a baby, but they represent by this the rising of the sun, referring enigmatically to its kindling out of liquid.'

the Thessalian witches: see Glossary of Proper Names, s.v. 'Aglaonice'. To pull down the moon is a traditional feat of witches; according to Plato (*Gorgias* 513A), it was only accomplished at the sacrifice of something or someone very dear.

the children of Molione: these powerful Siamese twins, children of Actor and Molione, were killed by Heracles at Cleonae in the course of his expedition against King Augeas and his 'Augean stables'. The view Plutarch rejects is followed by Pausanias, 5. 2. 1–2.

Acanthians and Brasidas: this dedication dates from 423 BC, when the Spartan general Brasidas induced Acanthus to revolt from Athens.

Rhodopis: according to Herodotus (2. 135), this famous courtesan ('Rose-face') dedicated these iron bars as a tithe of her earnings.

401 *Aesop*: according to legend, Aesop and Rhodopis were both slaves of Iadmon of Samos. Aesop is said to have been thrown over the cliff by the Delphians, because of some quarrel or alleged sacrilege. The Delphians subsequently paid compensation to Iadmon's grandson for their action.

among the generals and kings: the gold statue of Phryne, by Praxiteles, on a column of Pentelic marble, stood between the statues of Archidamus, king of Sparta and Philip, king of Macedon.

Callias' house: the scene of Xenophon's *Symposium*, to which Plutarch alludes.

Croesus: the story is from Herodotus (1. 51). Croesus was one of Delphi's greatest benefactors.

402 *the first-fruits of their people*: this may refer to the story (found in the first-century writer Conon) that the Thessalian Magnesians sent a tenth of their countrymen, when they returned from the Trojan War, to Delphi; thence they travelled to Crete and to Asia Minor, where they founded a new Magnesia. Nothing seems to be known of any similar episode in the history of Eretria.

Scythinus: if these lines are a versification of Heraclitus' doctrine (cf. Heraclitus B 51), they have a philosophical meaning. The Stoics used similar analogies: Cleanthes called the sun a 'plectrum' which served to play the lyre of the universe.

403 *three of them would be tyrants*: Gelo was tyrant of Gela from 490 BC, and of Syracuse from 485, when his brother Hiero took over Gela. On Gelo's death in 478, Hiero became ruler of Syracuse; he died in 467, and his brother Thrasybulus succeeded, but was soon driven out, and a democratic government set up.

Stags . . . bury and hide their horns: 'where the stags drop their horns' was proverbial for a place hard to find. Aristotle (*Hist. An.* 611ᵃ25) says no one has ever found a *left* horn, which was believed to have some magical property.

a temple in Phocis of Heracles: after 'Heracles' the Greek text has an evidently corrupt word, which editors have 'emended' to *misogynou*, producing thereby an otherwise unknown (and very improbable) cult of 'Heracles the Woman-Hater'.

405 *Pandarus*: there is no known poet called Pandarus; the name is probably wrongly repeated from above. The line quoted is an iambic trimeter, presumably from tragedy or comedy. It may be Euripides (fr. 397 (*TGF*)) or Meander.

406 *golden hair-ornaments*: the example is taken from Thucydides (1. 6).

407 "*oblique*": this alludes to the supposed etymological connection between Apollo's title 'Loxias' and the fact that his sayings are 'oblique' (*loxos*); the same play on words was used to make the title refer to the 'obliquity' of the sun's path with reference to the equator.

Teucer, Cretines, Gnesiochus: these names are doubtful.

408 *Hoplites*: the word means 'heavily armed infantryman'. Plutarch tells this story of Lysander's death (395 BC) in his *Life of Lysander* (29).

our school exercises: the 'thesis', a common elementary exercise in rhetoric, took the form of debating just this sort of question, but in general terms.

409 *Pylaea*: this is the shrine of Demeter 'of the Gates', near Thermopylae, where regular meetings of the Amphictyones were held.

Galaxion: the place is unknown, but the name is from *gala*, 'milk'.

the initiator of this policy: who is meant? The most popular views are: 1. Plutarch himself, 2. the emperor Hadrian; but these are not very plausible, and the probability is that some person, possibly a Roman governor, but not identifiable by us, is meant. Whoever it is, he receives here a discreet but impressive compliment.

IV. Socrates' *Daimonion*

575 *too much inclined to the Boeotian cause*: Archedemus is a historical character, known to have been *proxenos* (official representative and host) of the Boeotians in Athens—'a capable speaker, who ran many political risks for the Thebans' (Aeschines 3. 138).

to seize the Cadmea: the Spartans seized this citadel in 382 BC.

577 *the Amphion*: a hill north of the Cadmea. In Plutarch's day, only the Cadmea was inhabited. In reconstructing the life of the classical city, he has doubtless used his imagination and his knowledge of the site.

578 *the lake*: i.e. Lake Copais.

hipparch: commander of the cavalry.

agnus castus: a shrub related to the willow, the name of which (*agnos*) suggests 'chaste' (*hagnos*); it was supposed to have anti-aphrodisiac qualities, and is sometimes called 'chaste tree' or 'monk's pepper'.

Plato and I . . . were studying: it was widely believed in Roman times that Plato spent time in Egypt and studied with the priests there, but the fact is very doubtful, and the story is probably based on references in the dialogues (especially *Timaeus*). Nothing is known of Ellopion.

579 "*if they doubled the altar at Delos*": the problem of the duplication of the cube was one of the most celebrated in Greek mathematics, and Plato was supposed to have offered a solution. See Ivor Thomas, *Greek Mathematical Works*, i. 257–308 (Loeb Classical Library, London, 1941).

580 *has Meletus convinced you . . . divine*: Meletus was one of the accusers of Socrates, and one charge brought against the latter was that he 'did not believe in the gods in whom the city believed, but introduced new divinities (*daimonia*)'.

the Crossroads: Symbolon, north-west of the agora.

581 *a sneeze*: the divinatory significance of sneezes was widely recognized; it is first mentioned in literature in the *Odyssey* (17. 541).

Delium: the scene of an Athenian defeat on the Boeotian front in 424 BC. The story of Socrates' bravery is told by Plato (*Symposium* 221A, *Laches* 181B).

by the Crossroads: I translate the emendation *schistēs* (sc. *hodou*) i.e. 'the divided road', proposed by E. R. Dodds.

583 *Pythagorean societies*: oligarchies of persons who shared Pythagorean beliefs governed some cities in Southern Italy, especially Croton, in the late sixth century. Plutarch's version of these events (like the other accounts which have come down to us) is highly romantic. He has indeed moved the scene of the fire from Croton to Metapontum, and put Philolaus (a well-known person, to whom important books were attributed) in place of an unknown Archippus.

certain sure signs: no doubt, a dream in which Lysis' figure appeared and cast no shadow. See below 585, and *God's Slowness to Punish* (41), 564B.

Jason, Prince of Thessaly: this seems to be an anachronism. Jason had been ruler of Pherae since 380, but is unlikely to have made a proposition like this to the Thebans before their liberation from Spartan occupation.

586 *sacrificing the ox to Demeter*: Demeter Thesmophoros had a temple on the Cadmea.

588 *not a vision but a perception of a voice*: Jeremy Taylor, 'Of Christian Prudence' (*Eniautos*: *Twenty-five Sermons*, xxii)

comments: 'There was some reason in his fancy, for God does not communicate himself by the eye to men, but by the ear: "Ye saw no figure, but ye heard a voice," says Moses (Deut. 4: 12).'

590 *Lamprocles*: in fact, Lamprocles survived Socrates, so this story is anachronistic.

Cave of Trophonius: a famous incubation oracle near Lebadea, and so well-known to Plutarch's circle. We have a detailed description by Pausanias (9. 39 = 1. 393 tr. P. Levi (Penguin, Harmondsworth, 1971)).

590–2 For a detailed exposition of the myth, see especially Einarson and de Lacy in the Loeb edition of the *Moralia*, VII. The astronomical setting is complex, and not very clear. The 'islands' are stars, the 'sea' is the celestial sphere, and the angle which it makes with the central space indicates the inclination of the ecliptic. Styx is the shadow of the earth. Plutarch combines with this setting a metaphysical speculation, the doctrine of the Four Principles, and an account of the relation of *daimon* to soul, presumably intended to support Simmias' account of the way in which Socrates was exceptionally privileged in being responsive to the calls and warnings of the *daimōn*.

591 *every 177 secondary measures*: i.e. every six months, the period between lunar eclipses. The 'secondary measure' is evidently a day.

592 *the soul of Hermodorus of Clazomenae*: this may be the person referred to as Hermotimus by Aristotle (*Metaph.* 984^b19) as having anticipated Anaxagoras in regarding *nous* (intellect) as the cause of order in the world.

595 *like Neoptolemus*: the son of Achilles and Deidamia was brought to Troy by Odysseus and Diomedes because it had been prophesied that Troy could not be captured without his aid. Like Charon's son, he went willingly to war as a boy.

V. 'Live Unknown'

1128 '*Don't write to your friends in Asia*': Epicurus' letters, some personal, some doctrinal, were very famous. His will contained instructions for the regular celebration of his birthday.

1129 *Hedea . . . Leontion*: Hedea seems to have been from Cyzicus, Leontion was an Athenian woman who lived with Epicurus, and was the wife or mistress of his disciple Metrodorus of Lampsacus.

1130 *'Delian' and 'Pythian'*: the first title suggests *delōs*, 'clear', 'plain', and the second the root *pyth-*, meaning 'inquire', 'ascertain'.

<that the soul . . . is told of> : this conjectural addition seems to give the likely connection of thought. But what follows is very difficult. We read of a 'Third Road', when the text has only mentioned one other sort of destiny. There must therefore be something missing, and there are two possibilities: 1. the Third Road is that of all the Wicked, those already mentioned are the Blessed, and the missing part of the text described the fate of those who have escaped the 'cycle of becoming' altogether, and achieved immortality; 2. the Third Road is that of the *incurably* wicked, and it is the *curable* cases who have not been mentioned. With 1. the missing sentence came at the beginning of this paragraph, and there is a considerably longer gap there than I have indicated; with 2. it came just before the mention of the Third Road. I have marked a gap there.

VI. The Fortune of Rome

316 *in a prose work*: this was a speculative work (*Triagmos*) which began by enunciating the proposition that 'all things are three'; *aretē* (virtue), for example, is made up of understanding, power, and fortune.

317 *'standing tiptoe on her globe'*: the phrases marked as quotations sound poetical, but their source is not known. The globe symbolizes Fortune's universal power, but also the uncertainty of her movement; it is when she steps down from it (318) that she becomes reliable. See Edgar Wind, *Pagan Mysteries in the Renaissance* (Penguin, Harmondsworth, 1967), 102.

318 *Horn of Plenty*: the cornucopia, the goat's horn given by Zeus to the nymph Amalthea, which was miraculously filled with all the fruits she desired.

Caecilius Metellus: consul 143 BC, his sons holding consulates in 123, 117, 115, and 113.

novus homo: i.e. the first member of his family to attain the consulate.

first man on the roll of the Senate: i.e. *princeps senatus*, the first senator to be called upon to speak, normally a patrician. This Scaurus, consul 115 BC, was of a patrician family which had fallen on evil times; his father was a dealer in charcoal.

Chaeronea: the battle was fought in 86 BC.

Ancus Marcius: it was in fact Servius Tullius who was supposed to have built the first temple to Fortune. Several of Plutarch's 'facts' in this paragraph are questionable.

319 *Rumour and Report*: Aius Locutius, the personification of the supernatural voice which announced the coming of the invading Gauls (391 BC). The warning was neglected, and disaster followed. The altar was at the north corner of the Palatine.

'Fortis': Plutarch misunderstands *Fors* ('Chance').

He had sailed out of Brindisi: see Plutarch, *Caesar* 38.

fifty-four years: Augustus died in AD 14, so that this indicates a beginning date of 40 BC, for which there seems no clear reason. We should perhaps read 'forty-four', dating the reign from soon after Actium.

his grandson: Gaius Caesar, sent to the east in AD 2.

320 *Heracles . . . in a long night*: Zeus prolonged the night when he slept with Alcmena and begot Heracles.

Nonae Capratinae: 7 July.

Ruminalis: one Ficus Ruminalis is said to have existed in Augustan times, at the south-west corner of the Palatine; another one (allegedly transplanted from its original site) was in the *comitium*.

321 *the fabled halcyons' brood*: the halcyon is a mythical bird, supposed to build its nest on the sea in midwinter, when the sea was miraculously calm for fourteen days.

made all Italy rise in arms: this refers to the war against the rebellious Italian allies (the Social War) of 90–89 BC, in which Papius Mutilus, Pompaedius Silo, and Telesinus were Samnite leaders.

322 *forty-three years*: Numa's reign, traditionally dated 715–673 BC.

Double Gate of Janus: the closing of the double gate (Janus Geminus) in the Forum symbolized peace. It was a rare event, supposed to have happened in 235 or 241 BC (after the First Punic War), and not again till Augustus closed it in 29 BC and again in 25 BC, after the Cantabrian campaign to which Plutarch refers.

Servius Tullius: before this sentence, the manuscripts give a passage which we have omitted; it is a briefer version of an earlier section (318).

Fortuna Obsequens: Fortuna, the power that brings (*fero*, I bring) good and evil, plenty and dearth, is an ancient Italian divinity, naturally identified with Greek *Tychē* ('Chance'). She had many titles in Rome, on some of which ('Primigenia', 'Auceps', 'Redux', 'Virilis') Plutarch comments.

323 *a Hero of the Household*: Plutarch uses the Greek word *hērōs* to express the Latin *lar familiaris*.

324 *one man in one campaign*: Pompey, 67–65 BC.

325 *a ceremonial procession*: according to Pliny (*Nat. Hist.* 29. 14) dogs paid the penalty annually for their failure by 'being fastened alive by the shoulder in a fork of alder wood, between the temple of Youth and that of Summanus'. Sacrifice of dogs was not uncommon in Roman religion. The honour to the geese is similarly described in other texts (e.g. Aelian, *Nat. An.* 12. 33).

326 *Alexander the Molossian*: in 330 BC.

Dionysus and Heracles: Dionysus was believed to have led an army to India, Heracles went to the far west.

VII. Rules for Politicians

798 *This passage*: these are the words of Nestor to Diomedes, approving his counsel, but adding to it from his own longer experience.

799 *The Athenians, for example*: cf. the speech of the Corinthians in Thucydides (1. 68–71), which is the earliest of these generalizations about 'national' characteristics. Plutarch is thinking of the change of heart towards Mitylene in 428 BC., and of the rise of vulgar demagogues (Cleon, Cleophon), as portrayed in Thucydides or in comedy.

If Cleon had asked them . . . If Alcibiades . . . speaking: see the stories in Plutarch, *Nicias* 7, *Alcibiades* 10.

Philip's couriers: the occasion is not known.

800 *You have heard how Themistocles*: *Themistocles* 3.

Miltiades' trophy: i.e. his victory at Marathon.

Pericles actually made a change in his appearance: *Pericles* 5, 7.

I hardly need mention Alcibiades!: Plutarch's *Alcibiades* is largely devoted to illustrating the diverse and contradictory features of its hero's character.

scratch his head with one finger: this was supposed to be a sign of a pervert. Cf. VIII. 89 (see below).

801 *He ought not to be like Iphicrates*: this refers to the prosecution of Iphicrates for allegedly refusing to engage in a sea-battle in 356 BC.

802 *the speech with which he tried to deter the people*: Plutarch has in mind the speech of Nicias in Thucydides (6. 9–14), and the acknowledgement (6. 19. 2) that it was ineffective.

'*smell of the lamp*': i.e. betray the hours of study by lamplight which had gone into its composition.

803 '*Do not put out one of the eyes of Greece!*': the two eyes are Athens and Sparta, and the author of this metaphor is Leptines, speaking on behalf of the Spartans when they sent an embassy to Athens in 369 BC., at the time of the Theban hegemony.

'*the shipwreck of the city*': Demades thus defended his subservience to Macedon by the weakness and helplessness of Athens.

the rock of Tantalus: Archilochus, it seems, gave Tantalus in Hades the punishment of an overhanging rock that threatened to fall. See Pausanias 10. 31.

'*the eyesore*': i.e. Aegina, visible from the Attic coast, and thus a reproach to Athenian ambitions. It was made tributary in 459 BC.

Ephorus and Theopompus: both these influential historians were pupils of Isocrates, the master of the polished style; Plutarch criticizes the unreality of the exhortations they put into the mouths of generals before battle.

Aristotle's friend Euxitheus: this reference is obscure. Euxitheus may be a character in a (lost) dialogue of Aristotle.

'*Athena and the pig*': *sus Minervam*, the stupid animal that tries to teach the goddess of wisdom, i.e. the fool who teaches his grandmother to suck eggs.

Xenaenetus: unknown.

804 *Leon of Byzantium*: in another version of this story (Philostratus, *Lives of the Sophists* 1. 2), Leon says he is fat, and his wife even fatter, and yet one bed holds them both in harmony.

the sprinter Ladas: there were two famous runners so called, one Achaean, one Spartan or Argive. This *bon mot* is used in an epigram on another sprinter, *Anthologia Palatina* 11. 86.

against the provisions of the law: in 147 BC.

805 *Alcmaeon*: in *Themistocles* 23 Plutarch gives a different account of the proceedings against Themistocles.

806 *quaestor under Marius in Libya*: i.e. in the Jugurthan War.

the wren in Aesop: this fable is not known from other sources, though there is a rather similar one in 'Aesop', in which a rat on an eagle's back sees better than the eagle and so avoids falling into a trap. See *Babrius and Phaedrus*, ed. B. E. Perry (Loeb Classical Library, London, 1965), 558. The passenger must have been a bird, since it flies ahead: *basiliskos*, the Greek word, may mean 'wren' or 'jay' as well as 'basilisk'.

808 *choose a friend, as Diomedes did*: the reference is to the episode related in *Iliad* 10, where Odysseus and Diomedes go out as spies behind the enemy lines.

Themistocles, after the battle: the battle of Salamis, 480 BC.

810 *Appius, contesting an election*: Appius lost the election for the censorship in 142 BC to the younger Scipio (son of L. Aemilius Paullus), but was elected in 136 BC.

Epaminondas' retort: Epaminondas turns against the Athenians two episodes in mythical history in which they took pride: their granting asylum to Oedipus (see Sophocles' *Oedipus at Colonus*), and their providing the court of the Areopagus which acquitted Orestes (see Aeschylus' *Eumenides*).

812 *like Cleon . . . Philopoemen . . . Hannibal . . . fails*: Cleon did have some success as a general, and died in action at Amphipolis (422 BC). Philopoemen was unsuccessful at sea (193/2 BC: see Plutarch's *Philopoemen* 14) Hannibal's poor oratory does not seem to be otherwise attested; he had some repute as a man of letters.

813 *to the sophists*: 'sophists' here means 'teachers of rhetoric', who performed practice speeches like those which Iphicrates practised.

Caesar's procurators: though Asia was a senatorial province, the emperor's *procuratores*, who managed his properties, exercised influence and power comparable to, and often in rivalry with, the governor's.

Pholegandrian . . . Sicinetan: the tiny Aegean islands of Pholegandrus and Sicinus are symbols of insignificance.

814 *the vote of amnesty*: the restored democracy of 403 BC granted an amnesty for supporters of the ousted oligarchic regime of the Thirty, though not for criminal acts committed by them.

for producing a tragedy: Phrynichus' play dealt with a recent event which had caused great distress, the fall of Miletus to the Persians after their suppression of the Ionian revolt in 494 BC.

Cassander's founding Thebes: in 316 BC., the Macedonian Cassander rebuilt the city, which had been destroyed by Alexander in 335 BC.

the 'clubbing' at Argos: in 370 BC., a violent internal revolution resulted in the brutal massacre of many prominent citizens by the mob.

Octavian . . . entered Alexandria: in August 30 BC.

the lines of Euripides: in *Phoenissae* 524 ff., the Theban prince Eteocles says: 'for if we *must* do wrong, 'twere best to do so for a tyranny.'

815 *fellow-tribesmen*: the 'tribe' (*phȳlē*) is here a subdivision of the urban population.

Pergamum in Nero's time: in AD 61/2, a freedman of Nero carried off works of art from Pergamum, and the people unwisely tried to stop him. The situations in Rhodes and the Thessaly, mentioned here, are not known.

'*you will not see*' . . . '*sleeping*': a hidden quotation of a familiar line of Homer (*Iliad* 4. 223).

Sthennon: in *Pompeius* 10, where Plutarch tells this story, the man is called Sthennis. He was a demagogue from Himera, and the events happened in the civil war of 82 BC., when Pompey (then aged 24) was clearing up Marius' supporters in Sicily.

816 *Praeneste*: captured by Sulla in Nov. 82 BC.

Scipio . . . Mummius: these were colleagues as censors, 142 BC.

817 *in going to rescue Messene*: in 203 BC (*Philopoemen* 12).

Epaminondas illegally prolonged . . . for four months: in the campaign of 370 BC., when the victory of Leuctra was won.

818 *the Feast of Choes*: this 'feast of flasks' was the second day of the festival of the Anthesteria, in early spring; it was a riotous and drunken occasion.

819 *Phocion . . . to invade Boeotia*: probably in the Lamian War, 322 BC.

Diomedes passed over the brave: in choosing his companions for the spying expedition related in *Iliad* 10, Diomedes passed over Ajax, Menelaus, and Meriones, and chose the 'man of sense', Odysseus.

find it hard to be convincing . . . like Callicratidas: this Spartan commander was unsuccessful in applying for help to the Persians and to Cyrus in the closing years of the Peloponnesian War (Plutarch, *Lysander* 6).

as Nicias chose Lamachus: viz. as a colleague in the expedition to Sicily, 415 BC.

the Argonauts: having left Heracles behind in Mysia, when he had gone to search for the missing boy Hylas, the Argonauts had, in the event, to depend, not on Heracles' strength, but on the charms of the witch Medea.

820 *the Trumpeter or the Doryphorus*: the *Trumpeter* was by Epigonus, a Pergamene sculptor of the 3rd cent. BC., the *Doryphorus* (youth with a spear) by Polyclitus (5th cent.).

If a man sails beyond Syrtis: Syrtis is the name given to the dangerous gulfs on the coast of Tripolitania, between Cyrenaica and what is now Tunisia. The 'crossing' which follows the voyage is presumably the passage over to Sicily, or (if the voyage is in the other direction) the passage to Crete or southern Greece.

Epimenides: was supposed to have purified Athens from the pollution incurred by the murder at the altar of some of the supporters of Cylon, who attempted to seize power in the early 6th cent.

the seven Persians who killed the Magi: this refers to the overthrow of a usurper in 521 BC, after which Darius became king: Herodotus 3. 76 ff.

Publius the Roman: i.e. Horatius Cocles, who 'held the bridge' against the army of Porsena.

recast as chamber-pots: so the statues of Sejanus according to Juvenal 10. 64.

821 *Lysimachus' dog . . . Achilles' horses*: the dog chose to die with his master; the horse Xanthus (*Iliad* 19. 404 ff.) is miraculously gifted with speech and promises to carry Automedon out of the battle, but prophesies death to Achilles himself.

822 *when Hermon sought to avoid office*: Hermon is not known. The four provinces of Thessaly are Thessaliotis, Hestiaeotis, Pelasgiotis, Phthiotis. This may well be an event near Plutarch's own time.

823 '*lovelier than Croesus' pieces of gold*': the Greek phrase is metrical, and this may therefore be a quotation (from a lyric poet).

where Callias or Alcibiades spends the money: this refers to Xenophon's *Symposium* (where Callias is the host) and perhaps to Plato's *Symposium*, though there it is Agathon who gives the dinner. A lost Socratic dialogue is a possible source.

824 *Theramenes' comfortable shoe*: Theramenes, a moderate politician who changed sides but who lost his life through not acquiescing in the extremism of the oligarchic revolution at Athens in 403 BC., was compared to a *cothornos*, a high boot that would fit either foot.

825 *The greatest revolution in the history of Delphi*: date unknown, but referred to by Aristotle, as also is the Syracusan story which follows.

Athena Pronaia: 'Athena Protectress of the Temple'; her shrine is at Marmaria, below the sanctuary and town of Delphi.

VIII. How to Profit from your Enemies

86 *though they say this of Crete*: lists of places from which certain animals were absent are a feature of ancient popular science: e.g. no moles in Boeotia (except at Coronea), no wolves or owls or any dangerous animal in Crete (Antigonus, *Collection of Strange Facts* 10).

87 '*my old cloak*': the cloak (*tribōn*) symbolizes simple living and the philosophical life.

'*how Priam and his children would rejoice!*': these are the words of Nestor to Achilles and Agamemnon when they are quarrelling.

because Carthage . . . and the Achaeans enslaved: the final defeat of Carthage and the destruction of the Achaean League and sack of Corinth happened in the same year, 146 BC.

89 '*the moray you were keeping*': this pet *muraena* was famous. Crassus adorned it with jewels, like a woman, and it would come to eat from his hand (Aelian, *On Animals* 8. 4). Plutarch

tells of it elsewhere (63, 976A); whether it was really a moray or a lamprey seems uncertain. Cf. VII. 811.

The god's injunction 'Know thyself': *Gnōthi seauton, nosce teipsum*: the most famous precept of Apollo at Delphi.

an enemy's spear: Telephus, king of Mysia, was wounded by Achilles, and the wound would not heal 'unless' (as the oracle said) 'the wounder healed it'. Telephus therefore went, as a beggar, to the Greek army, which was assembling at Aulis for the expedition against Troy, and offered to guide them, if Achilles would cure him. A touch of the rust of Achilles' spear healed his wound.

Prometheus of Thessaly: this story (a popular example of 'good coming out of evil') is told elsewhere of Jason of Pherae; 'Prometheus' may just be a nickname for that enterprising ruler.

Postumia's ready laughter: this is a story of early Rome (420 BC.), told also in Livy (4. 44).

91 *Scaurus refused to listen*: Plutarch has this story the wrong way round. It was Scaurus' servant who approached Domitius, and Domitius who sent the man back to his master (Cicero, *Pro rege Deiotaro* 31).

When Cato was prosecuting Murena: in Nov. 63 BC., Murena being defended by the consul Cicero.

IX. Curiosity

515 '*Where did I go wrong . . . done?*': This, according to the Pythagorean poem called 'Golden Verses', is what we should ask ourselves in our daily self-examination.

516 *Odysseus . . . talk to his mother*: in Odysseus' view of the souls in Hades (*Odyssey* 11), he prudently postpones satisfying his curiosity (10. 88) until he has heard Tiresias' counsel about his return home, which is what he had come to hear.

517 '*Thieving*': Klopidai, a mock place-name.

518 *cupping-vessels*: vessels of glass, horn, or bronze, with a narrow neck and a bell-shaped body, used for letting blood: a common medical procedure down to recent times.

the vice of gloating: *epichairekakia*, literally 'taking pleasure in troubles', *Schadenfreude*.

it is their loss if they do not: because they were private contractors, who had bought the contract for collecting the duties as an investment.

519 *the rulers of Locri*: Locri (in southern Italy) was famous for its wise laws, and boasted two famous lawgivers, Zaleucus and Charondas.

the lawgiver of Thurii: this was a Panhellenic colony in Italy (at or near the site of Sybaris), founded under Athenian leadership in 443 BC. It was designed by the town-planner Hippodamus.

520 *headless lines*: hexameters in which the first syllable is short instead of long.

'*Roguestown*': *Ponēropolis*. The story comes from the historian Theopompus, who wrote a colourful history of the age of Philip.

521 *like a badly-trained maidservant*: 'Our senses should not, like petulant and wanton girls, wander into markets and theatres without just employment' (Jeremy Taylor, *Holy Living*, II. ii. 5, 'Of Modesty').

'*the Aenian's hardmouthed horses bolted*': this description of a chariot race comes in Sophocles' *Electra*, as a false tale to persuade Electra of Orestes' death. The chariot crashes into another competitor's, and other collisions follow.

a red-hot mirror: mirrors were made of bronze.

Euphrone: a poetical word for 'night', perhaps meaning 'kindly' (so a euphemism for the evil darkness), rather than what Plutarch here suggests.

522 *It was curiosity that brought Oedipus to utter disaster*: the following passage is a commentary on Sophocles' *Oedipus Tyrannus*.

Once, when I was lecturing in Rome: Arulenus Rusticus was ordered to commit suicide by Domitian in AD 93; but he was a prominent person throughout the Flavian period. This passage therefore tells us that Plutarch was in Rome, lecturing, before 93, but gives no closer date. Jeremy Taylor (*Holy Living* I. i, 'Care of our Time') quotes Plutarch and compares Rusticus with Sir Thomas More, 'who, being sent for by the king when he was at his prayers in public, returned answer, he would attend him, when he had first performed his service to the King of Kings'.

X. Talkativeness

502 *Stoa of Seven Voices*: this was a colonnade on the east side of the Altis at Olympia, rebuilt in the 4th cent. BC.

'*Hermes has come in*': i.e (as we sometimes say when a sudden silence falls) 'an angel has passed by', 'es geht ein Engel durchs Zimmer'.

503 *'shining reins'*: a phrase from Homer (e.g. *Iliad* 5. 226). The word for 'shining', *sigaloenta*, resembles the word *sigē*, 'silence', and Plutarch seems to be playing on this.

504 *wrote a speech for a litigant*: in Athenian courts, litigants had to plead in person, and employed professional speech-writers (*logographoi*) to compose their plea for them. Lysias was particularly famous for writing speeches appropriate to the character and abilities of his client.

Aphrodite's magic belt: the *cestus*, symbolic of love of friendship.

505 *Sulla besieging Athens*: in 87 BC, in the war against Mithridates. 'Other labours pressed upon him' is a quotation from Homer (*Odyssey* 11. 54).

Seven Bronzes: Heptachalcon, a district near the gate leading to Piraeus.

Nero: this seems to refer to the conspiracy of AD 65 (Tacitus *Annals* 15. 53), but Plutarch's account is different. He had himself written a 'Life of Nero', in a collection of Lives of the Caesars (lost, apart from 'Galba' and 'Otho').

The philosopher Zeno: this is Zeno of Elea, not Zeno the Stoic.

Leaena: the name means 'lioness'. The reference is to the murder of Hipparchus, 514 BC.

506 *the king of Egypt*: Amasis (569–*c*. 525 BC).

Eumenes . . . giving them warning: see Plutarch's *Eumenes* 6–7.

507 *As the Monad . . . diversity*: cf. *Oracles in Decline*, II. 428–9 above. Here Plutarch seems to play on the word *monas*, 'unit', and relate it to the root of *meno*, 'I remain'.

The Roman husband: a version of this story, naming the senator as Papirius Praetextatus, is given by Aulus Gellius (1. 23) as coming from a speech by Cato.

508 *Augustus' friend Fabius*: the manuscripts have Publius or Fulvius, but it is pretty certain that Fabius Maximus is meant. Augustus, having lost his favourite grandsons, Gaius and Lucius, and banished his other grandson, Agrippa Postumus, reluctantly turned to his stepson, Tiberius, as the only possible successor. However, accompanied by Fabius, he visited the exiled Agrippa Postumus (Tacitus, *Annals* 1. 5). Fabius, on his return, reported the emperor's tears and distress to his wife. Tacitus adds that Fabius died soon after, 'perhaps by his own hand'.

508 *Needlefish*: the eggs of the needlefish or pipefish are deposited in a pouch under the belly of the male, and it is this which bursts and disperses the young. The idea that the viper's young gnaw through the mother's belly to get out was a piece of popular natural history from which it was easy to draw morals.

509 *Athenian disaster in Sicily*: 413 BC. The following quotation is from *Iliad* 23. 207.

Athena of the Bronze Shrine: the temple of Athena Chalcioecus was on the Acropolis of Sparta. It was here that Pausanias took refuge (Thucydides 1. 128).

the murderers of Ibycus: the poet Ibycus was said to have been murdered at Corinth, having predicted to his murderers that cranes would avenge him.

510 *geese . . . by night*: see *Intelligence of Animals* (63), 10.

Euthycrates: a slip for Lasthenes.

511 '*Dionysius at Corinth*': i.e. he is an exile, fallen from his high estate as monarch of Syracuse, and the same may happen to you.

512 *Theaetetus and Charmides*: young men who figure in the Platonic dialogues that bear their names.

the proverb about 'asking for buckets': 'They asked for buckets, and the others refused them tubs.' This was said 'of people who are asked for one thing, and reply that they haven't got something else.'

513 *Antimachus of Colophon*: author of an epic on the Theban legend, and other poems. Plato is said to have admired him, but many later critics regarded him as boring and long-winded.

the eighth book of Thucydides: the last book of Thucydides' history contains the narrative of events from the arrival in Athens of the disastrous news from Sicily (413 BC) to the victory of the Athenians at Cynossema in 411.

514 *the boy Cyrus*: in Xenophon's *Cyropaedia*, 1. 4. 4.

Ephorus: Ephorus' general history of Greece went down to the fall of Perinthus (341/0 BC). The events of the Theban hegemony (371–363 BC), so dear to Plutarch's friend, probably figured in Books 22–5.

writing or private discussion: Jeremy Taylor (*Eniautos*: *Twenty-five Sermons*, xxiii) enlarges on this: 'Plutarch advises that such men should give themselves to writing, that making an issue in the arm it should drain the floods of the head.'

XI. Bashfulness

528 *'had whores . . . not pupils'*: the Greek for 'pupil' (*kore*) is the word for 'girl', so that the point made is a play on the word.

529 *next there appeared*: this is from a parody of Homer's underworld (*Odyssey* 9) by Timon of Phlius, in which philosophers appear in various monstrous guises, like the monsters and sinners of Hades.

a premature love of money: avarice is a natural failing in the old, perverse in the young.

530 *the penitent adulteress*: who? we do not know what Sophoclean play this comes from.

the case of Antipater: this seems to be a mistake for Antipater's brother Alexander (Plutarch, *Demetrius* 36).

531 *'Violence and Necessity'*: Antigonus puns on the name of Bion, which suggests *bia*, 'violence'.

534 *Athena Polias*: her temple was the Parthenon, and the sacrifices had to be brought up to the Acropolis.

What young Cato did to Catulus: as quaestor, 64 BC.

a clash between vowel and vowel: Plutarch is thinking of Isocrates and his followers; but in his own writing he avoids clashes of vowels (hiatus) quite carefully. See Introduction, p. xvi.

XII. Against Borrowing Money

827 *from your own table*: *trapeza*, 'table', also means 'bank', and so there is a play on the word.

828 *Colias or Tenedos*: Colias is a promontory of Attica, Tenedos an island in the northern Aegean, both famous for pottery.

'so that . . . we can restore no less afterwards': this is how Pericles explained his action in having the ornaments made detachable, Thucydides 2. 13.

the women of Rome: this is supposed to have happened in 394 BC (Plutarch, *Camillus* 6).

'wait not for the horses to ride': a quotation from the oracle given to the Athenians at the time of the Persian invasion of 480 BC (Herodotus 7. 141).

not asking for earth and water: these were the symbols of submission demanded of the Scythians by Darius (Herodotus 4. 126).

829 *interest is created*: the Greek *tokos* means both 'interest' and 'birth', so that there is again a play on two senses.

the Persians: Plutarch misquotes Herodotus 1. 138, who says that the Persian thought lying the worst thing, and indebtedness second worst.

830 '*And Micylus I saw*': a parody of Odysseus' vision of the sinners in Hades (*Odyssey* 11. 582, 593).

832 *waiting for Arcturus to rise*: i.e. waiting for the rising of Arcturus, the traditional beginning of autumn, and so vintage time.

XIII. Eroticus

748 *the shrine of the Muses*: in the upper valley of the Permessus, once well-wooded, now largely bare.

749 *Plato's Ilissus*: the reference is to the opening scene of Plato's *Phaedrus*, in which Socrates and his friend sit down by the stream, in a beautiful spot just outside Athens, to listen to the reading and discuss it.

The Mother of the Muses: Mnemosyne (Memory).

750 *as bastards do to Cynosarges*: Cynosarges was a gymnasium at Athens dedicated to Heracles, which was open to illegitimate sons or sons of foreign mothers.

'*rub down*': i.e. take part in gymnastic exercises.

752 *raises its eyebrows*: a gesture of superciliousness or disdain, not surprise or shock.

as in Ethiopia: this refers to the description of the country in Herodotus 3.23.

753 *like cultivating figs or dates*: the text is defective here, and the exact sense uncertain. But Plutarch presumably refers 1. to 'caprification', the practice of attaching a wild fig to an edible fig, so that the gall-insects can pollinate the flowers; 2. to the need to have male palms in close proximity to female palms, or the practice of grafting one on the other.

scattering the nuts: nuts, figs etc. were showered over the newly married, like rice or confetti today.

the woman who shares the shrine of Eros: Phryne (see III. 401). Her lover Praxiteles made statues of her for Delphi and for Thespiae.

754 *Munychia*: a fort at Piraeus, garrisoned by the Macedonians under Antigonus Gonatas.

the nurse rules the child . . . the general the grown man: no age of life is without control of authority. The *ephēbi* are young men of 18–20 undergoing military training or (in post-classical Greece) a period of organized physical and musical education under the discipline of a magistrate (here the gymnasiarchs).

As Boeotians . . . we ought to respect Heracles: Heracles was born at Thebes, though his cult was widespread, and indeed strongest in the Peloponnese.

he was freshly anointed: after his exercise (and ?bath) he would anoint himself again with olive oil.

chlamys and cloak: the chlamys was a light garment, worn as a cape or scarf, probably of bright colours; Bacchon also wears a dibolia, apparently a warmer cloak. The himation, which they put on him, is the regular formal outdoor dress of the grown man.

755 *Independence is proving the road to anarchy*: this may refer to the liberty granted to the Greek cities by Nero and withdrawn by Vespasian, but more probably to the special status of Thespiae as a *civitas libera*.

Lemnos is nothing to this: Lemnos was the scene of the murder of their husbands, the sons of Aegyptus, by the fifty daughters of Danaus, acting on their father's orders; only Hypermnestra disobeyed, and spared her husband, Lynceus.

a physical disease that is called 'sacred': this is epilepsy.

756 *through the agency of hermaphrodites and women*: the priests of Attis were castrated, the worship of Adonis was largely a cult for women, and these were two of the most prominent cults of oriental origin which spread over the Greek world in Hellenistic and Roman times.

'*I go not far away*': as this is a somewhat unexpected way of saying 'I shall stick to my subject', and as the Greek words form part of an iambic line, I suspect this is a quotation from tragedy or (less likely) comedy.

757 *Cypris*: a title of Aphrodite, from her cult in Cyprus.

on a bronze model: by *pinax*, 'tablet', Plutarch seems to mean some kind of plan or diagram or model made in bronze, in which the positions of the things represented are significant: cf. the *pinax* brought by Aristagoras to Sparta (Herodotus 5. 49) on which lands and seas and rivers were marked.

Enualios . . . Stratios: Enualios was perhaps originally a distinct war-god; Stratios is a 'god of armies'.

Agrotera: a title of Artemis.

758 *Ilithyia and Locheia*: Ilithyia is a goddess of childbirth, identifiable with Artemis; Locheia is a title of Artemis, as goddess of the delivery of children.

the god who says: Death, who, like sleep, was the child of Night.

Plato's words may well latch on to our argument: interpretation unsure, but the reference is clearly to *Phaedrus* 244 ff., Plato's discussion of the 'kinds of madness'.

760 *the famous Roman Gabba*: celebrated for his wit or fooling at the court of Augustus. The basic story here is, however, older: the satirist Lucilius (*c.* 180–102 BC) wrote of a complaisant husband whom he called Pararrhenchon ('snorer on the side'), and *non omnibus dormio* became proverbial.

the brother of Proteas: Proteas was a boon-companion of Alexander, son of his nurse Lanice.

at the height of the Thessalian war: this is the so-called 'Lelantine' war, between the Euboean cities of Chalces and Eretria and their respective allies in the 7th cent. BC; it led to a long conflict involving many cities. (The text is uncertain hereabouts.)

761 *Aristotle*: probably not the philosopher, but a historian of the same name, from Chalcis.

Aitia: i.e. a collection of stories explaining customs or origins by mythological or historical events. Callimachus' *Aitia* is the best-known poetical example. Plutarch's treatises on Greek and Roman antiquarian problems (18) are also called *Aitia*. Little is known of this Dionysius, not even when he lived.

Heracles . . . his medical skill: this is a rationalization of the legend told in Euripides' *Alcestis*, where Heracles wrestles with Death to save Alcestis.

762 *my family feud with Anytus*: Zeuxippus regards himself, as a philosopher, as one of 'Socrates' family', and so has a feud with Socrates' principal accuser.

Telemachus' words: in *Odyssey* 19. 29 ff., Odysseus and Telemachus are guided by Athena when they go to collect arms from the store. The building is lit miraculously 'as though with burning fire'.

763 *beautiful Sappho*: this refers to a very famous poem, preserved (incompletely) in Longinus, *On the Sublime* 10 (*Classical*

Literary Criticism, (World's Classics; Oxford, 1989)), p. 154, and imitated by Catullus (51).

They do not admit Strife or Prayers . . . Ares: this alludes to allegories found in Hesiod (*Works and Days* 11 ff.) and Homer (*Iliad* 9. 502 ff.; 13. 29; 15. 119).

765 *an oscillation that generates sperm*: this, and what follows, is Epicurean language: cf. Lucretius 4. 1041 ff.

766 *like the nightmarish fantasies*: Plutarch adapts for his own purposes a passage of Plato (*Phaedo* 81D) which describes 'shadowy images' of souls not wholly freed from bodily corruption as haunting tombs and graves.

Euxynthetus and Leucocomas: this story comes from what seems to have been a well-known book of Theophrastus *On Love*. Leucocomas imposed on his lover Euxynthetus the task of bringing back 'the dog of Prasus'; in another version, Leucocomas commits suicide because his rejected lover consoles himself with another young man.

what happened to the Peeper: the story of the woman who 'leans out of the window' to watch her rejected lover's funeral is told of an Arsinoe by the poet Hermesianax, and of an Anaxarete by Ovid (*Metamorphoses* 14. 698). It is clearly an explanatory myth (*aition*) to account for a mysterious stone.

767 *Podargus . . . Aithe*: 'Swift-foot' and 'Bay', names of horses in *Iliad* 23. 295. Aithe is a mare.

'the bloom of virtue': a definition given by the Stoic Chrysippus in his work *On Love* (Diogenes Laertius 7. 129).

behave like cicadas: cf. Plato, *Symposium* 191C. Plutarch, like Plato, seems to confuse the cicada with the grasshopper, and the ovipositor with a male organ. Such is popular natural history.

"mine" and "not mine": for Plato, the best city is one in which the greatest number of people say 'mine' and 'not mine' of the same things, i.e. have most interests in common.

and the two seas fought over her: Lais was from Corinth, which is on the isthmus between two seas.

768 *You people who are Eros' neighbours*: i.e. the people of Thespiae.

Camma: see below (XVI, 257) for a somewhat differently told version of this story.

"Hybris does this, not Cypris": *hybris* is aggression or assault; the word translated 'assault' just above, *epipēdēsis*, means literally 'jumping on' or 'mounting' the victim.

769 *What scientists call "total integration"*: *krāsis di' holōn* is a phrase used especially in Stoic physics of the complete interpenetration of two substances. Cf. XIV. 142.

770 *"earth is in love with rain", and heaven with earth*: Euripides (in an unknown play) gave the classical exposition of this idea (fr. 898):

Do you not see how great is Aphrodite?
Her greatness and her power cannot be spoken
nor measured; me, and you, and all mankind
she nurtures. You want proof? No need of words,
I'll show the goddess' power by what she does.
When the proud heaven fills with rain, it craves
to fall on earth; that's Aphrodite's doing.
And when the two are joined, they bear and nurture
all things by which man lives and flourishes.

"Harmodius and Aristogeiton": the assassins of Pisistratus' son Hipparchus (514 BC), and so archetypal 'tyrannicides'.

Civilis, the man who raised the rebellion in Gaul: AD 70; see Tacitus *Histories* 4. 67.

771 *here with us in Delphi only the other day*: as this event must be at the earliest in the 90s (the young man must be grown up), and Plutarch's marriage was clearly earlier, this is an anachronism, as is the subsequent allusion to the destruction of the Flavian dynasty with Domitian's murder in AD 96. Neither Plato nor Plutarch avoids such anachronisms in dialogues.

XIV. Advice on Marriage

138 *words*: by *logos* here, Plutarch means rational, philosophical discourse as opposed to the solemn injunctions of the ritual.

"The Rampant Stallion": there are several references in ancient literature to a 'wedding-song' performed to encourage horses to mate (e.g. Aelian, *On the Nature of Animals*, 12. 44).

asparagus: this is *asparagus acutifolius*, not our cultivated form; it has a black fruit.

jointed articles: Jeremy Taylor ('The Marriage Ring', *Eniautos: Twenty-five Sermons*, xvii) gives a clearer image: 'Plutarch compares a new marriage to a vessel before the hoops are on.'

141 *The Roman who was reproached by his friends*: see Plutarch, *Aemilius Paullus* 5.

nor yet with the fingers: there were conventional ways of counting on the fingers which made it possible to calculate large numbers, so that this is a natural way of speaking of 'marrying for money'.

the tyrant of Sicily: Dionysius I.

what adorns a woman is what makes her better ordered: *kosmos* means both 'order' and 'adornment', and Plutarch plays on the range of meaning.

142 *Phidias' statue of Aphrodite*: this was Aphrodite Ourania, 'Heavenly Aphrodite', in gold and ivory, in the city of Elis.

143 *The Roman lawgiver*: Ulpian (*Digest* 24. 1–2) writes that is customary that gifts between man and wife shall have no validity, and that the emperor Antoninus explained the rationale of this provision on the ground that 'our ancestors judged honourable love solely by feeling, and also took thought for the reputation of the parties', so that they should not be thought to have made a mercenary contract.

Cyrus' Greek troops: i.e. the Greek forces who formed part of the army of Cyrus the younger in 401 BC, in his attempt to win the crown of Persia: Xenophon's *Anabasis* (1. 7. 4, 1. 8. 11) is Plutarch's source.

ran into a mill: mills were places for penal hard labour, so that the master has a point in saying that he expects to find the bad slave there.

a speech at Olympia: date uncertain, probably 392 BC.

bees . . . are believed to become angry . . . woman: this is a widespread belief, cf. Keith Thomas, *Man and the Natural World* (London, 1983), 98.

145 *Timoxena*: Plutarch's wife, here apparently an author in her own right.

XV. A Consolation to His Wife

608 *my niece*: the word translated (*thugatridē*) often means 'granddaughter', but may also mean 'niece' or 'daughter-in-law', and the probability is that it is one of these here, since there is unlikely to be a grown-up grandchild when Plutarch's wife has had an infant daughter two or three years ago. Tanagra lies on a route which Plutarch could reasonably take from Athens to Chaeronea.

'no child of oak or rock': this proverbial phrase is found in Homer (*Odyssey* 19. 162), though in a slightly different sense.

609 *Aesop*: this fable is also found in the pseudo-Plutarchan 'Consolation to Apollonius' (10), and is clearly a commonplace of consolatory literature.

610 *the 'entrance of bad women'*: in Euripides' *Andromache*, where this phrase comes from, the reference is to malicious gossip; here the danger is rather moral weakness and indulgence in grief or superstitious cult. Cf. XIV, 143 above.

611 *'headless' . . . lines*: cf. IX. 520

others say . . . dissolution: the Epicureans are meant.

XVI. Virtues in Women

242 *the Roman custom*: *laudationes* of women, as well as men, of good family were a feature of Roman life which attracted the notice of Greek observers (cf. Polybius 6. 52). They fostered family pride, and, though not necessarily of high rhetorical quality, were carefully preserved. Two *laudationes* of women survive as inscriptions.

243 *works of a great craft*: cf. IV. 575.

Irene did not show her love: there is no convincing identification of this Irene.

Rhome: the name means 'strength' in Greek, a point often made by Greek eulogists of Rome. This story of the burning of the ships is best known from Virgil (*Aeneid* 5), though there it is set in Sicily, and the moving spirit is the goddess Iris in the guise of a Trojan matron. See also Plutarch's *Romulus* 1.

244 *Elaphebolia*: 'Stag-Shooting', a festival held in many places in honour of Artemis as huntress.

indications of divine anger: perhaps a plague or crop failure, which made the Chians consult 'the god', no doubt Apollo at one of his oracles. The date of these events is unknown; it is clearly in the archaic period.

245 *when Philip . . . was besieging the city*: Philip V of Macedon besieged Chios in 202/1 BC.

when king Cleomenes . . . in battle: the battle of Sepeia, *c.* 494 BC.

Pamphyliacum: Pamphyloi was the name of one of the three tribes in which many Dorian communities were organized (the others were Hylleis and Dymanes), and this building or area is presumably the centre of this tribe in Argos.

246 *fled into the city*: Persepolis.

Ochus: Artaxerxes III (359–338 BC).

the area of Italy they now occupy: Gallia Cisalpina, the Po valley and some areas to the south.

in their treaty with Hannibal: on his march from Spain into Italy in 218 BC, Hannibal met the Gaulish chieftains in what is now Roussillon, and negotiated with them to ensure his safe passage.

247 *The Women of Lycia*: This curious chapter consists of various rationalizing versions of the story of Bellerophon's killing of the monster Chimaera, at the bidding of Iobates, king of Lycia. The Chimaera (*Iliad* 6. 181) was 'lion in front, snake behind, wild goat [*chimaira*] in the middle'. For the setting of the story, see G. E. Bean, *Turkey's Southern Shore* (London, 1979), 94.

249 *the so-called Sacred War*: the Phocians under Philomelus seized Delphi in 356 BC. The following year, the Amphictyonic Council declared a 'sacred war' against the occupation, but Philomelus, using the temple treasures, raised a large mercenary army, and captured Amphissa in 354 or 353 BC. The war dragged on till 346.

Thyiades: Clea, the addressee of this book, was the leader of just such a group of votaries at Delphi.

250 *Valeria and Cloelia*: see Plutarch, *Publicola* 19, Livy 2. 9–14.

Micca and Megisto: these events took place around 271 BC.

251 *Lucius by name*: the name suggests he was an Italian mercenary, perhaps Lucanian.

253 *Pieria*: This story (a version of which was told by the poet Callimachus) seems to have been developed in the form in which Plutarch gives in order to support Milesian claims to the small, independent city of Myus. In any case, it is designed to explain an old custom.

the sons of Neileus: descendants of the founder of Miletus, who was said to be a son of Codrus, king of Athens.

Naxos and Miletus went to war: this war belongs to an early period, 7th or 6th cent. BC.

255 *the Leucadian Rocks*: the proverbial setting for the leap of a disappointed lover into the sea. It is the promontory of Leucas, in the far west of Greece. Some said that Sappho was the first to jump over the cliff here; tradition gave many other names. See Ovid, *Heroides* 15. 171.

heroic honours . . . as a goddess: worship as a hero or heroine is essentially worship of the dead, and the cult is connected with a known grave. As a goddess, Lampsace received different forms of sacrifice, altar, and worship.

the age of Mithridates: the date is probably between 96 and 86 BC.

any of the heroines: Plutarch uses the word *herois* here, but not in any theological sense. He merely means a 'great woman' of the past.

256 *he was a fratricide, but no tyrannicide*: the point is that a true tyrannicide is a liberator, not just the man who kills the tyrant and then takes his place.

257 *Camma*: These events belong to the early 1st cent. BC. Tennyson's 'The Cup' is a dramatic version of this story, which Plutarch tells also in 'Eroticus' (XIII, 768).

priestess of Artemis: Artemis here is the Asiatic goddess Ma. The Galatians, who were Celtic invaders, had taken over the cults of the earlier inhabitants.

258 *it was a honey drink*: *melikrāton*, milk and honey, or honey and water.

wife of Deiotarus: Stratonice's husband was Deiotarus II Philopator, co-regent with his father (who died in 39 BC). Despite these efforts, he left no heir to succeed to the kingdom.

the Romans under Gnaeus: we go back to an earlier period of Galatian history. Gn. Manlius Vulso defeated the Galatians in 189 BC. This story is told in Livy (38. 24), though he calls the husband Orgiagon and does not name Chiomara. Polybius, whom Plutarch quotes, may have met Chiomara much later, when she was a captive.

259 *The Woman of Pergamum*: These events happened in 80 BC, when Mithridates apparently sought to eliminate the Galatian nobility, for fear they should go over to Rome. The names are uncertain: 'Tosiopi' may be a mistake (of Plutarch or a scribe) for Tolistobogii or Tectosagi, both known names of Galatian tribes. Eporedorix, a known Gaulish name, is a probable correction for Poredorax, the form given in the manuscripts—though, once again, the mistake may be Plutarch's.

fell at Chaeronea: 338 BC. This story is told by Plutarch in *Alexander* 12. In 335 BC, when Alexander razed the city, he sold the population into slavery, and apportioned the territory among its neighbours. Stories like the present one are meant to do something to save his reputation for humanity.

260 *Eryxo*: this story is set in the time of Arcesilaus II of Cyrene in the 6th cent. BC.

sea-hare: a kind of sea-slug (perhaps *Aphysia depilans*), producing a supposedly poisonous secretion, said to kill in 'as many days as the sea-hare has lived'.

261 *korōnistai*: this word elsewhere means men or children begging 'for the crow' or singing the 'crow song', a kind of ritualized begging with menaces, like 'a penny for the guy'. So Plutarch's point about the long hair is not clear.

262 *Pythes' wife*: see Herodotus 7. 27 ff.

XVII. Gryllus

985 *that mortal wife*: Penelope.

986 *By Hecate*: a very suitable oath for the sorceress Circe.

King of the Cephallenians: Cephallenia was part of Odysseus' kingdom.

Cyclopes: *Odyssey* 9. 106 ff.

987 *Ithaca*: *Odyssey* 4. 606, 9.21 ff.

the wild sow of Crommyon: on his way from Troezen to Athens, the young Theseus encountered various perils, among them this sow, offspring of Typhon and Echidna, which he killed with the sword. Plutarch elsewhere (*Theseus* 9) makes it a 'sideshow' for Theseus.

988 *the Teumessian vixen*: this monster was hunted by Amphitryon, and turned to stone.

your king: Agamemnon (*Iliad* 23. 295 ff.) accepted the horse Aithe from Echepolus, the rich ruler of Sicyon, (whose name means 'colt-owner'), in exchange for excusing him from service in the expedition against Troy.

And she is a Spartan!: Penelope was the daughter of Icarius, and thus niece of Tyndareus and Leda, and cousin of Helen and Clytemnestra.

Caria or Maeonia: these Asiatic countries were traditionally associated with a softer, less aggressive, and less virile culture.

anger is . . . the way to temper or hone the edge of courage: *thumos* is the quality of the 'spirited' part of the soul in Plato's psychology. It implies aggressiveness or being 'keyed up' for the fight.

989 *the he-goat of Mendes*: it was the common Greek belief (e.g. Herodotus 2. 46) that this goat (or ram), which was the incarnation of Osiris in the Egyptian religion, copulated openly with women. Plutarch's version saves his reputation.

far away . . . from the sea of vain desires: this alludes to the idea (found, e.g. in Plato's *Laws*, where the ideal city is to be sited a safe distance from the sea) that proximity to the sea leads to a society corrupted by bad customs brought in from outside.

I remember seeing you in Crete: this refers to the false story told by Odysseus in disguise (*Odyssey* 19. 177 ff.), where the grand cloak and gold clasp (representing a dog seizing a fawn) are carefully described. In making Gryllus be witness to a fiction, Plutarch perhaps intended to stress the fantasy of his imagined dialogue.

990 *malobathrum*: tamala leaf, an Indian spice, used as unguent or medicine.

the Arabian reed: many perfumes came from Arabia; this may be 'sweet flag' (*Acorus calamus*).

Heracles . . . pursued a beardless friend: Hylas, son of Theodamas, king of Dryopes. Heracles had captured him, and took him with him on the voyage of the Argo, but he disappeared in Mysia, drawn down into the water of a spring by nymphs who admired his beauty. Heracles looked for him in vain, and was left behind when the ship sailed on.

991 *Aegipans*: 'goat Pans', supposed to live in Africa.

992 *that Corinthian Homer*: though 'seven cities' claimed to be Homer's birthplace, Corinth is not one of them. The person meant is, presumably, a simpleton, to make a contrast with Autolycus, who 'excelled in theft and perjury'. The point of the joke is therefore uncertain, although it is possible that Gryllus means to ridicule Homer by saying that he comes from a city renowned chiefly for immorality. Haupt conjectured 'that fool Coruebus'—a proverbially stupid fellow—but it is difficult to account for the corruption which this assumes.

Sisyphus: was supposed to be an atheist.

SOURCES OF QUOTATIONS

This list is intended to be used in conjunction with the Notes. References to fragments are to standard collections, not necessarily the most recent. The following list explains the abbreviations used.

von Blumenthal	A. von Blumenthal, *Ion von Chios* (Stuttgart, Berlin, 1939)
CAF	T. Kock, *Comicorum Atticorum fragmenta* (Leipzig, 1880–8)
Decleva Caizzi	F. Decleva Caizzi, *Antisthenis fragmenta* (Milan, 1966)
Diehl	E. Diehl, *Anthologia lyrica Graeca* (Leipzig, 1925–52)
F Gr Hist	F. Jacoby, Fragmente der griechischen Historiker, Leiden, 1926–1958
Kaibel	G. Kaibel, *Comicorum Graecorum fragmenta* (Berlin, 1899)
Kern	O. Kern, *Orphicorum fragmenta* (Berlin, 1922)
Kindstrand	J. F. Kindstrand, *Bion of Borysthenes* (Uppsala, 1976)
Lobel–Page	E. Lobel and D. Page, *Poetarum Lesbiorum fragmenta* (Oxford, 1955)
Merkelback–West	R. Merkelbach and M. L. West, *Fragmenta Hesiodea* (Oxford, 1967)
PMG	D. L. Page, *Poetae Melici Graeci* (Oxford, 1962)
Sandbach	Plutarchus, *Moralia VII*, ed. F. H. Sandbach (Leipzig, 1967)
Schneider	O. Schneider, *Callimachea* (Berlin, 1873)
Snell	B. Snell, *Pindari fragmenta* (Leipzig, 1962)
SH	H. Lloyd-Jones and P. J. Parsons, *Supplementum Hellenisticum* (Berlin, 1983)
SVF	H. von Arnim, *Stoicorum Veterum fragmenta* (Leipzig, 1903–24)
TGF	A. Nauck, *Tragicorum Graecorum fragmenta*, 2nd edn. (Leipzig, 1889)
VS	H. Diels and W. Kranz, *Fragmenta der Vorsokratiker*, 6th edn. (Berlin, 1951–2)
Wehrli	F. Wehrli, *Die Schule des Aristoteles* (Basel, 1944–53)

West — M. L. West, *Iambi et elegi Graeci* (Oxford, 1971–2)

Many of Plutarch's quotations are otherwise unknown, and many cannot be assigned to particular authors or works. The references in this list are to the *marginal* page-numbers of our text, in which the relevant places are indicated by [1], [2], [3], etc.

Superstition

165 1. *TGF* adespota 374
 2. Euripides *Orestes* 211
166 1. *TGF* adespota 375
 2. Euripides *Troades* 764
 3. *CAF* adespota 150
 4. Heraclitus B 89 (*VS*)
 5. *TGF* adespota 376
167 1. Pindar *Pyth.* 1.25
 2. Pindar fr. 143 Snell
168 1. *Carmen aureum* 42
 2. Bion F 30 Kindstrand
169 1. Archilochus fr. 105 West
 2. *TGF* adespota 377
 3. Hesiod *Works and Days* 465
 4. *Iliad* 7. 193
 5. *Iliad* 2. 382
 6. *Iliad* 2. 414
 7. Sophocles *Oedipus Tyrannus* 4
170 1. Timotheus: *PMG* 778(b)
 2. *Iliad* 24. 604
 3. *Iliad* 24. 212
 4. Sophocles *Antigone* 291
 5. *Iliad* 22. 20
171 1. Empedocles B 137 (*VS*)
 2. Plato *Cratylus* 403A
 3. Xenophanes A 13 (*VS*)

Oracles in Decline

409 1. Epimenides B 11 (*VS*)
410 1. Alcaeus Z 115 Lobel–Page.
 2. razor *Iliad* 10. 173
 3. *Odyssey* 3. 367

412 1. *Odyssey* 4. 140
413 1. Pindar fr. 149 Snell = *Paean* 16. 6
415 1. Hesiod fr. 304 Merkelbach–West
2. Pindar fr. 165
3. *Iliad* 20. 8
416 1. Euripides fr. 971 (*TGF*)
2. Plato *Politicus* 260D
417 1. Hesiod *Works and Days* 123, 126
2. Herodotus 2. 171
3. Pindar, *Dithyramb* 2. 13
4. Aeschylus *Supplices* 214
5. Sophocles fr. 767 (*TGF*)
418 1. Empedocles B 24 (*VS*)
420 1. Theophrastus fr. 263 Fortenbaugh (*Theophrastus of Eresus*, Leiden, 1992)
422 1. *Odyssey* 21. 397
426 1. *PMG* adespota 998 = Pindar fr. 140c Snell
430 1. Plato *Timaeus* 52E
431 1. Euripides fr. 972 (*TGF*)
2. Euripides fr. 970 (*TGF*)
3. Hesiod, *Works and Days* 125
4. Ibid. 123
432 1. Euripides fr. 973 (*TGF*)
2. Euripides *Bacchae* 298
433 1. Heraclitus B 118 (*VS*)
2. Empedocles B 93 (*VS*)
3. Theogony 117
434 1. Aeschylus fr. 356 (*TGF*)
435 1. Euripides *Cyclops* 331
436 1. Simonides (= *Anth. Pal.* 9. 700)
2. *Odyssey* 9. 393
3. Plato *Republic* 507D
4. Orphica fr. 21 Kern

Why Are Delphic Oracles No Longer Given in Verse?

395 1. *CAF* adespota 461
396 1. *Odyssey* 7. 107
397 1. Heraclitus B 92 (*VS*)
2. Pindar fr. 32
398 1. Aristotle *Rhetoric* 1411^{b}–1412^{a}
400 1. *Odyssey* 3. 1

2. Plato *Timaeus* 90A
3. Empedocles B 44 (*VS*)

402 1. Scythinus fr. 1 West
2. Simonides: *PMG* 577

403 1. Pindar fr. 275 Snell
2. Thucydides 5. 16

404 1. Heraclitus B 93 (*VS*)

405 1. Xenophon, *Oeconomicus* 7. 5
2. Euripides fr. 663 (*TGF*)
3. Pindar *Isthmians* 2. 3

406 1. Chaeremon fr. 16 (*TGF*)
2. Pindar *Isthmians* 1. 48
3. Sophocles fr. 704 (*TGF*)

407 1. Euripides *Phoenissae* 958

409 1. *PMG* 997 (Pindar fr. 104b Snell)

Socrates' *Daimonion*

575 1. Pindar *Isthmians* 1. 2

580 1. *Iliad* 10. 279
2. *Odyssey* 13. 301
3. *Iliad* 20. 95

581 1. Euripides fr. 282 (*TGF*)

583 1. *Odyssey* 9. 27

593 1. *Iliad* 7. 44
2. *Iliad* 7. 53
3. Hesiod *Works and Days* 122

'Live unknown'

1128 1. Euripides fr. 905 (*TGF*)

1129 1. Sophocles fr. 780 (*TGF*)
2. *SH* 1046
3. Democritus B 158 (*VS*)

1130 1. *PMG* adespota fr. 996
2. Pindar fr. 129
3. Ibid. 130
4. *Odyssey* 11. 220

The Fortune of Rome

316 1. Ion of Chios fr. 22 von Blumenthal
2. Plato *Timaeus* 28B, 32B

317 1. Democritus B 148 (*VS*)
2. *Odyssey* 11. 41
3. Aeschylus (Diehl, i. 1. 80), see E. Fraenkel, *Aeschylus: Agamemnon* (Oxford, 1950) 830

318 1. Pindar fr. 40
2. Alcman: *PMG* 64
3. Sophocles *Oedipus Tyrannus* 1090
4. Menander fr. 739 *CAF*

322 1. Pindar fr. 39

323 1. Timotheus: *PMG* 789

324 1. *Iliad* 1. 10

325 1. Polybius 2. 18. 22

326 1. Livy 6. 1
2. *Odyssey* 18. 149
3. *Odyssey* 9. 49

Rules for Politicians

798 1. *Iliad* 9. 55
2. *Iliad* 9. 443
3. *PMG* adespota 1005

801 1. Plato comicus fr. 185 (*CAF*)
2. Menander fr. 472 (*CAF*)
3. Plato *Critias* 109c
4. *Iliad* 9. 441
5. Hesiod *Theogony* 80

802 1. Euripides fr. 987 (*TGF*)
2. Euripides fr. 439 (*TGF*)
3. Sophocles fr. 760 (*TGF*)
4. *Odyssey* 2. 69
5. Thucydides 2. 65

803 1. Archilochus fr. 91 West
2. Thucydides 1. 86, 2. 72, 2. 60–4
3. Euripides fr. 282 (*TGF*)

804 1. Aristophanes *Knights* 137
2. Pindar *Olympians* 6.4
3. *Anthologia Palatina* 11. 86

805 1. *Odyssey* 10. 495

806 1. Plato *Laws* 6. 762 E

807 1. Aristophanes *Wasps* 1033
2. *CAF* adespota fr. 11
3. *SH* 1150

4. Pindar fr. 57 Snell
5. Euripides fr. 309 (*TGF*)

808 1. *Iliad* 10. 242
2. Ibid. 10. 558
3. [Plato] *Epistles* 4, 321B

809 1. Xenophon *Agesilaus* 4
2. Simonides: *PMG* 538
3. *TGF* adespota 411
4. *Iliad* 17. 171
5. *Iliad* 7. 358

810 1. *Iliad* 5. 880
2. Sophocles fr. 771 (*TGF*)

811 1. Antisthenes fr. 193 Decleva Caizzi
2. Euripides fr. 974 (*TGF*)

812 1. Euripides fr. 988 (*TGF*)

813 1. Sophocles *Trachiniae* 1058
2. *TGF* adespota 412
3. Solon fr. 2 West

814 1. Metiochus: *CAF* adespota 1325

815 1. *Iliad* 17. 157
2. Ibid. 4. 223
3. unidentified, anon. 383 Schneider

817 1. *Iliad* 4. 415
2. Demosthenes 21. 31
3. Xenophon *Anabasis* 3. 1. 4

818 1. *TGF* adespota 413
2. Plato *Republic* 552 C–D

819 1. *Odyssey* 5. 350

820 1. Plato *Republic* 3. 416E
2. Empedocles B 9 (*VS*)

821 1. Democritus B 153 (*VS*)
2. *Iliad* 19. 404
3. Demosthenes 6. 24
4. *TGF* adespota 414 (prob. Euripides, *Alexander*)
5. *Iliad* 4. 130

822 1. Plato *Republic* 3. 398 ff.

823 1. *TGF* adespota 415
2. *TGF* adespota 75

824 1. Hesiod *Works and Days* 235

How to Profit from your Enemies

86 1. Xenophon *Oeconomicus* 1. 15
2. Aeschylus fr. 207 (*TGF*)

87 1. *Iliad* 1. 225
88 1. Aeschylus *Seven against Thebes* 593 ff.
2. Pindar fr. 229
3. Demosthenes 19. 208
4. Euripides *Orestes* 251
5. Euripides fr. 1086 (*TGF*)
6. *TGF* adespota 75
7. *TGF* adespota 358
89 1. Sophocles fr. 843 (*TGF*)
2. Antisthenes fr. 77 Decleva Caizzi
90 1. Euripides fr. 458
2. Plato *Laws* 731E
3. Callimachus (?), fr. 784 Pfeiffer
4. unidentified (cf. *Odyssey* 5. 412–7
91 1. Pindar fr. 123
2. Simonides: *PMG* 538
3. Pindar fr. 212
92 1. Hesiod *Works and Days* 25
2. Plato *Laws* 728A
3. Solon fr. 15 West
4. Plato *Laws* 731E

Curiosity

515 1. Empedocles A 14 (*VS*)
2. *CAF* adespota 359
3. unidentified
4. Xenophon *Oeconomicus* 8. 19
5. *Carmen aureum* 42
516 1. *Odyssey* 11. 278
2. *SH* 1142
3. Ariston of Ceos fr. 16 Wehrli
4. Hesiod *Works and Days* 519
517 1. Aristophanes *Knights* 79
2. Sophocles fr. 787 (*TGF*)
3. Aeschylus *Supplices* 937
518 1. *SH* 1143
2. *TGF* adespota 386
3. Ibid. 387
519 1. *CAF* adespota 347
520 1. *TGF* adespota 388
2. Euripides fr. 996 (*TGF*)
3. Empedocles B 101 (*VS*)

521 1. Euripides fr. 790 (*TGF*): from *Philoctetes*
2. Sophocles *Electra* 724
3. Xenophon *Cyropaedia* 5. 1. 8
4. Sophocles *Oedipus Tyrannus* 1169–70
5. Euripides *Orestes* 213

Talkativeness

502 1. Euripides fr. 899 (*TGF*)
2. *TGF* adespota 361
3. Sophocles fr. 78 (*TGF*)
503 1. *PMG* adespota 1000
2. Archilochus fr. 233 West
3. Euripides *Bacchae* 386
4. *Odyssey* 15. 463–5
504 1. Sophocles fr. 771 (*TGF*)
2. *PMG* adespota 1001
3. *Odyssey* 12. 452–3
505 1. *Odyssey* 11. 54
2. *SH* 1156
3. Plato *Laws* 717D, 935A
4. Hesiod fr. 61 Merkelbach–West
506 1. *Odyssey* 19. 494
2. Ibid. 19. 210–12
3. Ibid. 20. 13
4. Ibid. 20. 23
5. Euripides fr. 413 (*TGF*)
507 1. Archilochus fr. 181 West
2. Euripides fr. 411 (*TGF*): from *Ino*
508 1. *Iliad* 10. 457
509 1. Sophocles *Antigone* 317 ff.
510 1. *CAF* adespota 774
2. Demosthenes 19. 265
3. Epicharmus fr. 274 Kaibel
4. Plato *Protagoras* 342 E
511 1. *CAF* adespota 347
2. Sophocles fr. 772 (*TGF*)
3. dumb cf. Herodotus 1. 47
513 1. Menander fr. 164 (*CAF*)
2. *CAF* adespota 151
514 1. Euripides fr. 183 (*TGF*)

Bashfulness

528 1. Timaeus fr. 122 (F Gr Hist)
529 1. *SH* 832 (Timon of Phlius)
2. *Iliad* 24. 44–5
3. Euripides fr. 309 (*TGF*)
530 1. Sophocles fr. 773 (*TGF*)
2. Euripides *Medea* 290
3. Hesiod *Works and Days* 342
532 1. Demosthenes 3. 19
2. Euripides fr. 977 (*TGF*)
533 1. Thucydides 2. 40
2. *TGF* adespota 389
3. Euripides fr. 595 (*TGF*)
4. Hesiod *Works and Days* 371
5. [Plato] Epistles 13. 360c
6. Euripides *Medea* 1078
534 1. Epicharmus (?) fr. 275 Kaibel
2. Plato *Clitopho* 407c
535 1. Thucydides 2. 64
536 1. Antisthenes fr. 26 Decleva Caizzi

Against Borrowing Money

827 1. Plato *Laws* 844B
828 1. Plato *Republic* 615E
2. *Odyssey* 11. 579
829 1. See Aristophanes *Knights* 1059
2. *Iliad* 1. 154
830 1. Crates fr. 5 = *SH* 349
2. Empedocles B 115 (*VS*)
831 1. (Calypso): *Odyssey* 5. 264
2. *Odyssey* 5. 291, 295

Eroticus

749 1. Plato *Phaedrus* 229–30
750 1. See *TGF* p. 632 (Euripides, *Chrysippus*?)
2. Archilochus fr. 181 West
3. *TGF* adespota 401
4. Philippides fr. 31 (*CAF*)
5. *Iliad* 21. 252, 24. 315
751 1. Anacreon: *PMG* 444

2. Solon fr. 25 West
3. Aeschylus fr. 135 (*TGF*)
4. (?)Pindar *Pythians* 2. 42; Hesiod *Theogony* 927
5. Sappho fr. 49 Lobel–Page
6. *TGF* adespota 402
7. Plato *Phaedrus* 250E
8. Plato *Laws* 839B
9. Solon fr. 26 West

752 1. *TGF* adespota 403
2. *TGF* adespota 404

753 1. Hesiod *Works and Days* 696

755 1. Euripides fr. 986 (*TGF*)
2. Heraclitus B 85 (*VS*)

756 1. Euripides *Bacchae* 203
2. Euripides fr. 480–1 (*TGF*)
3. Empedocles B 17, B 20 (*VS*)
4. Euripides fr. 898 (*TGF*); cf. *Hippolytus* 449
5. Empedocles B 151 (*VS*)
6. Sophocles fr. 763 (*TGF*)
7. Aeschylus *Choephori* 295
8. Parmenides B 13 (*VS*)
9. Hesiod *Theogony* 120

757 1. Euripides fr. 322 (*TGF*)
2. Sophocles fr. 855, 754 (*TGF*)
3. Sophocles fr. 754
4. Homer: *Iliad* 5. 31, 831
5. Chrysippus: *SVF* II 1094
6. *SH* 1147
7. Aeschylus fr. 200 (*TGF*)
8. Pindar, fr. 165
9. Ibid. 153

758 1. *TGF* adespota 405
2. Euripides *Bacchae* 66
3. Melanippides, *PMG* 763
4. Sophocles fr. 778 (*TGF*)
5. Plato, *Phaedrus* 244
6. *Phaedrus* 265
7. Aeschylus *Supplices* 681

759 1. *TGF* adespota 406
2. *Iliad* 7. 121
3. Euripides *Hippolytus* 478
4. Sophocles *Trachiniae* 497
5. Plato *Republic* 439E

6. *TGF* adespota 407
7. *Iliad* 17. 57

760 1. Euripides fr. 322 (*TGF*)
2. Sophocles *Antigone* 783
3. *TGF* adespota 408
4. Sophocles fr. 410 (*TGF*)

761 1. *PMG* 873
2. Dionysius: see *SH* 388
3. *Iliad* 13. 131, 16. 215
4. Anon. fr. 380 Schneider (cf. Panyasis, fr. 3 in A. Bernabé, *Poetae Epici Graeci*, i (Leipzig, 1987))
5. Sophocles fr. 703 (*TGF*)

762 1. Euripides fr. 663 (*TGF*)
2. *Certamen Homeri et Hesiodi* (p. 236 in T. W. Allen, *Homeri Opera*, v, Oxford, 1911)
3. *Odyssey* 19. 40
4. Pindar *Pythians* 1. 5
5. Phrynichus fr. 17 (*TGF*)
6. Philoxenus: *PMG* 822
7. Sappho fr. 31 Lobel–Page
8. Menander fr. 541 (*CAF*): cf. also Plutarch, *On Love*, fr. 134 Sandbach
9. Aeschylus fr. 351 (*TGF*)
10. Pindar fr. 143
11. Xenophanes A 13 (*VS*)
12. Alcaeus fr. 348 Lobel–Page
13. Euripides fr. 595 (*TGF*)

764 1. *Odyssey* 12. 453
2. Plato *Phaedrus* 235D
3. Euripides *Hippolytus* 193 ff.
4. *SH* 1148

765 1. Alcaeus fr. 227 Lobel–Page

766 1. Euripides *Hippolytus* 7
2. *SVF* 1. 390
3. *TGF* adespota 355 = *CAF* adespota 360

767 1. Aeschylus fr. 243 (*TGF*)
2. Plato *Republic* 462c
3. Sophocles fr. 785 (*TGF*)
4. Euripides fr. 1084

768 1. *TGF* adespota 409
2. Sophocles fr. 779 (*TGF*)

769 1. *CAF* adespota 222–4
2. Ibid. 221

770 1. *Odyssey* 15. 183
2. Euripides fr. 898 (*TGF*)

Advice on Marriage

139 1. Herodotus 1. 8
140 1. Plato *Republic* 462c
141 1. Sophocles fr. 762 (*TGF*)
143 1. Euripides *Medea* 190
2. *Iliad* 15. 205, 209
3. Hermione: Euripides *Andromache* 930
144 1. Plato *Laws* 729B
145 1. *Iliad* 6. 429
146 1. Sappho fr. 55 Lobel–Page

A Consolation to His Wife

608 1. Euripides fr. 785 (*TGF*): from *Phaethon*
609 1. Euripides *Bacchae* 317
610 1. Euripides *Andromache* 930
611 1. Theognis 427

Virtues in Women

242 1. Thucydides 2. 45
2. Gorgias B 22 (*VS*)
243 1. Euripides *Hercules Furens* 673
245 1. Herodotus 6. 83

Gryllus

988 1. e.g. *Iliad* 4. 253, 5. 639

GLOSSARY OF PROPER NAMES

An asterisk indicates that further information may be found in *The Oxford Companion to Classical Literature*, ed. M. C. Howatson (Oxford, 1989). References to *marginal pages* are given where there could be some doubt about the identification of a name. Some very obvious names (e.g. Athens) are omitted, also some of which nothing is known but what is stated in Plutarch's text.

Acanthus: city in Macedonia, near the isthmus of the peninsula of Acte (Chalcidice).

***Achaeans**: in Homer, name for the entire Greek army at Troy; later, the people of Achaea, a region of northern Peloponnese. The Roman province covering most of mainland Greece was also called Achaea.

***Acheron**: a river of the Underworld—the 'river of sorrow'.

***Achilles**: son of Peleus and Thetis, the hero whose 'wrath' is the theme of the *Iliad*.

***Acragas**: Greek city of south-west Sicily, founded *c.*580 BC.

Acrocorinth: the citadel of Corinth.

***Admetus**: mythical king of Pherae in Thessaly, husband of Alcestis, who died to save his life.

***Adrastus**: mythical king of Argos and Sicyon; led the army of the 'Seven' against Thebes to restore Polynices to the throne.

***Aegina**: island south-west of Athens, a maritime power in 6th cent. BC, subsequently conquered by Athens.

***Aegospotami**: 'Goat's Rivers', in Thracian Chersonese (Gallipoli peninsula), scene of decisive Athenian naval defeat in 405 BC.

Aemilianus: son of Epitherses, probably the rhetor known to the elder Seneca (*Controversiae* 10. 5. 25), active in Augustan times.

***Aemilius Paullus, L.**: consul 182 and 168 BC, defeated Perseus, king of Macedon, at Pydna, 168 BC. Life by Plutarch.

***Aemilius Scaurus, M.**: Roman noble, *princeps senatus*, consul 115 BC, died before 89 BC.

***Aeschines**: Athenian orator, *c.*390–322 BC, the great rival of Demosthenes.

***Aeschylus**: (525–456 BC); the tragic poet.

***Aetolia**: region of central Greece, north of Corinthian Gulf.

Afranius, L.: consul 60 BC, friend and supporter of Pompey.

***Agamemnon**: son of Atreus, brother of Menelaus and king of Mycenae or Argos; Greek leader in the Trojan war.

Agathoclea: a dancer, mistress of Ptolemy IV, king of Egypt 221–204 BC.

Agathocles: tyrant of *Syracuse 317–289 BC.

***Agathon**: Athenian tragic poet, whose first victory (416 BC) is the occasion commemorated in Plato's *Symposium*.

***Agaue**: mother of Pentheus, legendary king of Thebes, whom she helped to tear to pieces in the delusion of Bacchic frenzy (Euripides, *Bacchae*).

***Agesilaus**: king of Sparta 399–360 BC. Life by Plutarch.

Aglaonice: Thessalian witch, who was able to claim to 'pull down the moon' because she could foretell eclipses.

Agyrrhius: Athenian democratic politican, prominent 400–388 BC, best-known as an advocate of pay for attendance at assembly or festivals.

***Ajax**: son of Telamon, heroic Greek warrior in the Trojan War.

***Alcaeus**: Greek lyric poet from Mytilene in Lesbos, 7th cent. BC.

Alcamenes: sculptor, pupil and rival of Phidias.

***Alcestis**: wife of Admetus (q.v).

***Alcibiades**: (*c*.450–404 BC); Athenian statesman and general, of spectacular talents and conspicuous failings; the subject of one of Plutarch's best Lives.

Alcmaeon: 1. in myth, son of Amphiaraus, murderer of his mother Eriphyle. 2. Athenian nobleman (of the family of the *Alcmaeonids), sometimes stated to be an accuser of *Themistocles (q.v.).

***Alcman**: Greek lyric poet, 7th cent. BC; lived at Sparta, but may have come originally from Sardis.

Alcmena: wife of *Amphitryon, and mother of Heracles by Zeus.

Alexander: 1. Alexander of Pherae, successor of Jason (q.v.) and tyrant 369–358 BC; assassinated by his wife's brothers. 2. *Alexander III of Macedon, 'the Great', lived 356–323 BC. 3. Alexander I, king of Epirus (Molossia), killed at Pandosia (q.v.) 326 BC.

Alexinus of Elis: (4th–3rd cent. BC), logician and controversialist of the Megarian school (cf. Stilpo); supposed to have died as a result of being pricked by a reed while swimming in the Alpheus.

***Alexis**: (*c*.375–275 BC); A thenian comic poet; few fragments of his voluminous works survive.

***Allia**: tributary of the Tiber (now Fosso della Bettina), scene of the Roman defeat by the Gauls, 18 July 390 BC, a day of disgrace never forgotten.

***Alpheus**: the river of Elis near which Olympia stands.

Alyattes: king of Lydia (*c*.610–560 BC), the founder of the Lydian empire.

Amasis: king of Egypt (*c*.569–525 BC), had many Greek contacts and friends; the Persians conquered Egypt shortly after his death.

Ambracia: Corinthian colony in Epirus, later capital of the Molossian kingdom, modern Arta.

Amestris: wife of Xerxes (q.v.).

***Ammon**: the oracle of Zeus Ammon at Siwa was known to the Greeks from the 7th cent. BC, and much consulted, e.g. by Alexander the Great. There was a connection with the oracle of Amphiaraus at Oropus; so Plutarch's interest in Ammon was natural.

Ammonius of Cholleidae: Platonist philosopher, teacher of Plutarch, and three times general (*strategos*) at Athens. Said to have been of Egyptian origin.

***Amphiaraus**: son of Oecles, mythical Theban prophet, husband of Eriphyle.

***amphictyony**: the 'Amphictyones' are the 'dwellers around' the shrine of Demeter near Thermopylae; they were a league of peoples of northern Greece, which also administered the shrine at Delphi, and had considerable political importance.

Amphilochus: son of Amphiaraus (q.v.); with Mopsus, settled in Cilicia and established a famous oracle.

Amphissa: town north-west of Delphi (medieval Salona), a traditional ally of Thebes and enemy of Phocis; destroyed by Philip II in 339/8 BC.

***Anacharsis**: (6th cent. BC); Scythian prince who travelled in Greece and was regarded as a sage, and a type of the 'noble savage', prefiguring the Cynic ideal of an ascetic life.

***Anacreon**: (b. *c*.570 BC); lyric poet of Teos.

***Anaxagoras**: (*c*.500–*c*.428 BC); philosopher, born in Clazomenae, lived in Athens; friend of Pericles.

Anaxarchus of Abdera: philosopher, pupil of Democritus and teacher of the sceptic Pyrrho of Elis.

***Anchises**: Trojan prince, father of Aeneas by Aphrodite.

***Andocides**: (*c*.440–390 BC), Athenian orator, best-known for his part in the scandal of the mutilation of the Hermae, 415 BC.

Antalcidas: Spartan admiral, made peace and alliance with Persia 387 BC.

Antias, Valerius: Roman annalist, who wrote a history of Rome down to his own time (early 1st BC.).

Antigonus: 1. *Antigonus I, Monophthalmus ('One-eyed'); satrap of Phrygia under Alexander the Great, attempted to reunite Alexander's empire in the period after his death, but was finally defeated by a coalition of other rulers at Ipsus, 301 BC. 2. Antigonus II, Gonatas, grandson of Antigonus I; king of Macedonia, 266–239 BC, friend and patron of Stoic and Cynic philosophers.

Antileon of Metapontum (or Heraclea): lover of Hipparinus, murdered the tyrant of the city because he tried to seduce the young man (4th cent. BC).

***Antimachus of Colophon**: (*c*.400 BC); poet, who wrote both epic (*Thebaid*) and narrative elegy; much criticized as long-winded and dull, but admired by Plato.

Antipater: 1. general of Philip II and Alexander, governor of Greece in Alexander's absence, and after his death (d. 319 BC). 2. son of Cassander, involved in wars with Pyrrhus, king of Epirus and Demetrius Poliorcetes; murdered by his father-in-law, Lysimachus, 293 BC. 3. of Tarsus, Stoic philosopher, 2nd cent. BC.

Antisthenes: (*c*.445–*c*.360 BC); follower of Socrates, regarded as the first *Cynic philosopher; author of moralizing works on Heracles, Cyrus, and Aspasia.

***Antonius, M**: (83–31 BC); the triumvir, Octavian's opponent and Cleopatra's husband, Shakespeare's Mark Antony. Excellent Life by Plutarch.

***Anytus**: (5th–4th cent. BC); Athenian politician, one of the accusers of Socrates in 399 BC.

***Apelles**: (4th cent. BC); the greatest Greek painter; worked at the court of Philip and Alexander as well as at Athens and elsewhere.

***Aphrodite**: the goddess of love.

***Apollo**: the god of music, archery, prophecy, and medicine, and sometimes identified with the sun.

Apollonia: a common place-name, but in III. 401 the place meant is probably modern Pollina, a city of Illyria, founded from Corcyra (Corfu), 6th cent. BC.

Appius Claudius Pulcher: censor 136 BC, opponent of Scipio Aemilianus.

Araspas: prince of Media, a prominent character in Xenophon's *Cyropaedia*, suitor of the beautiful Panthea.

Aratus of Sicyon: (271–213 BC); statesman and general. Life by Plutarch, dedicated to Aratus' descendant Polycrates.

***Archelaus**: king of Macedon, 413–399 BC; murdered by a former favourite.

Archidamus: in XI, 535, probably Archidamus III, king of Sparta 361–338 BC. (For Archedemus in IV, see notes).

***Archilochus of Paros**: (7th cent. BC); Greek poet, famous especially for his wit and invective.

***Archytas of Tarentum**: Pythagorean philosopher, mathematician, and lawgiver, visited by Plato *c*.390 BC.

***Ares**: the Greek god of war.

Aretaphila of Cyrene: liberator of the city from tyranny (see XVI).

Argynnus: a beautiful Boeotian boy, loved by Agamemnon. The Boeotian cult of Aphrodite Argynnis is supposed to commemorate him.

***Aristaeus**: son of Apollo and the nymph Cyrene, divine patron of hunting and husbandry, and father of Actaeon.

***Aristarchus of Samos**: born *c*.320 BC, famous astronomer.

***Aristides**: Athenian statesman, rival of Themistocles, died *c*.468 BC. Life by Plutarch.

Aristion: supporter of Mithridates and tyrant of Athens, 86–83 BC. Also the name of a citizen of Tithora mentioned in XIII.

***Aristippus of Cyrene**: disciple of Socrates, believed to have founded the Cyrenaic (Hedonist) school.

Aristodemus: 1. king of Messenia, 8th cent. BC; supposed to have sacrificed his daughter in response to a Delphic oracle, and to have killed himself on her grave. 2. tyrant of Cumae in Italy, *c*.500 BC, defeated the Etruscans, gave asylum to the exiled Tarquin; killed by conspirators.

Aristogiton: Athenian noble, one of the assassins of Hipparchus (514 BC), executed (with his accomplice, Harmodius) by the surviving tyrant, Hippias.

Ariston: 1. of Chios, Stoic philosopher, pupil of Zeno. 2. of Ceos, Peripatetic (so in IX. 516).

Aristonice: the Pythian priestess who gave the oracle to the Athenians in 480 BC, bidding them flee the city before the advancing Persians.

***Aristophanes**: (*c*.445–*c*.385 BC); the greatest Athenian comic poet.

Aristophon: Athenian politician and general, accuser of Timotheus and Iphicrates (356/5 BC), later opponent of Hyperides; lived to nearly 100.

Aristotimus: tyrant of Elis in 272 BC, supported by Antigonus Gonatas.

Aristotle (Aristoteles): 1. *the philosopher, 384–322 BC. 2. an obscure historian from Chalcis in Euboea.

Aristylla: friend of Plutarch, perhaps the wife of Timon.

Aristyllus: astronomer, 3rd cent. BC.

Arius Didymus: philosopher of Alexandria, friend of Augustus, author of an extant summary of Stoic and Peripatetic ethics.

Arne: town in Thessaly (II. 432).

Arruns: Etruscan prince, son of Porsena (q.v.).

Artaphernes: Persian commander killed at Marathon, 490 BC.

Artaxerxes III: Ochus, king of Persia 359–337 BC.

***Artemis**: daughter of Zeus and Leto, twin sister of Apollo, goddess of hunting and childbirth, identified also with Hecate and the Moon.

***Asclepius**: the god of healing.

Astyages: king of Media 584–550 BC, overthrown by Cyrus.

***Athamas**: legendary king of Thebes, husband of 1. Nephele ('Cloud'), by whom he had Phrixus and Hebe, 2. Ino, daughter of Cadmus, who hated her stepchildren. Athamas, made mad by Dionysus, mistook Ino for a lioness and the children for cubs, and killed the children.

***Athena**: daughter of Zeus, patron goddess of Athens, goddess of wisdom and all arts.

Atropos: one of the three *Fates (Moirai), with Clotho and Lachesis.

Autobulus: name of Plutarch's father and of his eldest son.

Autolycus: son of Hermes, master thief, grandfather of Odysseus.

Bacchis: courtesan of Samos or Miletus.

***Bacis**: name given to various male prophets whose divination depended on ecstatic possession: cf. the female Sibyls.

Bastarnae: Germanic people of the lower Danube, enlisted by Mithridates against the Romans, not subdued by Rome till 29–28 BC.

***Battus**: name given (because of his stammer) to Aristoteles of Thera, founder of Cyrene (631 BC.); succeeding rulers took the names Arcesilaus and Battus alternately.

Bebryces: a people of north-west Asia Minor, figuring in the saga of the Argonauts.

Belestiche: mistress of Ptolemy Philadelphus (king of Egypt 283–246 BC), worshipped after her death as Aphrodite Belestiche.

***Bellerophon**: mythical Corinthian hero, falsely accused by Proetus' wife, Stheneboea, of seducing her, and then sent by Proetus to Iobates, king of Lycia, who set him hard tasks: he killed the Chimaera (q.v.), and defeated the Solymi (q.v.), always with the help of the winged horse Pegasus (q.v.).

Bias of Priene: one of the *Seven Sages.

Bion of Borysthenes: (= Olbia, on the Dnieper estuary); writer of popular moral sermons, died *c*.246 BC, aged about 80.

Bocchoris: an unjust ruler of Egypt, (8th cent. BC). It was said that Isis sent a serpent to wrap itself round his head, as a warning to him to give just decisions.

Bocchus I: king of Mauretania, *c*.110–80 BC; betrayed Jugurtha to the Romans, 105 BC.

Boulis: a Spartan who, with Sperchis, surrendered voluntarily to the Persians in requital for the murder of a Persian herald sent by Darius. Cf. Sperchis. (Herodotus 7. 134).

***Brasidas**: Spartan general of great courage and spirit, killed at Amphipolis, 422 BC.

***Brauron**: place on east coast of Attica, site of important cults; Iphigenia is said to have brought here the statue of Artemis which she and Orestes stole from Tauris.

Briareos: a hundred-handed Giant, one of the children of Uranus and Gaea.

Bruttium: region of south-west Italy, modern Calabria.

***Brutus**: 1. L. Junius Brutus, prime mover in the overthrow of Tarquin, and one of the first consuls, 509 BC; the legendary liberator of Rome. 2. M. Junius Brutus (85–42 BC), one of the assassins of Caesar, and a leader of the army defeated by Antony and Octavian at Philippi (42 BC). Life by Plutarch.

***Cacus**: fire-breathing monster, supposed to have lived on the site of Rome. He stole the cattle Hercules had taken from Geryon, and was himself killed by Hercules.

***Cadmus**: son of Agenor, king of Tyre; legendary founder of Thebes, supposed to have introduced writing from his native Phoenicia.

***Caesar, C. Julius**: (100–44 BC); the statesman and general. Life by Plutarch.

Caligula (= *Gaius Caesar): Roman emperor, AD 37–41.

Callias: son of Hipponicus, a wealthy and influential Athenian, who figures as host or friend in Socratic dialogues by Plato and Xenophon. Died *c.*370 BC.

Callicles: Athenian moneylender, 4th cent. BC.

Callicratidas: Spartan admiral, defeated and killed at Arginusae, 406 BC.

***Calliope**: one of the nine Muses, traditionally associated with epic poetry (but not in Hesiod, *Theogony* 80, which Plutarch quotes, VII. 801).

Callippus: Callippus, an Athenian pupil of Plato and friend of the Syracusan Dion (q.v.) against whom he conspired; ruled Syracuse briefly (354 BC), but was murdered by his own soldiers, whom he could not pay.

Callistratus: nephew of Agyrrhius (q.v.); Athenian politician, financier, and orator; played a large part in Athens' relations with Sparta and Thebes; condemned to death 361 BC, and executed on his return to Athens from Macedonia.

***Calypso**: the nymph of the island of Ogygia, who kept Odysseus with her seven years.

***Camillus, M. Furius**: 'the second founder of Rome', who saved the city in the Gallic invasion, 390 BC, and was dictator five times. Life by Plutarch.

Camma: Galatian heroine, wife of Sinatus, murderer of her treacherous lover Sinorix.

Carbo, C. or Cn. Papirius: in VII. 801, *either* the consul of 120 BC, supporter of C. Gracchus, *or* the consul of 85–4 BC, supporter of Cinna.

Caria: region of south-west Asia Minor.

***Carneades of Cyrene**: (*c*.213–129 BC); sceptical philosopher, the head of the Academy (once Plato's school), who opposed the dogmatism of Stoics and Epicureans.

Carystus: town in Euboea, famous for its marble quarries.

***Cassandra**: Trojan princess, daughter of Priam, the truthful prophetess doomed never to be believed, taken home to Argos as captive and concubine by Agamemnon.

***Catiline (L. Sergius Catilina)**: Roman noble who headed the conspiracy against the senatorial government which Cicero, as consul, suppressed in 63 BC.

***Cato**: 1. M. Porcius Cato, 234–149 BC, Roman statesman and moral reformer, famous for his opposition to luxury and Greek fashions; the first historian to write in Latin. Life by Plutarch. 2. M. Porcius Cato, 95–46 BC, great-grandson of 1, a committed Stoic, opponent of Caesar; defeated in Africa in the civil war, he committed suicide at Cetica. A hero of the losing cause. Life by Plutarch.

Catulus, Q. Lutatius: 1. consul 102 BC, an opponent of Marius and a famous orator. 2. consul 78 BC, colleague of Crassus as censor, 65 BC.

***Cebes**: Pythagorean from Thebes (of Simmias); present at the death of Socrates, according to Plato's *Phaedo*.

Celtiberians: a general name for the peoples of the Spanish plateau, a mixture of Celts (from north of the Pyrenees) and Iberians (from the Mediterranean coast).

***Centaurs**: mythical creatures with human head and horse's body; symbols of a savage way of life.

Cephallenia: large island off the west coast of Greece, near Ithaca.

Cephalus: Athenian politician, 4th cent BC, ridiculed by the comic poet Plato (see VII. 801).

Cephisodorus: Boeotarch 364/3 BC; loved by Epaminondas, according to XIII. 761.

***Cephissus (Cephisus)**: the name of various rivers, notably 1. a river near Athens; 2. a river that rises in the Parnassus (q.v.), and waters Phocis and northern Boeotia.

***Ceramicus**: an area of Athens north-west of the Acropolis, best-known for the cemetery, containing many graves of the archaic and classical periods. The name means 'Potters' Quarter'.

Chabrias: (*c*.420–357 BC); Athenian general who fought many land and sea campaigns. Died at the battle of Chios.

Chaereas: Cassius Chaerea, assassin of Caligula (AD 41).

Chaeremon: tragic poet, 4th cent. BC, a colourful and inventive writer, very little of whose work survives.

Chaeron: the eponymous hero of Chaeronea; also the name of a son of Plutarch.

***Chaeronea**: Plutarch's home town, in Boeotia.

***Chalcis**: the principal city of Euboea, commanding the narrow channel separating the island from the mainland; an important colonizing power, 8th–7th cent. BC, and famous for metal work.

Charinus: supporter of Pericles, proposer of a decree directed against the Megarians shortly before the outbreak of the *Peloponnesian War.

***Charon of Lampsacus**: historian, 5th cent. BC, author of works on the Persian war and on Lampsacus. Few fragments survive.

***Chersonese**: a word meaning 'land-island', i.e. peninsula, applied especially to the peninsula of Gallipoli, but also to other similar geographical features (e.g. the site of Lyctus in N.E. Crete).

Chilon of Sparta: one of the *Seven Sages, the wise men of early Greece (7th or 6th cent. BC).

***Chimaera**: mythical fire-breathing monster (lion, goat, and snake) killed by Bellerophon (q.v.).

***Chios**: large Greek island off the coast of Asia.

***Chrysippus of Soli**: (*c*.280–207 BC); Stoic philosopher, the main formulator of the doctrines of the school.

***Cicero, M. Tullius**: (106–43 BC); the Roman politician, orator, and philosopher.

***Cilicia**: region of south-east Asia Minor.

Cimbri: a Germanic people (probably from Scandinavia), who invaded Gaul and were ultimately defeated by Marius, 102–101 BC. Cf. Teutones.

***Cimmerians**: a nomad people of southern Russia who invaded Asia Minor, 7th cent. BC. A traditional example of northern barbarians, who hardly ever see the sun (*Odyssey* 11. 15–19).

***Cimon**: Athenian statesman, son of Miltiades, d. 449 BC. Life by Plutarch.

Cinaethon of Sparta: poet to whom some early epic poems were attributed. Date uncertain.

***Cincinnatus, L. Quinctius**: dictator of Rome, 458 BC.

***Cinesias**: (*c*.450–*c*.390 BC); poet, composer of the type of lyric called 'dithyramb', honouring Dionysus.

***Circe**: the goddess-sorceress of Aeaea who changed Odysseus' men into swine. See XVII.

***Cithaeron**: mountain chain dividing Boeotia from Attica and the Megarid, a region rich in legend.

Cius (Ceos): island of the Cyclades (now Kea), celebrated for the good manners and morals of the people.

Civilis, C. Julius: leader of the Batavian revolt, AD 69–70.

Claudia: in XIV. 145, *either* the Vestal Virgin who rescued her father from an attack on him during his triumph (Val. Max. 5. 4. 6), *or* the Claudia Quintia who proved her virtue by helping to carry the statue of Cybele into Rome, 203 BC.

Clazomenae: Ionian city of Asia Minor, on an island in the Gulf of Smyrna, later joined to the mainland.

Clea, Flavia: Plutarch's friend, addressee of XVI.

***Cleanthes of Assus**: Stoic philosopher, 3rd cent. BC, pupil and successor of Zeno; also a poet.

Cleobulina: also called Eumetis, daughter of Cleobulus of Lindos, one of the Seven Sages; famous for her clever riddles. A character in Plutarch's 'Banquet of the Seven Sages'.

***Cleomenes I**: king of Sparta, reigned *c*.519–490 BC, victor over the Argives at Sepea (*c*.494 BC).

***Cleon**: Athenian politician, prominent after the death of Pericles; defeated by Brasidas and killed at Amphipolis, 422 BC.

Cleonae: city of the Peloponnese, near Argos; site of the Nemean Games.

***Cleopatra VII**: (69–30 BC); the last queen of Egypt, loved by both Caesar and Antony.

***Cleophon**: Athenian politician, prominent as a demagogue 410–404 BC.

Clio: one of the nine *Muses, traditionally patroness of history.

***Clisthenes**: Athenian statesman who introduced important democratic reforms 508/7 BC.

***Clodius Pulcher, P.**: (92–52 BC); Roman politician, supporter of Caesar, and enemy of Cicero, who defended his murderer, Milo.

Cloelia: Roman girl who was given as hostage to Porsena (q.v.) but escaped and was returned to his keeping, earning her liberty then by her brave bearing before him.

Clotho: one of the three Fates (Moirai), with Atropos and Lachesis.

Clymene: wife of Cephalus, and mother of Phaethon by the sun-god, Helios.

***Cnidus**: town of south-west Asia Minor, scene of Conon's naval victory over the Spartans in 394 BC.

***Cocles:** see Horatius.

***Codrus**: mythical king of Athens at the time of the Dorian invasions (? 11th cent. BC).

Colophon: city of Asia Minor, between Smyrna and Ephesus, briefly very rich in the 7th and 6th cents. BC.

***Conon**: (*c*.444–392 BC.), Athenian general at Aegospotami (q.v.) and Cnidus (q.v.); rebuilt the Long Walls joining Athens and Piraeus.

Copais: lake in Boeotia, now drained.

***Coriolanus, Cn. Marcus**: hero of early republican Rome. Life by Plutarch.

Cornelia: daughter of Scipio and mother of Tib. and C. Gracchus.

Corniculum: town of Latium, home of Servius Tullius' mother; site perhaps Monte dell' Incastro.

***Corybantes**: dancing priests in various orgiastic cults, especially those of Cybele; sometimes confused with the Curetes, whose clashing weapons drowned the infants cries of Zeus, committed to their care by his mother Rhea.

Cotys: king of the Odrysae in Thrace, ruled Thrace 383–360 BC, murdered by Pytho and Heraclides of Aenus, in revenge for their father's death.

***Crassus, M. Licinius**: 115–53 BC; consul in 70 BC, killed at Carrhae, fighting the Parthians, 53 BC. Life by Plutarch.

Craterus: (321–*c*.255 BC); son of Alexander's general Craterus; governor of Peloponnese (and later of Attica) under Antigonus II.

Crates of Thebes: (*c*.365–285 BC); Cynic philosopher, husband of Hipparchia.

***Creon**: a name ('Ruler') given to many rulers in legend and in tragedy, notably the king of Corinth killed by Medea.

***Critias**: (*c*.460–403 BC). Athenian aristocrat, connection of Plato, and one of the Thirty Tyrants (404 BC); also author of tragedies and other poems; held sceptical views about traditional religion and ethics.

Critolaus of Phaselis: Peripatetic philosopher, 2nd cent. BC.

***Croesus**: the last king of Lydia (*c*.560–546 BC), defeated by the Persians under Cyrus.

Cromnus: place in Arcadia, on the Messenian border.

***Cronus**: a Titan, son of Uranus and Gaia, and father of Zeus.

***Croton**: Greek city of southern Italy, a centre of Pythagoreanism; flourished 6th–5th cent. BC, especially after the destruction of its rival Sybaris, 510 BC.

Cryassus: city in Caria.

***Cumae**: the earliest Greek colony in Italy (*c*.750 BC), near Naples; opposed Etruscan power in 5th cent. BC, but later succumbed to its Italian neighbours; Roman from 338 BC. See s.v. Aristodemus.

***Cyclopes**: one-eyed giants, living without law or organized society; the most notable was Polyphemus, who imprisoned Odysseus and his men and ate some of them. Traditional location, east coast of Sicily.

Cydnus: river of Cilicia, on which Tarsus stands.

Cylon of Croton: opponent of the Pythagoreans, 5th cent. BC.

***Cyprus**: the large island in the eastern Mediterranean.

***Cypselus**: tyrant of Corinth, 657–625 BC.

***Cyrene**: Greek city of north Africa, colonized from Thera *c.*630 BC.

***Cyrus**: 1. king of Persia 559–529 BC, founder of the Persian empire. 2. second son of Darius II, rebelled against his brother Artaxerxes II and was killed at the battle of Cunaxa, 401 BC. His Greek troops, led by Xenophon, made good their retreat to the Black Sea.

Cyzicus: city of north-west Asia Minor, on the coast of the Sea of Marmara; scene of Athenian naval victory in 410 BC.

Daiphantus: Phocian leader in the wars with the Thessalians, 6th cent. BC. Life by Plutarch (lost).

***Darius**: 1. Darius I, son of Hystaspes, king of Persia 521–486 BC. 2. Darius II, Nothus, king of Persia 423–404 BC. 3. Darius III, king of Persia 336–330 BC, defeated by Alexander and killed.

Datis: one of the generals of Darius I in the Greek campaign of 490 BC.

Daulis: town in Phocis, on a spur of Mt. Parnassus.

Deinomenes: ruler of Gela in Sicily, and father of the tyrants Gelo, Hiero, and Thrasybulus.

Deiotarus: 1. Deiotarus I, son of Sinorix, made king of Galatia by Pompey, died 39 BC. 2. Deiotarus Philapator, son of 1, co-regent with his father but predeceased him.

Delium: a name common to sanctuaries of Delian Apollo, but especially 1. Boeotian town, near the Attic border, scene of a defeat of the Athenians in 424 BC. (IV. 581); 2. a sanctuary on Naxos (XVI. 254).

***Demades**: (*c.*380–319 BC.); Athenian orator, supported a pro-Macedonian policy.

Demaratus: king of Sparta, colleague of Cleomenes I, accompanied Xerxes on the expedition to Greece, 480 BC.

***Demeter**: sister of Zeus, goddess of agriculture and of the Eleusinian mysteries.

Demetrius: *1. Demetrius I of Macedonia, Poliorcetes, 'the Besieger', son of Antigonus, hailed as 'saviour' at Athens 307 BC, regent with his father 306 BC; after Antigonus' death at Ipsus (301 BC), established a kingdom in Greece, and ruled as king of Macedonia and Thessaly, 293–287 BC. Life by Plutarch. 2. Demetrius II of Macedonia, regent from 262, king 238–229 BC. *3. Demetrius of Phalerum, Athenian statesman and philosopher, governor of Athens under Macedonians, 317–307 BC, expelled by 1, and went to Egypt. 4. Demetrius of Tarsus, character in II, identifiable with the

Demetrius who made a dedication to Ocean and Tethys and the gods of the governor's headquarters, known from an inscription found at York (R. G. Collingwood and R. P. Wright, *The Roman Inscriptions in Britain* (Oxford, 1965) 662–3).

Democrates: Athenian orator, 4th cent. BC, pro-Macedonian.

***Democritus of Abdera**: (*c*.460–360 BC); the atomist and hedonist philosopher.

Demos of Chios: politician, date unknown.

***Demosthenes**: (384–322 BC), the greatest Athenian orator.

Diagoras of Melos: known as 'the atheist'; late 5th cent. BC, lived in Athens.

Dicaearchia: Greek name for Puteoli (Pozzuoli), seaport on the Bay of Naples

***Diogenes of Sinope**: (*c*.400–*c*.325 BC), founder of the Cynic school.

Diogenianus: character in III, son of Diogenianus of Pergamum, grammarian, friend of Plutarch.

***Diomedes**: son of Tydeus, a prominent Greek hero in the *Iliad*.

Dion: (*c*.408–354 BC), brother-in-law of Dionysius I of *Syracuse; pupil of Plato; liberated Syracuse from tyranny, 357 BC, but was murdered by Callippus (q.v.) in 354.

***Dionysius**: 1. Dionysius I, tyrant of Syracuse, 406–467 BC. 2. Dionysius II, tyrant of Syracuse, 367–57 BC, and again 347/6–344 BC. Lived in exile at Corinth. 3. Poet, author of *Aitia*: date unknown.

***Dionysus**: son of Zeus and Semele, god of wine and of ecstasy.

Dioxippus of Athens: Olympian victor, 4th cent. BC.

***Dirce**: wife of Lycus, ruler of Thebes; killed by Amphion and Zethus, sons of Antiope. Changed into a river called by her name.

***Dolon**: Trojan spy killed by Odysseus and Diomedes (*Iliad* 10).

Domitian: Roman emperor AD 81–96.

Dromoclides of Sphettus: Athenian politician, flatterer of Demetrius Poliorcetes.

Echinades: islands off West coast of Greece, near mouth of R. Achelous (Aspropotamos).

***Egeria**: a nymph, supposedly visited by Numa Pompilius.

***Eleusis**: town West of Athens, seat of the mysteries of Demeter and Persephone.

***Elis**: city and region in north-west Peloponnese.

Emathion: son of Eos (the Dawn goddess) and Tithonus, and brother of Memnon; ruler of Ethiopia; killed by Heracles.

***Empedocles of Acragas**: (*c*.493–*c*.433 BC); philosopher and poet.

***Enyalius**: a god of war, identified or associated with Ares.

***Epaminondas**: the greatest Theban statesman and general, victor of Leuctra (371 BC), killed at Mantinea (362 BC). Life by Plutarch, lost.

***Ephialtes**: Athenian statesman of democratic tendency, whose reforms reduced the powers of the Areopagus, 462/1 BC. He was murdered shortly afterwards.

***Ephorus of Cyme**: (*c*.405–330 BC): an important historian.

Epicaste: Homer's name for Jocasta, the mother and wife of Oedipus.

***Epicharmus**: comic writer, of Syracuse, 5th cent. BC.

***Epicurus**: (341–270 BC); philosopher, founder of the Epicurean (atomist and hedonist) school; opposed by Plutarch as a denier of divine providence.

***Epidaurus**: city of the Peloponnese, famous for its sanctuary of Asclepius.

***Epimenides**: of Phaestus in Crete; religious teacher and prophet, 6th–5th cent. BC, said to have slept miraculously for 57 years.

***Erasistratus of Ceos**: physician, 3rd cent. BC.

Eretria: city in Euboea.

Erythrae: city on the Asiatic coast, opposite Chios.

Euboea: large island of northern Greece, off the coast of Attica and Boeotia, from which it is separated by a narrow channel (Euripus), now bridged.

***Eubulus**: (*c*.405–*c*.335 BC): Athenian statesman and financier, pro-Macedonian.

***Eudoxus of Cnidus**: (*c*.400–*c*.350 BC): mathematician and astronomer.

Eumenes of Cardia: (*c*.362–316 BC); secretary of Alexander, later a general; defeated and executed 316 BC by the soldiers of Antigonus. Life by Plutarch.

***Euripides**: (*c*.485–406 BC); the tragic poet.

Eurotas: the river on which Sparta stands.

Eurycles: a prophet and ventriloquist, mentioned by Plato and Aristophanes (*Wasps* 1019).

Eurydice: *1. in myth, the wife of Orpheus. 2. the addressee (with her husband Pollianus) of XIV.

***Eurymedon**: river of southern Asia Minor, near which the Greeks under Cimon defeated the Persian fleet, *c*.467 BC.

Euthyphro: Athenian diviner (*mantis*), name-character of Plato's dialogue *Euthyphro: On piety*.

Euxitheus: said (VII. 803) to be a friend of pupil of Aristotle, but perhaps a character in one of his dialogues.

Fabius Maximus, Paullus: consul 11 BC, close friend of Augustus.

***Fabius Maximus Cunctator, Q.**: Roman general, consul 233 BC, dictator 221 BC, successful general against Hannibal, thanks to his caution and patience. Life by Plutarch (who pairs him with Pericles).

***Fabricius, C.**: hero of the war with *Pyrrhus, consul 282 and 278 BC.

Gabii: small town between Rome and Praeneste (Palestrina), a deserted village in imperial times.

***Galatia**: part of Phrygia (Asia Minor), occupied in 3rd cent. BC by invading Gauls (Tolistobogii, Tectosagi, Trocmi). Defeated by the Romans 190 BC, these tribes were generally ruled by kings who favoured Rome (v. Deiotarus), and in 25 BC the region became a Roman province.

Gegania: wife of Servius Tullius.

***Geryon**: a three-bodied giant living in the far west, whose cattle Heracles stole.

Glauce: lyre-player, singer, and composer, from Chios; active at the court of Ptolemy II (late 3rd cent. BC).

Gnatho: 'Big Jaw'; name of a Sicilian glutton, and of 'parasites' (professional diners-out) in comedy, e.g. in Terence's *Eunuchus*.

***Gorgias of Leontini**: (*c*.483–*c*.385 BC); sophist and teacher, famous for his artificial and highly antithetical prose style.

Gorgo: 1. wife of Leonidas, the Spartan king who commanded at Thermopylae (480 BC). 2. a Cretan woman, subject of a love story alluded to in XIII. 766.

***Gorgons**: three female monsters, with glaring eyes and serpents in their hair; one of them, Medusa, was killed by Perseus.

***Gracchus, C.**: younger brother of Tib. Gracchus; Roman reformer, *tribunus plebis* 123–2 BC, died in a riot 121 BC. Life (of both brothers) by Plutarch.

***Gyges**: king of Lydia (*c*.685–657 BC), the founder of the dynasty that ended with Croesus (q.v.).

Habrotonon: mother of Themistocles (q.v.).

Haliartus: town of Boeotia, south of Lake Copais.

***Hannibal**: (247–182 BC); the great Carthaginian general in the Second Punic War. Defeated at Zama (202 BC) he left Carthage shortly after. His suicide in Bithynia (182 BC?) prevented his surrender to the Romans by King Prusias.

Hanno: son of Hamilcar, Carthaginian commander who conquered large territories in Africa, 5th cent. BC. Doubtfully identified with the Hanno who sailed down west coast of Africa, 6th–5th cent. BC.

***Harmodius**: see Aristogiton.

Harpalus: (*c*.355–323 BC); disloyal Macedonian nobleman, entrusted by Alexander with the central treasury; fled to Athens, and bribed Athenian politicians. Demosthenes was among those involved in the scandal.

***Hecate**: a goddess of the Underworld, associated with magic or necromancy, often identified with Artemis and Selene (the moon).

***Hector**: eldest son of Priam, and the principal defender of Troy against the Greeks; his death at the hands of Achilles is the climax of the *Iliad*.

***Hecuba**: wife of Priam, king of Troy.

***Helen**: daughter of Zeus and Leda, wife of Menelaus; her seduction by Paris led to the Trojan war.

***Helicon**: mountain range in Boeotia, sacred to Apollo and the Muses.

Helicon of Cyzicus: mathematician and astronomer, contemporary and associate of Plato.

***Hephaestus**: son of Zeus and Hera, the god of fire and of metal-work.

***Hera**: wife and sister of Zeus (= Latin Juno).

***Heracles** (= Latin **Hercules**): 1. the greatest Greek hero, son of Zeus and Alcmena. 2. a son of Alexander the Great by Barcine.

***Heraclitus of Ephesus**: (*c*.500 BC); philosopher, noted for his obscure aphorisms.

***Hermes**: son of Zeus and Maia, messenger of the gods, guide of souls in Hades, patron of eloquence, thieves, and athletes.

Hermione: daughter of Menelaus and Helen, wife of Orestes.

Hermolaus: member of Alexander's guard, who conspired against the king and was put to death in 327 BC.

***Herophilus of Chalcedon**: doctor who practised in Alexandria *c*.290 BC.

***Hesiod**: Boeotian poet (8th cent. BC?), author of *Theogony, Works and Days* (on which Plutarch wrote a commentary), and other works.

Hiero: tyrant of Gela (485 BC) and Syracuse (478 BC), one of the sons of Deinomenes.

***Hipparchus**: 1. son of Pisistratus, tyrant of Athens, assassinated by Harmodius and Aristogiton (514 BC). 2. of Nicaea, astronomer, 2nd cent. BC.

***Hippocrates of Cos**: (*c*.460–*c*.370 BC); the most famous Greek doctor, reputed author of many medical works.

***Hippys of Rhegium**: historian, 5th cent. BC.

***Hirtius, A**: consul 43 BC, one of Caesar's officers; wrote the completion (Book VIII) of the *Gallic War*; killed in fighting against Antony at Mutina.

***Homer**: the poet of the *Iliad* and *Odyssey*.

Horatius Cocles: Roman hero who 'held the bridge' against Porsena's army in 509 BC.

Hyampolis: city in Phocis, north-west of Lake Copais.

***Hyperides**: (389–322 BC); Athenian orator, anti-Macedonian; among his surviving speeches is a funeral oration on the war-dead of the Lamian campaign (322 BC). Put to death after the Macedonian victory.

Hyrcania: region of Asia, south of Caspian Sea.
***Ibycus of Rhegium**: lyric poet, 6th cent. BC.
***Ictinus**: the architect who designed the Parthenon.
Ilithyia: Greek goddess of childbirth.
Imbros: island of northern Aegean.
***Ino**: daughter of Cadmus and Harmonia, wife of Athamas (q.v.).
Iolaus: companion and charioteer of Heracles, worshipped in Boeotia.
***Ion of Chios**: tragic poet and prose writer, 5th cent. BC.
Iphicrates: (*c*.415–353 BC); Athenian general, successful commander of light troops and mercenaries in many campaigns.
***Iris**: the goddess of the rainbow.
Ischomachus: Athenian, the principal personage in Xenophon's *Oeconomicus*, who probably figured in other (lost) Socratic dialogues.
Ismenias: name of several distinguished Thebans: 1. a patriot, put to death after the occupation of the Cadmea (IV. 576). 2. his son, a friend of Pelopidas. 3. a famous piper, 4th cent. BC. 4. a Boeotian leader, 2nd cent. BC.
Ismenus: river of Thebes, from whose name many personal names (e.g. Ismenias, Ismenodora) are derived.
Ister: the river Danube.
Istros: 3rd cent. BC, scholar and antiquarian, pupil of *Callimachus.
***Ithaca**: island off west coast of Greece, home of Odysseus.
***Ixion**: mythical ruler of the Lapiths (Thessaly), a great sinner, who murdered a kinsman and attempted to rape Hera (but was deceived into embracing a phantom); punished in Hades, tied to a revolving fiery wheel.
***Jason of Thessaly**: tyrant of Pherae, *c*.385–370 BC, friendly to Thebes. Assassinated.
***Jugurtha**: king of Numidia who provoked war with Rome (112 BC) and was finally defeated by Marius in 105, and then executed.
Laander: brother and successor of Nicocrates, tyrant of Cyrene *c*.90 BC.
Laarchus: tyrant of Cyrene, 6th cent. BC.
Lacedes: king of Argos, one of the suitors of Agariste, and son of Pheidon, 6th cent. BC.
Laches: Athenian politician and general, supporter of peace with Sparta; killed at Mantinea, 418 BC. Principal character of Plato's *Laches*.
Lachesis: one of the three *Fates (Moirai), cf. Atropos, Clotho.
***Laelius C.**: friend of Scipio Aemilianus and consul 140 BC.
Lais: the name of two celebrated courtesans, the elder from Corinth, the younger a Sicilian (both 4th cent. BC).

***Laius**: father of Oedipus.

***Lamachus**: Athenian general, killed at Syracuse, 414 BC.

***Lamia**: 1. a town in Thessaly. 2. 'The Strangler', a bogy-figure used to frighten children, whom she is supposed to devour; according to one myth, she was the daughter of Poseidon; and she is often associated with Libya.

Lampon: Athenian diviner, friend of Pericles.

Lampsacus: city on eastern shore of Hellespont, facing Callipolis (Gallipoli).

***Lasus of Hermione**: lyric poet and musician, 6th cent. BC.

Lebadea: important town of Boeotia, west of Lake Copais, modern Livadia.

***Leda**: wife of Tyndareus, king of Sparta; mother (by Zeus, who came to her as a swan) of Helen, Castor, and Polydeuces.

***Lemnos**: large island of northern Aegean.

Leon of Byzantium: pupil of Plato, friend of Phocion; hanged himself, 340 BC, because he was accused of letting the Athenians into Byzantium.

Leontis: friend of Plutarch and Clea, whose death occasioned the writing of XVI.

Leosthenes: Athenian general, victorious in the futile war against the Macedonians 323–322 BC, but killed in the *Lamian War 322 BC.

***Lepidus, M. Aemilius**: (*c*.90–12 BC); Caesar's colleague as consul, 46 BC, joined Antony and Octavian in the second triumvirate, Oct./Nov. 43; lost power 36, but continued in office as *pontifex maximus*.

Leptis: city of north Africa, Phoenician colony, on Roman side in Jugurthan war, very prosperous in imperial times.

***Lethe**: 'forgetfulness', the name of one of the mythical rivers of Hades.

Leuconia: town of Ionia, probably Leucas or Leuce, near Phocaea (XVI. 244).

***Leuctra**: plain near Thespiae in Boeotia, where Epaminondas and the Thebans defeated the Spartans in 371 BC.

Libya: Greek name for the continent of Africa.

Lichas: rich Spartan, chariot victor at Olympia 420 BC, died 411 BC at Miletus (VII. 823).

***Livia Drusilla**: wife of Ti. Claudius Nero, subsequently wife of Augustus.

Livius *Drusus, M.: *tribunus plebis* 91 BC, a reformer who aimed at reconciling the Italian allies to Rome.

Locri: Greek city of southern Italy, near modern Gerace, colonized from western Locris.

Locris: two areas of central Greece: 1. eastern Locris, on the coast between Thessaly and Boeotia. 2. western Locris, on northern coast of gulf of Corinth, east of Aetolia.

Lucania: region of southern Italy, between Tyrrhenian Sea and Gulf of Tarentum.

***Lucretia**: wife of L. Tarquinius Collatinus, whose rape by Sextus, son of Tarquinius Superbus, led to the revolution which ended the monarchy, 510 BC.

***Lucullus, L. Licinius**: (*c.*114–57 BC); Roman general and statesman, follower of Sulla, consul 74 BC, conqueror of Mithridates. Life by Plutarch.

Lycia: coastal region of south-west Asia Minor.

Lyctus (Lyttus): city of northern Crete, south-east of Cnossus.

***Lycurgus**: Spartan lawgiver (8th cent. BC?), founder of the 'good order' (*eunomia*) of Spartan society. Life by Plutarch.

Lynceus: mythical hero who took part in the Argonauts' expedition; proverbial for sharp sight—he could see through a piece of wood.

***Lysander**: Spartan commander, victorious in the Peloponneisan War, killed at Haliartus in the Corinthian War, 395 BC. Life by Plutarch.

***Lysias**: (*c.*459–*c.*380 BC); Attic orator, son of a Syracusan immigrant; supporter of democracy in 404 BC; famous for the purity of his style and the excellence of his portrayal and representation of character.

Lysimachus: (*c.*355–282 BC); one of Alexander's generals, king of Thrace from 306 BC, occupied eastern Macedonia 285 BC, but was attacked by other 'successor' kings, and died in battle, 282 BC.

Lysis of Tarentum: Pythagorean who fled from Croton (q.v.) to Thebes after the destruction of the Pythagorean communities in Italy.

Lysithides: Athenian, nephew of the democratic politician Thrasybulus.

***Maecenas, C. Cilnius**: (d. 8 BC); friend of Augustus, patron of Virgil and Horace.

Maeonia: ancient name for Lydia.

Magnesia: a district of Thessaly. (Also a common place-name in other areas).

Malis: coastal region of northern Greece, bounded on north by Thessaly.

***Mamertines**: mercenaries who occupied Messina after the death of Agathocles (289 BC), and resisted Pyrrhus. They were loyal to Rome in the First Punic War.

Mantias: Athenian politician, 4th cent. BC, known from a joke in comedy (VII. 801).

***Mantinea**: principal city of Arcadia, destroyed in 385 BC, rebuilt in 371 after Theban victory at Leuctra. Scene of important battles in 418 BC and 362 BC. (the Theban defeat).

***Marathon**: place on north-east coast of Attica, scene of the defeat of the Persians by Miltiades (q.v.), 490 BC.

***Marcellus, M. Claudius**: consul 222 BC, captured Syracuse 211 BC. Famous general; Life by Plutarch.

Mardonius: son-in-law of Darius I, and Xerxes' chief commander in the Greek campaign of 480–479 BC.

***Marius, C.**: (157–86 BC); Roman general, first promoted in the war with Jugurtha; victor over Cimbri and Teutones; rival and opponent of Sulla, six times consul. Life by Plutarch.

Masaesylians: a people of the coast of Mauretania (Morocco).

***Medea**: daughter of Aeetes, king of Colchis; a sorceress who helped Jason to win the Golden Fleece, and subsequently married him; she later killed their children and Jason's new wife.

***Megara**: city on the eastern side of the Isthmus of Corinth.

Megisto: wife of Timoleon of Elis, (XVI, [15]).

Melanippe: daughter of Aeolus, who bore twins by Poseidon. Euripides wrote two (lost) plays on her story.

Melanippides of Melos: lyric poet, 5th cent. BC.

Melanippus of Acragas: assassin of the tyrant Phalaris, 6th cent. BC.

Melanthius: Athenian tragic poet, 5th cent. BC (XIV, 144; uncertain identification).

***Meleager**: son of Oeneus and Althaea, famous for his part in the hunting of the Great Boar of Calydon; died when his mother burnt the brand on which his life was fated to depend.

Melos: island in the Sporades, brutally subdued by the Athenians, 416 BC.

Memphis: city of Lower Egypt.

***Menander**: 1. Athenian comic poet (342–*c*.290 BC), the principal writer of New Comedy, i.e. the comedy of everyday manners and domestic life. 2. king of Bactria, the Greek Buddhist ruler of the Indo-Greek kingdom, 155–130 BC (VII. 821).

Meneclides: Theban orator, opponent of Pelopidas and Epaminondas, involved in the liberation of Thebes, 379 BC.

Menedemus of Eretria: (*c*.350–278 BC); philosopher.

***Merope**: wife of Cresphontes, subject of a (lost) play by Euripides. Forced to marry Polyphontes, the murderer of her husband and children, she subsequently conspired with her surviving child, Aepytus, to kill him. See Matthew Arnold, *Merope*.

***Messene**: 1. region of Peloponnese, subjugated by Sparta, 7th cent. BC, but revived as an independent power, 369 BC. 2. city of Sicily on the 'Straits of Messina'.

Metapontum: city of southern Italy, west of Tarentum; site of Pythagoras' grave.

Metellus Macedonicus, Q. Caecilius: consul 143 BC; had four sons who were consuls (VI. 318).

Metiochus: friend of Pericles, known only from the abuse of him in comedy.

Metrodorus of Lampsacus: (331/0–278/7 BC); pupil of Epicurus.

***Midas**: legendary king of Phrygia, whose touch turned all to gold.

***Miletus**: Ionian city of Asia Minor, a great colonizing power, especially in the Black Sea region.

***Miltiades**: Athenian general, the victor of Marathon (q.v.).

***Mithridates VI Eupator**: (120–63 BC); king of Pontus, and lifelong opponent of Roman power in the east; finally defeated by Pompey 67 BC.

Mitylene (or Mytilene): principal city of Lesbos.

Mnesarete: see Phryne.

***Mopsus**: Cretan prophet, who founded the oracle at Claros and (with Amphilochus) that of Mallus in Cilicia.

Mucius Scaevola, C.: hero of early republican Rome, who plunged his right hand into flames in order to show the Etruscan King Porsena (q.v.) how cheaply he held life (Livy 2.12).

***Mummius, L.**: the Roman consul who sacked and destroyed Corinth (146 BC).

***Musonius Rufus, C.**: (*c.*30–100 AD); Roman Stoic, exiled by Nero (AD 65–6) to the island of Gyaros. Teacher of Epictetus; author of some moral lectures which have survived.

Myrina: a place in Lemnos (III. 401); but also the name of a coastal city of north-west Asia Minor.

Myus: Ionian city at mouth of R. Maeander.

Nabis: ruler of Sparta 207–192 BC; a revolutionary despot.

Naxos: island of the Cyclades, centre of the cult of Dionysus.

Neileus: legendary founder of Miletus, younger son of Codrus, king of Athens.

***Neoptolemus**: 1. son of Achilles. 2. general of Alexander, later satrap of Armenia, who fell in battle fighting Eumenes.

***Nero**: the Roman emperor AD 54–69.

Nesiotes: sculptor, worked in Athens, 5th cent. BC.

***Nestor**: mythical king of Pylos, the wise old warrior of the *Iliad*.

Nicander: priest at Delphi in Plutarch's time.

Niceratus: probably the son of Nicias, put to death by the Thirty Tyrants, 404 BC (VII. 823).

***Nicias, son of Niceratus**: Athenian statesman and general; defeated, captured, and put to death at Syracuse 413 BC. Life by Plutarch.

Nicocles: tyrant of Sicyon, ruled for four months after murdering his predecessor; was then deposed by Aratus, 251 BC.

Nicocrates: tyrant of Cyrene, *c*.90 BC.

Nicomachus of Thebes: painter, late 4th cent. BC.

Nicostratus of Argos: 1. Argive commander in 4th cent. BC; cf. Archidamus (XI. 535). 2. perhaps the same as 1, perhaps an Argive politician of the time of Philip V (XII. 760).

Ninus: legendary founder of Nineveh.

***Niobe**: daughter of Tantalus, wife of Amphion, mother of six children, of whom she boasted to Leto; Apollo and Artemis, Leto's twins, then killed all six. Niobe wept for them, and was turned into a rock on Mt. Sipylus in Lydia.

***Numa Pompilius**: second king of Rome, traditionally dated 715–673 BC, lawgiver and religious reformer.

***Numantia**: town on upper Douro, besieged by Romans on several occasions, finally taken by Scipio Aemilianus, 133 BC.

Numitor: father of Rea Silvia, and so grandfather of Romulus; king of Alba Longa, deposed by Amulius, reinstated by Romulus and Remus.

Nymphis: historian of Alexander and his successors, and of his own native city, Heraclea on Pontus (3rd cent. BC).

***Odysseus**: the cunning hero from Ithaca, whose wanderings and return home are the theme of the *Odyssey*.

Oechalia: city sacked by Heracles, whence he captured Iole, daughter of Eurytus; most often supposed to be in Euboea.

Oedipus: mythical king of Thebes, son of Laius (whom he unknowingly killed) and Jocasta (whom he unknowingly married).

Oenanthe: mother of Agathoclea (q.v.).

***Olympias**: wife of Philip II of Macedon and mother of Alexander the Great; murdered 316 BC.

***Olynthus**: city in Chalcidice (northern Greece), destroyed by Philip II, 348 BC.

***Onomacritus**: Athenian, collector of oracles (*chrēsmologos*), supposed to have been involved in Pisistratus' recension of Homer (6th cent. BC).

Opus: principal town of eastern Locris.

Orchomenus: ancient city of Boeotia, at western end of Lake Copais.

***Orestes**: son of Agamemnon, murderer of his mother, Clytemnestra.

***Orion**: giant and hunter, loved by Eos (the Dawn) and killed by Artemis out of jealousy: chased the seven Pleiades (daughters of Atlas) and, like them, became a constellation.

Ornea (Orneae): city of Peloponnese, north-west of Argos.

***Orpheus**: mythical poet and prophet, to whom poems of religious content were attributed.

Orsilaus of Delphi: killed by the father of the bride he refused to marry; date and circumstances unknown (VII. 825).

***Osiris**: Egyptian god, incarnated in the sacred bull Apis. Plutarch wrote extensively on his cult in *Isis and Osiris* (= *Moralia* 23).

Ortiagon: Galatian chieftain, captured by Romans 189 BC.

Pammenes of Thebes: supporter of Epaminondas, whom he succeeded as commander-in chief of the Theban army (362 BC).

***Panaetius of Rhodes**: (*c.*185–109 BC); Stoic philosopher, friend of Scipio Aemilianus, influential teacher of ethics.

Pandosia: city of Bruttium, scene of battle in which Alexander of Epirus was killed (326 BC).

Pansa, C. Vibius: consul 43 BC, colleague of A. Hirtius (q.v.).

Panthea: see Araspas.

Pardalas of Sardis: unfortunate politician who evidently fell foul of the Roman power (VII. 813, 825).

***Paris**: Trojan prince, son of Priam and Hecuba, seducer of Helen.

Parium: city of Asia Minor, on the Hellespont.

***Parmenides of Elea**: philosopher-poet, 5th cent. BC.

Parnassus: mountain near Delphi, associated with the cult of Apollo and the Muses.

***Pasiphae**: wife of Minos and mother of Ariadne and (by a bull) of the Minotaur.

Patrae: city of Achaea, northern coast of Peloponnese.

***Patroclus**: in *Iliad*, the close friend of Achilles whose death at the hands of Hector led Achilles to rejoin the battle.

Pausanias: member of Philip II's guard, who assassinated the king at Aegae 336 BC, and was himself killed.

Pauson: painter (Athenian?) who, according to Aristotle, painted people 'worse than they are'.

Paxi: Paxos and Antipaxos, two islands south of Corfu.

***Pegasus**: winged horse, child of Poseidon and Medusa, ridden by Bellerophon in his attack on the Chimaera (q.v.).

***Pelasgians**: a name given to pre-Greek inhabitants of the Aegean area, especially the northern islands and Crete; sometimes identified with the Tyrrhenians (Etruscans).

***Peleus**: hero of the region of Mt. Pelion, husband of the goddess Thetis, and father of Achilles.

***Pelopidas**: Theban statesman, friend and collaborator of Epaminondas. Life by Plutarch.

***Penelope**: wife of Odysseus.

Peparethus: small island in the Sporades.

***Pergamum**: city of north-western Asia Minor, capital of the Attalid kingdom from 3rd cent. BC; a great centre of the cult of Asclepius.

***Periander**: 1. tyrant of Corinth, son of Cypselus, ruled *c*.625–*c*.585 BC. 2. tyrant of Ambracia, nephew or grandson of 1.

***Pericles**: (*c*.490–429 BC); the Athenian statesman. Life by Plutarch.

Persaeus of Citium: Stoic philosopher at the court of Antigonus Gonatas.

***Persephone**: daughter of Demeter, wife of Pluto.

***Perseus**: king of Macedon 179–168 BC; defeated and deposed by the Romans, died in captivity.

Petraeus: 1. a Thessalian, burnt alive in the time of Augustus (VII. 815). 2. C. Cassius Petraeus, friend of Plutarch (III. 409).

***Phaestus**: town of southern Crete, site of a Minoan palace; home of Epimenides.

Phalanthus: legendary founder of Tarentum.

***Phalaris**: tyrant of Acragas in Sicily, *c*.570–554 BC, noted for his cruelty.

Phanias: of Eresus in Lesbos (*c*.375–300 BC); philosopher, pupil of Aristotle.

***Pharsalus**: city of Thessaly.

***Phidias of Athens**: (5th cent. BC); the great sculptor, famous especially for Athena Parthenos at Athens and Zeus at Olympia.

***Philip**: 1. *Philip II of Macedon, father of Alexander the Great, king 359–336 BC. 2. *Philip V of Macedon, (238–179 BC); father of Perseus (q.v.), became embroiled with Rome and was defeated in 197 BC by Q. Flamininus (see Plutarch's Life) at Cynoscephalae.

Philippides: Athenian comic poet, 4th–3rd cent. BC, favourite of King Lysimachus.

***Philochorus of Athens**: (*c*.340–*c*.267 BC); writer of Athenian history.

Philolaus of Croton: Pythagorean philosopher, (5th–4th cent. BC).

Philomelus: leader of the Phocians in the Third Sacred War, occupied Delphi (356–348 BC).

***Philopoemen of Megalopolis**: (253–183 BC); statesman and general of the Achaean League, greatly admired by Polybius. Life by Plutarch.

Philoxenus: *1. of Cythera (435–380 BC), lyric poet. 2. poet at court of Dionysius I of Syracuse, perhaps the same as Philoxenus son of Eryxis, a noted glutton; wrote a poem entitled 'Dinner'. 3. an official of Alexander, charged with financial affairs and relations with the Aegean cities *c*.333 BC.

***Phineus**: legendary Thracian king, plagued by the Harpies, who stole or defiled his food.

***Phocaea**: city of Asia Minor, near mouth of R. Hermus.

***Phocion**: Athenian general (held office 45 times), a powerful influence, especially 345–318 BC, generally advocating accommodation with Macedon. Life by Plutarch.

***Phocis**: region of central Greece, adjoining Boeotia, and including Delphi.

Phoebidas: Spartan commander who seized the citadel of Thebes, 382 BC; killed at Thespiae, 378 BC.

Pholegandros: small island in the Cyclades, now Polykandro.

Phormio of Elis: disciple of Plato (VII. 805).

***Phryne**: a famous courtesan, 4th cent. BC. Her real name was Mnesarete. 'Phryne' means 'toad'.

***Phrynichus**: Athenian tragic poet, who was fined for the depressing impact of his play on the fall of Miletus (492 BC).

***Pindar Theban**: (518–*c*.446 BC); lyric poet, perhaps Plutarch's favourite author.

***Pisa**: city of Elis, a little north-east of the site of Olympia.

***Pittacus**: (*c*.650–570 BC); ruler of Mytilene, one of the Seven Sages; violently opposed by the poet Alcaeus.

***Plataea**: town of Boeotia, near the Attic frontier; scene of battle with Persians, 479 BC.

***Plato**: 1. comic poet, contemporary with Aristophanes. 2. the philosopher (428–348 BC.).

Pleistoanax: king of Sparta, 458–408 BC.

Pollianus: see Eurydice.

Polus: tragic actor, 4th cent. BC.

***Polybius**: (*c*.200–*c*.120 BC); the historian, the first to chronicle the rise of Rome as a world power.

Polycrates: 1. *tyrant of Samos, 6th cent. BC. 2. of Sicyon, friend of Plutarch (III. 409).

Polyeuctus of Sphettus: Athenian orator, anti-Macedonian, colleague of Demosthenes in embassy to Peloponnese 343/2 BC, survived at least to 320 BC.

***Polygnotus of Thasos**: painter (active 480–440 BC); son and pupil of Aglaophon.

Polyperchon: Macedonian commander who succeeded Antipater as regent 319 BC; unable to maintain his position, he became a mercenary leader, serving now Antigonus, now Cassander.

***Polyphemus**: see Cyclopes.

***Pompeius Magnus, Cn.**: (106–48 BC); Pompey, the great Roman general and statesman, Caesar's defeated opponent in the civil war of 49–8 BC. Life by Plutarch.

***Porcia**: daughter of Cato (2), and wife of Brutus (2), committed suicide 43 BC.

***Porsena (Porsina, Porsenna)**: Etruscan ruler of Clusium (Chiusi), who tried to restore Tarquinius Superbus to his kingdom of Rome.

***Poseidon**: the god of the sea (= Latin *Neptunus*), brother of Zeus and Aidoneus (Hades).

Praeneste: town of Latium, east of Rome; now Palestrina.

***Praxiteles of Athens**: (4th cent. BC); the famous sculptor.

***Priam**: king of Troy.

Procles: tyrant of Epidaurus, whose daughter Melissa married Periander (1).

Prodicus of Ceos: *sophist, contemporary of Socrates. (The person mentioned III. 407, if the reading is right, is different).

***Protesilaus**: Greek hero, killed in landing at Troy; his wife Laodamia was miraculously allowed to see him again for three hours, after which she killed herself.

***Proteus**: a sea-god, with power to change himself into any shape; also decribed as a king of Egypt.

Ptoion: mountain area in Boeotia, east of Lake Copais, site of oracle of Apollo.

***Ptolemy**: 1. Ptolemy I, Soter, Macedonian general, king of Egypt 304–282 BC. 2. Ptolemy XIII, king of Egypt 51–47 BC, whose ministers killed Pompey.

Publicola, P. Valerius: one of the first consuls, 509 BC; lawgiver. Life by Plutarch.

Pupius Piso, M.: consul 61 BC, died before 47 BC, orator and wit (X. 511).

***Pylos**: area in western Peloponnese, centre of Nestor's kingdom according to Homer.

Pyrilampes: a rich Athenian, son of Antiphon, and friend of Pericles.

***Pyrrhus**: (319–272 BC); king of Epirus. Life by Plutarch.

***Pythagoras of Samos**: the philosopher and religious teacher, 6th cent. BC.

Pytheas: Athenian orator and politician, 4th cent. BC, at first supporter of Demosthenes, then pro-Macedonian.

Pythes: 1. a wealthy Lydian at the time of Xerxes' invasion of Greece. 2. of Aenus, assassin of the Thracian prince Cotys, 360 BC.

Raria: 'the field of Rarus', Rarus being the father of Triptolemus (q.v.); a sacred area at Eleusis, where ritual ploughing was carried out.

***Rhea**: daughter of Uranus and Gaia (Heaven and Earth), mother of Zeus; identified with Cybele or (in Egypt) with Nut, the mother of the gods.

***Rhodopis**: 'Rose-face', a famous courtesan, said to have been a fellow slave of Aesop.

Romulus: the founder of *Rome.

Rutilius Gallicus, C: *praefectus urbi* 89 AD, d. AD 92.

Sabinus, Julius: chieftain of the Lingones (tribe of Gaul), ally of Julius Civilis in the revolt of AD 70.

Salmantica: Salamanca.

***Samos**: large and fertile Greek island off the Asiatic coast, facing Mt. Mycale.

***Sappho**: the Lesbian poetess (b. *c*.612 BC).

Sarapion (Serapion): Athenian poet, friend of Plutarch; perhaps the author of a poem on the duties of a doctor known from an inscription.

***Sarapis (Serapis)**: god worshipped in Egypt from time of Ptolemy I, who is said to have introduced the cult, which later became very important throughout the Mediterranean world.

Sardis: capital of Lydia, in the plain of the R. Pactolus.

Sarmatians: nomadic Iranian people of the steppes, who spread from the region north of the Caucasus across southern Russia.

Scilurus (Scylurus): powerful Scythian king, late 2nd cent. BC, whose capital was Neapolis (near Simferopol, in Crimea), but who minted coins also at Olbia.

***Scipio**: 1. P. Cornelius Scipio Africanus (236–184/3 BC), successful opponent of the Carthaginians in Spain, finally defeated Hannibal at Zama, 202 BC. 2. P. Cornelius Scipio Aemilianus (185/4–129 BC), adopted by the son of 1; friend of Polybius, Laelius, Panaetius; captured Numantia 133 BC; died in mysterious circumstances, 129 BC. Plutarch wrote a 'Life of Scipio', as a parallel to Epaminondas; it is lost, and it is not sure whether 1 or 2 was the subject, but it seems certain that he wrote a life of 2 at least.

***Sciron**: a legendary brigand, said to kick travellers over the cliff near Megara.

Scythinus of Teos: philosophical poet, 5th–4th cent. BC.

Seleucus II: 'the Victorious'; king of Syria, 246–225 BC, fourth king of the *Seleucid dynasty.

Selinus: city of south-west Sicily, flourished 5th cent. BC until destroyed by Carthaginians.

Semiramis: the legendary queen supposed to have built Babylon (legend based on Sammuramat, regent of Assyria, 810–805 BC).

Sertorius, Q.: Roman general, who led a revolt against Roman rule in Spain; murdered 73 or 72 BC. Life by Plutarch.

***Servius Tullius**: sixth king of Rome (traditional dates 578–535 BC), of Latin origin, lawgiver and reformer.

Sesostris: Egyptian king, and conqueror of Asia; in Herodotus (2. 102–111), Sethos I (Nineteenth Dynasty) seems to be meant, but Greek notions of Egyptian history were confused.

***Sibyl**: the name given to a number of inspired prophetesses, including one at Delphi.

***Sicyon**: a city of the northern Peloponnese, west of Corinth, powerful in 7th and 6th cent. BC.

Simmias: 1. Athenian, an accuser of Pericles in 430 BC. 2. of Thebes, character in Plato's *Phaedo* and in IV.

***Simonides of Ceos**: (556–468 BC); lyric poet.

***Sisyphus**: son of Aeolus, seduced Autolycus' daughter Anticlea, and was believed to be Odysseus' real father; cheated Death, but was eventually punished in Hades by being made to push a rock which always rolled down on him.

Soclarus, T. Flavius: of Tithora in Phocis, close friend of Plutarch.

Socrates: 1. *the teacher and philosopher, 470–399 BC. 2. historian of Argos (XVI. 245).

***Solon**: (*c*.640–*c*.560 BC); Athenian lawgiver, archon 594 BC. Life by Plutarch.

Solymi: people of south-west Asia who fought against Bellerophon.

Sphodrias: Spartan governor of Thespiae who attempted to seize Piraeus 379 BC.

***Sphinx**: in Greek legend, a female monster (woman, lion, bird) sent by Hera to torment Thebes. Oedipus solved her riddle, and she threw herself off the rock.

Spintharus: Pythagorean, of Tarentum, 4th cent. BC, perhaps father of Aristoxenus, the Peripatetic philosopher and musical theorist.

Sthenelaidas: Spartan ephor at the time of the outbreak of war with Athens, 432 BC.

Stilpo: (*c*.380–300 BC); philosopher of the Megarian school, a brilliant logician.

Stratocles: Athenian orator, flatterer of Demetrius Poliorcetes, influential in Athens from 307 BC, and still active in early 3rd cent. BC.

***Styx**: 'River of Hate', 'Loathsome', one of the legendary rivers of the Underworld.

***Sulla, L. Cornelius**: (138–78 BC); Roman general and dictator, conqueror of Mithridates, lifelong opponent of *populares* and of Marius. Life by Plutarch.

Taenarum: promontory in southern Greece, (Cape Matapan).

Tanagra: town of Boeotia, near Attic border.

***Tanaquil**: wife of Tarquinius Prisius, mother-in-law of Servius Tullius, a woman of great influence and strength of character.

***Tantalus**: son of Zeus, father of Niobe; he offended against the gods, and is punished in Hades by being 'tantalized' by food and drink he cannot reach.

***Tarquin**: 1. Tarquinius Priscus, fifth king of Rome (by tradition) 616–579 BC; son of Demaratus of Corinth, a Greek immigrant in Etruria. 2. Tarquinius Superbus, 'The Proud', last king of Rome (524–510 BC), expelled as a tyrant.

Tarsus: city of Cilicia on R. Cydnus.

Taygetus: mountain range of southern Peloponnese, separating Laconia from Messenia.

Tegyrae (Tegyra): Boeotian town at north-western end of Lake Copais; oracle of Apollo.

***Telemachus**: son of Odysseus.

***Telesilla of Argos**: lyric poetess, 5th cent. BC.

Tempe: valley of the lower Peneus (north-east Thessaly), between Mt. Olympus and Mt. Ossa; famous for its natural beauty.

Tenedos: island off the coast of the Troad, north-west Asia Minor.

Terentius Priscus: friend of Plutarch, patron of the poet Martial; a Spaniard who spent many years in Rome.

Terpsion of Megara: pupil of Socrates.

***Teucer**: son of Telamon, founder of Salamis in Cyprus.

Teutones: northern people, invaded Germany, Gaul, and Italy (with Cimbri, q.v.) *c.*100 BC.

***Thales of Miletus**: philosopher, 6th cent. BC.

***Thasos**: large island of northern Aegean.

***Theagenes of Thasos**: athlete, boxing champion at Olympia 480 BC; his statue at Olympia fell on a man who vandalized it.

Theano: 1. wife of Pythagoras (XIV, 142, 145). 2. an Athenian priestess who refused to curse Alcibiades.

***Thebe**: daughter of Jason of Pherae, she induced her stepbrothers to murder her wicked husband, Alexander, 358 BC.

***Thebes**: principal city of Boeotia.

***Themis**: in myth, a goddess (daughter of Earth and mother of the Fates) who once held the oracle at Delphi. She is the personification of Law.

***Themistocles**: (*c.*525–459 BC); Athenian statesman, the hero of the Persian War of 480–479 BC, later exiled. Life by Plutarch.

Theocritus of Chios: (4th cent. BC); sophist and politician, pupil of Isocrates. (Distinguish from 1. the Hellenistic pastoral poet *Theocritus, 2. the character of this name in IV).

Theodorus: famous tragic actor, 4th cent. BC.

***Theognis of Megara**: elegiac poet, 6th cent. BC.

Theon: friend of Plutarch, character in several dialogues (though it is not certain whether the same person is always intended).

***Theophrastus of Eresus**: (*c*.371–287 BC); Peripatetic philosopher of wide-ranging learning, Aristotle's successor as head of the Lyceum.

Theopompus: 1. king of Sparta, 770–*c*.720 BC, conqueror of Messenia. 2. *Theopompus of Chios, 378–after 323 BC, historian, author of *Hellenica* and *Philippica*.

***Thera**: volcanic island in Aegean (Santorini).

***Theramenes**: son of Hagnon, Athenian politician, prominent in the oligarchic government of 411 BC, but condemned to death by the more extreme oligarchs of 404 BC.

***Thermopylae**: mountain pass in central Greece, of great strategic importance, scene of battle in 480 BC, and again in the Gaulish invasion of 279 BC.

***Theseus**: legendary king and unifier of Attica, the national hero of Athens. Life by Plutarch.

Thespiae: town in Boeotia, near Mt. Helicon.

***Thrasea Paetus**: Roman Stoic of republican sympathies, consul AD 56, committed suicide when condemned by Nero, AD 66.

Thrasybulus: 1. son of Deinomenes, Sicilian tyrant (III. 403). 2. of Elis, supporter of the tyrant Aristotimus (XVI. 253).

Thrasymedes of Heraea: the man who 'never had a dream' (II. 437).

Thucydides: 1. son of Melesias, Athenian politician, opponent of Pericles (VII. 802). 2. *son of Olorus, (*c*.460–400 BC), the famous historian.

***Thurii**: city of southern Italy, founded as a panhellenic colony, 443 BC.

Thyiades: group of women devoted to the orgiastic worship of Dionysus.

***Tiberius**: the Roman emperor, AD 14–37.

Tigranes I: king of Armenia, *c*.95–55 BC, ally of Mithridates.

Timesias of Clazomenae: leader of a colony to Abdera in Thrace, 7th cent. BC.

Timocharis: astronomer, 3rd cent. BC.

Timoclea: sister of Theagenes, Theban general who fought and fell at Chaeronea 338 BC.

Timoleon: 1. *Timoleon of Corinth, overthrew the tyranny of his brother, and later (345 BC) liberated Syracuse from Dionysius II; defeated the Carthaginians 341 BC, and brought peace to Greek Sicily before retiring into private life. Life by Plutarch. 2. Timoleon of Elis, husband of the heroine Megisto (see XVI).

Timon: 1. *Timon of Phlius, sceptical philosopher and humorous poet, *c*.320–230 BC. 2. brother of Plutarch.

***Timotheus**: 1. of Miletus, lyric poet, *c*.450–360 BC.; 2. son of Conon, Athenian general 378 BC, active till 356 BC (IV. 575).

Timoxena: name of Plutarch's wife and of the daughter whose death was commemorated by XV.

***Tiresias**: legendary blind Theban prophet.

Tiribazus: satrap of Armenia and later of Sardis under Artaxerxes II; killed for his alleged participation in a conspiracy (I. 168).

Tithorea (Tithora): modern Velitsa, small town of Phocis, home of Plutarch's friend Soclarus.

***Triptolemus**: Eleusinian hero, supposed to have been taught by Demeter how to grow wheat and make bread.

Troglodytes: 'Cave-dwellers', a people of Ethiopia.

***Trophonius**: oracular divinity whose shrine was at Lebadea in Boeotia.

***Tydeus**: Argive hero, father of Diomedes.

Tyndareus: husband of Leda (q.v.).

***Typhon**: a hundred-headed monster, sometimes identified with the Egyptian Seth.

Tyro: daughter of Salmoneus, king of Elis, and mother by Poseidon of Pelias and Neleus.

***Uranus**: 'heaven'; in Greek mythology, the husband of Gaia (Earth) and father of the Giants and Titans.

Valeria: daughter of Publicola (q.v.), sent with Cloelia as hostage to Porsena.

Veii: Etruscan city, about 12 miles north of Rome, destroyed by Romans, according to the usual tradition, in 396 BC, after a ten years' war.

***Vespasian**: the Roman emperor, AD 69–79.

***Vulcan**: Latin god identified with the Greek Hephaestus (q.v.).

Xanthippe: wife of Socrates, traditionally represented as a shrew.

Xanthus: town of Lycia, captured by Brutus in the civil war, 42 BC.

Xenaenetus: Athenian general (VII. 803).

Xenocrates of Chalcedon: philosopher, pupil of Plato, head of the Academy 339–312 BC.

***Xenophanes of Colophon**: poet and philosopher, 6th cent. BC.

***Xenophon of Athens**: (430–*c*.355 BC); the historian and writer of Socratic dialogues and other prose writings; leader of the Greek troops of Cyrus (2) after the defeat at Cunaxa (401 BC), on their long march back to the Greek world.

Xerxes: king of Persia, 486–465, at the time of the second *Persian War against the Greeks.

Zelea: town in Mysia (north-west Asia Minor), said to be birthplace of the Homeric character Pandarus; supposed to be a colony from Lycia (south-west Asia Minor).

***Zeno**: 1. of Elea, philosopher, *c*.495–*c*.445 BC. 2. of Citium, Stoic philosopher, 333–262 BC.

***Zeuxis of Heraclea**: painter, late 5th cent. BC.

Zoroaster (Zarathustra): the prophet of Zoroastrianism, probably 6th cent. BC; known to the Greeks from Persian sources, and often mentioned by philosophers from Plato onwards.

THE WORLD'S CLASSICS

A Select List

JANE AUSTEN: Emma
Edited by James Kinsley and David Lodge

J. M. BARRIE: Peter Pan in Kensington Gardens & Peter and Wendy
Edited by Peter Hollindale

WILLIAM BECKFORD: Vathek
Edited by Roger Lonsdale

JOHN BUNYAN: The Pilgrim's Progress
Edited by N. H. Keeble

THOMAS CARLYLE: The French Revolution
Edited by K. J. Fielding and David Sorensen

GEOFFREY CHAUCER: The Canterbury Tales
Translated by David Wright

CHARLES DICKENS: Christmas Books
Edited by Ruth Glancy

MARIA EDGEWORTH: Castle Rackrent
Edited by George Watson

ELIZABETH GASKELL: Cousin Phillis and Other Tales
Edited by Angus Easson

THOMAS HARDY: A Pair of Blue Eyes
Edited by Alan Manford

HOMER: The Iliad
Translated by Robert Fitzgerald
Introduction by G. S. Kirk

HENRIK IBSEN: An Enemy of the People, The Wild Duck, Rosmersholm
Edited and Translated by James McFarlane

HENRY JAMES: The Ambassadors
Edited by Christopher Butler

JOCELIN OF BRAKELOND:
Chronicle of the Abbey of Bury St. Edmunds
Translated by Diana Greenway and Jane Sayers

BEN JONSON: Five Plays
Edited by G. A. Wilkes

LEONARDO DA VINCI: Notebooks
Edited by Irma A. Richter

HERMAN MELVILLE: The Confidence-Man
Edited by Tony Tanner

PROSPER MÉRIMÉE: Carmen and Other Stories
Translated by Nicholas Jotcham

EDGAR ALLAN POE: Selected Tales
Edited by Julian Symons

MARY SHELLEY: Frankenstein
Edited by M. K. Joseph

BRAM STOKER: Dracula
Edited by A. N. Wilson

ANTHONY TROLLOPE: The American Senator
Edited by John Halperin

OSCAR WILDE: Complete Shorter Fiction
Edited by Isobel Murray

VIRGINIA WOOLF: Mrs Dalloway
Edited by Claire Tomalin